Italian Gothic

Edinburgh Companions to the Gothic

Series Editors
Andrew Smith, University of Sheffield
William Hughes, Bath Spa University

This series provides a comprehensive overview of the Gothic from the eighteenth century to the present day. Each volume takes either a period, place, or theme and explores their diverse attributes, contexts and texts via completely original essays. The volumes provide an authoritative critical tool for both scholars and students of the Gothic.

Volumes in the series are edited by leading scholars in their field and make a cutting-edge contribution to the field of Gothic studies.

Each volume:
- Presents an innovative and critically challenging exploration of the historical, thematic and theoretical understandings of the Gothic from the eighteenth century to the present day
- Provides a critical forum in which ideas about Gothic history and established Gothic themes are challenged
- Supports the teaching of the Gothic at an advanced undergraduate level and at masters level
- Helps readers to rethink ideas concerning periodisation and to question the critical approaches which have been taken to the Gothic

Published Titles
The Victorian Gothic: An Edinburgh Companion
   Andrew Smith and William Hughes
Romantic Gothic: An Edinburgh Companion
   Angela Wright and Dale Townshend
American Gothic Culture: An Edinburgh Companion
   Joel Faflak and Jason Haslam
Women and the Gothic: An Edinburgh Companion
   Avril Horner and Sue Zlosnik
Scottish Gothic: An Edinburgh Companion
   Carol Margaret Davison and Monica Germanà
The Gothic and Theory: An Edinburgh Companion
   Jerrold E. Hogle and Robert Miles
Twenty-first-century Gothic: An Edinburgh Companion
   Maisha Wester and Xavier Aldana Reyes
Gothic Film: An Edinburgh Companion
   Richard J. Hand and Jay McRoy
Twentieth-century Gothic: An Edinburgh Companion
   Sorcha Ní Fhlainn and Bernice M. Murphy
Italian Gothic: An Edinburgh Companion
   Marco Malvestio and Stefano Serafini

Visit the Edinburgh Companions to the Gothic website at:
www.edinburghuniversitypress.com/series/EDCG

Italian Gothic

An Edinburgh Companion

Edited by
Marco Malvestio and Stefano Serafini

EDINBURGH
University Press

Edinburgh University Press is one of the leading university presses in the UK. We publish academic books and journals in our selected subject areas across the humanities and social sciences, combining cutting-edge scholarship with high editorial and production values to produce academic works of lasting importance. For more information visit our website: edinburghuniversitypress.com

© editorial matter and organisation, Marco Malvestio and Stefano Serafini 2023, 2024
© the chapters their several authors, 2023, 2024

Edinburgh University Press Ltd
13 Infirmary Street
Edinburgh EH1 1LT

First published in hardback by Edinburgh University Press 2023

Typeset in 10.5/13pt Sabon LT Pro
by Cheshire Typesetting Ltd, Cuddington, Cheshire

A CIP record for this book is available from the British Library

ISBN 978 1 4744 9016 0 (hardback)
ISBN 978 1 4744 9017 7 (paperback)
ISBN 978 1 4744 9018 4 (webready PDF)
ISBN 978 1 4744 9019 1 (epub)

The right of Marco Malvestio and Stefano Serafini to be identified as the editors of this work has been asserted in accordance with the Copyright, Designs and Patents Act 1988, and the Copyright and Related Rights Regulations 2003 (SI No. 2498).

Contents

Acknowledgements   vii

Introduction. 'A systemic disorder, an extravagant research, and an abjuration of common sense': Defining the Italian Gothic   1
Marco Malvestio and Stefano Serafini

PART I: HISTORY

1. Gothic Beginnings: 1764–1827   19
   Fabio Camilletti
2. The Gothic and the Historical Novel: 1828–1860   30
   Morena Corradi
3. Early Developments: 1861–1914   48
   Stefano Serafini
4. The Age of Permutations: 1915–1956   63
   Fabrizio Foni
5. The Golden Age of the Gothic: 1957–1979   76
   Roberto Curti
6. The Decline of the Gothic: 1980–2020   89
   Marco Malvestio

PART II: MEDIA

7. Gothic Poetry   107
   Simona Di Martino

8. The Gothic in Periodicals and Magazines 123
   Fabrizio Foni

9. Gothic Cinema 138
   Giulio Giusti

10. Comics and the Gothic 154
    Fabio Camilletti

11. Gothic Music 167
    Eduardo Vitolo

PART III: THEMES

12. The Gothic Body 185
    Catherine Ramsey-Portolano

13. The Female Gothic 197
    Francesca Billiani

14. Gothic Criminology 210
    Stefano Serafini

15. Ecogothic and Folk Horror 225
    Marco Malvestio

Notes on Contributors 241
Index 245

Acknowledgements

This project was born one warm evening in a small pub facing London Euston Station in September 2019. We had just completed our PhDs and we had no idea what would happen to us. Needless to say, these have been three exceptionally complicated years so thanks are due, first and foremost, to the individual contributors, who have produced extraordinary pieces of scholarship under the most distressing historical circumstances. We are also deeply grateful to Andrew Smith and William Hughes, the general editors of the Edinburgh Companions to the Gothic, for their support, help and guidance with this volume. We would finally like to thank Fabio Camilletti, mentor and friend, who honoured us with two magnificent contributions; when we asked him about the potential feasibility of such a project, he simply answered, 'If you don't, I will, and it's better you do it.' This is the final result.

These projects, however, rarely have clear points of origin. This one has, in fact, much deeper roots. It has been fed over the years by an immense, perhaps obsessive, passion for the Gothic in all its forms, nuances and manifestations. In the late 1990s and early 2000s Italian cultural landscape, the one in which we grew up, the Gothic was critically marginalised, if not openly ostracised, and confined to the corners of para-literature, popular publishing, comics and low-budget cinema. Luckily enough, there was a small number of rebellious figures, including editors, experts and translators, who thought otherwise. Above all others, the occasionally chaotic, but always open-minded, anthologies by Gianni Pilo and Sebastiano Fusco, with their flashy covers and eclectic flavour, had an impact on our taste and upbringing that could hardly be underestimated. This book is dedicated to all the fans and enthusiasts of the Italian Gothic who came before us and paved the way we took with this book.

Introduction: 'A systemic disorder, an extravagant research, and an abjuration of common sense': Defining the Italian Gothic

Marco Malvestio and Stefano Serafini

> First principles, Clarice: simplicity. Read Marcus Aurelius, 'Of each particular thing, ask: What is it in itself? What is its nature?'
>
> — *The Silence of the Lambs*

Over the past forty years, at least since the appearance of David Punter's ground-breaking *The Literature of Terror* (1980), the field of Gothic Studies has grown in a variety of different directions. Explorations of its transnational dimension (Camilletti, *Trans-National Gothic*; Elbert and Marshall), trans-medial aspects (Och and Strayer; Botting and Spooner; Punter, *The Edinburgh Companion to Gothic and the Arts*) and interactions with other literary forms (Ascari) and fields of knowledge (Hogle and Miles) have contributed to complicating and problematising traditional understandings of the Gothic. Critical studies have also started going beyond the Anglo-American paradigm, bringing to light manifestations of the Gothic in other cultural contexts, such as France (Gibson; Hale, 'French and German' and 'Translation in Distress'; Hall; Horner; Horner and Zlosnik; Wright), Spain (Aldana and Rødtjer; Curbet; Davies; Lee Six; López Santos; Roas) and Latin America (Casanova-Vizcaíno and Inés Ordíz). Thus, it is surprising that, with the exception of a 2007 volume edited by Francesca Billiani and Gigliola Sulis and a small number of articles and book chapters, scholarly research on the Italian Gothic seems non-existent. For instance, the monographic issue of the journal *Gothic Studies* dedicated to 'Italy and the Gothic' is, in reality, exclusively concerned with Italy *in* the Gothic, which is to say Italy as a setting for Gothic novels written in other languages. In its application to Italian cultural artefacts, the term *gotico* is almost never used in bookshops, which tend to privilege labels such as 'fantastic' or 'horror', and it is just as rare in mainstream journals, newspapers and academic criticism.

Without doubt, the very idea of an Italian Gothic will sound like an oxymoron to most readers. This is in many ways paradoxical given the widespread presence of the Gothic in Italian art, literature, film, television series, graphic novels and music. In both high and popular culture, the Gothic intrudes upon and pervades an extraordinary variety of cultural products, from the short stories that appeared in forgotten magazines of the *fin de siècle* to literary classics such as Alessandro Manzoni's *I promessi sposi* (1827) or Antonio Fogazzaro's *Malombra* (1881). These texts are rarely, if ever, recognised as Gothic because of a two-fold tendency among Italian critics: first, the refusal to take seriously, from a rigorous, academic perspective, what is conventionally called 'genre fiction'; second, the difficulty of fitting the irrationalism that is inherent to the Gothic into the larger picture of Italian culture, which, from the Renaissance onwards, has viewed itself as innately 'rational'. As Alessandra Aloisi and Fabio Camilletti argue, discourses on Italian identity tend to configure 'Italianness', at least since the Napoleonic age, as 'the encounter between the legacy of Classical antiquity, Catholic religion, and philosophical rationalism', which had the effect of 'rooting cultural identity in the worship of aesthetic "measure", the refusal of superstition, and philosophical/theological rigour' (2). As a consequence, Italian culture, particularly during the long nineteenth century, exhibited a strong propensity to negate the potentially dangerous drives of 'Northern' forms of knowledge and discursive practices (Aloisi and Camilletti 4–5). Over time, this led to the ostracism, rejection or intellectual manipulation of entire disciplines, domains and cultural experiences, such as the history of religions, folklore, postmodernism and, crucially, the Gothic. However, as Camilletti notes, Italy's repudiation of the literary paradigms of Northern Europe facilitated the autonomous and different re-articulation of Gothic tropes and themes in Italian culture ('"Timore" e "terrore"' 244). This complex cultural process of appropriation and re-working has remained largely understudied. In this companion, we intend to provide the first extensive analysis of the Gothic in Italian culture, examining its major aspects and themes, delineating its historical development and exploring the media it has infiltrated. At the same time, in line with the aforementioned new developments in Gothic Studies, this companion will propose an understanding of the Gothic as a transnational phenomenon. The chapters of this volume insist on the complex network of influences and remediations, translations and adaptations that defines the Italian Gothic. Thus, we challenge the traditional Anglo-centric idea of the Gothic and hopefully pave the way for further explorations of the Gothic in Continental and especially Latin Europe, where the interactions, interchanges and mutual influences between cultures have remained unexplored.

Volumes such as this can hardly ignore the fundamental question: what is the Gothic? In terms of definitions, the Gothic can refer to a specific period in the history of English literature, which ranges approximately from the second half of the eighteenth century to the first half of the nineteenth century. At the same time, the Gothic is seen as a genre, characterised by a more or less fixed set of tropes and conventions that have been adapted and varied over the years in literary, cinematic and televisual texts. For instance, film production and distribution companies, such as Universal Pictures in the 1930s, Hammer in the 1950s and 1960s, and a group of Italian directors in the 1960s, produced movies that were markedly Gothic in terms of atmosphere, themes, plots and characters, by incorporating and adapting elements and devices of classical Gothic texts. However, scholars now generally agree on the modal, rather than generic, nature of the Gothic: the Gothic is not something that *is* in the text, but something that the text *does*. Originally described by Horace Walpole in the preface to the 1765 edition of *The Castle of Otranto* (1764) as 'an attempt to blend the two kinds of romance, the modern and the ancient' (9), the Gothic has since experienced an exceptional number of theoretical conceptualisations. Sigmund Freud, 'the last of the great Victorian Gothic writers' (Warwick 36), played a major role in drawing attention to the connections between the Gothic and psychoanalysis and to the idea of Gothic literature as the return of the repressed, as theorised in the celebrated 1919 essay 'The Uncanny'. Even Howard Phillips Lovecraft, who can hardly be described as a follower of Freudian psychoanalysis, writes in 'Supernatural Horror in Literature' (1927) that the best Gothic horror elicits the most 'inner instincts' embedded in our 'subconscious minds' from the earliest, bestial stages of human evolution (141–3). Post-Freudian psychoanalytic theories have equally generated extraordinarily important readings of the Gothic, as testified by Julia Kristeva's *Powers of Horror* (1980). Alongside psychoanalysis, a different theoretical scheme – Marxism – has been fruitfully used to both interpret and stimulate Gothic fiction during the twentieth century, with Jerrold E. Hogle arguing that Marx 'was plainly influenced by earlier Gothic when he wrote in the 1860s that capitalism was "vampire-like"' ('The Gothic-Theory' 6). Since the second half of the twentieth century, the combination of psychoanalysis and Marxist theory has represented one of the most valuable ways of looking at Gothic narratives. It is not a coincidence that these two conceptual frameworks form the theoretical foundations of Punter's *The Literature of Terror* (1980, expanded in 1996), the book that 'most helped to launch the world-wide acceleration in the study of the Gothic over the last four decades' (Hogle, 'The Gothic-Theory' 8). Feminist Theory, particularly since the 1970s, has become a crucial lens through which to explore the territories of Gothic writing (Fleenor; Ellis; Williams), giving shape to what is now called the Female Gothic, meaning a sub-category of the Gothic that takes as its focus female protagonists wrestling with familial histories and problematic social and institutional pressures relating to female sexuality and gender roles. The rise of fields of research and theories in the last fifty years – New Historicism, Cultural Studies, Queer Theory, Critical Race Studies, Postcolonial Theory, Ecocriticism – has made it possible to unveil previously marginalised dynamics in the many forms of Gothic fictions. The diverse scope and characteristics of these different, often conflicting, theories illustrate the essentially unstable nature of the Gothic and, crucially, the impossibility of inserting it into the strictly defined, and hence often reductive, categories of Italian literary criticism.

Rather than using a particular lens through which to define the Italian Gothic, this volume embraces its modal, composite and multifarious nature, exploring its trans-medial and transdisciplinary dimension. This is necessary to challenge the intellectualistic, highbrow approach that Italian-speaking scholars have adopted to explain what the Gothic is and why it never actually transgressed the borders of Italian culture. The reference to 'transgression' is not coincidental; the Gothic, in its very essence, is a deviant form that resists systematic theorisation and defies accepted, natural assumptions. The Gothic explores the dark, disturbing side of individuals, cultures and societies to interrogate socially dictated and institutionally entrenched attitudes and laws relating to gender, class, race and power. Its engagement with the controversial is the result of its ability to tap into deep-seated, sometimes repressed, desires and anxieties. As Jerrold E. Hogle argues, the Gothic forces readers to 'confront what is psychologically buried in individuals or groups, including their fears of the mental unconscious itself and the desires from the past now buried in that forgotten location' ('Introduction' 3). The Gothic gives positive value to disorder and chaos, to violent emotions and forbidden desires, in open opposition to the harmony, equilibrium and moderation of neoclassicism and the Enlightenment. 'Gothic', David Punter writes, 'was the archaic, the pagan, that which was prior to, or was opposed to, or resisted the establishment of civilised values and a well-regulated society' ('The Literature' 3). In the Gothic, the historically, socially and psychologically repressed makes a disturbing return. The Gothic's obsession with the past, in the form of ruins, ghosts, the undead, or lost manuscripts, is also quite literally a return of something that was believed to be surpassed, historically absorbed, and yet that still pervades and haunts the present. The Gothic allows the uncontrollable emergence, in simultaneously terrifying and inviting forms, of that which societal roles seek to control: female sexuality, queerness and gender instability, the occult, class conflict and the agency of nature. The Gothic is not limited to the arts, as it permeates a variety of cultural phenomena, from local folklore to non-fiction, as Christopher Partridge highlights when discussing the key concept of 'occulture', that is, the circulation and re-articulation of occult and esoteric phenomena in periods of secularisation: 'occulture includes those often *hidden, rejected,* and *oppositional* beliefs and practices associated with esotericism, theosophy, mysticism, New Age, Paganism, and a range of other subcultural beliefs and practices' (68).

While Italy has historically been a privileged setting for Gothic tales, the Gothic as a form of writing has been, since its inception, received with suspicion within the Italian literary establishment. At the beginning of the nineteenth century, during the so-called *polemica Classico-Romantica* [Classicist-Romantic quarrel], Italian intellectuals debated the merits of Classicism and Romanticism, which, in its essence, included the Gothic. Most rejected Romanticism, dismissing it as a disordered manifestation of the Nordic imagination that was fundamentally alien to Italian sensibilities. As Camilletti has maintained, 'fin dall'inizio della Restaurazione, qualsiasi influenza 'nordica' sulla cultura italiana dovette fronteggiare un ostracismo che non ha equivalenti nel resto dei paesi europei' [since the beginning of the Restoration period, every 'Nordic' influence on Italian culture faced ostracism that had no equivalent in other European countries] ('"Timore" e "terrore"' 244).[1] It is significant that, when Romantic poetics finally took root in Italy, artistic creations were almost entirely deprived of supernatural and irrational features (Camilletti, '"Timore" e "terrore"'). In a famous letter sent from Alessandro Manzoni to the Marchese D'Azeglio in 1823, the author expresses disdain for these manifestations of Romanticism. He labels them as 'non so qual guazzabuglio di streghe, di spettri, un disordine sistematico, una ricerca stravagante, una abiura in termini del senso comune; un romanticismo insomma, che si sarebbe avuta molta ragione di rifiutare, e di dimenticare, se fosse stato proposto da alcuno' [an unimaginable muddle of witches, spectres, a systemic disorder, an extravagant research, and an abjuration of common sense. In short, a kind of Romanticism that one would have much reason to refute and forget, had it ever in fact been proposed by anyone] (886). It should not come as a surprise, then, that although Manzoni's *I promessi sposi* is strongly imbued with elements typical of the Gothic novel – ruined castles, superhuman villains, unspeakable passions, forced monachisations and secret murders[2] – scholars have tended to neglect these features or put them under the strict control of stylistic equilibrium and Catholic ethics.

In fact, Italian critics have long struggled to even acknowledge the existence of the Gothic mode in Italian literature. Monica Farnetti, for instance, has identified 'la natura sostanzialmente parodica e citazionale – quando non meramente esornativa – del gotico italiano' [the substantially parodic and 'citational' – when not merely decorative – nature of the Italian Gothic], which essentially failed to make an impact in the nineteenth century (360). The term *gotico* is hardly found in Italian literary criticism and is often utilised in its restrictive, eighteenth-century sense. In Francesco Orlando's posthumous *Il soprannaturale letterario*, which collects a series of lessons from 1984 onwards, the word 'Gothic' appears only ten times, mostly as an adjective to qualify the works of Ann Radcliffe. More importantly, since 1977, when Tzvetan Todorov's seminal volume *Introduction à la littérature fantastique* (1970) was translated into Italian, it has been often used as a synonym of *fantastico* to define an increasingly homogenous group of literary texts.[3] In the 1980s, the work of writers and scholars such as Italo Calvino, Enrico Ghidetti and Gianfranco Contini contributed to constructing the canon of the *fantastico* by denying much of its irrational, hybrid and popular character in order to emphasise its rational, purely intellectual and markedly elitist nature. Calvino dismisses the fantastic in the nineteenth century as a 'campo veramente "minore"' [a very 'marginal' domain] ('Racconti fantastici' 210), characterised by the 'controllo della ragione sull'ispirazione istintiva o inconscia' [by reason's control of instinctive or unconscious inspiration] and 'disciplina stilistica' [stylistic discipline] (Calvino, 'Il fantastico' 224). In Calvino's opinion, the only notable nineteenth-century Italian author of fantastic tales is, quite surprisingly, Giacomo Leopardi, with his *Operette morali* (Calvino, 'Il fantastico'). Enrico Ghidetti and Leonardo Lattarulo have equally denied the existence of Gothic fictions during the nineteenth century, arguing that, unlike in the rest of Europe, explorations of Gothic themes and devices in Italy were conducted exclusively by Decadent artists at the beginning of the twentieth century (xii). Gianfranco Contini, in the 1988 reprint of his *Italia magica*, which originally appeared in France in 1946 and was almost unknown in Italy, identifies the fantastic as an ironic genre, practised by 'umoristi e balordi' [humorists and buffoons], bordering surrealism and humour, that must be characterised by being 'espressivamente validi' [stylistically valid] (1). Giuseppe Lo Castro has pointed out that 'la maggior parte degli scrittori italiani che hanno subito il fascino del fantastico si confrontano comunque con una istanza irriducibilmente logico-razionale, che tende a confinare il potenziale perturbante in ambienti ristretti e in situazioni-limite' [the vast majority of Italian writers who have been fascinated by the fantastic have to meet an irreducibly logical-rational demand that tends to restrict the uncanny into narrow environments and liminal situations] (8).

As Camilletti has pointed out, such Italian theorisations of the Gothic/fantastic as an exclusively '"alto", intellettualistico e razionale' [high, intellectual, and rational] form, which have marginalised the 'contaminazione con altri codici e la cultura 'popolare', il manieristico e l'irrazionale' [contamination with other modes and popular culture, the manneristic, and the irrational] (Camilletti, *Italia lunare* 9), are historically problematic and critically inadequate. Scholars have lost sight of the complexity of the Gothic, its hybrid nature and its tendency to combine high and low culture. One of the most prominent and influential theorists of the Italian Gothic/fantastic is Remo Ceserani, who has consistently ignored developments in international Gothic Studies in order to promote a relatively outdated critical paradigm that is rooted in the Italian tradition of literary criticism. In the pioneering and significant *The Italian Gothic and Fantastic: Encounters and Rewritings between Narrative Traditions* (2007), edited by Francesca Billiani and Gigliola Sulis, the theoretical keys are given to Ceserani, who argues that the difference between the Gothic and the fantastic resides in their very essence. The Gothic is a genre that 'constructed its tradition for the most part using the model of the romance (and, if necessary, combining it with elements of the fable or fairy tale, of the extraordinary and the horrific)'. The fantastic, on the other hand, is a 'new, unmistakably modern literary mode which is also found in texts belonging to different genres, even those characterized by the clearest mimetic realism' (Ceserani, 'The Boundaries' 41).[4] Not only does Ceserani privilege the fantastic over the Gothic, but he also uses the term 'Gothic' in its restrictive sense, dismissing its manifestations in the Italian context. These equivocal statements are ostensibly contrasted by the way in which the Gothic mode has been theorised and studied in Anglo-American scholarship since the 1990s. Nonetheless, this theoretical approach has created, as Stefano Lazzarin writes, an 'amalgama di abbagliante prestigio' [an amalgam of dazzling prestige] that continues to be largely undisputed in Italian literary criticism (Lazzarin 31).

However, the last few years have seen a number of scholars attempt to challenge existing preconceptions and accepted assumptions. The work of Fabrizio Foni and Fabio Camilletti, who have contributed chapters to this volume, seeks to do this. In his studies on early twentieth-century periodicals, Foni has got his hands dirty in 'le cantine della "paraletteratura", quella che una volta si definiva letteratura d'intrattenimento' [the basements of para-literature, which once was defined as literature of entertainment] (Ghidetti vii),[5] bringing to the fore a huge variety of forgotten popular texts situated at the intersection of crime, Gothic and supernatural fiction that appeared in obscure newspapers and journals between approximately 1899 and 1919. Camilletti has explored the occult in popular culture in the late 1950s and the 1960s, highlighting the wide diffusion of occultural interests among the general public and their influence on 'highbrow' authors and directors, from Mario Soldati to Federico Fellini.[6] Francesca Saggini, in her contribution to the recent *The Cambridge History of the Gothic* (2020), has provided a general yet valuable overview of the Gothic in nineteenth-century Italy, offering brief analyses of authors such as Manzoni and Carlo Collodi.

This companion does not exist in a vacuum, then, but rather builds on these important studies in order to innovatively address, and account for, the textual, cultural and intellectual diversity that constitutes the Italian Gothic. This volume is divided into three parts, called 'Histories', 'Media' and 'Themes'. In Part I, our contributors adopt interdisciplinary, transnational and trans-medial approaches to offer an account of the historical developments of Gothic narratives in the Italian context from the second half of the eighteenth century, when early examples of the genre started to appear and circulate globally, to the present day. In the first chapter, Fabio Camilletti discusses the period between about 1764, in which Walpole's *The Castle of Otranto* was originally published, and 1827, when Manzoni's *I promessi sposi* appeared. Camilletti provides the historical framework for contextualising late eighteenth- and early nineteenth-century Italy's relationship with the Gothic as a field of tensions, arguing that refusal and resistance, rather than being viewed as symptoms of a constitutive incompatibility based on apparently innatist premises, should be seen as the consequences of specific cultural-historical processes, which had determined complex and oblique forms of incorporation, adaptation and metamorphosis. In Chapter 2, Morena Corradi considers the years between 1828 and 1860, before Italy's unification, a period characterised by the increasing production and circulation of Gothic texts, both home-grown (like the work of the *Scapigliati*) and foreign, as testified by the stories of Edgar Allan Poe, Theophile Gautier, E. T. A. Hoffmann and many others. In particular, Corradi examines the close relationship between the Gothic and the nineteenth-century historical novel in the work of Giambattista Bazzoni, Diodata Saluzzo Roero, Cesare Balbo and Francesco Domenico Guerrazzi. In their work, national history becomes a source of uncanny memories, shocking stories and emblematic characters. While the Middle Ages were usually considered a moment of national shame, these authors recover them as the setting for stories of heroism and romance that aim to educate the new national readership of the forming nation. In Chapter 3, Stefano Serafini takes us through the years between Italy's unification in 1861 and the outbreak of the First World War in 1914, a cultural moment characterised by invasive processes of industrialisation and urbanisation that dramatically changed the texture of cities while at the same time being marked by important developments in science, medicine and technology that paradoxically mirrored the resurgence of apparently discarded occult beliefs and practices. As this chapter shows, contrary to what scholars have repeatedly claimed, Italian Gothic literature eagerly and variously participated in these debates, responding to the enormous interest in the disproportionate, alarming expansion of the new city and the complicated interplay of science and the occult and thereby tapping into the fears and anxieties that characterised this period of dramatic socio-political transitions and transformations. In Chapter 4, Fabrizio Foni considers a large number of authors active between 1915 and 1956 who tried to adapt the traditional topoi and motifs of the nineteenth-century Gothic to socio-cultural and historical contexts that were rapidly and irrevocably mutating. By unearthing stories by both popular writers (Italo Toscani, Vasco Mariotti) and canonical authors (futurists like Paolo Buzzi and Persio Falchi) who delved into the terrains of the Gothic, Foni provides us with the coordinates to better understand a literary moment that, due to its complexity and problematic historical legacy, has remained largely unexplored. In Chapter 5, Roberto Curti investigates the extraordinarily rich period between 1957 and 1979. These years saw the birth and development of a national Gothic cinema (Riccardo Freda's *I vampiri*, the first truly Italian Gothic film, was originally released in 1957) and the simultaneous renaissance of all things Gothic in the literary market, which coincided with the boom of popular publishing. Through cinema, literature, magazines and comics, Curti shows the power of the Gothic to infiltrate different cultural phenomena and respond to the most dramatic changes in Italian history – the Second World War, 1968 and the 'years of lead'. Finally, Chapter 6 by Marco Malvestio, which concludes the historical trajectory of the Gothic in Italy, explores the Gothic from the 1980s to the present in literature and cinema. These decades saw the general decline of the Gothic in Italy, with the termination of several popular publications and comics, and, most importantly, the dissolution of national genre cinema, which lost its battle against private television and international productions. At the same time, the intensification of debates on the fantastic and the coeval reutilisation of Gothic themes and devices by postmodern authors in the 1980s did not prompt a renaissance of the Italian Gothic; rather, it resulted in the exacerbation of the dichotomy between popular fiction, which has continued to receive no critical attention, and 'highbrow' literature, which seems to ignore the history and nature of the Gothic.

Part II of this companion is devoted to the different media in which Gothic forms have appeared, specifically poetry, periodicals and magazines, cinema, comics and music. Simona Di Martino paints an accurate and nuanced picture of how the Gothic permeates late eighteenth- and early nineteenth-century Italian sepulchral poetry, which is heavily reliant on deadly motifs associated with the ideas of excess and abjection. Discussing the work of exceptionally popular yet forgotten poets such as Alfonso Varano and Salomone Fiorentino through these lenses, Di Martino demonstrates the central role played by authors now considered lowbrow and marginal in terms of their influence on the taste of an entire epoch. Fabrizio Foni, in Chapter 8, reconstructs the symbiotic relationship between Italian Gothic literature and popular periodicals. Through a wide-ranging examination of a vast array of journals, reviews and magazines published between Italy's unification and the post-war period, Foni shows us that popular publishing was, for many decades, the privileged territory of Gothic writing and significantly concludes with RAI's 1971 miniseries *Il segno del comando*, which contributed to finally opening the doors to occultism and the Gothic on Italian television, which would become, in the following years, a very fertile site for Gothic manifestations. In Chapter 9, Giulio Giusti explores the Gothic in Italian cinema, focusing on the 1960s and 1970s, conventionally described as the decades of the Gothic and the *giallo* respectively. Instead of reinforcing traditional distinctions between a truly Gothic cinema, produced by directors such as Riccardo Freda and Mario Bava, and the *giallo*, best represented by the *maestro* Dario Argento, Giusti examines the Gothic influence on the *giallo*, as well as the close intertwining of the narratives and styles of the two *filoni*. The result is a detailed historical account of the development of the Gothic and the *giallo* in a domestic context, the dynamics of their production and their major thematic affinities and shared practices. Chapter 10 is concerned with the Gothic in Italian comics. Fabio Camilletti takes us through the history of Italian Gothic-horror comics, concentrating on what he considers the Golden Era, stretching from 1962, when *Diabolik*, in a watershed moment, was first published, at the peak of the economic miracle, to 1992, when Tiziano Sclavi published issue 69 of *Dylan Dog*, titled 'Caccia alle streghe'. By remaining relatively untouched by intellectualism and engagement, these cultural artefacts were able to develop their discourses outside of pre-made ideological frameworks and thus intercepted abject tensions and desires that lay under the radar of 'highbrow' culture. Chapter 11 ends the media section with an analysis of Italian Gothic music. Eduardo Vitolo provides an overview of the Gothic in Italian Progressive, New Wave and Heavy Metal music. These popular, but understudied, genres are pivotal to understanding the influence of the international Gothic in twentieth- and twenty-first-century Italy. By focusing on the constant interplay of music, lyrics, album covers and practices of self-fashioning, Vitolo highlights the inherently trans-medial nature of the form. Moreover, by underlining the recurring references made by Italy's musical Gothic to national Gothic cinema, Vitolo offers a picture of the Italian Gothic as a homogenous and coherent phenomenon undergoing continuous processes of remediation.

Part III, devoted to some of the major themes of the Italian Gothic, begins with a chapter on the female body. Catherine Ramsey-Portolano focuses on the work of late nineteenth- and early twentieth-century writers active within the *Scapigliatura* and Naturalist movements, such as Igino Ugo Tarchetti, Luigi Capuana, Antonio Fogazzaro and Matilde Serao, who explore the suffering female body as a means of addressing issues associated with female oppression in society. In a period characterised by the circulation of derogatory theories about women's nature, these authors' portrayal of femininity significantly interweaves themes of contaminated beauty, illness and madness with plot structures that combine romance, mystery, suffering, alienation and sometimes death. As a sort of natural continuation of Ramsey-Portolano's contribution, the following chapter is devoted to the Female Gothic. Francesca Billiani considers similar authors – Tarchetti, Capuana, Arrigo Boito – but reads their work through a different lens, with the aim of examining how their female protagonists conveyed critical socio-political messages. By drawing on feminist theories, she argues that the female protagonists of Italian Gothic novels only occupy a seemingly subaltern position; it is precisely from such a position that they have the power to articulate forms of social critique and thus make their voices heard publicly. Chapter 14 is devoted to Gothic criminology. Stefano Serafini focuses on the controversial figure of Cesare Lombroso, the founder of criminal anthropology and one of the most influential late nineteenth-century thinkers. Starting from the premise that the *fin de siècle* was distinguished by the interplay of scientific and Gothic discourses, he explores why and how Lombroso's criminology is deeply Gothic in its methods, applications and implications. Discussing the literary, visual and occult components of Lombroso's multifarious and far-reaching work, Serafini seeks to show how Gothic narratives on the construction of deviance affected Lombroso's criminological thinking and had a major, disturbing influence on the way in which Italians conceptualise the origins of evil. Finally, the fourth and last chapter of Part III is concerned with folk horror and the ecogothic. Marco Malvestio analyses the recurring presence of an ecogothic approach to the environment in Italian nineteenth- and twentieth-century fiction, especially in the tradition of *Verismo*. Even when the authors in question cannot be labelled as Gothic, Malvestio argues, their treatment of landscape and the nature-culture dynamics can be understood within the critical framework of the ecogothic and ecophobia. This attitude towards the national landscape is paralleled by a re-discovery of folklore, both in fiction and non-fiction, that has contributed to the creation of a truly Italian folk horror scene. This is particularly evident in Italian Gothic and *giallo* cinema, which dramatises the environmental and cultural effects of the post-war economic boom.

This book, the first in the *Edinburgh Companions to the Gothic* series to focus on a non-English-speaking culture, appears at a strange time. While recent years have witnessed a growing academic interest in the Gothic and a renewed attention to its manifestations in national cultures other than English and American culture, the popularity of the Gothic in Italy has declined since the 1980s as a result of the crisis of specialised publishers and genre cinema. In this sense, our goal is both to challenge the dominant Anglo-centric paradigm and to revitalise debates on the Gothic in Italian culture. We thus hope to provide a sustained analysis that could serve as an introductory volume for both teaching and research purposes. It is worth underlining that attempts at comprehensiveness are utopic, if not counterproductive, and our book simply cannot cover every single aspect of the Gothic in Italy – no book could. For instance, its influence on the visual arts and theatre (including plays, showmanship and phantasmagorias) deserves closer attention, particularly considering the lack of scholarship on these subjects. Our aim is, rather, to show the richness and discursive potential of a field of study that has long been at the margins of critical literature. For decades, indeed, the Gothic in Italy has been repressed and rejected, only to resurface, powerfully and mysteriously, in different guises and forms. Scholars have denied its existence or sought to establish generic boundaries in a vain attempt to control its deviant potential, reducing the Gothic to a genre or a sub-genre and confining it to the despicable corners of para-literature. The contributors to this book, by applying a transversal gaze and a diverse body of critical and historical approaches, have challenged decades of criticism in order to offer a more complex and nuanced understanding of the Italian Gothic, thus opening new routes of research that can be further explored. Much more work needs to be done. It is our hope that the time to break barriers and transgress boundaries is finally upon us.

Bibliography

Aldana, Xavier, and Rocío Rødtjer, 'The Gothic in Nineteenth-Century Spain', in Angela Wright and Dale Townshend (eds), *The Cambridge History of the Gothic*, 3 vols (Cambridge and New York: Cambridge University Press, 2020–1, II, 2020), pp. 285–302.
Aloisi, Alessandra, and Fabio Camilletti, 'Introduction', in Alessandra Aloisi and Fabio Camilletti (eds), *Archaeology of the Unconscious: Italian Perspectives* (New York: Routledge, 2019), pp. 1–12.
Ascari, Maurizio, *A Counter-History of Crime Fiction: Supernatural, Gothic, Sensational* (Basingstoke and New York: Palgrave, 2007).
Botting, Fred, and Catherine Spooner (eds), *Monstrous Media/Spectral Subjects: Imaging Gothic Fictions from the Nineteenth Century to the Present* (Manchester: Manchester University Press, 2015).
Calvino, Italo, 'Il fantastico nella letteratura italiana', in Italo Calvino, *Mondo scritto e mondo non scritto* (Milan: Mondadori, 2002), pp. 219–30.
Calvino, Italo, 'Racconti fantastici dell'Ottocento' [1983], in Italo Calvino, *Mondo scritto e mondo non scritto* (Milan: Mondadori, 2002), pp. 198–211.
Camilletti, Fabio, 'Guerre, sequestri e tavolette *ouija*. Contributo a una storia parapsicologica del Novecento italiano', *The Italianist*, 39.1, 2019, pp. 1–14.
Camilletti, Fabio, 'Il sorriso del conte zio. Manzoni, Sade e l'omaggio alla Vergine', *Enthymema*, 14, 2016, pp. 231–46.
Camilletti, Fabio, *Italia lunare. Gli anni Sessanta e l'occulto* (Oxford: Peter Lang, 2018).
Camilletti, Fabio, '"Timore" e "terrore" nella polemica classico-romantica: l'Italia e il ripudio del gotico', *Italian Studies*, 69.2, 2014, pp. 31–45.
Camilletti, Fabio (ed.), *Trans-National Gothic*, Compar(a)ison, 1–2 (2009).
Casanova-Vizcaíno, Sandra, and Inés Ortíz (eds), *Latin American Gothic in Culture and Literature* (New York: Routledge, 2018).
Ceserani, Remo, 'The Boundaries of the Fantastic', in Francesca Billiani and Gigliola Sulis (eds), *The Italian Gothic and Fantastic: Encounters and Rewritings of Narrative Traditions* (Madison, NJ: Fairleigh Dickinson University Press, 2007), pp. 37–45.
Ceserani, Remo, *Il fantastico* (Bologna: Il Mulino, 1996).
Contini, Gianfranco, 'Prefazione', in Gianfranco Contini (ed.), *Italia magica* (Turin: Einaudi, 1988), p. 1.
Curbet, Joan, '"Hallelujah to Your Dying Screams of Torture": Representations of Ritual Violence in English and Spanish Romanticism', in Avril Horner (ed.), *European Gothic: A Spirited Exchange 1760–1960* (Manchester: Manchester University Press, 2002), pp. 161–82.
Davies, Ann, *Contemporary Spanish Gothic* (Edinburgh: Edinburgh University Press, 2016).
Del Principe, David, *Rebellion, Death and Aesthetics in Italy. The Demons of Scapigliatura*, (Madison, WI: Fairleigh Dickinson University Press, 1996).

Del Principe, David (ed.), 'European and Italian EcoGothic in the Long Nineteenth Century', monographic issue of *Gothic Studies*, 16.1, 2014.

Demata, Massimiliano (ed.), 'Italy and the Gothic', *Gothic Studies*, 8.1, 2006.

Elbert, Monika, and Bridget M. Marshall (eds), *Transnational Gothic: Literary and Social Exchanges in the Long Nineteenth Century* (Farnham and Burlington, VT: Ashgate, 2013).

Ellis, Kate, *The Contested Castle: Gothic Novels and the Subversion of Domestic Ideology* (Chicago: University of Illinois Press, 1989).

Farnetti, Monica, 'Patologie del romanticismo. Il gotico e il fantastico fra Italia ed Europa', in Gian Mario Anselmi (ed.), *Mappe della letteratura europea e mediterranea. Dal Barocco all'Ottocento*, 4 vols (Milan: Bruno Mondadori Editore, 2000–1, II, 2000), pp. 340–66.

Fleenor, Juliann E. (ed.)., *The Female Gothic* (Montréal: Eden Press, 1983).

Foni, Fabrizio, *Alla fiera dei mostri: racconti pulp, orrori e arcane fantasticherie nelle riviste italiane 1899–1932* (Latina: Tunué, 2007).

Foni, Fabrizio, *Piccoli mostri crescono. Nero, fantastico e bizzarrie varie nella prima annata de 'La Domenica del Corriere' (1899)* (Ozzano dell'Emilia: Perdisa, 2010).

Frangipani, Maria Antonietta, *Motivi del romanzo nero nella narrativa lombarda* (Rome: Elia, 1981).

Ghidetti, Enrico, 'Prefazione', in Enrico Ghidetti (ed.), *Notturno italiano Racconti fantastici dell'Ottocento* (Rome: Editori Riuniti, 1984), pp. vii–xii.

Ghidetti, Enrico, and Leonardo Lattarulo, 'Prefazione', in Enrico Ghidetti and Leonardo Lattarulo (eds), *Notturno italiano. Racconti fantastici del Novecento* (Rome: Editori Riuniti, 1984), pp. vii–xii.

Gibson, Matthew, *The Fantastic and European Gothic: History, Literature and the French Revolution* (Cardiff: University of Wales Press, 2013).

Giovannoli, Renato, *Il vampiro innominato. Il 'Caso Manzoni-Dracula' e altri casi di vampirismo letterario* (San Giorgio a Cremano: Medusa, 2008).

Hale, Terry, 'French and German Gothic: The Beginnings', in Jerrold E. Hogle (ed.), *The Cambridge Companion to Gothic Fiction* (Cambridge: Cambridge University Press, 2002), pp. 63–84.

Hale, Terry, 'Translation in Distress: Cultural Misappropriation and the Construction of the Gothic', in Avril Horner (ed.), *European Gothic: A Spirited Exchange 1760–1960* (Manchester: Manchester University Press, 2002), pp. 17–38.

Hall, Daniel, *French and German Gothic Fiction in the Late Eighteenth Century* (Oxford: Peter Lang, 2005).

Hogle, Jerrold E., 'The Gothic-Theory Conversation: An Introduction', in Jerrold E. Hogle and Robert Miles (eds), *The Gothic and Theory: An Edinburgh Companion* (Edinburgh: Edinburgh University Press, 2019), pp. 1–32.

Hogle, Jerrold E., 'Introduction: The Gothic in Western Culture', in Jerrold E. Hogle (ed.), *The Cambridge Companion to Gothic Fiction* (Cambridge: Cambridge University Press, 2002), pp. 1–20.

Horner, Avril (ed.), *The European Gothic: A Spirited Exchange, 1760–1960* (Manchester: Manchester University Press, 2002).

Horner, Avril, and Sue Zlosnik (eds), *Le Gothic: Influences and Appropriations in Europe and America* (Basingstoke: Palgrave, 2009).

Kristeva, Julia, *Powers of Horror: An Essay on Abjection* [1980] (New York: Columbia University Press, 1982).
Lazzarin, Stefano, 'Trentacinque anni di teoria e critica del fantastico italiano (dal 1980 a oggi)', in Stefano Lazzarin et al. (eds), *Il fantastico italiano. Bilancio critico e bibliografia commentata (dal 1980 a oggi)* (Florence: Le Monnier, 2016), pp. 1–58.
Lee Six, Abigail, *Gothic Terrors: Incarceration, Duplication, and Bloodlust in Spanish Narrative* (Cranbury, NJ: Bucknell University Press, 2010).
Lo Castro, Giuseppe, 'Introduzione', in Antonio D'Elia et al. (eds), *La tentazione del fantastico: racconti italiani da Gualdo a Svevo* (Cosenza: Pellegrini, 2007), pp. 5–18.
López Santos, Miriam, *La novela gótica en España (1788–1833)* (Pontevadra: Academia del Hispanismo, 2010).
Lovecraft, Howard Phillips, *Dagon and Other Macabre Tales* [1916–39] (London: Gollancz, 1967).
Manzoni, Alessandro, *Opere*, ed. Lanfranco Caretti (Milan: Mursia, 1965).
Och, Dana, and Kirsten Strayer (eds), *Transnational Horror across Visual Media: Fragmented Bodies* (New York: Routledge, 2014).
Orlando, Francesco, *Il soprannaturale letterario: storia, logica, forme* (Turin: Einaudi, 2017).
Partridge, Christopher, *The Re-Enchantment of the West: Alternative Spiritualities, Sacralization, Popular Culture, and Occulture* (London and New York: T&T Clark International, 2004).
Pompeo Giannantonio, 'Manzoni e il romanzo "nero"', *Otto/Novecento*, 3.2, 1979, pp. 5–37.
Punter, David, *The Literature of Terror* (London and New York: Longman, 1980).
Punter, David (ed.), *The Edinburgh Companion to Gothic and the Arts* (Edinburgh: Edinburgh University Press, 2019).
Roas, David, *De la maravilla al horror. Los inicios de lo fantástico in la cultura española (1750–1860)* (Madison, WI: Mirabel Editorial, 2006).
Saggini, Francesca, 'The Gothic in Nineteenth-Century Italy', in Angela Wright and Dale Townshend (eds), *The Cambridge History of the Gothic. Volume II: The Gothic in the Nineteenth Century*, 3 vols (Cambridge: Cambridge University Press, 2020–1, II, 2020, pp. 303–27).
Simonetti, Gianluigi, *La letteratura circostante* (Bologna: Il Mulino, 2018).
Todorov, Tzvetan, *The Fantastic: A Structural Approach to a Literary Genre* [1970], trans. Richard Howard (Ithaca, NY: Cornell University Press, 1975).
Walpole, Horace, *The Castle of Otranto: A Gothic Story* [1764], ed. by W. S. Lewis and E. J. Clery (Oxford: Oxford University Press, 1996).
Warwick, Alexandra, 'Victorian Gothic', in Catherine Spooner and Emma McEvoy (eds), *The Routledge Companion to Gothic* (London: Routledge, 2007), pp. 29–37.
Williams, Ann, *Art of Darkness: A Poetics of Gothic* (Chicago, IL: The University of Chicago Press, 1995).
Wright, Angela, *Britain, France and the Gothic: The Import of Terror* (Cambridge: Cambridge University Press, 2016).

Notes

1. All translations, unless otherwise stated, are written by the chapters' contributors.
2. On Manzoni's debt to the Gothic tradition, see Giannantonio; Frangipani; Giovannoli; Camilletti, 'Il sorriso del conte zio'; and Saggini.
3. For Todorov, the fantastic is a threshold genre that relies heavily on the tension between the real and the imaginary. The fantastic is created in between these two notions, when a story introduces an event that seems not to respect the natural laws of our world without providing a conclusive explanation. If the event were to be satisfactorily explained, the narrative would stop being fantastic and fall into one of two closely related genres: the uncanny or the marvellous. He thus defines the fantastic as 'a hesitation common to reader and character, who must decide whether or not what they perceive derives from "reality" as it exists in the common opinion' (41).
4. Remo Ceserani, in his influential study *Il fantastico* (1996), deliberately refuses to discuss popular fiction because it apparently contaminates the supposedly pure identity of the form (10).
5. The concept of *paraletteratura* has often been employed by Italian critics to dismiss the study of certain cultural products; it is the result of an aesthetic prejudice that has nonetheless contributed to the marginalisation of entire fields of research. Surprisingly, it is still widely used by scholars. See, among others, Simonetti.
6. See Foni, *Alla fiera dei mostri* and *Piccoli mostri crescono*; Camilletti, *Italia lunare* and 'Guerre, sequestri e tavolette *ouija*'.

Part I

History

Chapter 1

Gothic Beginnings: 1764–1827
Fabio Camilletti

The relationship between Italian culture and the Gothic in the years 1764–1827 – the years of Horace Walpole and E. T. A. Hoffmann, of Ann Radcliffe and Mary Shelley – is a history of reciprocal misconstructions, determining the perception of an alleged Italian 'delay', generally stated by scholars without any substantial historical problematisation.

Eighteenth- and early nineteenth-century Italy is not a nation, but the laboratory of a nation, primarily defining its own identity by means of exclusion. Through a narrative formalised in the Renaissance by Giorgio Vasari, and reiterated by the eighteenth-century reaction against the Baroque, the Italian 'mode' in the arts (and by extension in literature) is localised in Italian culture's un-mediated continuity with Classical antiquity, expelling as other-than-self whatever does not fall within the organic cycle of sleep and rebirth of the 'Classic': primarily, the 'maniera tedesca' [German style] characterising the art of those centuries when the memory of antiquity seemed to be forgotten (Belting 73). It is immediately clear that, as a term derived from the architectural jargon, Horace Walpole's use of the adjective 'Gothic' perfectly matches Vasari's definition of 'maniera tedesca'. From this viewpoint, the act of labelling *The Castle of Otranto* as a 'Gothic' novel does not only mean setting it in the 'long period of barbarism, superstition, and anarchy dimly stretching from the fifth century [. . .] to the Renaissance' (Clery 21), but also proposing a deeply anti-Classicist image of Italy, directly challenging the primacy of Classicism as the dominant aesthetics of eighteenth-century Europe (Scianatico 16–22).

Hence the discrepancy between the image of Italy featuring in Gothic novels, from Walpole to Radcliffe and beyond – a 'Meridionist' (Pfister 3), Baroque and papist theatre of miracles (Pezzini) – and the actual country, where, in the absence of a unified nation and in a context of linguistic de-territorialisation, literate élites conceptualise Italianness as the un-mediated legacy of Classical tradition in the name of 'reason'.

Established as a keyword in Giovanni Vincenzo Gravina's influential treatise *Della ragion poetica* (1708), 'ragione' ('reason', but also 'rationale') is employed, throughout the long eighteenth century, as a remarkably open term, progressively constructed as the pivot of philosophical, conceptual, ideological and aesthetic normativity (Aloisi and Camilletti 3–4). One of the consequences of this process is the unappealable refusal, on the part of the Italian cultural élites, of the 'irrational' and 'superstitious' drives of 'Northern' cultures, broadly coinciding with our contemporary understanding of the 'Gothic': to speak in Alessandro Manzoni's terms, that Germanising 'guazzabuglio di streghe, di spettri' [hodge-podge of witches and spectres] Italian literature should irrevocably reject, finding an 'Italian way' to literary modernity based, instead, on rationalism, aesthetic measure, and avoidance of excess (Manzoni, 'Sul Romanticismo' 189). The legacy of such an approach is still to be found in contemporary criticism about the Italian 'fantastic' or 'weird'.[1]

In this chapter, I will not attempt a survey of more or less explicit 'Gothicising' elements in Italian literature of the time span in question – an approach which, provided that it might be of any use, would only lead to reiterating the established narrative about Italy's isolation from the trans-national circuits of the Gothic. I will, instead, provide the historical framework for contextualising Italy's relationship with the Gothic as a field of tensions, that is, 'as an unstable equilibrium on the verge of transformation, providing the condition, energy, and direction for processes that can be productive as well as destructive' (Holzhey 7). From this viewpoint, refusal and resistance – rather than symptoms of a constitutive incompatibility based on more or less veiled, unacceptable innatist premises – may rather be seen as the consequences of specific cultural-historical processes, determining oblique forms of incorporation, adaptation and metamorphosis. Undertaking an archaeology of the Italian Gothic means, therefore, to explore the ways Italian-speaking literature incorporates and discusses those very same tensions inhabiting Gothic literature in other cultural domains, even where one would not expect them: the long-lasting influence of the Baroque and its morbid imaginary in religious-moral poetry;[2] the afterlife of Dante as a paragon in stylistic hybridism, and the influence of the *Inferno* in the representation of monstrosity, abjection and excess; the exploration of anti-Classical models of antiquity; or the historical novel as a negotiation of the national past and the way it haunts modernity.

In this chapter, I will primarily focus on the quarrel between Classicists and Romantics inflaming the Italian-speaking periodical press from 1816 to the late 1820s, when the publication of Manzoni's *I promessi sposi* re-directs the debate towards the mission of historical novels and the problem of national language. As a palimpsest and a laboratory of Italian identity, the Classicist-Romantic quarrel is the first context where the alleged, constituent alienness of Italian culture to the Gothic is theorised.[3] Such reaction takes the shape of a literary skirmish, but its sphere is that of the imaginary: and its vocabulary is made of specific metaphorical fields – of climatological, military, and medical order – by which Italian culture conceptualises the contrast between South and North, identity and otherness, classical tradition and the temptation of modernity. The Classicist-Romantic quarrel outlines, thus, an intellectual geography of post-revolutionary Europe, an imaginary territory wherein Italy tries – in a still hesitating way – to find its own place. Post-Napoleonic Europe is (as we will see, quite literally) a colder continent, dominated by technicality and artifice, in which the unravelling of political *authority* and of its self-legitimisation has corresponded an equal erosion of literary *authoriality* and its meticulous normative apparatus (Camilletti, 'Authorship and Authority'): the Gothic, a *plague* of taste, is the most evident symptom of the contagion by which modernity tries to seduce the peninsula, undermining its deepest identity.

The Frost

Il giorno 22 d'Ottobre di quell'anno 1629, Pietro Antonio Lovato [. . .] entrò in Milano, carico di vesti rubate o comperate dai soldati alemanni; e andò a porsi in una casa di suoi parenti nel borgo di Porta Orientale. Appena giunto s'ammalò; fu portato allo spedale; e morì nel quarto giorno. Nel cadavero si scoperse un carbone che diede sospetto di peste [. . .]. (Manzoni, *Fermo e Lucia* 651)

[On 22 October of that year 1629, Pietro Antonio Lovato [. . .] made his entrance into Milan, with a load of clothes stolen or bought from German soldiers; and he went to stay at the place of some relatives in the neighbourhood of Porta Orientale. As soon as he got there, he got sick; they brought him to the hospital; and on the fourth day he died. In the corpse they found a bubo, which raised the suspicion of plague.]

In the years when Manzoni was drafting *Fermo e Lucia* (1821–3), no Milan citizen could certainly remember Pietro Lovato, an obscure character mentioned in seventeenth-century chronicles of the plague. Still, when approaching Porta Orientale – now Porta Venezia – they could nonetheless perceive it as a passage whence something foreign, *German* and infernal had once entered the city. 'Maledett Bonapart' [damn Bonaparte], ladies exclaimed along the avenue leading from Porta Nuova to Porta Orientale, following Stendhal's testimony as included in

Rome, Naples, Florence (I, 113). The First Consul was, for them, the cause of the frost experienced in Lombardy '*depuis la Révolution*' [since the Revolution]; when opening the route of the Simplon, Napoleon must have opened a breach (*brèche*) from whence Northern winds had violated the natural shelter formed by the Alps. Years later, in *The Charterhouse of Parma* (1839), Stendhal would pay credit to another breach opened by Napoleon – in 1796, at the bridge of Lodi – the opening of a deeper and far more incisive *breach* in Italy's national consciousness, slumbered by centuries of political servitude and literary Classicism. Together with modernity, however (and with a literary praxis that could be perfectly labelled as *Romantic*), the French army had also brought the winds of the North, transforming a once sunny and Mediterranean city into a frosty land.

Partially, Milanese ladies were right. The early nineteenth century was still amid the 'little ice age' following the 'medieval warm period' (Fagan). In particular, 1816 would become globally known as the 'year without a summer' – rains and floods on the whole Atlantic area, destroying economies already weakened by the Napoleonic wars. Literary works of 1816 bear the traces of such uncustomary weather. In Byron's lodgings in Geneva, the weather propitiates the abandonment to a 'Northern' and Gothic imaginary, and the narratives produced in that summer – the thunderstorms of Mary Shelley's *Frankenstein*, the blackened sun of Byron's 'Darkness', the Swiss glaciers of Percy Shelley's 'Mont Blanc' and of John Polidori's *Ernestus Berchtold* – are all marked by the vestiges of something obscure and apocalyptic that is impacting Europe, deeply interweaving reality and imagination (Clubbe).

The 'year without a summer' had most probably been caused by the eruption, on 10 April 1815, of Indonesian volcano Tambora: ashes and toxic gases would cause, for several years, a remarkable lowering of temperatures all over the world, while volcanic ashes would give sunsets a brightly red colour, as portrayed in William Turner's canvases (Serres). Two months later, on 18 June, an unexpected night rain had transformed the area surrounding the village of Mont Saint-Jean, near the Belgian town of Waterloo, into a sort of morass: the French army had had to wait for the sun to dry the wet ground, and when Napoleon had finally been able to draw his attack, late in the morning, cannons had remained blocked by the mud, leaving the Prussian troops the time to re-join the British infantry. On that evening, both armies had lost many men, but the British-Prussian coalition of Wellington and von Blücher had won.

The connection between Waterloo and Tambora is beyond every possible demonstration. There remains its involuntarily symbolic charm, and the idea that only some apocalyptic fatality could destroy the power of Napoleon, a sort of Icarus or Phaethon who had fallen the more ruinously, the more he had attempted to ascend. Not incidentally, when commemorating Napoleon's death in 'Il Cinque Maggio' (1821), Manzoni would surreptitiously evoke the mythologem of the reckless son of Apollo: Napoleon, once 'folgorante in solio' [shining in his throne] (v. 13), has fallen; in his exile at Saint Helena, 'al tacito / morir d'un giorno inerte' [at the silent dying of a useless day] (vv. 73–4) the Emperor's 'rai fulminei' [lightning eyes, but also rays] decline, subtly delineating the image of a dying sun (Manzoni, *Tutte le poesie* 201–4). By so doing, Manzoni transforms the chariot of Napoleon-Apollo of imperial iconography into the wrecked carriage of Phaethon, making the emperor an emblem of hybris and impiety (Nigro, *La tabacchiera* 127).

Not only literature bears the traces of such symbolic short-circuit. In the 'year without a summer' all Europe seems to be crossed by apocalyptic fears, a sort of post-traumatic aftermath of Waterloo mixing science and superstition, political metaphors, and the entire panoply of the age's taste – from the grotesque to the sublime, and through the Gothic. Popular imagination points to the sun, a seemingly dying star on the point of extinguishing or exploding. Rumours had spread about the planet getting colder, and between 1815 and 1816 spots had been seen on the surface of the sun. Both phenomena could be perfectly explainable (Riccati II, 328–34): still, the idea that the sun was extinguishing, and that a fragment of it was about to fall on Earth, had run all over the continent, fuelled by the eschatological prophecies of German occultist Heinrich Stilling (Anonymous, 'Superstizioni'). Rumours fixed the catastrophe for 18 July; their very distribution is eloquent – Paris, Alsace and Belgium: the military geography, in other words, of the Hundred Days – as if an unconscious but tenacious knot encompassed, in the collective imaginary of 1816, the falling sun and the ruination of Napoleon's star. On 11 July, the citizens of Gand (less than 45 miles from Waterloo) had mistaken the trumpet of a cavalry regiment for that of the angel of the last day (Riccati II, 336). And although, of course, no apocalypse would occur, the collective imaginary was clearly trying to express, in a confused way, the idea of a fracture from whence it was impossible to come back. The falling sun, the Northern winds coming from the Simplon, the very idea of something terrible and fateful that has forever changed Europe and the world are nothing but ways of metaphorising (and, therefore, metabolising) a historical transition: Napoleon – and, more broadly, the French Revolution and the war, in a word: modernity – has dissolved the timeless connection binding humankind and nature, opening a fissure between a pre-modern Arcadia and a new, technicised world.

Romanticism

On 29 February 1816, in Milan, weather had been fine; temperature, however, had remained low, oscillating between 2 degrees in the morning and 5.5 in the afternoon. Measurements were made by the observatory of Brera and published every three months in *Biblioteca italiana*, the journal funded by the newly restored Austrian government and directed by Giuseppe Acerbi (Bizzocchi). Although the first issue was dated January 1816, it precisely appeared on that frosty day: it was opened by a short text by Madame de Staël, translated by Pietro Giordani. As the following months would make clear, it was the inaugural act of the so-called Classicist-Romantic quarrel. De Staël made a conventional praise of Italian culture, but could not help but notice how it had lost its propulsive role, and how the most lively cultural experiences were now taking place elsewhere, 'di là dall'Alpi' [beyond the Alps] (16). Even Italy's sun, an already outworn Grand Tour cliché, was almost useless for a people slumbered by centuries of Classicism, and was presently nothing but a motionless star, shining over a landscape of ruins and tombs (Luzzi, *Romantic Europe* 87–123). The fracture between North and South, cold and warm, aimed thus at delineating a specific politico-cultural geography, placing Italy in a subaltern position against transalpine Europe: an equation between climate and national inclinations grounded in the thought of the Enlightenment, but which in 1816 could possess far more literal resonances. Germinated in a year marked by apocalyptic tensions, the Classicist-Romantic quarrel seems to incorporate them within the metaphorical fields that dominate the debate since the beginning: the clash between an Arcadia-like, mild south and a cold, shadowy, transalpine North; the images of invasion, siege and expoliation of those very vestiges in which the proto-national community finds the foundations of its own identity; and, finally, the very problem of literary *authoriality* (who, in other words, is legitimised to write, whether those who make appeal to the heritage of a timeless tradition or those who claim their own right to newness) behind which one can easily perceive the post-revolutionary disaggregation of political *authority* and of its sources of legitimisation.

It is telling that many of the critics received by de Staël – the most relevant of which, although it remained unpublished at that time, is Giacomo Leopardi's *Discorso di un italiano intorno alla poesia romantica* – amplify this geo-climatic notation, opposing to the Gothicising North a Mediterranean temper that would make Italy intrinsically alien to transalpine novelties. In the following issue of *Biblioteca italiana*,

Giordani polemicises against the folly of those who would like to import foreign imaginaries in countries where 'nature' bids otherwise (12–14); in 1817, Carlo Giuseppe Londonio defines Romanticism as the literature of peoples living in cold climates, who are naturally brought to see everything in a melancholy light (46–7). That we should read 'Romanticism' as 'Gothic' is implicitly confirmed by Giovanni Gherardini, who notes in 1820 how the tempers of Northern people need 'colpi gagliardi' [strong shocks], 'immagini gigantesche' [Gargantuan images], 'oggetti d'orrore' [horrid objects], 'stravaganze' [eccentricities] and 'cose fuor dalle leggi della natura' [things outside natural laws] (154). In 1818, jurist Pier Luigi Mabìl rhetorically asks whether Romantic innovators would require Italian dramatists to 'ingombr[are] le [. . .] scene di patiboli, di carnefici, di teschi, di stregoni e di fantasmi' [clutter theatrical stages with gallows, hangmen, skulls, sorcerers, and ghosts] (470).

The same geo-cultural opposition animates Leopardi's *Discourse*, whose apocalyptic closure warns Italians against the temptations of modernity and fashion (in the *Operette morali* [1827], Leopardi would identify *Moda* as the sister of Death). 'Ancora', Leopardi writes, 'beviamo quest'aria e calchiamo questa terra e godiamo questa luce che godé un esercito d'immortali; [. . .]; ancora non è cambiata quell'indole propria nostra' [we still drink this air and tread this earth and enjoy the same light that an army of immortals enjoyed [. . .]; that character that belongs to us is unchanged] (*Discorso* 161–2). For Leopardi, like Stendhal, the breach opened by Napoleon has allowed modernity to irrupt into Italy. Whereas, however, Stendhal saw the battle at Lodi as a possibility of reawakening, Leopardi views modernity as the most threatening menace to the Italian specificity: the French army itself, which he never names directly, is dissolved into the almost archetypal one of a Northern, imperial, and foreign Europe that has *always* threatened Italy's identity, and now tries to barbarise it through the 'sterco sentimentale e poetico [che] ci scola giù dalle alpi' [sentimental and poetic dung dripping down to us from the Alps] (161), finding in Milan its point of entrance.

The Plague

The story of Lovato, who enters Milan from Porta Orientale bringing on his shoulders the contaminated clothes of *German* soldiers, possesses a central position in *Fermo e Lucia*: the plague enters the city in a specific and determinable moment and place, for the negligence of a single individual, and the passage is emblematically placed as the opening of the chapter. In 1827, in *I promessi sposi* Manzoni compares different sources, concluding that neither can be completely trustworthy: in the published novel, the date, the man's name, and the very historical truth of the episode are covered with doubt, while the occurrence shifts to the middle of Chapter XXXI, thereby losing all narrative centrality, dispersed among the 'particolarità [. . .] indifferenti' [irrelevant circumstances] bearing so much significance for posterity (Manzoni, *I promessi sposi* 589).

Among these 'circumstances' we could maybe add the mentioning of Porta Orientale, which in 1823 – as per the date by which the manuscript of *Fermo e Lucia* is signed – possessed very specific geo-cultural features: unlike *I promessi sposi*, *Fermo e Lucia* fully belongs to the Classicist-Romantic quarrel, conceived as it is after the forced closure of *Il Conciliatore* and the Austrian repression plaguing Milan from October 1820 onwards. The abusive nature of power exemplified by the trial against the 'plague-spreaders' in seventeenth-century Milan mirrors the violent reprisal annihilating the circle of the Milanese Romantics, of which Manzoni had discreetly but actively been part, thereby explaining the haste in which Manzoni completes his first draft, as a testimony and an accusation.

Thus, in *Le mie prigioni* (1832), Silvio Pellico relates his last night in Milan, while he is being transferred – date is February 1821 – from Milan to Venice, whence he will be deported to the Spielberg fortress, in Moravia:

> Oh corsìa di porta Orientale! Oh pubblici giardini, ov'io avea tante volte vagato con Foscolo, con Monti, con Lodovico di Breme, con Pietro Borsieri, con Porro e co' suoi figliuoli, con tanti altri diletti mortali, conversando in sì gran pienezza di vita e di speranze! (70–1)

> [Oh, you avenue of Porta Orientale! Oh, you the public gardens, where I had often walked with Foscolo, Monti, Lodovico di Breme, with Pietro Borsieri, with Porro and his children, and with so many other beloved mortals, talking in the fullest of life and of hope!]

In the topography of Milan, Porta Orientale and its *Corso* are remarkably connoted from a cultural viewpoint, not only in that they recall – as we have seen – the memory of Napoleon's invasion and the route of Simplon, but also the later one of Milan's Romantic scene (Ravesi 20).[4] Unlike Classicists, Milanese Romantics always express a connection between their literary praxis and the territory in which they operate: such relation makes the emphasis of Porta Orientale in *Fermo e Lucia* – eloquently historicised, and therefore minimised, in *I promessi sposi* – less innocent than it could seem at first glance. Porta Orientale is the doorway whence something innately *other* enters Milan: the metaphorical fields of climate, of invasion, and of pestilence reciprocally intersect in the writings of the quarrel as much as in the novel, in which the plague is not incidentally presented as a side-consequence of the foreign invasion of German Landsknechts.

Equally, in *I promessi sposi*, the ambiguity surrounding the theme of the plague echoes the ambiguity by which Manzoni views Romanticism, a 'hodge-podge of witches' possessing, nonetheless, the merit of having swept away the provincial junk plaguing Italian literature (Manzoni, 'Sul Romanticismo' 189). Such ambiguity will remain unresolved throughout the entire course of Italian modernity, between defence of tradition and yearning for renovation, intellectual autarchy and foreignising temptations, South and North – and, of course, 'ragione' and the Gothic. 'Questa pestilenza è stata un flagello, figliuoli, un flagello' – comments Don Abbondio in the closure of Italy's least and, at the same time, greatest Gothic novel – 'ma è stata anche una scopa: ha spazzato via certa gente, che, figliuoli miei, non ce ne liberavamo più' [this pestilence has been a curse, my sons, a curse, but it was also a broom: it swept away certain people whom, my sons, we'd never got rid of] (Manzoni, *I promessi sposi* 732).[5]

Bibliography

Aloisi, Alessandra, and Fabio Camilletti, 'Introduction', in Alessandra Aloisi and Fabio Camilletti (eds), *Archaeology of the Unconscious: Italian Perspectives* (New York: Routledge, 2020), pp. 1–12.

Anonymous, 'Superstizioni, Fattucchieríe [sic], Maleficii, ec.', in *Lo Spettatore ovvero Mescolanze di viaggi, di storia, di statistica, di politica, di letteratura e di filosofia*, V (1816), p. 425.

Bellorini, Egidio (ed.), *Discussioni e polemiche sul romanticismo*, 2 vols (Rome and Bari: Laterza, 1943).

Belting, Hans, *The End of History of Art* (Chicago and London: The University of Chicago Press, 1987).

Bizzocchi, Roberto, *La 'Biblioteca italiana' e la cultura della restaurazione (1816–1825)* (Milan: Franco Angeli, 1979).

Bollati, Giulio, *L'italiano. Il carattere nazionale come storia e come invenzione* (Turin: Einaudi, 2011).

Camilletti, Fabio, 'Authorship and Authority in the Classicist/Romantic Quarrel', *Forum for Modern Language Studies*, 54.3, 2018, pp. 307–19.

Camilletti, Fabio, *Classicism and Romanticism in Italian Literature* (London: Pickering & Chatto, 2013).

Camilletti, Fabio, 'Italians and the Irrational', in Teresa Franco and Cecilia Piantanida (eds), *Echoing Voices in Italian Literature: Tradition and Translation in the 20th Century* (Newcastle-Upon-Tyne: Cambridge Scholars, 2018, pp. 159–79).

Camilletti, Fabio, '"Timore" e "terrore" nella polemica classico-romantica: l'Italia e il ripudio del gotico', *Italian Studies*, 69.2, 2014, pp. 231–45.

Clery, Emma, 'The Genesis of "Gothic" Fiction', in Jerrold E. Hogle (ed.), *The Cambridge Companion to Gothic Fiction* (Cambridge: Cambridge University Press, 2002), pp. 21–39.

Clubbe, John, 'The Tempest-toss'd Summer of 1816: Mary Shelley's "Frankenstein"', *The Byron Journal*, 19, 1991, pp. 26–40.

Fagan, Brian, *The Little Ice Age: How Climate Made History, 1300–1850* (New York: Basic Books, 2000).

Gherardini, Giovanni, 'Poesia classica e poesia romantica', in Egidio Bellorini (ed.), *Discussioni e polemiche sul romanticismo*, 2 vols (Rome and Bari: Laterza, 1943, II, 1943), pp. 135–65.

Giordani, Pietro [Un italiano], 'Sul discorso di Madama di Staël. Lettera ai Compilatori della "Biblioteca"', *Biblioteca Italiana*, 2, February 1816, pp. 3–14.

Holzhey, Christoph, 'Preface', in Christoph Holzhey (ed.), *Tension/Spannung* (Vienna: Turia + Kant, 2010), pp. 7–12.

Lazzarin, Stefano, 'Trentacinque anni di teoria e critica del fantastico italiano (dal 1980 a oggi)', in Stefano Lazzarin et al. (eds), *Il fantastico italiano. Bilancio critico e bibliografia commentata (dal 1980 a oggi)* (Florence: Le Monnier, 2016), pp. 1–58.

Leopardi, Giacomo, *Discorso di un italiano intorno alla poesia romantica*, ed. by Rosita Copioli (Milan: Rizzoli, 1997); trans. Gabrielle Sims and Fabio Camilletti, in Camilletti, *Classicism and Romanticism*, pp. 113–73.

Londonio, Carlo Giuseppe, *Cenni critici sulla poesia romantica* (Milan: Pirotta, 1817).

Luzzi, Joseph, *Romantic Europe and the Ghost of Italy* (New Haven and London: Yale University Press, 2008).

Mabìl, Pier Luigi, 'Una tirata contro il romanticismo', in Egidio Bellorini, *Discussioni e polemiche sul romanticismo*, 2 vols (Rome and Bari: Laterza, 1943, I, 1943), p. 470.

Manzoni, Alessandro, *Fermo e Lucia*, ed. by Salvatore Silvano Nigro (Milan: Mondadori, 2002).

Manzoni, Alessandro, *I promessi sposi*, ed. by Salvatore Silvano Nigro (Milan: Mondadori, 2002).

Manzoni, Alessandro, 'Sul Romanticismo. Lettera al marchese Cesare D'Azeglio', in Adelaide Sozzi Casanova (ed.), *Scritti di teoria letteraria* (Milan: Rizzoli, 1981), pp. 155–91.

Manzoni, Alessandro, *Tutte le poesie 1797–1872*, ed. by Gilberto Lonardi and Paola Azzolini (Venice: Marsilio, 1992).

Nigro, Salvatore, *La tabacchiera di Don Lisander. Saggio sui 'Promessi sposi'* (Turin: Einaudi, 1996).

Oropallo, Lorenzo, 'La questione romantica in Italia. Appunti di storia della critica', *Studi sul Settecento e l'Ottocento*, 6, 2011, pp. 99–112.

Pellico, Silvio, *Le mie prigioni* [1832], ed. by Angelo Jacomuzzi (Milan: Mondadori, 1986).

Pezzini, Franco, 'Il signor Walpole, il redattore & il Dark Italy', in Danilo Arona et al. (eds), *Dark Italy: Best Italian Horror* (Milan: Acheron Books, 2017). Kindle edn.

Pfister, Manfred, 'Theoria: To Go Abroad to See the World', in Manfred Pfister (ed.), *The Fatal Gift of Beauty: The Italies of British Travellers. An Annotated Anthology* (Amsterdam and Atlanta, GA: Rodopi, 1996), pp. 3–8.

Ravesi, Marcello, 'La polemica classico-romantica in Italia', in Sergio Luzzatto and Gabriele Pedullà (eds), *Atlante della letteratura italiana*, 3 vols (Turin: Einaudi, 2010–12, III, 2012), pp. 14–25.

Riccati, Charles, *Tableau historique et raisonné des événemens qui ont précédé et suivi le rétablissement des Bourbons en France, et de la paix en Europe, depuis mars 1815, jusqu'au 8 juillet 1816*, 2 vols (Paris: Delaunay, 1817).

Scianatico, Giovanna, *La questione neoclassica* (Venice: Marsilio, 2010).

Serres, Michel, 'Science and the Humanities: The Case of Turner', *SubStance*, 83, 1997, pp. 6–21.

Staël, Germaine de, 'Sulla maniera e la utilità delle Traduzioni', *Biblioteca italiana*, 1, January 1816, pp. 9–18.

Stendhal, *Rome, Naples et Florence*, ed. by Paul Arbelet and Édouard Champion, 2 vols (Paris: Honoré Champion, 1919).

Notes

1. I have extensively discussed this matter in my 'Italians and the Irrational' and '"Timore" e "terrore" nella polemica classico-romantica'. A comprehensive account of the critical debate on the Italian fantastic can now be found in Lazzarin.
2. For this aspect, I address the reader to Chapter 8 of this volume, by Simona Di Martino.
3. On the Classicist-Romantic quarrel as a palimpsest of Italian identity see Bollati, *L'italiano*. I have adopted Bollati's perspective in *Classicism and Romanticism in Italian Literature*. Most of the texts contributing to the quarrel are collected in Bellorini, from whence I cite. The critical history of the quarrel is extremely interesting on its own: see Oropallo.
4. Today, north-east of Porta Orientale are located via Alessandro Tadino, via Lazzaretto, and via Lodovico Settala, all names connected to the plague.
5. I will return in a forthcoming work on *I promessi sposi* as a Gothic novel.

Chapter 2

The Gothic and the Historical Novel: 1828–1860
Morena Corradi

This chapter addresses the Gothic in Italian literature in the first half of the nineteenth century (between 1828 and 1860 in particular), before the *Scapigliati* welcomed the genre in their work in post-unification Italy and a widespread interest in both Gothic and fantastic literature was enhanced and testified by the circulation of foreign works by Edgar Allan Poe, Theophile Gautier, and E. T. A. Hoffmann, among others. Earlier in the century, as Fabio Camilletti shows in Chapter 1 of this volume, there was an ostensive lack of literary examples of the Gothic genre which had been spreading in Europe thanks to authors such as Horace Walpole, Ann Radcliffe, Matthew Lewis and Charles Maturin. And yet, several Italian literary texts from the 1820s and 1830s, without offering a fully fledged expression of the Gothic, still represent a significant, and to this day largely under-investigated, body of work. Among the authors who engage with this genre, four appear of particular interest: Giambattista Bazzoni, Diodata Saluzzo Roero, Cesare Balbo, and Francesco Domenico Guerrazzi. All significant figures in their own right, their narratives are informed by the rising interest in Italian history.

The famous expression used by Alessandro Manzoni to define, and dismiss, Gothic literature ('un [. . .] guazzabuglio di streghe, di spettri, un disordine sistematico, una ricerca stravagante, una abiura in termini del senso comune' [a mishmash of witches and ghosts, a systematic disorder, a recherché extravagance, an abdication of common sense], from the 22 September 1823 so-called 'Letter on Romanticism' to the Marchese D'Azeglio, *Lettere* 344) has become paradigmatic of the widespread scepticism towards the role of imagination in the first half of the nineteenth century, scepticism which characterised the lively debate in the pages of *Il Conciliatore* at the dawn of Italian Romanticism. A revealing article, addressing Romantic poetry from the Orient ('Poesia romantica dall'Oriente'), dated 26 November 1818, mocks its 'bizzarre invenzioni' [bizarre inventions] and deems 'l'apparizione degli spettri dei morti' [the apparition of the ghosts of the dead] to be among 'le superstizioni del volgo' [the superstitions of the common people] (97). In the often-quoted letter to Marco Coen (2 June 1832), Manzoni comes to distinguish between literature based on invention (imagination) and literature based on 'invenimento' [finding]. The former, the 'letteratura che ha per iscopo [...] componimenti detti d'immaginazione' [a literature whose goal is the so-called imaginative composition] (*Lettere* 665) is described as fostering falsehoods such as 'immagini dei centauri e degli ippogrifi' [images of centaurs and hippogryphs], dangerous, as the letter reports, since the fantastic could affect the minds of those insufficiently educated (in these minds, we read, it is likely that 's'appigli lo strano' [the uncanny seizes them], 665–6). Manzoni will come to theorise that art cannot create, only discover, or uncover, what already exists.

Utterly unacceptable are, therefore, the 'storture' [distortions] and 'stranezze' [oddities], especially when applied to prose:

> alcuni poi [...] i quali hanno trasportate quelle storture nella prosa [...] hanno certamente potuto con ciò dilatarne il regno per qualche tempo, ma avranno, se non erro, contribuito ad abbreviarlo; perché il senso comune, che ha potuto lasciar correre molte stranezze nella poesia [...] quando esse voglion far di buono, e cacciarsi per forza in casa sua, le respinge per modo, e per modo le nega, e imprime loro un tal marchio di falsità, che non posson più mostrarsi nemmen dove prima. (*Lettere* 670)
>
> [Those who have carried those distortions into prose [...] certainly could thereby expand their kingdom for some time, but might have, if I am not mistaken, helped to shorten it; because common sense, which has allowed many oddities to flow into poetry, [...] when they want to really force their way into its house, it rejects them, and denies them, and marks them as false, to the extent that they cannot even appear where they used to appear before.]

This line of criticism is apparently not dissimilar from what Walter Scott claims in his 'On the Supernatural in Fictitious Composition', focused on the works of E.T.A. Hoffmann, where the Scottish author reads narratives such as 'The Sandman' as the result of a 'wild imagination' (which is counterposed to the 'common sense' exemplified by Clara's character). Scott ends his essay by defining Hoffmann's works as a 'warning [on] how the most fertile fancy may be exhausted by the lavish prodigality of its possessor' (353). The Scottish novelist, however, appreciates a mixing of the marvellous and the real, as is evident in his praise for Hoffmann's story 'An Entail', 'an instance of a tale in which the wonderful is, in our opinion, happily introduced, because it is connected with and applied to human interest and human feeling' (349). As Carlo Bordoni points out in his analysis of the essay, Scott is a rationalist and can only conceive of magic and superstitious manifestations in fiction as 'rari, brevi e indeterminate' [rare, short, and undefined] (Bordoni in Scott, *Del soprannaturale* 58) – also in order to preserve their effect – and rooted, so to speak, in a realistic context, as is the case of the Italian narratives of the early nineteenth century, greatly influenced by Radcliffe and Lewis, as well as by Scott.[1] The Scottish author himself had vastly read and reviewed the English Gothic, which could easily complement the romance he so greatly valued (55–6).

The Gothic and the Historical Novel

The relation between the Gothic genre and historical fiction has long been established. If György Lukács defines as a historical novel what is considered the first Gothic story, *The Castle of Otranto*, Walter Scott himself, in his introduction to Walpole's text, famously writes about the correspondences between the historical novel and the Gothic. Walpole's purpose (and ultimate achievement), in Scott's reading, is not so much to excite 'surprise and horror' ('Walpole' 87), but rather 'to draw [. . .] a picture of domestic life and manners, during feudal times' (87). Scott remarks that 'the natural parts of [Walpole's] narrative are so contrived, that they associate themselves with the marvellous occurrences; and [. . .] render those *speciosa miracula* striking and impressive' (87). While also Manzoni in his essay *Del romanzo storico* (1830) will write about 'speciosa miracula' commenting on the 'apparizioni fantastiche' [fantastic apparitions] as elements that Virgil 'trovava nel soggetto medesimo' [would find in the subject itself] (*Del romanzo storico* 37) of a poem about ancient Rome, the author of *The Betrothed* will famously reject epic and mythology in the name of the 'vero poetico' ['poetic truth']. An admirer of Ann Radcliffe, whose *The Mysteries of Udolpho* (1794) is itself an example of the close connections between the Gothic and the historical novel, Scott particularly praises Walpole's attempt to create 'a tale of amusing fiction upon the basis of the ancient romances of chivalry' ('Walpole' 84), a fiction carrying a 'tone of feudal manners and language' (93) that results in a virtuous blend of novel and romance. Something that Scott would claim for his own works as well.

Preparing the Ground: Ludovico di Breme's *Il Romitorio di Sant'Ida*

One of the most prominent Italian intellectuals of the turn of the century and one of the main contributors to *Il Conciliatore*, Ludovico Di Breme, whose work appears seminal in many respects for the authors and the period here addressed, proves receptive of the Gothic suggestions of northern literature. His *Romitorio di Sant'Ida*, if probably initially meant to be a sentimental novel, then converted to a moral one, as Piero Camporesi (who edited the manuscript, until then unpublished, in 1961) maintains, is nonetheless rich in images evoking sepulchral atmospheres and describing unsettling feelings. Based on a play titled *Ida*, this 'romanzo di un romanzo' [novel of a novel], in Camporesi's definition, a text that was never developed into a full novel, presents several 'accidenti mostruosi' [monstrous events], as the narrator characterises them, from the night spent 'in compagnia di un morto' [in the company of a dead person] (*Il Romitorio* 45) to the presence of a 'immane fantasma' [giant spectre] (42). The idées fixes ('idee fisse')[2] of the female central character, Teresa, are compared by Di Breme's narrator to the visions of the 'frate di Lewis o alla Eleonora del Bürger' (48), calling explicitly into question Gothic images by seminal authors of the genre, namely Matthew Lewis and Gottfried August Bürger. Interestingly, Di Breme met the author of *The Monk* in the very same year in which the *Romitorio* was published.

Nevertheless, the macabre elements in Di Breme's writing present strong ties with reality ('legami con la realtà') and are affected by the author's scepticism towards the so-called 'romanticismo lugubre' [lugubrious Romanticism] (Camporesi in Di Breme l). While appreciating foreign literature and welcoming with enthusiasm Mme de Staël's theories, Di Breme confirms the urge to keep faith to the *verosimiglianza* that later Manzoni will foster in his essay *Del romanzo storico*. The very character of Teresa, certainly ambiguous and even mysterious, finds herself in a situation quite common for a woman of her time, somewhat led to choose the convent over a forced marriage, as prosaically explained. Furthermore, Di Breme assigns a primary pedagogical goal to literature, as do many other authors of the period addressed here. The eerie and gloomy atmospheres underlying the pages of the *Romitorio* inform the works of writers such as Diodata Saluzzo di Roero (friend of Di Breme, and whose Gothic tale *Il Castello di Binasco* is published in 1819), Cesare Balbo and Giambattista Bazzoni, works in which the Gothic elements are even more explicitly intertwined with historical events, resounding evident patriotic undertones (not foreign to the *Romitorio*, where the revered Don Adriano's 'istinto patriottico' [patriotic instinct] leads him to support the cause of the local people and even to get arrested). Many of the authors in question, from Bazzoni to Balbo to Guerrazzi, are patriots who actively participated in the *moti* of 1820–1 or 1848, and even experienced imprisonment, as in the case of Guerrazzi. It is with him, the initiator of the *Risorgimento* novel ('romanzo storico risorgimentale'), that this literary Gothic 'vein' will culminate, and at the same time acquire a more prominent character.

The Gothic and Italian Early Historical Fiction: Saluzzo Roero, Bazzoni, Balbo

Most Italian popular literature of the first half of the nineteenth century features (alleged) supernatural elements, borrowed by the Gothic novel and framed, if loosely, by historical narratives, which are notably influenced by Scott's works. The collection *Romanzi storici di Walter Scott* was published by Vincenzo Ferrario (a renowned publisher of the time) starting in 1821 (Romagnoli 8), while other publishers such as Giovanni Campiglio and Giuseppe Antonelli issued novels by the famous Scot in the following years (8n). It has been pointed out, nevertheless, that examples of historical fiction in Italy predated the encounter with the Scottish novelist: a genealogy of authors had already been looking back at Italy's past, with a pedagogical intent, starting from Ugo Foscolo's *Orazione* held in Pavia in 1809 (Romagnoli 10); moreover, Saluzzo's *Il Castello di Binasco* predates Scott's *Ivanhoe*. Influences of this tradition can be found in several authors, from Ottavio Falletti and his historical 'digressions' (Romagnoli 18) to Davide Bertolotti, author of what is considered the first Italian historical novel, *La calata degli Ungheri in Italia nel Novecento*, published in 1822 (Romagnoli 16). Romagnoli has traced a picture of the (often inconsistent) treatment of history within Italian Romanticism. Even Di Breme's *Romitorio* presents features of a historical narrative, as the excursus on events from the Repubblica Subalpina to the narrator's present (1811) clearly shows. Unlike Di Breme, however, many authors of the following three decades, after Scott's model, prefer to look back at a past (notably the Middle Ages as well as the fifteenth and sixteenth centuries) that is often idealised and at the same time paralleled with the contemporaneous political phase.

The Medieval setting is prominent in the narratives of Diodata Saluzzo Roero (1775–1840), a writer close to Di Breme and admired by many of her contemporaries, including Foscolo. Saluzzo portrays 'un Medioevo misterioso di castelli e ruderi, di atmosfere inquietanti e di figure enigmatiche' [mysterious Middle Ages made of castles and ruins, unsettling atmospheres and enigmatic characters] (Nay in Saluzzo Roero, *Novelle* 17), elements that are framed in 'modelli arcaici del racconto' [archaic narrative models] (Zaccaria 81) and are conveyed by 'descrizioni [...] convenzional(i)' [conventional descriptions] (78), as Zaccaria points out, continuing Francesco De Sanctis's critique. Even during her time, Saluzzo was often associated with excessive Romantic overtones (Nay 100). The presence of her renowned lyrics within her novellas contributes to the archaic trait of her narrative style.[3]

Paradigmatic, in this respect, is *Il castello di Binasco, novella storica inedita di cui i principali avvenimenti e i personaggi sono tratti dalla storia del 1360* (first published in 1819 in *Il Ricoglitore*). It tells the story of Beatrice, Countess of Tenda, who is tricked into marrying Filippo Visconti and eventually executed on Visconti's order. These characters and events will populate the stories of other authors, Bazzoni for one (Beatrice di Tenda is also the protagonist of Bellini's 1833 opera of the same name). As the title of the novella suggests, and as critics have pointed out, Saluzzo privileges setting over characterisation, and highlights the story's Gothic features with ghostly appearances, castle ruins and gloomy weather. A popular story at the time, *Il castello di Binasco* was also included in a collection of novellas that Saluzzo published in 1830 under Manzoni's aegis, a collection which asserts the 'esigenza di un recupero della tradizione storica, come verifica delle aspirazioni o delusioni del presente' [need to recover a historical tradition as a way to assess the aspirations or the frustrations of the present] (Zaccaria 79), the same need shared by several historical narratives of the following years. Nevertheless, in most of Saluzzo's stories, medieval chivalric society seems to prevail, as the celebrated novella *La Valle della Ferrania* (1830) exemplifies. In spite of its loose historical frame (critics have pointed out the Radcliffean trait of the novella), with its gloomy castle, evil characters (the Marchesa, Ugo del Carretto, or the *Mago degli Appennini*), and with an innocent, young man victim of his heartless mother as main character, the story clearly traces a codifed medieval setting with its widespread folkloric and superstitious beliefs ('tendenze immaginose della plebe' [imaginative tendencies of the common people], 87). Significantly, the short story, which also presents the typical pre-Romantic quality of Saluzzo's poetics ('sublime ma selvaggia apparisce la natura [...], canta l'upupa selvaggia nei merli e nei muri cadenti' [sublime and yet wild nature appears [...], the wild hoopoe sings on the battlements and crumbling walls], 97), ends with Antonino asking his beloved and her father to teach him chivalric arts.

Medieval settings and Gothic topoi populate the works of Giambattista Bazzoni (1803–50), deeply influenced by Scott. Gothic elements and undertones in his stories are often directly correlated to the superstition and magical thinking that characterised people's mindset in ancient times, and further enhanced by a more explicit historical frame of the stories themselves. This is noticeable in the story 'Magaruffo Venturiello o la corte del Duca Filippo Maria' (1832), which is inspired by the same events echoed by Saluzzo's *Il castello di Binasco*, although there are differences, starting with the title. Significantly Magaruffo, who Bazzoni chooses as his protagonist, embodies valour and love for the fatherland. Filippo Maria Visconti, on the other hand, is portrayed as superstitious, more than evil, with a 'mente [. . .] esaltata' [fanatical mind] (*Racconti* 132), relying on advisors such as the 'philosopher' Elia who deals in 'astrologia', 'chiromanzia', 'scienze occulte' [astrology, chiromancy, occult sciences] (131–2) and is capable of insane cruelty. In a historical setting with clear medieval features, the characters are moved by their sense of duty, and, more often, by their feelings of revenge that reflect the hostility between cities, which in turn reflects the hostility between factions (the Guelphs and the Ghibellines).

History and historical narratives are indeed of great interest to Bazzoni, writer and patriot, who earned respect and admiration in his time for the role he played as judge in the trials that followed the Five Days of Milan. His first novel, *Il castello di Trezzo*, which narrates the story of the end of Bernabò Visconti's reign at the hands of Giovan Galeazzo and which has at the centre the troubled love story of Palamede and Ginevra, proved to be a great success (Bazzoni was even introduced to the famous Salotto Maffei). First published in the *Nuovo Ricoglitore* starting from 1826, it was then released in twelve editions over the course of the following years (three editions were issued in one year). Inspired by Scott (whose novel *Waverley* was published in 1830 in Italy with Bazzoni's translation), *Il castello di Trezzo* is set in 1385, in that 'età di mezzo, età d'armi e di fanatismo' [Middle Ages, age of weapons and fanaticism] that constitutes the backdrop of so many a narrative of this period (1). Here the Gothic elements (the castle and its dungeons, the victimised innocent maiden, the evil lord) add to the creation of a narrative that mixes 'nei limiti della verisimiglianza [. . .] la storia con fatti d'invenzione' [within the limits of verisimilitude [. . .] history with fictional events] as Bazzoni himself defines the historical novel in the introductory chapter to his *Il falco della rupe, o la guerra di Musso* (1828–9) (20). In this introduction, the conversation about the historical novel among four aristocratic characters seems to counter the general scepticism and moral concern raised by this genre at the time, particularly in the words of Don Annibale, clearly conveying the author's point of view.[4] The historical novel is praised as a genre containing other genres: *Racconto del lago*, a reading Don Annibale recommends to the Countess (interested in learning about the region of Lake Como as well as in fighting boredom), represents an example of a novel where the 'fatti d'invenzione' [fictional events] make history 'più studiata e proficua' [more studied and useful] (20). A novel,

Racconto del lago, which, in a quite intriguing mise en abyme, proves to be nothing other than *Il falco della rupe*.

The 'imaginary events' take on Gothic traits, especially in Bazzoni's historical short stories published in 1832 (conversely, the stories published in 1839 carry a more distinctive historical trait, bringing the author to define them 'delineamenti storici' [historical traits] in his *dedica* to Sigismondo Karis). Significantly, in his note to Bazzoni's 1832 *Racconti storici* (the volume which also contains the already mentioned 'Magaruffo Venturiello'), the publisher Omobono Manini writes that the stories in question meet the favour of an audience that demonstrates a love for 'storiche cognizioni, specialmente quando vengono presentate sotto forma di dilettevoli e animati quadri' [historical notions, especially when presented in the shape of entertaining and animated pictures] (5). Next to a very short and peculiar narrative such as 'Un cadavere antico (Estore Visconti)', which in a playful more than sepulchral overtone tells the story of Estore's corpse preserved for over four centuries in the Monza cathedral, there are narratives in which the historical and the Gothic genre are more successfully intertwined. In one of the most interesting stories of the collection, 'Il sotterraneo di Porta Nuova', the Marchese Reginaldo Buoso, while chasing his wife of whom he is morbidly jealous, finds himself in a dark and narrow space which evokes 'antichi riti' [ancient rites]. He is described in a delirious state (271), and the narrator notes that 'né mancò [. . .] chi lo attribuì ad effetto di malia, di sortilegio o d'altro diabolico potere; alla quale credenza [. . .] già inclinavano [. . .] le menti in quella età' [some attributed it to the result of a spell, witchcraft, or of another diabolic power, which minds were already inclined to believe in at that time] (271).

The 'entertaining and animated pictures' of the publisher's note previously mentioned could be read as a reference to Gothic topoi which populate the historical novellas circulating in Italy in the 1830s. Animated pictures (like animated objects) namely characterise both Gothic and fantastic literature, starting from the picture of Alfonso, the original Prince of Otranto of Walpole's novel who sighs and steps out of his portrait, much to the dismay of his illegitimate successor, Manfred, led astray by his lust and conceit. Animated images are called into question in Diodata Saluzzo's 'La valle della Ferrania' as well, where Antonino del Carretto, the main character, while prisoner in a castle tower, believes that he sees moving figures on the wall tapestry. And indeed the *Mago degli Appennini* comes out of the wall and leads Antonino out of the castle through 'gallerie lunghe ed oscure [e] stretti corridoi' [long galleries and dark, narrow hallways] (95). However, here the Gothic topos seems to function more as a plot device rather than as an eerie component of the story, given the conventional style of the novella. In Bazzoni's 'Il sotterraneo di Porta Nuova', on the other hand, the paintings on the cellar walls 'sembravano muoversi' [seemed to be moving] (*Racconti* 270) in front of Reginaldo's eyes, creating a suggestive and uncanny scene. Moreover, in Bazzoni's novella, the alleged supernatural event carries moral undertones, just like in Walpole's novel: the cruel and ambitious Reginaldo, while in the cellar, hears a mysterious voice inviting him to abandon 'il pensiero della vendetta' [vengeful thoughts] (268).

A moral and overtly pedagogical intent frames the historical novellas of another author of the period, Cesare Balbo (1789–1853). Prime Minister, if briefly, of the Kingdom of Sardinia in 1848, Balbo wrote several history books and, together with Cavour, founded the journal *Il Risorgimento* in 1847. Certainly a minor component within Balbo's body of work, his short stories, which are of interest here, were published in 1829 and eventually released in six further editions with additional novellas. Not only Balbo's history books, largely addressing the history of Italy and its foreign occupation, but his novellas as well became hugely popular, as the publishers of the 1857 posthumous edition point out.[5] They recall the great success met by Giuseppe Pomba's 1829 edition of Balbo's *Quattro novelle narrate da un maestro di scuola*, which had several, almost contemporaneous editions (both luxury and economic ones). The same publishers also highlight the fact that they are publishing Balbo's novellas (reprinting the 1854 Le Monnier edition with the addition of a few unpublished works) within the *Biblioteca Popolare*, a series dedicated to the best Italian and international literature ('opere classiche d'ogni nazione e di ogni tempo' [classical works of all nations and times], Balbo 5).

Narrated by a school teacher, the original four novellas have a frame which bridges between a distant past and the narrator's present and aims to enhance the didactic purpose of the stories, leaving the historical and patriotic components in the background. The typical Gothic topoi, from the victimised innocent woman to the haunting settings (such as the forest in the novella 'La bella Alda'), if present, are not prevalent. The novellas 'Francesca' and 'Margherita', on the other hand, seem to anticipate themes that will inform fantastic narratives of the following decades. This is the case for the evil character's hand that no longer responds to the individual's command or for the protagonist's inexplicably fading health and beauty (themes that will later be found in Arrigo Boito's and Tarchetti's works, for instance). Rambaldo, the rejected lover who taints the reputation of the innocent Francesca, promised to Manfredi who is fighting in the Holy Land, causes the death of the young woman. When

Rambaldo sees her, her body has lost its beauty and the flowers surrounding it are withering. Shocked and in disbelief, Rambaldo touches Francesca's hand, which suddenly clutches his own. Only when the young man realises the harm he has done and starts praying (and returns the golden cross he had stolen from Francesca), does the woman's body regain its beauty and glow and Rambaldo's hand is released: 'parve quasi di verginal gioia il celeste volto suffondersi; e la mano vendicatrice dolcemente cadendo s'aprì, e lasciò libera quella di Rambaldo' [her heavenly face looked almost filled with virginal joy; and the vengeful hand softly opened and released that of Rambaldo] (Balbo 31).

A mysterious fading of beauty and health also characterises the destiny of Margherita, the protagonist of the novella of the same name, married to the unfaithful and insensitive Manfredi. Already suffering from a mysterious disease, Margherita gives birth to a girl as her husband persists in leading his dissolute life. The woman dies (while embracing him and falling at his feet, suppliant) during one of Manfredi's dishevelled parties. The tragic event caused the husband to leave the 'Castello Verde', where he lived with his wife, but not to change his behaviour. Back at the castle, on the night of the anniversary of Margherita's death, Manfredi suffers from a mysterious seizure, similar to the one that killed his wife, and from which he will never recover. In fact, from that day, 'pare che ogni notte intorno alla medesima ora si rinnovassero i medesimi accidenti o castighi' [it seems that every night, around the same time, the same events or punishments recurred] (Balbo 103), punishments which lead him to his death. And an old wives' tale narrates that, on the fatal night,

> lo spirito di lei, non veduto da nessun altro, comparì ad un tratto a Manfredi, e a lui corse abbracciandolo e baciandolo come soleva in vita, ed avea fatto all'ultima notte; poi l'accompagnò quando il portarono al suo letto, ed ivi con lui giacque quasi mogliera tutta la notte. (Balbo 103)
>
> [Her spirit, invisible to others, suddenly appeared to Manfredi and ran to him embracing and kissing him as she used to do when she was alive, and as she also did on her very last night; then she followed him when he was taken to his bed, and lay there with him all night as a wife would do.]

These novellas, characterised by the reassuring narrating voice of a teacher, tend to dim the frightening and even captivating component present in so many stories that were popular at the time. In his preface to the 1829 edition of the novellas, also reported by the editors of the 1857 edition, Balbo writes that his stories (regardless of their definition as 'classiche o romantiche, storiche, immaginate, miste' [classical or romantic, historical, imagined, mixed]), are meant to be read 'per ozio' [for entertainment], and yet they might as well improve the reader, who may find herself 'migliore' [improved]: 'tieni buona ogni cosa che non t'annoi, e non ti guasti' [cherish everything that does not bore you or spoil you] (10), is the author's advice for his audience. Interestingly, the teacher-narrator of 'Margherita', in the prologue to the story, explicitly criticises the idea that fear is the most effective pedagogical tool. He remarks that this common belief is a sign of 'stolta pigrizia' [stolid laziness] (85). On the other hand, he is convinced that some 'insegnamento virtuoso' [virtuous teaching] (85) hides in 'superstizioni popolari' [popular superstitions] since, as the narrator argues, 'quel po' di bene [. . .] si trova quasi sempre anche nel male' [some good can almost always be found in evil as well] (85). This prologue to the teacher's tale (based on an alleged folk tale set in a castle in 'mezzo a' neri boschi' [in the middle of dark woods] 86) seems to evoke the encountering of 'supernatural agency' and 'human interest' that Scott praises in Walpole's Gothic novel.

The Gothic in the Works of Francesco Domenico Guerrazzi: The *Risorgimento* Novel

A very different approach to historical narratives is found in Guerrazzi's novels, in which horror and fear notably play an important role. 'Dopo Mazzini e Manzoni, Guerrazzi. Dopo l'iniziatore della rivoluzione politica, dopo il poeta del cristianesimo, un'altra irreparabile perdita ci ha colpiti: quella del più grande romanziere d'Italia' [After Mazzini and Manzoni, Guerrazzi. After the initiator of the political revolution, after the poet of Christianity, another irreparable loss fell upon us: that of the greatest Italian novelist] (Cameroni 1). These opening lines of an article (which continues in the issue of 4 October) commemorating the passing of Guerrazzi (1804–73) emphatically praise an author who, if not the greatest, was certainly one of the most popular and influential writers of the first half of the nineteenth century. In honouring his valour as a novelist and as a patriot, the democratic journalist and poet Felice Cameroni, author of the piece, underlines 'il rimpianto di una generazione che non seppe realizzare i voti del repubblicano livornese, del sommo romanziere italiano' [the regret of a generation who was not able to achieve the aspirations of the Livornese Republican, of the greatest Italian novelist] (1). This statement, if clearly partial, conveys the deep connection between the life and the work of Guerrazzi. A patriot and a politician, as well as a journalist and novelist, Guerrazzi is considered the father of the *Risorgimento* historical novel, where the political and patriotic component is brought to the foreground while heavily relying on Gothic images and language.

As the narrator of Guerrazzi's first book *La battaglia di Benevento* (1827) explicitly states, the novel has to portray the events 'con quanto di fantastico può immaginare il poeta' [with as much fantastical as the poet can create] but the writer has to 'svilupparl[o] con naturale spiegazione' [develop it with a natural explanation] (*La battaglia di Benevento* II, 149). What follows this remark is a reference to a 'pergamena antichissima' [very ancient parchment] (II, 149), an element which ostensibly recalls the connection between the Gothic and the historical novel – even though, as Giovanna Rosa points out, the first edition of *La battaglia di Benevento* did not feature a preface to claim its authenticity (183). Published in 1827, this seminal book (the first example of the *Risorgimento* novel but also of the Italian popular novel) had several more editions (including one in 1852, an edition that Guerrazzi prepared while in prison), which not only indicate its popularity but are also suggestive of its influence. Ostensibly enhancing that 'mixed genre' praised by Bazzoni, Guerrazzi's novels present a strong link with the *melodramma* as well. Not insignificant in this respect is the fact that Guerrazzi first started writing for the theatre. A strong theatrical element informs (and amplifies) the Gothic tropes in *La battaglia di Benevento* as well as in most of Guerrazzi's production, from *L'assedio di Firenze* (first published in 1836) to *Beatrice Cenci* (1854), tropes that are often represented as if they were staged.

The moral message underlying Guerrazzi's literary production is deeply intertwined with the 'pedagogy of fear', as Rosa and Scappaticci, among others, have pointed out. *La battaglia di Benevento* significantly ends as follows: 'morale di questo libro? [...] nessun argomento per contenere l'uomo dal mal fare torn[a] più acconcio che spaventarlo con gli effetti stessi del male, frenarlo in somma col terrore' [the moral of this book? [...] to prevent man from doing harm, no argument is more suitable than to scare him with the very consequences of his evil doing, to finally restrain him through terror] (*La battaglia* II, 405). Frightening images and vengeful characters are meant to attract a wider, often uneducated public while heroic historical figures and events are meant to elicit interest and provide inspiration. Amid the numerous ghosts, skeletons and gloomy under-passages that populate the pages of Guerrazzi's first novel, though, there is hardly any uncanny or actual supernatural trait, Radcliffe being his most influential model. Revealing in this regard is the prevalence of static images, mostly of the 'supernatural explained' (Macchioni Jodi 403). The haunting voice that keeps telling the young protagonist, Ruggiero, 'rammentatevi di vostro padre' [remember your father], is a well-known and effective example in this respect: there is not a supernatural entity behind it, but rather a spy acting on behalf of the evil Count of Cerra. At the end of the novel, however, even 'real ghosts' appear to mark the solemnity of the moment: the scene of the *anima scettrata* [sceptred soul] of the emperor that frees the spirits of his children from their tombs sombrely anticipate the revenge that the Ghibellines will obtain with the Sicilian Vespers.

The obtrusive narrator, which characterises Guerrazzi's novels, often intervenes to underline the reason or the moral behind the Gothic images. We read, for example, that 'schiere [di] spiriti malefici [. . .] la superstizione e il rimorso hanno posto nell'aria sotto il cerchio della luna' [superstition and remorse have placed [. . .] a multitude [of] evil spirits under the circle of the moon], where the reference is to the widespread beliefs characterising the time (*La battaglia* II, 202). And a moral undertone informs the episode of the big spear stuck in the ceiling with a threatening message for the treacherous Caserta (235); an episode reminiscent of the giant helmet that falls on Conrad in *The Castle of Otranto*.

Past events and characters in Guerrazzi's novels are notably meant not so much to recreate a realistic historical setting, but rather to convey dramatic atmospheres and powerful, often gory images. If the latter are particularly evident in a 'domestic' narrative such as *Beatrice Cenci*, which features some of the most shocking themes and images of Italian popular literature (from incest to extremely graphic descriptions of violence – elements which nonetheless mark the author's breaking away from the moral code of his time; Rosa 220), they also heavily inform *L'assedio di Firenze*, whose resonance with the nineteenth-century political situation would appear evident to its readers. These traits, along with their melodramatic style, greatly contributed to the popularity of Guerrazzi's historical narratives (Vanden Berghe). The opening chapter of *L'assedio di Firenze* features a significant plea to the (Italian) people to act like a lion that does not rest 'finché non abbia divorato la preda, e bevuto il sangue degli uccisi' [till it has devoured its prey and drunk the blood of its victims] (I, 28). This is just one of countless horrific images that populate this novel where vampiric scenes add to the sepulchral and ghostly ones.

The theme of revenge acquires a prominent role in the novel, as the famous episode of *Morticino degli Antinori* proves with its lengthy and detailed description of Sassatello's son's murder. 'Mi lavai nel suo sangue le mani, me lo posi su i labbri e lo bevvi [. . .]. Chi intende pregustare nel mondo i diletti ineffabili del paradiso, arda prima di odio e si disseti poi nel sangue dell'odiato!' [I washed my hands in his blood, I brought it to my lips and drank it [. . .]. Whoever wishes to taste on earth the ineffable delights of heaven, should first deeply hate and then quench their thirst with the hated person's blood] (*L'assedio* II, 25): these are the terrible words spoken by Morticino after taking his revenge. In a novel full of shocking and grandiose scenes, including spectres rising from their tombs (an iconography which will become paradigmatic in *Risorgimento* literature throughout the following decades), the vampiric theme is recurrent. The scene involving the traitor Giovanni Bandino is namely quite powerful, as well as reminiscent of Lewis's and Maturin's narratives. Disguised as a friar, Bandino is compared to 'uno di quei corpi scomunicati, dalla superstizione greca detti vampiri, i quali nella notte, derelitti gli avelli, irrompono per virtù diabolica nelle stanze più segrete a pascersi col sangue delle persone ch'ebbero care in questa vita' [one of those excommunicated bodies, called vampires by an old Greek superstition, who break out of their tombs at night and diabolically enter the most secret rooms to feed on the blood of those who were dear to them in this life] (I, 362).[6]

While such scenes might seem gratuitous, and clearly undermine the pedagogical claim of Guerrazzi's literature, they somewhat aim to highlight figures and behaviours that resonate with the author's times. This is certainly the case for the epilogue of *L'assedio di Firenze*, focused on treason, which, together with political freedom and foreign occupation, is a central theme of the novel. Spectres and severed heads are haunting the treacherous Malatesta (whose own head is later found in the woods):

> Tra le nuvole appariscono i fantasmi di tutti coloro che egli aveva menato a morte a cagione del suo tradimento [...], larve infinite lo tormentano [...], ma sopra le altre uno spettro gli sta attaccato alla vita con l'ardore del vampiro che sugge il sangue alla vittima [...] – e questo spettro è il Pieruccio. (II, 452–3)
>
> [from the clouds the ghosts of all the ones who died as a consequence of his betrayal appear [...], endless ghostly figures torment him [...], but above all a spectre is on him with the ardor of a vampire who sucks his victim's blood [...] – and this ghost is Pieruccio.]

Pieruccio is a prophet-figure who is killed by a mob instigated by Malatesta.

Central to many of Guerrazzi's pages, images of killings and blood can be read as an expression of the pessimism that, according to Mazzini's appreciative review of *La battaglia di Benevento*, characterises the author's perspective: 'più veemente forza si vuole che non è la voce della virtù' [it is necessary a much stronger force than the voice of virtue] is a famous line from Guerrazzi's first novel (*La battaglia* I, 42).[7]

Significantly, a reference to blood and wars features in the opening issue of the short-lived *Indicatore Livornese*, inspired by Mazzini's *Indicatore Genovese* and founded by Guerrazzi in 1829. The *prospetto* of this newspaper, while asserting its educational and revolutionary inspiration, evokes the image of the 'ebbrezza di sangue' [bloodlust] that has characterised a century (the nineteenth) with the many wars that filled Europe with 'le ossa di milioni di caduti' [the bones of millions of dead] (1–2), only then to significantly state that nations by now would wage war only to free their homeland.

Traces of what we have called the 'Gothic vein' are also present in the *Risorgimento* novels of Massimo D'Azeglio (1798–1866), a writer as well as a politician, painter and cousin of Cesare Balbo, whose interest is otherwise much more focused on Italian history and political emancipation (see Romagnoli 65). D'Azeglio describes his first novel as a 'lento lavoro di rigenerazione del carattere nazionale' [a gradual work of regeneration of the national character] (*I miei ricordi* 415–16), which came to constitute, together with the works of other writers of the time, such as the ones here considered, what De Sanctis defined 'un medio evo della rivoluzione italiana, dove scrittori, principi e guerrieri parlano il nostro linguaggio ed operano e vogliono secondo i nostri desiderii' [the Middle Ages of the Italian revolution, where writers, princes and warriors speak our language and act and want according to our wishes] (287). De Sanctis highlights the resonance of narratives based on medieval characters and events with the hearts and minds of patriots during the *Risorgimento*. Even a novel like *Ettore Fieramosca, ossia la disfida di Barletta* (1833) reveals the influence of the Gothic in the portrayal of the medieval context: Radcliffian scenes are still intertwined with the historical narrative, but are handled with a certain detachment and even irony by the author (Romagnoli 62–3). The novel features ghosts which prove to be made of flesh and blood, as in the episode of the *bravo* Boscherino who frees himself from a sheet that covers him; or dead people who are very much alive, as in the case of Ginevra, who revives when kissed by Fieramosca while in the coffin. For D'Azeglio, who will also reflect on the essence of the historical novel, the 'favole' [fairy tales] (387), as they are defined in *I miei ricordi*, created by the author's imagination, make history more interesting and accessible to the readers. Once again, the Gothic component can be read within a pedagogical and moral frame.

This brief overview of some of the most celebrated (at the time) Italian literary works of the first decades of the nineteenth century shows how images and tropes that came to define the Gothic genre and populate the pages of Walpole, Radcliffe, Lewis and Maturin, among others, accompanied the evolution of Italian historical fiction with a striking persistence. The evident clichéd and formulaic character that these tropes assume, especially within Italian popular fiction, as exemplified by Guerrazzi's novels, does not detract from the interest that the phenomenon bears, holding ties both with the Romanticism of the early nineteenth century and the post-unification *Scapigliati* intellectual and artistic circle.

Bibliography

Balbo, Cesare, *Novelle. Nuova edizione, coll'aggiunta di una novella e due drammi sinora inediti* (Turin: Unione Tipografico-Editrice Torinese, 1857).
Bazzoni, Giambattista, *Il castello di Trezzo* (Paris: Baudry Libreria Europea, 1838).
Bazzoni, Giambattista, *Il Falco della rupe, o la guerra di Musso*, 1828–9 (Como: Lariologo, 2007).
Bazzoni, Giambattista, *Racconti storici* (Milan: Omobono Manini, 1832).
Billiani, Francesca, 'Il testo fantasticizzato e goticizzato come metafora della destrutturazione del discorso "nazione": attorno agli scrittori scapigliati', *California Italian Studies*, 2.1, 2011, https://doi.org/10.5070/C321008924.
Cameroni, Felice (Pessimista), 'Francesco Domenico Guerrazzi', in *L'Arte drammatica*, 48.2, 27 September 1873, p. 1.
D'Azeglio, Massimo, *Ettore Fieramosca ossia la disfida di Barletta* (Florence: Felice Le Monnier, 1850).
D'Azeglio, Massimo, *I miei ricordi*, ed. Silvia Spellanzon (Milan: Rizzoli, 1956).
De Sanctis, Francesco, *Nuovi saggi critici* (Naples: Morano e figlio, 1872).
Di Breme, Lodovico, *Il Romitorio di Sant'Ida*, ed. Piero Camporesi (Bologna: Commissione per i Testi di Lingua, 1961).
Guerrazzi, Francesco Domenico, *La battaglia di Benevento. Storia del secolo XIII*, 2 vols (Livorno: Poligrafia Italiana, 1849).
Guerrazzi, Francesco Domenico, *L'assedio di Firenze*, 2 vols (Milan: Guigoni, 1874).
Guerrazzi, Francesco Domenico, 'Prospetto', *L'Indicatore Livornese* 1, 12 January 1829, pp. 1–2.
Macchioni Jodi, Rodolfo, 'Dal romanzo gotico al romanzo storico italiano', *Italianistica: Rivista di letteratura italiana*, 23.2/3, 1994, pp. 389–416.
Manzoni, Alessandro, *Del romanzo storico e, in genere, de' componimenti misti di storia e d'invenzione* ed. Silvia De Laude, *Edizione nazionale ed europea delle opere di Alessandro Manzoni*, vol. 14 (Milan: Centro Nazionale Studi Manzoniani, 2000).
Manzoni, Alessandro, *Lettere*, ed. Cesare Arieti, in Alberto Chiari and Fausto Ghisalberti (eds), *Tutte le opere di Alessandro Manzoni*, 7 vols (Milan: Mondadori, 1970, vii, book 1).
Marini, Quinto, 'Un'occasione mancata. La narrativa risorgimentale ligure tra racconto storico, autobiografia e romanzo, (Mazzini, Canale, Ruffini, Barrili, Abba)', in Luca Lo Basso (ed.), *Politica e cultura nel Risorgimento italiano. Genova 1857 e la fondazione della Società Ligure di Storia Patria* (Atti del Convegno, Genoa, 4–6 February 2008, Atti della Società Ligure di Storia

Patria, Nuova Serie XLVIII (CXXII).I, 2008, Società Ligure di Storia Patria), pp. 285–315.

Nay, Laura, 'Storia d'Elza la Bella e della terribile sua Comitiva', in Marziano Guglielminetti and Paola Trivero (eds), *Il Romanticismo in Piemonte: Diodata Saluzzo* (Atti del Convegno di Studi, Saluzzo, 29 September 1990, Olschki, 1993), pp. 89–102.

Romagnoli, Sergio, 'Narratori e prosatori del Romanticismo', in Emilio Cecchi and Natalino Sapegno (eds), *Storia della letteratura italiana*, 9 vols (Milan: Garzanti, 1965–9, 1968, viii), pp. 5–192.

Rosa, Giovanna, *Il romanzo melodrammatico. F.D. Guerrazzi e la narrativa democratico-risorgimentale* (Florence: La Nuova Italia Editrice, 1990).

Saluzzo Roero, Diodata, *Novelle*, ed. Laura Nay (Florence: Olschki, 1989).

Scappaticci, Tommaso, *Un intellettuale dell'Ottocento romantico. Francesco Domenico Guerrazzi. Il pubblico, l'ideologia, la poetica* (Ravenna: Longo Editore, 1978).

Scarsella, Alessandro, 'Manzoni, Guerrazzi, Tenca. Ricezione del gotico e resistenze al fantastico in Italia', in Michela Vanon Alliata and Giorgio Rimondi (eds), *Dal gotico al fantastico: tradizioni, riscritture e parodie* (Venice: Cafoscarina, 2015), pp. 215–27.

Scott, Walter, *Del soprannaturale nel romanzo fantastico*, ed. Carlo Bordoni (Cosenza: Luigi Pellegrini Editore, 2004).

Scott, Walter, 'On the Supernatural in Fictitious Composition; and Particularly on the Works of Ernest Theodore William Hoffmann', in Ioan Williams (ed.), *Sir Walter Scott on Novelists and Fiction* (London: Routledge & Kegan Paul, 1968), pp. 312–53.

Scott, Walter, 'Walpole', in Ioan Williams (ed.), *Sir Walter Scott on Novelists and Fiction* (London: Routledge & Kegan Paul, 1968), pp. 84–93.

Vanden Berghe, Dirk, 'Enfasi e teatralità: *La battaglia di Benevento* di Guerrazzi', in *Nuova Corrente*, LXVII, 165, 2020, pp. 37–46.

V., E. (Ermes Visconti), 'Idee elementari sulla poesia romantica' (Articolo terzo. Definizione della poesia romantica), *Il Conciliatore* 25, 26 November 1818, pp. 97–100.

Zaccaria, Giuseppe, 'Diodata Saluzzo e i modelli del racconto', in Marziano Guglielminetti and Paola Trivero (eds), *Il Romanticismo in Piemonte: Diodata Saluzzo* (Atti del convegno di studi, Saluzzo, 29 September 1990, Olschki, 1993), pp. 75–87.

Notes

1. In fact, a realistic component also characterises post-unification fantastic literature so much so that the definition of 'testo fantasticizzato e goticizzato' [a fantasticised and gothicised text] (Billiani), and not merely of 'fantastic' or 'Gothic', has often been applied to Iginio Ugo Tarchetti's works.
2. 'Idee fisse' interestingly evokes the title that several years later Arrigo Boito would consider for a collection of fantastic tales that will never see the light and that was supposed to focus on obsessive thoughts recalling the concept of 'monomania'.

3. Theatre, more than prose, first welcomed Gothic instances in the pre-Romantic period (Scarsella 215).
4. The year 1827 has famously been defined as the year of the historical novel in Italy since, besides Bazzoni's novel, Alessandro Manzoni's *Fermo e Lucia* and Francesco Domenico Guerrazzi's *La battaglia di Benevento* were published, as well as Carlo Varese's *Sibilla Odaleta*.
5. This edition includes stories that the author defines as 'moralizzanti' [moralising] (Balbo 196). In the preface, titled 'Prefazione alle nuove novelle' and reported in the 1857 volume here quoted, the author maintains that the 'eventi strani [...] sono più rari che non si crede' [strange events [...] are rarer than believed] (196–7), and therefore focuses on moralising stories set in his own times.
6. Interestingly enough, in his 1830 anthology (*Antologia romantica e classica*), Guerrazzi includes the novella 'Storia d'Elza la bella', a peculiar story within the Italian landscape where vampirism is the dominant theme (see Saluzzo 15n) and whose style led some readers to attribute it to Saluzzo (see Nay's essay here cited).
7. Mazzini's piece on Guerrazzi's novel, titled '*La battaglia di Benevento*, storia del secolo XIII, scritta dal Dottore F.M. Guerrazzi, vol. 4 Livorno 1827', is published in the *Indicatore Genovese*, between 23 August and 30 August 1828. Mazzini, however, came to favour 'contemporary' novels over historical ones in the name of the urgency of the cause of Italian independence (see Marini 289).

Chapter 3

Early Developments: 1861–1914
Stefano Serafini

In the period between 1861 and 1914, two major interlinked traumas caused the fracture that led to the proliferation and multiplication of Gothic discourses. The first, of a historical and political nature, was national unification, which initiated a long and controversial process of state-building that eventually revealed the fragmented character of a country in which extremely diverse regions had been forcibly integrated into a single political entity. Rapid and invasive processes of industrialisation and urbanisation dramatically changed the texture of cities, particularly the largest ones, such as Milan, Florence and Naples; they also exacerbated social and economic disparities, caused a sharp increase in crime and generated strong concerns among Italians. The Gothic, as I will show, arises as an acknowledgement of such disquiet. The second trauma, of a social and historical nature, was the result of significant advancements in the fields of science, medicine and technology, which paradoxically aided or mirrored the resurgence of occult beliefs and practices.

In fact, far from being a monolithic discourse founded on purely rational and empirical thinking or a coherent set of methods and approaches, what scholars refer to as science at the *fin de siècle* was, rather, an extremely diverse series of stances, knowledges and practices (mesmerism, spiritualism and psychical research) that blurred the binary distinctions between natural and supernatural.[1] Although many questioned the scientific status of occult practices, 'there was no unequivocal position', as Martin Willis remarks, 'from which these beliefs could be denied a place within the scientific hierarchy' (11). Both telegraphy and spiritualism, as Richard Noakes points out, permitted invisible communication from a distance (422). While inventions such as laryngoscopes and stomach illuminations allowed physicians to explore the inside of the living body, clairvoyants claimed to be capable of identifying diseases through their gaze. Photography broadened the realm of the visible and proved to be an instrumental tool in distributing scientific knowledge, such as bacteriology, but it also became a crucial resource for spiritualists, who saw it as proof of psychic phenomenology.[2]

This was, all in all, an ambivalent and problematic period of contradictions, markedly characterised by a tension between the natural and the supernatural; the rise of spiritualist and occult discourses increasingly encouraged people to see unknown manifestations simply as phenomena governed by laws that were not yet fully grasped by humans.[3] It is revealing that the slow, difficult construction of the new-born state and the process of 'making Italians' in the name of scientific progress and secularisation were translated into attempts by positivist science to deprive the world of its mysterious and supernatural aura by drawing attention to phenomena that had previously been ascribed to superstition and religion, thus engendering a new form of syncretism. It was precisely the development of science and technology, then, that facilitated the resurgence of popular, discarded beliefs and traditions, which were re-evaluated in the light of recent discoveries and reassessed within a new, apparently more scientific system of knowledge.

As Stephen King reminds us, such periods of crisis and serious sociopolitical strain are extremely fertile for the development and spread of Gothic literature (43). This chapter will thus explore the broad spectrum of incarnations of the Italian Gothic in the late nineteenth and early twentieth centuries with the aim of revealing how these stories powerfully betray some of the deepest fears and anxieties of the Italian people at a pivotal moment in the definition of Italy's cultural and political identity. Here, I will focus neither on the so-called *Scapigliatura* movement nor on Antonio Fogazzaro's *Malombra* (1881), both of which are explored in Chapters 13 and 14 of this volume.[4] What I aim to show is how, in those times of uncertainty, Italian literature eagerly and variously responded to the enormous interest in the disproportionate, alarming expansion of the new city and the unaccomplished disjunction of science and the occult, rational and irrational practices, thriving on and shaping the contemporary heated debates on the degenerative and contagious nature of the underclasses and the existence of ghosts and vampires, metempsychosis and witchcraft, psychic and mesmeric powers. In so doing, this chapter will bring to light a multifaceted and heterogeneous literary landscape that arose between two competing systems of values – Gothic and modernity, the rational and the irrational – whose underlying tension signals the difficulty, if not the impossibility, of building a new, modernised and finally secularised Italy.

Urban Gothic

Violent crime constituted the most pressing issue in post-unification Italy, with the ruling class, as Paul Garfinkel underscores, considering it 'the defining feature of Italian lawlessness, if not the country's "incontestable" primacy in comparison with "civilized" Europe' (55). The increasing proximity and frequent interaction between delinquents and indigents within the poorest districts of the largest cities, caused by rapid and often inconsiderate processes of urbanisation, became a growing concern for the government and generated a vast number of discussions and theorisations about the potential perilousness of that great multitude of subversives, which came to be known as the 'dangerous classes'.[5]

This all-encompassing label was widely used to describe perpetrators of very different unlawful acts that frequently occurred in cities, such as murder, vagrancy, larceny and political violations.[6] Thus, the new enemies of the state, which were perceived as responsible for the country's socio-political weakness, were identified as a vast range of people that included criminals but also prostitutes, brigands, anarchists, idlers, vagrants and beggars. Their backwardness constituted a menace to the creation of a homogenous, normal population.

Discourses on the characteristics, recognisability and potential dangerousness of the dangerous classes engendered an unprecedented response in the literary field. Many writers promptly intervened in the debate, exploring the city-crime nexus and its implications for the construction of the state. The association between the city and crime represents one of the constitutive features of nineteenth-century Gothic literature. Outside of Italy, discussions on the dangerous classes dominated throughout the first half of the century, inspiring some of the most popular novels of the period, including Eugène Sue's *Les Mystères de Paris* (1842), whose publication and immediate translations gave rise to an array of adaptations, imitations and re-writings that have been grouped under the label 'city-mysteries'.[7] Here, I will use the critical term 'urban Gothic novels' to describe texts in which the Gothic is removed from the remote castle or the sublime forest and relocated to the new, labyrinthine nineteenth-century city, where it permeates the urban environment and demarcates social hierarchies.[8]

Many Italian authors – from Carlo Lorenzini (Carlo Collodi's real name) with *I misteri di Firenze* (1857) to Alessandro Sauli with *I misteri di Milano* (1857–9) – were ready to capitalise on the widespread success of the literary trend of the 'city-mysteries', which quickly took hold in Italy, and played on the threatening dimension of the urban environment, constructing a varied low-life topography of urban terrors.[9] The most interesting examples, however, were published between the early 1860s and the mid-1880s, in conjunction with the beginning of a contested process of state-building that generated new tensions in urban Italy. These include Francesco Mastriani's *I vermi. Studi storici su le classi pericolose in Napoli* (1863–4) and *I misteri di Napoli. Studi storico sociali* (1869–70); Lodovico Corio's *La plebe di Milano* (1876–7), which was published in a single volume as *Milano in ombra. Abissi plebei* (1885); Paolo Valera's *Milano sconosciuta* (1878–9); Giulio Piccini's *Firenze sotterranea* (1884); and Matilde Serao's *Il ventre di Napoli* (1884).

These texts are distinguished by their attempt to hybridise seemingly incompatible elements, such as objectivity, scientific detachment, crude realism, melodrama and Gothic sensationalism, in order to convey a stronger political message. Indeed, the urban investigations carried out by these writers do not aim to exacerbate the already tumultuous sociopolitical climate. Instead, they appropriate realism in service of a larger social reform agenda, with a view to raising awareness of the condition of the lower classes and redressing poverty and backwardness. However, the outcome is rather ambiguous. The profoundly Gothic dimension of these texts undermines their realistic and polemic character, while also weakening the authors' political stance.

The ambivalent nature of these novels was not merely the result of impassioned participation and sensationalism at the expense of realism. What is interesting is that their supposedly denunciatory and reformatory purpose collides with the textual representations of poverty, crime, and the slums and their inhabitants. In all these texts, dangerous individuals are portrayed as demoralised, alienated, morally degenerated and far more threatening than the real ones (which were mostly petty criminals). Notwithstanding the areas of prosperity and wealth in late nineteenth-century Italian cities, such as Naples, Milan and Florence, novelists remain firmly focused on the depressed conditions of impoverished, dreadful districts that are a breeding ground for delinquents of every kind. Novels such as Mastriani's *I misteri di Napoli*, a lengthy reconstruction of Neapolitan society between 1846 and 1862, are written in crude and somatic language, particularly when horrific effects are deployed in order to convey the horror of living in the city slums.

In the Urban Gothic, as Jamieson Ridenhour suggests, 'the cityscape replaces the classic Gothic edifice, or rather multiplies it' (10). The labyrinthine nature of the criminal underworld constitutes an obsessive concern in many of these texts. The unhealthy, overcrowded and densely packed districts of Naples, particularly those with the highest rates of poverty in the city, are at the centre of Serao's *Il ventre di Napoli*, written right after a major epidemic of cholera hit the city. Here the metaphor of the labyrinth becomes a way of establishing the city as the modern urban equivalent of the Gothic mansion: remote, impenetrable and dangerous. The irregularity of the alleys, courts and by-ways is cause for alarm and dismay, and 'the secrecy of the labyrinth', as Richard Maxwell points out, always 'signifies crime' (16). Serao claims that 'i napoletani istessi [...] non conoscono *tutti* i quartieri bassi' [the Neapolitans themselves do not know all the lowest neighbourhoods] (11), hinting at the unfamiliarity, inaccessibility and unknowability of certain areas of the city, where crime spreads like a wildfire. In describing the old *Via dei Mercanti*, she emphasises its convoluted character and uses words associated with the idea of the labyrinth: 'sarà larga quattro metri, tanto che le carrozze non vi possono passare, ed è sinuosa, si torce come un budello' [it's about four metres wide, so that carriages can't pass, and winding: it twists like an intestine] (10).

By depicting the back-room life of inner-city districts, made up of storerooms, basement tenements, narrow and winding alleys, secret passages, hidden doorways, subterranean chambers and small squares, Italian writers plunge the reader into an enclosed, claustrophobic, labyrinthine and ultimately Gothicised space from which it seems to be impossible to escape. Within such disorientating and alienating cities, the purposeful walker is transformed into a helpless victim, a version of the Gothic heroine trapped in a dark and threatening environment. In these texts, the uncanniness of the city, in the words of Anthony Vidler, 'finally became public' (6). These places are essentially de-familiarised – as Piccini writes in *Firenze sotterranea*, 'lungo le mura di San Rocco [...] vi credereste a mille miglia da Firenze!' [within the walls of San Rocco [...] you would believe that you were far away from Florence] (88) – which has the effect of bolstering the strangeness of the environment and its inhabitants, which are rendered as remote as the castles and monasteries of the Gothic landscape, and of establishing a fundamental distance between the civilised and the barbarous, the observer and the observed.

The people who inhabit the low-life locales are in themselves Gothic objects of horror. A strong orientalising gaze is frequently employed to depict the underclasses. Following Sue, who, in *Les Mystères de Paris*, relates 'some episodes from the lives of *French* savages who are as far removed from civilizations as the Indians Cooper so vividly depicts' (1), Piccini uses the label 'selvaggi d'Europa' [European savages] to describe 'gente che prova della legge le pene e non il beneficio [...] gente dannata dalla ingiustizia, o dalla improvidenza di chi dovrebbe pensare a educarla' [people who receive the punishments and not the benefits of the law [. . .] people condemned by injustice or by the short-sightedness of those who should educate them] (xxi). Corio, in his *Milano in ombra*, equally draws a parallel between the plebeians of Milan and some of the most remote populations of the world: 'riguardo ad ignoranza e ad abbiettezza' [regarding ignorance and baseness], he puts it, 'la feccia plebea di qualsiasi grande città può dare dei punti ai Papuas, agli Akka ed agli Esquimesi' [the plebeian dregs of any large city can claim superiority to Papuans, Asua, and Eskimos] (11). The inhabitants of the slums are exoticised as foreign or savage threats to Italy from within. They appear, in the words of Michel Foucault, both 'as very close and quite alien, a perpetual threat to everyday life, but extremely distant in its origin and motives, both everyday and exotic in the milieu in which it takes place' (286).

Italian writers' appropriation of elements of the Urban Gothic serves to organise a dichotomous city, in which the distance between the horrible and the horrified, the respectable and the outcast, is repeatedly emphasised. By way of the metaphor of the underbelly, through which social investigators descend into hell, the city is imagined as a contaminated body, which must be gutted and sanitised in order to make it safe. Thus, these texts reveal a very pessimistic view of the prospects of the new-born state at large. The South, in particular, emerges as a dark and hopeless region, devastated by injustice and corruption. Mastriani, for instance, is deeply sceptical of the possibility that his homeland could ever improve: 'non è quistione né di forma di governo, né di riforme politiche, né di più accomodata amministrazione. Sia questo o quel governo, sia monarchia assoluta o repubblica, le cose non muteranno giammai in bene, ove il sistema sociale resti il medesimo' [it's not a question of the type of government or of political reform or of more efficient administration. Under any kind of government, whether an absolute monarchy or a republic, things will never change for the better if the social system remains the same] (II, 548). Here, the Urban Gothic is used to form a strong critique of the unificatory process. The way in which cities are represented in these novels symbolises the worrying prospects of the country, a place that remained fragmented, plagued by criminality, social and economic inequalities, and an inescapable sense of pessimism.

Spiritualism, Mesmeric Villains and Vampires

In 1848, in the house of John D. Fox, a farmer who lived in the State of New York, the spirit of a pedlar who had been murdered in that building managed to establish communication with one of the farmer's daughters, famously giving rise to the extraordinary nineteenth-century resurgence of spiritualism, first in the United States and then in Europe. This revival took hold in Italy in the early 1850s, but it reached its peak in the 1890s, when both the scientific community and the Catholic Church intervened in the debate. Positivists and confident materialists, on the one hand, saw the ultimate understanding of the biology of occultism as the final stage of scientific development. Renowned figures such as Cesare Lombroso and Enrico Morselli started devoting more and more attention to the investigation of poltergeists and ghosts using a rigorously empirical approach.[10] The Roman Catholic Church, on the other hand, felt undermined by the rise of spiritualism and other occult practices, and constantly sought to disprove their validity and plausibility, with the effect, as Massimo Biondi (75) underlines, of rendering the subject unavoidable.

However, most Italians believed that they were expanding or improving their religious practices through séances, rather than replacing them. Thus, attempts to combine two worldviews that were as apparently irreconcilable as occultism and Catholicism were far from sporadic, as testified by the work of writers such as Antonio Fogazzaro and spiritualists and practitioners such as Enrico Dalmazzo, who published his *Lo spiritismo in senso cristiano* in 1889 under the pseudonym Teofilo Coreni and founded the journal *Luce e ombra* in 1900 in order to promote a form of Christian spiritualism that owed much to the lessons of the French thinker Allan Kardec.[11]

Although these positions remained peripheral, it is true that occultism and religion were far more coterminous than is generally acknowledged today. This is reflected in many late nineteenth-century Gothic stories in which the revival of spiritualism and the possibility of communicating with the dead are intertwined with the religious principle of divine justice. While Marchesa Colombi (the pseudonym of Maria Antonietta Torriani) plays with the motif of the retributive ghost in her 'I morti parlano' (1879) – in which it turns out that the voice of a murdered man, which drives his killer to confess, comes from a phonograph – Amilcare Lauria firmly sets revenge within the frame of supernatural justice. In his 'Notizie dall'altro mondo' (1887), for instance, the ghost of a young man appears during a séance to accuse his mother's new husband of having killed him and disguised his death as suicide. Catholic undertones are present in most of Mastriani's novels, many of which deal with supernatural occurrences, such as communication with the dead (as in *La maschera di cera*, 1879) and reincarnation (as in *Rediviva*, 1876).

The theories formulated by Madame Blavatsky and Henry Steel Olcott, who founded the Theosophical Society in 1875, circulated widely in Italy in the 1890s, as testified by the establishment of two centres for Theosophical studies in Milan (1891) and Rome (1897) and the interview that Olcott gave to the popular journal *La Domenica del Corriere* on 8 April 1900. Thus, it is not surprising that the concept of metempsychosis, meaning the transmigration of the soul, fascinated an exceptional number of both popular and mainstream writers, from Pietro Crespi ('Metempsicosi', 1899) and Luigi Capuana ('Creazione', 1901) to Italo Toscani ('La mano di sangue', 1906) and Carlo Merlini ('Metempsicosi', 1907).

The popular and scientific interest in mesmerism, which shared with spiritualism the common ambition to scrutinise the depths of an invisible energy underlying and governing material existence, resurfaced in the second half of the nineteenth century. Mesmerism, or animal magnetism, in the view of its inventor, the eighteenth-century German doctor Franz Mesmer, represented a material influence that animate or inanimate bodies exercise upon each other through the mediation of a universal and extremely fine fluid. In the 1840s, mesmerism was refashioned as hypnotism by the Scottish surgeon James Braid, who demonstrated in his *Neurypnology, or the Rationale of Nervous Sleep Considered in Relation with Animal Magnetism* (1843) that hypnotic sleep could be induced through simple fixation on a luminous object.[12]

In the 1880s, hypnotism acquired an increasingly prominent yet controversial role in the discourse of crime, as lively debates about who could be hypnotised and the ramifications this had on human will and autonomous agency escalated. While Jean-Martin Charcot and his disciples at the Paris school maintained that only those who were already hysterical (mainly female patients) were hypnotisable and that hypnosis was a manifestation of illness, the exponents of the Nancy school, including Ambroise-Auguste Liébault and Hippolyte Bernheim, challenged the notion that hypnosis was rare and pathological, claiming that everyone was hypnotisable under specific circumstances and that suggestibility was a universal human condition.

The Western debate on hypnosis – its definition, appropriate uses and potential dangers, particularly those posed by hypnotic and post-hypnotic suggestions – provided new possibilities for Gothic writing in terms of language, plot and narration, as shown by the increasing appearance, towards the end of the nineteenth century, of menacing criminal hypnotists, from Svengali in George du Maurier's *Trilby* (1894) to Dracula in Bram Stoker's famous novel of the same name, originally published in 1897. In Italy, where scientists followed, albeit cautiously, the Nancy school, the debate was extremely heated and eventually had an enormous effect on the popular imaginary, raising the issue of whether and to what extent a person could be hypnotised into committing criminal acts, creating major problems for the law.[13] Hypnotism was hugely appealing to people. The newspaper *Il Corriere della Sera* successfully serialised du Maurier's novel between 20 July and 11 September 1898, whilst *La Domenica del Corriere* published a wealth of fictional and non-fictional contributions devoted to hypnotism and telepathy, including the anonymous 'Fra le ombre' (1899), a short story that presents, in pseudo-scientific terms, the theory according to which human beings have a sixth sense, *il telesenso*, which allows the transmission of thought across distance.

Mesmeric powers can be employed as instruments of investigation in the service of a higher form of justice, as shown by Franco Mistrali's 'Caino' (1861), which associates detection with the biblical belief in the premonitory value of dreams as divine messages.[14] More frequently, however, the discovery of the ambiguous power of hypnotism, which promised one mind's complete control over another and its possible criminalisation, encouraged the perception of mesmerism as a dangerously powerful criminal tool. Most Italian Gothic stories explore the terrible consequences of this dark skill in the hands of mesmeric characters, such as the villains in Gastone Rossi's 'Morte' (1906), Guglielmo Stocco's 'L'ammaliatore' (1907) and Matilde Serao's *La mano tagliata* (1912), which probe the dreams and fears of sexual dominance that fascination and influence inevitably imply. In texts such as Capuana's 'Ofelia' (1893), in which a painter hypnotises his unfaithful wife and forces her to commit suicide, hypnotism is still treated as a scientifically explicable process that is nonetheless uncanny in its workings and effects. In other texts, such as Carlo Dadone's 'L'invincibile' (1902), in which a wicked spiritualist fails to possess sexually a woman and kills her by gaining control of her husband's mind before vanishing into thin air, hypnotism is seen as a weird, inexplicable force that causes the plot to veer towards the realm of the supernatural.

In a period marked by an increasing number of both amateur and professional incursions into the occult, it is unsurprising that a typically Gothic figure such as the vampire, which had appeared only sporadically in the Italian literary sphere throughout the nineteenth century, resurfaced.[15] The literary vampire is resurrected in a variety of texts, from those published in popular magazines and journals such as Francesco Morando's 'Vampiro innocente' (1885), Giuseppe Tonsi's 'Il vampiro' (1902), Daniele Oberto Marrama's 'Il dottor Nero' (1904) and Luigi Capuana's 'Un vampiro' (1904) to bestsellers like Gabriele D'Annunzio's *L'innocente* (1892). The very limited circulation of classic British Gothic texts in nineteenth-century Italy is one of the reasons why Italian writers developed vampirism in a different and autonomous way. These texts are more an echo of European folklore than of the literary vampires created by Anglophone writers. Common motifs associated with folkloric vampires that are central in these literary stories include the appearance of vampire fantasies in circumstances of acute object loss and intense grief on the part of the survivors; the marginalisation of blood, with vampires mainly being recognised due to their consumption of the victim's life force; and the idea that the recently deceased vampire's recurring visitations to family members brings malevolence, bad luck, or death.[16]

During the nineteenth century, the vampire, a figure that transgresses the categories that make the world intelligible, escaping attempts at identification and engendering unease and panic in those who confront it, mutated and adapted to the Italian environment to challenge not simply its rationality, but also accepted assumptions about family, gender and sexuality. It is not a coincidence that both Marrama's 'Il dottor Nero' and Capuana's 'Un vampiro' depict the vampire as a dead man who comes back from the grave and attacks his widow as a consequence of her recent new marriage. Far from merely being stories of a 'forte impronta positivistica' [markedly positivistic nature], as Giuseppe Tardiola suggests, in these narratives vampirism constitutes a disruptive element through which male writers seek to conceal, contain and exorcise objects of anxiety associated with the emergence of feminism and a new model of womanhood. In her demand for economic, political and notably sexual independence, the late nineteenth-century woman destabilised the very concept of femininity and simultaneously posed a threat to the socio-culturally constructed concept of male virility. In *L'innocente* (1892), for instance, the figure of Tullio Hermil's illicit son takes on vampiric attributes and is portrayed as an intruder who threatens to infiltrate and destroy the protagonist's entire world. As in Morando's 'Vampiro Innocente' – in which a widowed father murders his son as soon as he realises that the latter has been assuming the form of a vampire and is responsible for his sister's death, having absorbed her vital essences – in *L'innocente*, Tullio must kill the monstrous intruder in order to recover his masculinity and, as a direct consequence, survive.

In this chapter, I have sought to reveal the Gothic presence that lurks in the shadows of late nineteenth- and early twentieth-century Italian literature. Even in texts such as the 'city-mysteries' that do not exhibit the obvious outer signs of the Gothic, authors draw on Gothic motifs with a range of effects that, sometimes paradoxically, serve to enhance the realistic component of the plot. Moreover, the relationship between scientism and occultism was particularly conflictual and the resulting tension informed the literary landscape, with the Gothic assuming a myriad of different connotations and capturing the unstable and ever-changing interaction between science, human reason, religion and the occult world. The coexistence of rational and supernatural elements, of Catholic rhetoric, Gothicism and modernity, in these texts bespeaks the hybrid status of Gothic writing and the ambivalent nature of *fin-de-siècle* Italian culture, in which the spectre of the barbarous, the irrational and the unknown continued to loom large and constituted an obstacle in its slow, laborious process of modernisation.

Bibliography

Alongi, Giuseppe, *La maffia nei suoi fattori e nelle sue manifestazioni: studio sulle classi pericolose della Sicilia* (Turin: Bocca, 1887).

Alongi, Giuseppe, *Polizia e delinquenza in Italia* (Rome: Cecchini, 1887).

Ania, Gillian, and Brian Moloney, 'Analoghi vituperî: la bibliografia del romanzo dei misteri in Italia', *La bibliofilia*, 106.2, 2004, pp. 173–213.

Anonymous, 'Fra le ombre', *La Domenica del Corriere*, 26 February 1899, p. 8.

Ashley, Susan A., *'Misfits' in the Fin-de-Siècle France and Italy. Anatomies of Difference* (London: Bloomsbury Academic, 2017).

Baudi di Vesme, Cesare, *Storia dello spiritismo*, 2 vols (Turin: Roux Frassati e co., 1896–7).

Beames, Thomas, *The Rookeries of London: Past, Present and Prospective* (London: Thomas Bosworth, 1850).

Beresford, Matthew, *From Demons to Dracula: The Creation of the Modern Vampire Myth* (London: Reaktion, 2008).

Biondi, Massimo, *Tavoli e medium: storia dello spiritismo in Italia* (Rome: Gremese, 1988).

Bolis, Giovanni, *La polizia e le classi pericolose della società* (Bologna: Zanichelli, 1871).

Botting, Fred, *Gothic* (London: Routledge, 1996).

Bown, Nicola, Carolyn Burdett and Pamela Thurschwell, 'Introduction', in Nicola Bown, Carolyn Burdett and Pamela Thurschwell (eds), *The Victorian Supernatural* (Cambridge: Cambridge University Press, 2004), pp. 1–19.

Bringhenti, Marianna, 'Antonio Fogazzaro presidente della Società di Studi Psichici: un documento inedito sul rapporto tra spiritismo, religione, scienza', *Atti dell'Accademia roveretana degli Agiati*, 255.8, 2005, pp. 153–71.

Brofferio, Angelo, *Per lo spiritismo* (Modena: Briola, 1892).
Cigliana, Simona, *La seduta spiritica: dove si racconta come e perché i fantasmi hanno invaso la modernità* (Rome: Fazi, 2007).
Cigliana, Simona, *Due secoli di fantasmi: case infestate, tavoli giranti, apparizioni, spiritisti, magnetizzatori e medium* (Milan: Edizioni mediterranee, 2018).
Coreni, Teofilo, *Lo spiritismo in senso cristiano*, (Rome: Unione tipografico-editrice, 1889).
Corio, Lodovico, *Milano in ombra. Abissi plebei* (Milan: Civelli, 1885).
Corradi, Morena, *Spettri d'Italia. Scenari del fantastico nella pubblicistica postunitaria milanese* (Ravenna: Longo Editore, 2016).
Curcio, Giorgio, *Delle persone sospette in Italia*, Tip. edn (Milan: Tipografia Lombarda, 1874).
Del Principe, David, *Rebellion, Death, and Aesthetics in Italy: The Demons of Scapigliatura* (Madison, WI: Fairleigh Dickinson University Press, 1996).
Finzi, Gilberto (ed.), *Fogazzaro e il soprannaturale: pagine di narrativa fra spiritismo e spiritualismo* (Cinisello Balsamo: San Paolo, 1996).
Foni, Fabrizio, *Alla fiera dei mostri: racconti pulp, orrori e arcane fantasticherie nelle riviste italiane 1899–1932* (Latina: Tunué, 2007).
Foucault, Michel, *Discipline and Punish: The Birth of the Prison* [1975], trans. Alan Sheridan (Harmondsworth: Penguin, 1979).
Frègier, Antoine, *Les classes dangereuses de la population dans les grandes villes* (Paris: Cans et Compagnie, 1840).
Gabrielli, Eugenio, *Ipnotismo e spiritismo* (Bari: Pasini, 1892).
Gallini, Clara, *La sonnambula meravigliosa: magnetismo e ipnotismo nell'Ottocento italiano* (Milan: Feltrinelli, 1983).
Garfinkel, Paul, *Criminal Law in Liberal and Fascist Italy* (New York: Cambridge University Press, 2016).
Gauld, Alan, *A History of Hypnotism* (Cambridge and New York: Cambridge University Press, 1992).
Gottlieb, Richard, 'The European Vampire: Applied Psychoanalysis and Applied Legend', *Folklore Forum*, 24.2, 1991, pp. 39–58.
Guarnieri, Patrizia, 'Theatre and Laboratory: Medical Attitudes to Animal Magnetism in Late-Nineteenth-Century Italy', in Roger Cooter (ed.), *Studies in the History of Alternative Medicines* (Oxford: Palgrave, 1988), pp. 118–39.
King, Stephen, *Danse Macabre* [1981] (London: Hodder, 2012).
Knight, Stephen, *The Mysteries of the Cities: Urban Crime Fiction in the Nineteenth Century* (Jefferson, NC: McFarland, 2012).
Kontou, Tatiana, and Sarah Willburn, *The Ashgate Research Companion to Nineteenth-Century Spiritualism and the Occult* (Farnham and Burlington, VT: Ashgate, 2012).
Locatelli, Paolo, *Miseria e beneficenza. Ricordi di un funzionario di pubblica sicurezza* (Milan: Dumolard, 1878).
Locatelli, Paolo, *Sorveglianti e sorvegliati. Appunti di fisiologia sociale presi dal vero* (Milan: Brigola, 1876.
Lombroso, Cesare, *Ricerche sui fenomeni ipnotici e spiritici* (Turin: Unione Tipografico-Editrice Torinese, 1909).

Luckhurst, Roger, *The Invention of Telepathy 1870–1901* (Oxford: Oxford University Press, 2002).
Mastriani, Francesco, *I misteri di Napoli* [1869–70], 2 vols (Naples: G. Nobile, 1870).
Maxwell, Richard, *The Mysteries of Paris and London* (Charlottesville, VA and London: University Press of Virginia, 1992).
Mayhew, Henry, *London Labour and the London Poor* (London: George Woodfall and Son, 1851).
Melton, Gordon, and Alysa Hornick, *The Vampire in Folklore. History, Literature, Film and Television: A Comprehensive Bibliography* (Jefferson, NC: McFarland, 2015).
Mighall, Robert, *A Geography of Victorian Gothic Fiction: Mapping History's Nightmares* (Oxford: Oxford University Press, 1999).
Mighall, Robert, 'Gothic Cities', in Catherine Spooner and Emma McEvoy (eds), *The Routledge Companion to Gothic* (London and New York: Routledge, 2007), pp. 54–62.
Morselli, Enrico, *Psicologia e spiritismo*, (Milan and Rome: Bocca, 1908).
Noakes, Richard, 'Telegraphy is an Occult Art: Cromwell Fleetwood Varley and the Diffusion of Electricity to the Other World', *History of Science*, 32.4, 1999, pp. 421–59.
Oppenheim, Janet, *The Other World: Spiritual and Psychical Research in England 1850–1914* (New York: Cambridge University Press, 1985).
Pappalardo, Armando, *Spiritismo* (Milan: Hoepli, 1898).
Parrino, Maria, '"L'orrida magnificenza del luogo": Gothic Aesthetics in Antonio Fogazzaro's *Malombra*', *Gothic Studies*, 16.1, 2014, pp. 85–97.
Piccini, Giulio, *Firenze sotterranea. Appunti, ricordi, descrizioni, bozzetti* [1884] (Florence: Bemporad, 1900).
Ridenhour, Jamieson, *In Darkest London: The Gothic Cityscape in Victorian Literature* (Lanham: Scarecrow Press, 2013).
Saggini, Francesca, 'The Gothic in Nineteenth-Century Italy', in Dale Townshend and Angela Wright (eds), *The Cambridge History of the Gothic. Volume II: Gothic in the Nineteenth Century* (Cambridge: Cambridge University Press, 3 vols, 2020–1, II, 2020), pp. 303–27.
Serao, Matilde, *Il ventre di Napoli* [1884] (Pisa: ETS, 1995).
Sue, Eugene, *The Mysteries of Paris* [1842] (London: Penguin, 2015).
Tardiola, Giuseppe, *Il vampiro nella letteratura italiana* (Anzio: De Rubeis, 1991).
Thurschwell, Pamela, *Literature, Technology, and Magical Thinking, 1880–1920* (Cambridge: Cambridge University Press, 2001).
Tucker, Jennifer, *Nature Exposed: Photography as Eyewitness in Victorian Science* (Baltimore: Johns Hopkins University Press, 1995).
Turiello, Pasquale, *Dello spiritismo in Italia* (Naples: Golia, 1898).
Vidler, Anthony, *Architectural Uncanny: Essays in the Modern Unhomely* (Cambridge, MA and London: MIT Press, 1992).
Violi, Alessandra, 'Storie di fantasmi per adulti: Lombroso e le tecnologie dello spettrale', in Silvana Turzio (ed.), *Lombroso e la fotografia* (Milan: Mondadori, 2005), pp. 43–69.
Willis, Martin, *Mesmerists, Monsters, and Machines: Science Fiction and*

the Culture of Science in the Nineteenth Century (Kent, OH: Kent State University Press, 2006).

Winter, Alison, *Mesmerized: Powers of Mind in Victorian Britain* (Chicago: University of Chicago Press, 1998).

Notes

1. As Nicola Bown, Carolyn Burdett and Pamela Thurschwell have argued, the complexity of the term 'supernatural' in the nineteenth century was part of its appeal. They define it as 'slipper[y]' and 'resistant to definition', suggesting that it had a 'protean quality of being a cause, a place, a kind of being, a realm, a possibility, a new form of nature, [and] a hope for the future' (8).
2. See Tucker; Violi.
3. For a panoramic overview, see Oppenheim; Winter; Thurschwell; Luckhurst; Kontou and Willburn. With regard to the Italian case, see Gallini; Foni; Cigliana; Corradi.
4. The *Scapigliatura* is the central object of inquiry of the only monograph devoted to the Italian Gothic. See Del Principe 1996. For an interesting reading of Fogazzaro's *Malombra* as a Gothic text see Parrino 2014. Another novel of the period that may acquire new meanings through a Gothic reading is Carlo Collodi's classic *Le avventure di Pinocchio*, serialised in 1881 and published in book format in 1883. In this respect see the brief analysis of Saggini.
5. Original discussions on the dangerous classes were conducted in France and Great Britain in the first half of the nineteenth century, when journalists, novelists, travellers, and reformers started producing analytical studies of the lower classes and the underworld, identifying the reasons that generated a marginalised and self-replicating underclass and explaining why it caused crime. See Frègier; Beames; Mayhew. In Italy, theorisations on the dangerous classes began in the early 1870s. See Bolis; Curcio; Locatelli; Alongi.
6. See Ashley 114, 125.
7. The genre includes novels such as Paul Féval's *Les Mystères de Londres* (1843), Eugène Vidocq's *Les Vrais Mystères de Paris* (1844), G. M. W. Reynolds's *The Mysteries of London* (1844–8), George Lippard's *The Quaker City* (1845) and Edward Zane's *The Mysteries and Miseries of New York* (1848). For an overview of the genre, see Maxwell; Knight.
8. The term and concept of Urban Gothic is foreshadowed in Botting 74–87. The most relevant theorisation of the Urban Gothic is that of Robert Mighall. See also Ridenhour.
9. For an overview of the 'Italian mysteries', see Ania and Moloney.
10. Scientists who made forays into the world of spiritualism include Gabrielli; Brofferio; Baudi di Vesme; Turiello; Pappalardo; Morselli; Lombroso.
11. With regard to the work of Fogazzaro, see Finzi; Brighenti. Allan Kardec, the pen name of Hippolyte Léon Denizard Rivail (1804–69), crafted a more

Christian-influenced spiritualism that also embraced reincarnation and vehemently opposed the increasing materialism of the nineteenth century.
12. See Gauld 11.
13. See Guarnieri.
14. Franco Mistrali is mainly remembered for *Il vampiro. Storia vera* (1869), the first Italian variation on the theme of vampirism.
15. See Tardiola 33.
16. See Gottlieb 42; Melton and Hornick 39; Beresford 100.

Chapter 4

The Age of Permutations: 1915–1956
Fabrizio Foni

The Long Nineteenth Century

Writing in French in 1970 – and then translating into Italian, in 1980 – Italo Calvino, one of the major authors and theorists of Italian fantastic literature, maintained that

> [n]ineteenth-century fantasy, a refined product of the Romantic spirit, soon became part of popular literature. (Poe wrote for the newspapers.) During the twentieth century, intellectual (no longer emotional) fantasy has become uppermost: play, irony, the winking eye, and also a meditation on the hidden desires and nightmares of contemporary man. (Calvino)

If this is the case for a group of now canonical writers, it is equally true that popular fiction, for the whole first half of the twentieth century, tended to adapt the deep-rooted topoi and motifs of the nineteenth-century Gothic and fantastic to a mutated socio-cultural and historical context.[1] Moreover, many highbrow authors who were active between the late 1910s and the late 1950s did not shy away from genuinely disquieting and horrific effects, situations and descriptions; and – even when there is an insistence on the grotesque and citationism – the result is as often as not more uncanny than ironic.

In 1915, Carolina Invernizio, Italy's queen of the *feuilleton*, wrote *L'atroce visione*, published by Salani, after debuting as a novelist in 1877. The atrocious sight that gives the novel its title is the telepathic apparition of the dying mother of the protagonist, at the very moment of her death, claiming that she has been treacherously murdered. As is the case for many of her works, the novel takes the form of a stereotypical and gentrified Gothic narrative, but it is no less effective for that, with its numerous plot twists and its both real and fake supernatural apparitions. Invernizio herself passed away in 1916, but her books continued to be successfully reprinted for several decades.

A more curious case is that of Carlo H. De' Medici, whose narrative output, between the 1920s and 1930s, had little (if not minimal) impact on the publishing market and yet he can now be regarded as one of the most accomplished exponents of the Italian Gothic. His novel *Gomòria*, originally published in 1921 by the Milanese Facchi, and his collection *I topi del cimitero. Racconti crudeli*, first issued in 1924 by Bottega d'Arte in Trieste (with a new, revised edition appearing in 1927, released by Milan's La Sfinge under the title *Crudeltà*), were recently rediscovered by the Roman publisher Cliquot. Exquisitely illustrated by the author himself, both works are characterised by their decadent and occultist tones, evidently inspired by Edgar Allan Poe, Jules Barbey d'Aurevilly, Auguste de Villiers de L'Isle-Adam and Jean Lorrain. It is no coincidence that De' Medici also translated *Là-bas* (1891) by Joris-Karl Huysmans in 1929 and that, for the title of *Gomòria*, he drew inspiration from Johannes Wier's *Pseudomonarchia Daemonum* (1577).

Adventure literature, whose continued popularity was assured by the colonial backdrop, absorbed and re-elaborated the typical paraphernalia of Gothic and proto-science fiction. For instance, *La leggenda di un alchimista* by Antonio Ghersi, published in 1923 by Bemporad of Florence, tells the tale of a pair of friends – one a philologist, the other a chemist – trying to decipher the secrets of an alchemist monk. The setting shifts from Perugia to a Calabrian monastery, from the catacombs of the Nile to the peaks of Ruwenzori, all the way to Satapur in India. It is a novel that incorporates the clichés and narrative devices of authors such as Jules Verne and Emilio Salgari, as well as their many imitators.

Aimed at younger readers, Giovanni Corvetto's *Ridolini sotto terra* was the second of three instalments issued in 1923 by the Roman publishing house Mondini. Its protagonist – as evidenced by the cover illustrations – was modelled on the then famous American comedian Larry Semon, who was better known to Italian audiences by the stage name Ridolini. Corvetto constructs an astonishing, fable-like and deliberately absurd narrative that relinquishes all forms of realism to revel in sheer nonsense. More than Semon's own films, however, the result calls to mind the films of Georges Méliès, which are certainly not lacking in macabre situations, though these are presented in burlesque form. Exploring the underworld, Ridolini encounters, among others, some unusual bats and, at the *Club dei morti allegri* [Merry Dead's Club], he witnesses a veritable dance of skeletons and corpses.

For a more adult (or at least adolescent) audience, one may consider *Il cuore di Osiride* (1925) by Italo Toscani, an author who was already active in the early years of the twentieth century, mostly in popular periodicals, in which he published short stories with an often supernatural flavour that tap into the most marvellous or terrifying aspects of science. Toscani's novel, published by Rome's Edizioni 'Primavera', amalgamates both Gothic and adventure overtones, showing that the so-called Egyptomania was far from exhausted. The story – which focuses on a jewel that seems to possess a life of its own and a curse that haunts an English family (partly reminiscent of Arthur Conan Doyle's 1901–2 novel *The Hound of the Baskervilles*) – begins in an ancient castle before proceeding to Paris and eventually finding its resolution among the tombs in the land of the Pharaohs.

It is worth highlighting another work by Toscani, 'Il volto di Medusa', an epistolary tale, also set in England, that closes *Il cavallo dipinto* (1944), the second book in a series published by the Rome-based Consorzio Editoriale Italiano; the series was entitled *Romanzi di Avventure e di Mistero* and was entirely devoted to novels by Toscani. In this tale, an ophthalmologist conducts a diabolical experiment upon himself, which transforms his vision into an immensely powerful radioscopic instrument. Seen through his eyes, the world becomes an unsustainable danse macabre. 'Il volto di Medusa' seems to foreshadow, in a sense, Roger Corman's 1963 film *X: The Man with the X-Ray Eyes*, whilst also probably drawing inspiration from a short story by Sergio Bruno, 'L'occhio del dottor Scheinverborgen', which appeared on 21 August 1904 in *La Domenica del Corriere*, a Sunday supplement of the Milanese daily *Corriere della Sera*.

Although viewed with diffidence by many traditional intellectuals, cinema also came to play an increasingly important role in shaping the output of popular fiction writers and hence the popular imagination. The influence of certain German Expressionist films – especially those with the gloomiest and most eerie atmospheres – is felt in various literary works. In 1927, an issue of the fortnightly *Le Grandi Films*, a supplement to the weekly magazine *Cine-Cinema*, published by the Milanese imprint Gloriosa, featured a novelisation of F. W. Murnau's *Nosferatu, eine Symphonie des Grauens* (1922) entitled 'Lo Spettro della Morte nera'. Though fairly faithful to the film's plot, the text appears to have been rushed and contains many misprints. Nonetheless, it remains to all intents and purposes a Gothic novel, written specifically for an Italian audience. Its author, who signs off as Ivan Pissilenko (most likely a pseudonym), served as a French translator for the Milan-based publishing house Sonzogno and wrote other novelisations, as well as a book on the film star Rudolph Valentino, also for Gloriosa.

Elsewhere, two novellas by Giuseppe Senizza – which appeared in 1928 in *Il Romanzo Settimanale*, a weekly periodical issued by Nerbini of Florence – employ a naïve style and a pedantically didactic tone, and yet present decidedly Gothic elements. Both are set in the regional capital of Tuscany. The first ('Colui che voleva comunicare con gli spiriti') is redolent of a then still strong interest in not just spiritualism, but also Gnosticism, Hinduism, Zoroastrianism and the hypothesis of the plurality of inhabited worlds. The second, 'Il topazio fatale', concerns a precious stone retrieved from an Egyptian tomb, which induces misfortune and horrific nightmares, including visions of gelatinous and almost Lovecraftian monsters whose tentacles are covered in suckers.

Ugo De Amicis's *Storie infernali* (1930), published by the Milanese Treves, is a collection of short stories written by the second son of the more famous Edmondo, who authored the bestselling children's novel *Cuore* (1886). Ugo proposes philosophical positions that are antithetical to those of Edmondo, namely an individualistic and rather Nietzschean attitude, though he maintained close relations with his father. The influence of the nineteenth-century fantastic – Poe in particular – is undeniably found throughout the anthology, even if it tends to be diluted by allegorical and existentialist aims. Such influences nonetheless remain strong in 'Leggenda alpina' and 'Carnevale di morti', the latter dealing with the theme of premature burial and macabre Sicilian funerary customs.

One author who has been unjustly forgotten is Giuseppe Cassone, an esteemed journalist at Turin's *La Stampa* (not to be confused with the homonymous scholar who passed away in 1910). From 1921 onward, under the pseudonym Vittorio d'Arco, Cassone published several stories in that newspaper; these would eventually be collected, along with others, in *I racconti impossibili di gemme strane e corolle magate* (1930), published by the Società Editrice Torinese. The presence of flowers or precious stones is, in fact, a recurring feature of these narratives, which, despite being mostly derivative, are written in a confident, convincing style. The more or less explicit allusions throughout these stories – for example, to 'Le pied de momie' (1840) by Théophile Gautier, *Trilby* (1894) by George du Maurier, or *Le Fantôme de l'Opéra* (1909–10) by Gaston Leroux – do not undermine the genuinely emotional drive of their narrative flow. Corpses that have been decapitated, embalmed or petrified using the technique of Girolamo Segato, an anatomist, naturalist and Egyptologist of the first half of the nineteenth century; poisonous orchids and homicidal jewels; telepathic twins; the eyes of a gorilla transplanted into the sockets of a blind man – these are a few of the instruments in Cassone's arsenal, at the crossroads between exoticism, uncanny science and Grand Guignol.

But, as happened in the nineteenth century (as Corradi shows in Chapter 3), even the historical novel is frequently contaminated by

Gothic influences. One need only consider Gaetano Bernardi's 'Il veggente', which appeared in September 1940 in *Il Romanzo Mensile*, a successful monthly supplement to the *Corriere della Sera*. The titular character is modelled on the historical figure of Gerolamo Cardano, a sixteenth-century doctor, philosopher, astrologer and mathematician. Bernardi portrays him as a clairvoyant ghost-seer, whose soul is capable of leaving his body; he is in contact with superior beings and guided in particular by 'lo Splendore' [the Shining], which cannot but remind the contemporary reader, to some degree, of the famous 1977 novel by Stephen King.

'Giallo', but also Dark

As a result of the launch of Mondadori's series *I Libri Gialli* in 1929, the colour chosen for the covers rapidly became synonymous in Italy with detective and crime fiction, as also testified by the hugely popular trend of *giallo* films in the 1970s. However, the genre itself did not have an easy life under Fascism. In the 1930s, in fact, the *giallo* – considered an intrinsically foreign (and, in particular, anglophone) cultural product – was viewed with suspicion by the regime. Censors became increasingly worried about the enormous popularity of this genre, which was deemed 'anti-national' (but which many publishers were quick to exploit). As early as 1933, *I Libri Gialli* had already sold a million and a half copies; and by 1938, an average of two *gialli* were printed each day in Italy (Pistelli 160).

The publishing houses were eventually forced to reserve more space for home-grown writers and to follow numerous thematic restrictions. And yet, such limitations proved to be a creative stimulus for some writers. Several Italian authors decided to explore the terrains of crime fiction, mixing detection with sentimentalism and adventure (Pistelli 182), but also aspects of the Gothic, the macabre and science fiction.

Vasco Mariotti is certainly one of the most significant practitioners of this hybridisation. In *L'uomo dai piedi di fauno*, published on 8 August 1934 in the cheaper series *Gialli Economici Mondadori*, he combines the themes of mad science, dangerous radioactivity and serial killing, against the backdrop of a darkened Turin. In the novel, the mad doctor's experiments with human–animal hybrids call to mind H. G. Wells's *The Island of Doctor Moreau* (1896), but also Mary Shelley's *Frankenstein* (1818, 1823 and 1831) and Robert Louis Stevenson's *Strange Case of Dr Jekyll and Mr Hyde* (1886). In *La valle del Pianto Grigio*, which also appeared in *Gialli Economici Mondadori* (8 September 1935), Mariotti presents a sombre portrait of Sicily: the life of two former Italian colonists, who have made their fortune in South Africa, is seemingly affected by a chilling curse, which leaves a mysterious grey slime around the eyes of its victims. It is a tale of the 'explained supernatural' variety, which nonetheless sustains an atmosphere of sinister threat.

In 1941, the Florentine publishing house Nerbini issued Mariotti's *La catena spezzata* as part of the series *I Romanzi del Disco Giallo*. In this Paris-based novel, the author's imagination makes various analogies with *The Leopard Man* (1943), a film by Jacques Tourneur that drew inspiration from Cornell Woolrich's *Black Alibi* (1942). Once again, readers are presented with the manifestation of a disquieting past that originates in colonial sub-Saharan Africa, including a femme fatale, secret societies, human sacrifice and, above all, the legend of 'uomini leopardo' [leopard men].

Mariotti's propensity for the Gothic and the paranormal is fully expressed in the short 1949 fortnightly series *I Racconti dell'Occultismo*, also published by Nerbini, the four issues of which were entirely written by the author himself. However, he only signed the first, 'Ombre dell'aldilà' (1 May), with his real name. For the others, he used pseudonyms that respectively sound English (M. W. Arriott for 'Il castello dei fantocci viventi', 15 May); Arabic (Gaddàmek El Hkèir Sàhab for 'Il fantasma della notte Kadir', 29 May); and French (G. De Latour Sombrée for 'Una morta è tornata', 12 June). 'Il castello dei fantocci viventi' seems to almost prefigure the first Italian Gothic film in colour, Giorgio Ferroni's *Il mulino delle donne di pietra* (1960). Both the short story and the film are hinged on the uncanny exhibition of statues and puppets, hence proving a certain attunement to the coeval success of waxworks and *tableaux vivants* in popular museums as well as travelling shows and fairgrounds.

Esotericism would also play a leading role in *Il teschio d'argento* by Renato Umbriano, published on 23 June 1935 in the aforementioned *Gialli Economici Mondadori*. The novel opens with the discovery in Rome of a corpse, which is found clutching a piece of paper marked with mysterious symbols, followed by the theft from the morgue of part of the unidentified victim's skull. It is the prelude to a narrative that compellingly weaves together alchemy (viewed as a precursor of modern science), medieval legends, witchcraft, Satanism and Egyptomania. Two of the characters stand out in particular: an enigmatic monk with a long grey beard and a decadent polyglot adventurer born in Java to an Italian mother and a Russian father. The latter is an expert in the occult, having spent his youth in India, and counts among his former friends the notorious Rasputin. It is not surprising that Umbriano explicitly mentions Jean des Esseintes, the protagonist of Huysmans's *À rebours* (1884), and Oscar Wilde's *The Picture of Dorian Gray* (1890 and 1891).

High demand for crime stories led to the multiplication of publications that play with genre traits and created the space for imitators, such as Andrea Lavezzolo (also a successful comic-book scriptwriter), whose 'L'automa che uccide' is a perfect example of how widespread (and accepted) the fusion of detective fiction, psychical research, crime-news sensationalism, weird science and – presumably – cinematic influences had become. 'L'automa che uccide' (a title that is far from metaphorical and that reveals the story's final resolution) was published on 23 September 1939 in the fortnightly series *I Gialli Moderni* by the Milanese Casa Editrice Impero. It seems to echo Robert Wiene's *Das Cabinet des Dr. Caligari* (1920) and other films in which scientists make use of a human being, an animal or a robot to exact personal revenge. It also exhibits a morbid fascination with wax museums, which were viewed as veritable showcases of horrors, thus playing with the conventions of the Grand Guignol.

One of the main locations for Lavezzolo's story is, not coincidentally, the Parisian Musée Grévin, where the titular automaton is put on display in the form of a guillotined mannequin. Adding to the catalogue of clichés, there is also the hideout of the mad scientist, escaped from an asylum: a house that has previously been the scene of a crime and is believed to be haunted by the spirits of the damned.

Two completely different novels that are worth mentioning are Pietro Zampa's *Il tesoro dei Roccabruna: Primo romanzo poliziesco radiestesistico* and *Espiazione: Romanzo giallo radiestesistico*, published in 1940 and 1941 respectively by the Brescia-based Giulio Vannini. In the preface to the former, the author declares that he wrote this work of fiction as a means of popularising radiesthesia, a form of dowsing and divining that he practises using a pendulum. Both novels were released in the *Biblioteca di Radiestesia Vannini*, a series edited by Zampa himself, comprising studies devoted to this pseudoscientific field. Zampa's monograph *Elementi di radiestesia, teoria e pratica: Le meraviglie di una Scienza Nuova*, for example, first appeared in 1940 and was reprinted many times between then and 2017. Though the author does not want radiesthesia to be confused with spiritualism and the so-called mediumistic phenomena, his novels combine detection with the irrational, using typically Gothic scenarios, such as ruined castles belonging to ancient families, mediums, hypnotists and clairvoyants, fabulous treasures, theosophy and reincarnation. Zampa was, moreover, the umpteenth Italian popular author to explicitly follow the model provided by Jules Verne's novels, including, but not limited to, the Gothic story *Le château des Carpathes* (1892).

Gothic Futurism

As scholars have shown, futurists were fascinated by metapsychics and the occult in general. Spiritualism, theosophy, anthroposophy and other forms of esoteric thinking found their way into the anti-academic and transgressive movement (Cigliana; Pautasso). However, in their constant search for excess and desecration and in their attempts to shock the public, several futurists paradoxically ended up reclaiming, more or less consciously, the passionate, individualistic, libertarian and even Gothic traits of a Romanticism that had previously been provocatively dismissed as useless, antiquated sentimentalism by the futurist movement itself. From the 1920s onward, a significant number of writers adhering, or culturally indebted, to this movement would either abandon the *parole in libertà* [words-in-freedom] technique or choose to produce sensational, fantastic and detective stories.

Tullio Alpinolo Bracci – the journalist, poet and artist who collaborated with the more famous Fillia (Luigi Colombo) – authored many stories belonging to the *giallo* genre, though the latter are not highly original. Under the eccentric pseudonym of Kiribiri (he adopted a variety of *noms de plume* and occasionally wrote under his own name), he published 'Lo scheletro vivente' (10 May 1941) in the *Edizioni Gialli 'Tascabile'*, which was the name of both a Florentine publishing house and a fortnightly, sixteen-page series of short stories. There is very little that can be considered truly avant-garde about this narrative. The plot revolves around a human skeleton that is transferred from India to a castle in the vicinity of London; upon the death of its proprietor, the skeleton seems to come to life and commit a few murders, impervious to the bullets of Scotland Yard. This story is rendered even more banal by the inclusion of a secret passageway and an enigma left by the deceased to be resolved by his children in exchange for a handsome inheritance.

On the other end of the spectrum in terms of length is *La danza della jena*, a novel of over 370 pages published in 1920 by Vitagliano of Milan. Its author, the futurist Paolo Buzzi, puts on display his strong links to the most macabre forms of *Scapigliatura*. The novel is a compendium of vices and perversions that would not be out of place in the case histories collected by the German criminologist and sexologist Richard von Krafft-Ebing, and it includes, among other things, a fetish for physical deformity and an attraction to singing blind girls. The narrative's main setting is the cemetery, to which the characters seem to be magnetically drawn in order to commit suicide, to indulge in the most savage copulations or to satisfy their own necrophiliac urges in an even more outrageous way by having sex with the corpses. Will-o'-the-wisps hover among the tombstones and mysterious fluids simmer as they become ectoplasms, which, invoked by the mediumistic powers of one female protagonist, assume a dangerously tangible human form. Eventually, the ghosts of the dead are revealed in their entirety. It is practically impossible not to associate certain passages from *La danza della jena* – a grotesque text, though it is characterised by a strong corporeality – with Tiziano Sclavi's *Dellamorte Dellamore* and its homonymous 1994 cinematic adaptation, directed by Michele Soavi, which was distributed on the anglophone market under the title *Cemetery Man*.

Several short stories collected in Giuseppe Bevilacqua's *Allucinazioni*, published in 1939 by the Milanese La Prora, employ traditional Gothic and parapsychological paraphernalia as allegorical instruments for philosophical-moral reflections. 'L'ultimo giorno del dottor Brisk' focuses on the unpredictable and tragic consequences of the scientific possibility of mind-reading. In 'La vita è bella', the decrepit ninety-year-old Prof. Rodolfo Reitz takes up residence in the decaying *Castello del Diavolo* [Devil's Castle], near a river where many commit suicide, and hires a vigorous youth to save the lives of those who wish to die. His motives, however, are anything but philanthropic: as an old man who remains, in spite of his age, highly attached to life, his objective is to obsessively contemplate those who have decided to take their own. Characterised by a 'maschera mostruosa' [monstrous mask], he is described as a 'vampiro dello spirito' [vampire of souls] (Bevilacqua 105). Other tales that stand out in this anthology include 'Io e l'ipnotizzatore', 'Il macellaio dalla barba', whose titular character is uncannily reminded of the kiss of his deceased betrothed by a piece of severed tongue that hits him on the cheek while he is butchering, and 'La corsa dietro il morto', in which the protagonist-narrator finds himself madly pursued by a hearse after overtaking it in his car.

In *Le novelle del Demonio* (1914) by Persio Falchi, the founder of the futurist Florentine magazine *La Forca*, the supernatural is turned into a predominantly (a)moral allegory with an anti-bourgeois tone. In places, Falchi exalts vice and lust in a way that is more decadent than futurist, making numerous references to the Gospels that are intended to shock the public, especially more moderate and conformist readers. 'Un bicchiere di sangue' is, without doubt, the book's most Gothic text: a story with a gloomy atmosphere, in which an irresistible and diabolic femme fatale proposes a game of cards to the narrator-protagonist. Should he win, she will offer up her body for wild intercourse; should he lose, she will drink a glass of his blood. This vampiric dark lady reveals herself to be a non-human creature, metamorphosing into a snake with eyes that exude sulphurous flames. 'La canzone dell'annegato' recalls to some degree both 'The City in the Sea' (1831, 1836 and 1845) and 'A Descent into the Maelström' (1841) by Poe; whilst 'La solita coppia' narrates the protagonist's casual encounter, in a church, with a couple that arouses his morbid interest: he discovers that they are the ghosts of the Jesuit Luigi Gonzaga and the lascivious Messalina. In 'Tu morrai domani!', a woman with three lovers takes leave of her senses and is committed to a mental hospital. There, she prophesies the death of all three lovers, two of whom do, indeed, part with their lives, while the third realises that he has died in an inner spiritual way. 'Gli amori del Gentiluomo senza faccia' presents a lady who maintains that she is the mistress of a seventeenth-century portrait of a man whose face has been scraped off. A second edition of the book was published in 1921 by Taddei of Ferrara, with the addition of two tales, one of which, 'Tre croci', is rather disturbing: in the story, two lovers are attacked by an old, naked, skeletal madman in a secluded place near a monastery, regularly attended by witches and haunted by the ghosts of the dead friars, walking in procession. In the new preface, Falchi – who had, during the war, spent time in prison in Austria, at Hart bei Amstetten and Sigmundsherberg – ends up distancing himself from his own short stories. Evidently, he now found himself haunted by other ghosts.

Spectres of War

The brutality, blood and grief of the two world wars was inevitably reflected in works of fiction; and Gothic literature, in many cases, mirrored the pervasive feelings of alienation, indignation and loss. In a collection of short stories entitled *Ombre cinesi*, published in 1920 by Sandron of Palermo, the famous playwright, journalist and writer Roberto Bracco reveals his attraction to the afterworld, which is somewhat in contrast with the traditional image of him as a man who was sarcastic and sceptical about spiritualism – as shown by the book *Lo Spiritismo a Napoli nel 1886* (1907). In *Ombre cinesi*, examples of such an attraction include the grotesque story 'Il vecchione, la vergine e il pazzo (temi lirici)' and the sinister and decadent 'Il braccio troncato'. Strongly anti-militarist overtones are expressed in this anthology through a reliance on the uncanny and the supernatural. 'Barbarello', for instance, is set during the second year of Italy's participation in the

Great War, and the first-person narrator coincides with Bracco himself. Barbarello is the name of a character in a successful and controversial 1910 play by the same author, *Il piccolo santo*; in the story of the same name, the character is played by a former soldier who has been psychologically scarred by his experiences on the front. The nocturnal encounter between dramatist and actor assumes an increasingly uneasy tone, with descriptions of the bloodiest and harshest moments of battle. What emerges is the profound, mysterious relationship between the soldier and his captain, a bond that, upon the death of the latter, seems to be of a truly paranormal nature. In 'Il fantoccio', a Gothic castle provides the backdrop for the horrific hallucinations of the consumptive Lorenzo Del Varo, who, in the course of the First World War, gives vent to his feelings of inadequacy in relation to his own father – who died heroically in Libya during the Italo-Turkish War – in a conversation with an elderly Austrian, who turns out to be his natural father. Also from *Ombre cinesi*, 'Dopo' takes the form of a dialogue between the ghosts of two men who died in the conflict.

Active service in war likewise inspired the journalist, publisher and novelist Mario Puccini to write various works. In a few of the stories in *Racconti cupi*, issued in 1922 by the publisher Franco Campitelli of Foligno, the author describes spectral, ominous and eerie coincidences, situations and consequences that are directly linked – or otherwise traceable – to war. These stories include 'La civetta', 'Il vicolo cieco' and 'Il forte X . . .'. In the last of these, the first-person narrator is a sentry who, for twenty days, must stand guard over an abandoned Austrian military fort in complete solitude. The fact that the edifice is partially in ruins, isolated and perched on a rocky peak between mountains makes it a worthy substitute for the traditional Gothic castle. The sentry feels ever more oppressed by an 'atmosfera misteriosa e nemica' [mysterious and hostile atmosphere] (Puccini 62). Perturbing creaking noises and toads that disappear after being killed suggest that the place possesses a malignant form of life: a dog, barking at invisible presences, ends up horribly entrapped in barbed-wire fences, as though the fort had swallowed it whole. Monotony turns into obsession and then despair, until, at last, another soldier mercifully arrives to relieve the sentry. The new sentry and subsequent occupants of the fort will go on to meet grisly deaths, with the construction's final collapse evoking Poe's 'The Fall of the House of Usher' (1839).

The effects of war are also felt within the walls of the unusual Parisian abode of Alberto Savinio's *La casa ispirata*, a serialised novel that appeared in 1920 in the Milanese monthly *Il Convegno* and was published in book form in 1925 by Carabba of Lanciano. The younger brother of Giorgio de Chirico, and lauded by the surrealists, the painter, playwright and composer Savinio is undeniably an 'intellectual' author. Nonetheless, his imagination – which swirls with alchemy, hermeticism, Greek mythology, the fantastic and esotericism in general, all rendered through the grotesque and irony – is profoundly disquieting (De Bei). The titular house is 'inspired' in the purely etymological sense of the word, that is, animated by a divine influence. The building turns out to be inhabited by human and supernatural bizarre and terrifying presences, whose logic and nature are difficult to rationally grasp or decipher. The outbreak of war, and the tragic death of one of the house's occupants, the young Marcello, causes the divine forces to abandon the house (Cesaretti 129), thus putting an end to its 'inspiration'.

It is not surprising that, after numerous experiences as a war correspondent, another of Italy's main twentieth-century authors of the fantastic, Dino Buzzati, broaches the topic in a dramatically dark and otherworldly way, as in 'Il mantello'. This short story originally appeared in the *Corriere della Sera* (14 July 1940), of which Buzzati was an editorial staff member, and was later anthologised in the book *I sette messaggeri*, published in 1942 by Mondadori. In the story, Giovanni comes home from the war after a two-year absence; he is pale, exhausted and refuses to remove his cloak. More unusually still, he proclaims that he must leave at the earliest opportunity to follow a strange figure who stands waiting impatiently for him outside the door. It is the 'signore del mondo' [lord of the world] (Buzzati 162), namely Death. Giovanni's cloak, in fact, conceals a mortal wound.

The violence of the Second World War acts as a frame for the novel *Racconto d'autunno*, undoubtedly the most Gothic work produced by the eccentric and refined Tommaso Landolfi. In this case, too, the centrepiece of the narration is a house, a veritable topos that, as underscored by Enrico Cesaretti (131), serves as a source of fascination and obsession for the author, as it did for Savinio. Published in 1947 by Vallecchi in Florence, the novel was hastily written between September and October 1946. Landolfi's main (though not his only) inspiration was the deterioration of his family home, to which he would forever remain attached, after Allied bombings and the passage of troops. Fleeing from a pursuant patrol, *Racconto d'autunno*'s narrator-protagonist takes refuge in a house that turns out to be a labyrinthine site of apparitions and obscure magical rituals that exhibit sadistic, vampiric and incestuous aspects. With great efficacy – it is a work that meets both the expectations of an intellectual audience and the demands of a public seeking thrilling suspense – Landolfi unfolds and reworks the major themes and motifs of the supernatural. By the time the protagonist (and, with him, the reader) is deeply immersed in the exploration of this house-castle's meandering mysteries – which seem so far removed from the temporal and historical setting of the story – the war unexpectedly irrupts back onto the scene with extraordinary cruelty.

Bibliography

Bevilacqua, Giuseppe, *Allucinazioni* (Milan: La Prora, 1939).
Buzzati, Dino, *I sette messaggeri* (Milan: Mondadori, 1942).
Calvino, Italo, *The Literature Machine: Essays* [1997], trans. Patrick Creagh, Vintage, 2011, <https://www.penguin.co.uk/books/1035082/the-literature-machine/9781446414453.html> (last accessed 29 July 2022).
Cesaretti, Enrico, *Castelli di carta: Retorica della dimora tra Scapigliatura e Surrealismo* (Ravenna: Longo, 2001).
Cigliana, Simona, *Futurismo esoterico: Contributi per una storia dell'irrazionalismo italiano tra Otto e Novecento* (Naples: Liguori, 2002).
De Bei, Alessandro, *Conversazione con gli spettri: La poetica di Alberto Savinio* (Adria: Apogeo, 2021).
Gallo, Claudio, and Fabrizio Foni (eds), *Ottocento nero italiano: Narrativa fantastica e crudele* (Milan: Aragno, 2009).
Lazzarin, Stefano, et al., *Il fantastico italiano: Bilancio critico e bibliografia commentata (dal 1980 a oggi)* (Florence: Le Monnier Università, 2016).
Pautasso, Guido Andrea, *Vampiro futurista: I futuristi e l'esoterismo* (Albissola Marina: Vanillaedizioni, 2018).
Pistelli, Maurizio, *Un secolo in giallo: Storia del poliziesco italiano (1860–1960)* (Rome: Donzelli, 2006).
Puccini, Mario, *Racconti cupi* [1922] (Milan: Claudio Lombardi, 1992).

Notes

1. See Gallo and Foni 517–39, but also Lazzarin et al. 23–31.

Chapter 5

The Golden Age of the Gothic: 1957–1979
Roberto Curti

The years between 1957 and 1979 marked a dramatic boost of the Gothic within Italian popular culture. First and foremost, this period saw the birth and development of a national Gothic cinema, with some key auteurs standing out, and later of made-for-TV works with *fantastique* nuances. Moreover, the renewed interest in all things Gothic prompted a renaissance in the literary market, which coincided with the boom of popular publishing. Besides reprints of famous novels and the publication of anthologies collecting the work of noted foreign authors, a massive production of new material by Italian authors ensued, consisting of paperbacks, pulp novels and photo-novels, which allowed the Gothic to circulate among different audiences. Over the course of these two decades the Italian Gothic mutated substantially in response to different socio-cultural changes, from the growing interest in the paranormal to the new-found political awareness prompted by 1968. Moreover, new perspectives in the genre emerged, such as the inclusion of elements of the *giallo*, while the loosening of censorship resulted in an overemphasis on eroticism.

A Hybrid Founder: *I vampiri*

The birth of Italian Gothic cinema is commonly associated with the release of Riccardo Freda's *I vampiri* (1957), a low-budget film produced by Ermanno Donati and Luigi Carpentieri's company Athena Cinematografica with financial assistance from the distributor Titanus. Freda repeatedly claimed that the film was born out of a bet: 'le cinéma fantastique, c'était le privilège des Américains et des expressionnistes allemands. Je voulais prouver qu'on pouvait faire des films fantastiques en Italie' [fantastic cinema was the prerogative of the Americans and the German Expressionists. I wanted to prove that we could make fantastic films in Italy] (quoted in Poindron 258).

I vampiri was a novelty of sorts, for audiences were not wholly acquainted with the Gothic tradition, having been kept away from it by 'decenni di estetica crociana, di storicismo marxista e di moralismo cattolico' [decades of Crocian aesthetics, Marxist historicism and Catholic moralism] (Pezzotta, 'Il boom' 36). Foreign horror and *fantastique* movies had circulated in the national venues and spectators were familiar with Expressionism, but such works as *Nosferatu* by Friedrich Wilhelm Murnau (1922) and *Vampyr* by Carl Theodor Dreyer (1932) did not have a proper distribution and appeared only in festivals and film forums. Likewise, Hollywood vampire movies – including *Dracula* (1931) and *Mark of the Vampire* (1935) by Tod Browning, *Dracula's Daughter* by Lambert Hillyer (1936) and *Son of Dracula* by Robert Siodmak (1943) – were not released theatrically in the country. Therefore, the term 'vampire' was largely disconnected from tradition and Gothic mythology. It nevertheless retained the metaphorical allusiveness linked to the predatory figure of the bloodsucking creature and was used in correlation with crime news about murders of a probable sexual nature. Moreover, the term *vampira* (female vampire) was still associated with the image of the *femme fatale*, the man-eating seductress of Decadentist literature and early silent cinema.

Freda's film introduced a peculiar vampire figure, an elderly woman (Gianna Maria Canale) who receives blood transfusions from abducted young girls in order to recover her beauty, with the help of a mad doctor (Antoine Balpêtre) and a factotum (Paul Muller). *I vampiri* drew from varied sources, either traditional (the notorious Hungarian 'Bloody Countess' Erzsébet Báthory), literary (Edgar Allan Poe, the mystery popular literature which harks back to the *feuilleton* and the so-called sensation novel, from Wilkie Collins to Gaston Leroux), theatrical (the Parisian Théâtre du Grand Guignol) and cinematic, namely *L'Atlantide* by Georg Wilhelm Pabst (1932), *Mystery of the Wax Museum* by Michael Curtiz (1933) and *The Return of Dr. X* by Vincent Sherman (1939).

The film underwent severe tampering on the part of producers during the making. Freda left and Mario Bava took over the direction (Poindron 263); the plot was modified with the addition of detection elements which made it closer to a detective story; scenes were re-sequenced, and the dialogue was altered. The most controversial elements were discarded, including a pre-credit sequence in which Muller's character is guillotined (Poindron 262): originally an 'undead' man brought back from the grave in Freda and Piero Regnoli's original script, he was reimagined as a drug addict (Venturini 106). This resulted in a hybrid of sorts, labelled by some critics as 'il primo film "nero" del cinema italiano sonoro' [the first noir film of Italian sound cinema] (Morandini), which only highlighted the producers' uneasiness in dealing with the Gothic.

Vampires Are Among Us

I vampiri's underwhelming box-office failed to make it a prototype. Only after the surprising commercial success of Terence Fisher's *Dracula* (1958) did vampirism and horror cinema become popular. As a mundane newspaper article of July 1959 stated, 'quest'estate pullula di film di vampiri e la gente ne va matta anche se ostenta di prenderli in giro o persino di prendere in giro se stessa' [this summer is teeming with vampire movies and people are crazy about them even though they pretend to make fun of them or even to make fun of themselves] (De Feo 3). Distributors rushed to capitalise on the successful new trend, and so did publishers. Within a couple of years, the editorial market was flooded with books on the subject, including a new Italian translation of Bram Stoker's novel (the previous one dated from 1952), plus several anthologies on the horror genre. *I vampiri tra noi*, published in April 1960 and edited by renowned musicologist and essayist Ornella Volta and journalist Valerio Riva, proved highly influential in the development of the Gothic trend. Other anthologies released that same year were *Un secolo di terrore. 17 racconti del terrore* (edited by Bruno Tasso for the Milan-based SugarCo) and *Storie di fantasmi*, published by Einaudi and edited by Carlo Fruttero and Franco Lucentini. The interest in the Gothic prompted even idiosyncratic editorial initiatives such as *Io credo nei vampiri*, a 1961 book essay penned by Emilio de' Rossignoli, a journalist, film critic and writer who also produced several lurid thriller and horror novels under various pseudonyms. The book explored the vampire myth from its origins to the present day. As the author explained, 'il vampiro della curiosità mi succhiava il sangue: dovevo cercare, approfondire, sapere' [the vampire of curiosity sucked my blood: I had to search, to investigate, to know] (De' Rossignoli 22).

Accordingly, vampirism became almost immediately a target for parody. The musical stage play *Un juke-box per Dracula*, by Marcello Marchesi, Renzo Puntoni and Italo Terzoli, satirised the new horror fad alongside such diverse topics as Pier Paolo Pasolini, pop singers and Vladimir Nabokov's novel *Lolita* (1955). Likewise, the first proper Italian vampire film, Steno's *Tempi duri per i vampiri* (1959), was a spoof, packed full of jokes related to the erotic nuances of vampirism and co-starring Christopher Lee alongside comedian-singer Renato Rascel.

The editorial market represented fertile terrain for the Gothic. Cheap paperbacks, published by small independent publishers, explored horror as a viaticum for erotic innuendo. June 1959 saw the publication of *Il vampiro*, the first release in a series named *KKK. I classici dell'orrore*. Three years later the series would change its name to *I Capolavori della Serie KKK. Classici dell'Orrore* and continued its existence until 1972. Soon another similar paperback series ensued, *I Racconti di Dracula*, which was published until 1981. These books, which sported evocative titles and lurid, allusive covers, were cheaply priced and amply distributed at news stands. The authors, hiding behind an array of English pseudonyms, were Italian writers, sometimes credited as 'translators' of a non-existent English version. The endeavour to conceal the domestic origin of these works was a consequence of the perceived foreign nature of the Gothic on the part of the public. Gothic-themed photo-novels such as *Malìa. I fotoromanzi del brivido* (1961–7), which featured photo-novel versions of existing films and original photographic stories containing an abundance of scantily dressed ladies, were the link between pulp paperbacks and horror movies. Overall, these publications summarise the appeal the Gothic had on Italian audiences: an exotic source of forbidden thrills that arose from a new-found prosperity and constituted a fascinating novelty as opposed to the everyday-like backdrops of post-war neo-realism.

The Gothic Wave, 1960–1966

Alongside the release of old and new foreign titles, producers rushed to crank out homemade products. A quintet of Italian movies came out between May and November 1960 – *L'amante del vampiro* by Renato Polselli, *Seddok 'l'erede di Satana'* by Anton Giulio Majano, *La maschera del demonio* by Mario Bava, *Il mulino delle donne di pietra* by Giorgio Ferroni and *L'ultima preda del vampiro* by Piero Regnoli – which represented the first batch of homemade Gothic horror films. Besides, a couple of hybrids – *Ercole al centro della terra* by Mario Bava (1961), featuring Lee, and *Maciste contro il vampiro* by Giacomo Gentilomo and Sergio Corbucci (1961) – merged the Gothic with another commercially viable *filone*, the sword-and-sandal.

These early works showed different approaches to the Gothic and its tropes, some of which were soon to be abandoned. *L'amante del vampiro*, *L'ultima preda del vampiro* and *Seddok* were all set in the present day, and the latter featured a protagonist who undergoes a monstrous transformation recalling Robert Louis Stevenson's *Strange Case of Dr Jekyll and Mr Hyde* (1886); Polselli and Regnoli's films presented traditional bloodsuckers complete with long fangs in tune with the established screen image of the vampire. In turn, *Il mulino delle donne di pietra* (the only one shot in colour) and *La maschera del demonio* displayed a more original approach. The latter (a loose adaptation of Nikolai Gogol's short story 'Viy', 1835, which centres on a centuries-old, resurrected vampire witch) did away with the clichés related to vampire stories and proposed the theme of rejuvenation in a wholly supernatural setting, introducing or developing themes that would become central in Italian Gothic cinema: a centuries-old curse, a menace from the past which affects the protagonists, a female *doppelgänger* motif (the witch and the innocent heroine are played by the same actress), and the centrality of the female character, seen as a perturbing element.

Box-office results proved disappointing, so much so that only one Gothic film was released in 1961, the werewolf mystery *Lycanthropus* by Paolo Heusch; two more came out the following year, *La strage dei vampiri* by Roberto Mauri and *L'orribile segreto del dr. Hichcock* by Riccardo Freda. However, *La maschera del demonio* (picked up by American International Pictures and distributed overseas as *Black Sunday*) became the US company's biggest moneymaker (Lucas 317) and paved the way for the hunt for foreign low-budget horror films on the part of American distributors. The Gothic thread resumed, resulting in a rather homogeneous production aimed primarily at foreign markets: six films were released each year between 1963 and 1965 and four in 1966, which marked the end of the first wave of Italian Gothic.

Compared with the works produced in 1960, these were more homogeneous and had several elements in common. Production-wise, these were mostly low-budget projects on the part of small-time companies. Bava's films were an exception: *La maschera del demonio*, produced by Galatea Film, was a medium-budgeted work that allowed the director to take meticulous care with the formal aspects (Venturini, *Galatea Spa* 138), whereas *La frusta e il corpo* (1963) and *I tre volti della paura* (1963) were Italian/French ventures, and the latter—another Galatea production starring Boris Karloff – benefitted from an advance on the part of AIP. The disappearance of Galatea Film, who had invested in the Gothic more than any other Italian producer in the field, gave the *filone* a fatal blow and resulted in its most talented exponent, Mario Bava, adapting to much tighter production values for *Operazione paura* (1966), which would be his last Gothic film in some time. By the mid-1960s, as the *filone* was waning after the advent of other commercially reliable ones such as the western and the spy film, the fragility of many production ventures became manifest. Production-wise, the Gothic remained a marginal phenomenon that never secured a strong grip on the market.

A Web of Deception

On the surface, Italian Gothic cinema looks like a mere appropriation of clichés. The main settings are ominous old castles or villas, stories take place in foreign countries and revolve around vampirism and reincarnation, centring on the *doppelgänger* motif or avenging spirits returning from the grave. The films were shaped to resemble foreign ones such as Hammer productions and A.I.P.'s Edgar Allan Poe cycle, with casts and crews hiding behind Anglo-Saxon aliases so that audiences would perceive the results as 'authentic' additions to the *filone* given Italy's perceived extraneity with the Gothic tradition. As Freda himself liked to stress in an oft-quoted anecdote about *I vampiri*, 'molta gente entrava nella hall del cinema e si fermava a guardare le fotografie e a leggere i nomi. Quando arrivava al mio, esclamava: "Oddio, ma allora è un film italiano!" e se ne andava' [many people entered the theater lobby and stopped to look at the lobby cards and read the names on them. When they saw mine, they exclaimed: 'My God, but this is an Italian movie!' and left] (in Faldini and Fofi 200).

Regardless, the approach to the myths and archetypes of the Gothic is idiosyncratic and the results have several specificities and common elements. Firstly, the nonchalant attitude toward literary sources stands out. *La maschera del demonio* retains very little of 'Viy'; conversely, *La cripta e l'incubo* by Camillo Mastrocinque (1964) borrows liberally from Sheridan Le Fanu's *Carmilla* (1872, included in *I vampiri tra noi*) without crediting its source. Others merge highbrow and lowbrow literature in peculiar ways. The opening credits of *I tre volti della paura*, a three-part anthology in the vein of *Tales of Terror* (1962, Roger Corman), claim that the episodes are based 'on works by Maupassant, Tolstoy and Chekhov'. In reality, only the middle one, *I Wurdalak*, a grim vampire tale featuring Karloff as a patriarch bloodsucker who infects his whole family, comes from Aleksei Tolstoy's novella (also included in *I vampiri tra noi*), whereas the source for *Il telefono* (a short story by an 'F. G. Snyder') is merely nominal, and the last episode, *La goccia d'acqua*, draws from the short story *Dalle tre alle tre e mezzo* (included in *Storie di fantasmi*) by 'P. Kettridge', an alias for the anthology's co-editor – noted author, essayist and translator Franco Lucentini.

Such travesty was a recurring element. Several titles sport fake literary origins that would legitimise them to the eyes of the public. *Il mulino delle donne di pietra*'s opening credits mention 'the short story of the same name in *Flemish Tales* by Pieter Van Weigen', but neither the book nor the author exists; Alberto De Martino's *Horror* (1963) and Antonio Margheriti's *Danza macabra* (1964) claim to be adaptations of Edgar Allan Poe's stories whereas in fact they merely derive sparse elements from the American author. Margheriti's film even features Poe as a character, who in the opening sequence recites excerpts from his short story 'Berenice' (1835). Margheriti's *La vergine di Norimberga* (1963) is noteworthy as being the only adaptation of a paperback in the *KKK. I classici dell'orrore* series, penned by 'Frank Bogart' (alias Maddalena Gui): Marco Vicario, who scripted and produced it under the pseudonym of 'Gastad Green', was the co-founder and owner of the publishing house, G.E.I.

Furthermore, some plots salvage elements from other Gothic films, either reprising visual ideas or scenes – the witch's curse of *La Maschera del demonio* returns in *La cripta e l'incubo* and in Freda's Gothic-peplum hybrid, *Maciste all'inferno* (1962) – or even recycling whole chunks of plot: the climax of *Danza macabra* was reused almost to the letter in *La vendetta di Lady Morgan* by Massimo Pupillo (1965); in turn, *Operazione paura* reprises the theme of vengeance from beyond the grave from Pupillo's *Cinque tombe per un medium* (1965). A borderline case is Mario Caiano's *Amanti d'oltretomba* (1965), a summation of the situations, characters and narrative devices that Italian Gothic films made during the previous years.

Cinematic influences were equally varied and nonchalantly mixed. Besides Hammer films and A.I.P.'s Poe cycle, models range from *The Phantom of the Opera* (the blueprint for Renato Polselli's *Il mostro dell'opera*, 1964) to *Vampyr*, from Hitchcock's work (amply referred to in *L'orribile segreto del dr. Hichcock*, starting with the titular character's name) to Jean Cocteau, the latter being a noticeable influence of Bava's cinema. Stylistically, Bava's films stand out for their formal care and visual inventions, with plenty of surreal moments and elaborate colour compositions which are rarely, if ever, matched by his peers. Margheriti's works display a technique influenced by American cinema, with three cameras shooting at once, whereas the odd displays of style (such as a two-minute long take in *I lunghi capelli della morte*) seem dictated by timesaving needs rather than aesthetic pretences. This is understandable given the tight shooting schedules: Freda boasted about wrapping up his films in two or three weeks at most (Freda 90), a claim which (albeit exaggerated) was achieved by filming on one main location and keeping two units constantly at work.

Tales of Sex and Violence

The originality of Italian Gothic cinema can also be noticed in the way it employs the tools of the genre. Suspense is accessory, sometimes even marginal. Filmmakers often 'rifuggono dal climax articolato in un susseguirsi di momenti di tensione' [shun the typical climax based on a succession of tense moments] (Mora 186), seeking instead 'più di inquietare che di spaventare, di sfumare i confini tra realtà e allucinazione' [to unsettle rather than scare, to blur the boundaries between reality and hallucination] (Pezzotta, 'Doppi' 27). Sometimes the supernatural is only a decoy and the stories centre on human monsters. Elsewhere, most notably in *La frusta e il corpo*, the hesitation before an event which 'cannot be explained by the laws of this same familiar world' (Todorov 25) lingers even after the ending.

Conversely, the approach toward violence and eroticism is surprisingly bold. *La maschera del demonio* opens with a grisly torture scene where a witch (Barbara Steele) is put at the stake and a spiked metal mask is nailed onto her face by way of a huge sledgehammer, with spurts of blood spilling from it. In the prologue of *La vergine di Norimberga*, the protagonist (Rossana Podestà) discovers a dead woman inside the titular torture instrument, her eyeballs gouged out. In Freda's *Lo spettro* (1963), the evil heroine (Barbara Steele) savagely slashes her lover with a razor, the camera taking the victim's point of view and blood dripping on the lens. Moreover, there is a fetishistic attention to the effects of death on the human body, while the reworking of somewhat naïve macabre elements – skulls and skeletons, cobwebs and rat-infested crypts – is paired with a noticeable attention towards funeral practices and fetishes. This latter trait emphasises a deeper relationship with death and its social dimension, which goes beyond a mere imitation of the foreign models and results in a true aesthetic of decay.

Likewise, sensuality and eroticism acquire primary importance. The Gothic *filone* of the early to mid-1960s launched a diva, Barbara Steele, whose popularity was much bigger than that of the films in which she starred. The British-born actress embodied an aggressive and vindictive type of sexuality, in tune with the genre's depiction of gender relations. Compared with its Anglo-Saxon counterparts, in fact, Italian Gothic is often characterised by the representation of women as monsters: in contrast with the overemphasised, almost parodistic image of masculinity exhibited by the sword-and-sandal films, it deals with succubus male figures as opposed to dominating females who seduce and kill, in a path of transgression and atonement which mimics the nation's troubled relationship with sin and sexuality. Likewise, the supernatural element and period setting allowed the depiction of sexual behaviour, lesbianism and nudity which otherwise would not be tolerated. *La frusta e il corpo* revolves around a sadomasochistic liaison; the titular character in *L'orribile segreto del dr. Hichcock* is a necrophile; *La cripta e l'incubo* and *Danza macabra* feature openly lesbian characters. Filmmakers devoted ample footage to actresses wearing see-through nightgowns or briefly displaying a bare breast to the camera, and sometimes nude scenes were conceived for foreign versions. Such an imagery was complementary to the naïve sadistic one sported in pulp paperbacks and photo-novels of the period, explicitly evoked in Pupillo's *Il boia scarlatto* (1965).

Frankenstein and the Computer

Despite the drying up of the filmic thread in the mid- to late 1960s, the interest in the Gothic did not wane. Publishers continued their rediscovery of classics with series such as Bompiani's *Il Pesanervi* (1966–70), which collected works by William Beckford, Gustav Meyrink, Montague R. James, Charles Maturin and more, and similar editorial initiatives flourished. December 1969 saw the debut of *Horror*, a monthly magazine focusing on horror in all its aspects: comics, short stories, essays, poems and cinema. Created by Pier Carpi and Alfredo Castelli and published by the Milan-based Sansoni, it featured first-rate comic-book artists (Dino Battaglia, Marco Rostagno and Leo Cimpellin) and writers (Ornella Volta, Orio Caldiron, Piero Zanotto, Emilio de' Rossignoli, Gianfranco De Turris and Sebastiano Fusco). As Carpi wrote in the editorial column, these were 'perlopiù giovani o giovanissimi e, lo sbandieriamo con faziosità autarchica, tutti italiani' [mostly young or very young and, we stress it with autarchic bias, all Italian] (2). The time of deception was over.

Published up to October 1972 for a total of thirty-one issues, *Horror* proved a fundamental step in the resurgence of Italian Gothic, not the least because of its embracing of the new tendencies in the genre. Such was the growing fascination with all things paranormal, a remnant of hippie culture's mysticism that elicited disengagement and escapism as opposed to the decade's escalation of political struggle, and the dichotomous approach to technology, for, as Carpi argued, 'ai nostri giorni, i Frankenstein come il computer appartengono all'irrazionale' [nowadays, both Frankenstein and the computer belong to the irrational] (Carpi 2).

At the turn of the decade, the Gothic flourished on the small screen as well. The success of Claude Barma's mini-series *Belphégor ou le Fantôme du Louvre* (1965) prompted a new wave of Gothic-related, made-for-TV products such as Giorgio Albertazzi's *Jekyll* (1969), an experimental, modern-day rendition of Stevenson's classic, or Luciano Emmer's *Geminus* (1969), which revisited iconic Roman locations in a perspective akin to *fantastique*. Daniele D'Anza's mini-series *Il segno del comando*, aired in Spring 1971, drew from the themes of the Gothic novels as well as from nineteenth-century supernatural short stories, such as the *doppelgänger* motif, reincarnation, predestination and the inescapability of Fate. The story is set in present-day Rome and revolves around a Byron scholar (Ugo Pagliai) and an elusive woman (Carla Gravina) who appears and disappears mysteriously through the alleys of Trastevere.

With an audience of almost fifteen million viewers, *Il segno del comando* launched a new wave of mini-series with supernatural or paranormal elements, namely *La pietra di luna* by Anton Giulio Majano (1972), based on Wilkie Collins's novel *The Moonstone* (1868); *Ritratto di donna velata* by Flaminio Bollini (1975), exhibiting a similar plot as D'Anza's work and featuring a character who might be the reincarnation of an eighteenth-century dame portrayed in a painting; D'Anza's *L'amaro caso della baronessa di Carini* (1975), a tale of reincarnation based on the same folk story that inspired Giovanni Verga's novelette *Le storie del castello di Trezza* (1876); *Il fauno di marmo* by Silverio Blasi (1977), a modern-day adaptation of Nathaniel Hawthorne's novel *The Marble Faun* (1859); and Blasi's *La dama dei veleni* (1979), from John Dickson Carr's mystery novel *The Burning Court* (1937). Many of these employed Italian locations to perturbing effects, whether it be the Tuscan village of Volterra and its Etruscan necropolis, the Sicilian countryside, or the eerie, Mannerist Gardens of Bomarzo (already seen in Warren Kiefer's bizarre *Il castello dei morti vivi*, 1964).

A concurring factor in the mutation of Italian Gothic in the 1970s was the rise to prominence of the Dario Argento-inspired thrillers, which prompted a partial reshaping of the genre. Many *gialli* included such themes as precognition, séances, tarot and mind reading, whereas several crossovers borrowed the black-gloved killers and graphic murder scenes from Argento's films and transplanted them into typical Gothic scenarios, namely Emilio P. Miraglia's *La notte che Evelyn uscì dalla tomba* (1971) and *La dama rossa uccide sette volte* (1972) and Giuseppe Bennati's *L'assassino ha riservato nove poltrone* (1974), just to name a few. This change in perspective affected pulp literature as well: later issues in *I capolavori della serie KKK* used elements of the *giallo*, reshaping the stories and characters in present-day settings and even featuring references to 1968 and hippie culture.

The Changing Face of Old-Style Gothic

Meanwhile, veteran filmmakers struggled to keep up with the new tendencies, with mixed results. Mario Bava directed a couple of co-productions set in the present day and destined for foreign distribution, *Gli orrori del castello di Norimberga* (1972) and *Lisa e il diavolo* (1973). The former, an old-style yarn mostly devoid of graphic violence, had some commercial fortune overseas but was hardly noticed in Italy. The latter, a more ambitious and literate effort, was released in a heavily manipulated form as *La casa dell'esorcismo*, in the wake of William Friedkin's *The Exorcist* (1973). Bava returned to the Gothic with his final works, the modern-day, low-budget ghost story *Shock* (1977) and the made-for-TV *La Venere d'Ille* (1978), based on Prosper Mérimèe's 1837 short story and co-directed with his son Lamberto, aired only in 1981. Conversely, Freda's little-seen *Estratto dagli archivi segreti della polizia di una capitale europea* (1972) and Giorgio Ferroni's *La notte dei diavoli* (1972), a modern-day remake of *I Wurdalak*, amply resorted to gore. Margheriti, in turn, emphasised eroticism in his later Gothic efforts, namely *Contronatura* (1969), loosely inspired by Dino Buzzati's short story 'Eppure bussano alla porta' (1940); *Nella stretta morsa del ragno* (1971), a colour remake of *Danza macabra* featuring Klaus Kinski as Poe; and the mystery/Gothic hybrid, *La morte negli occhi del gatto* (1973). The latter, allegedly based on a non-existent short story by a British author, was in fact penned by the director and Giovanni Simonelli (himself a frequent contributor to *KKK* and *I Racconti di Dracula*) and showed a notable pulp atmosphere.

Most of these works highlighted eroticism as a key factor. Throughout the 1970s, the ongoing relaxation of censorship gave way to female nudity and simulated sex both on the big screen and in mainstream publishing. A key influence in this respect came in the form of adults-only comics such as *Jacula* (1969–82), *Oltretomba* (1971–86) and *Zora la vampira* (1972–85), which boldly mixed sex and horror, taking the place of the pulp paperbacks of the previous decade and pushing the limits in the depiction of nudity and violence. Sex turned into the main attraction in films that reworked Gothic stereotypes (sometimes in present-day settings) in a patently erotic way, such as *La notte dei dannati* by Filippo Ratti (1971), *Il plenilunio delle vergini* by Luigi Batzella and Aristide Massaccesi (1973), *Riti, magie nere e segrete orge nel Trecento* . . . by

Renato Polselli (1973), *Nuda per Satana* by Luigi Batzella (1974) or *La sanguisuga conduce la danza* by Alfredo Rizzo (1975). A common practice was filming more explicit material for the sex scenes, sometimes bordering on hardcore.

These low-budget products were mainly intended for independent or regional distribution and aimed at the so-called second- and third-run cinemas. By the end of the decade, these venues were converting to hardcore porn to face the continuing loss of moviegoers, most of whom had found a more satisfying alternative in television, after the rise of commercial broadcasters. The film industry's non-stop quest for on-screen excess resulted in such works as Andrea Bianchi's *Malabimba* (1979), a hardcore porn hybrid in which genre paraphernalia – including the setting in the Balsorano castle, a recurring location of 1960s Italian Gothic – are merely a tapestry for a parade of erotic attractions.

New Perspectives in the Genre

During the 1970s, some refreshing approximations of the Gothic emerged, in tune with the decade's political and sociological tendencies. Capitalism as vampire and the devilish repressive power of the élites were at the centre of *Il delitto del diavolo* by Tonino Cervi (1970), *... hanno cambiato faccia* by Corrado Farina (1971), *La corta notte delle bambole di vetro* by Aldo Lado (1971), *Il prato macchiato di rosso* by Riccardo Ghione (1973) and *Il cav. Costante Nicosia demoniaco ovvero: Dracula in Brianza* by Lucio Fulci (1975). Other peculiar works – such as Francesco Barilli's *Il profumo della signora in nero* (1974) – embraced the so-called 'Female Gothic' (Kavka 219), focusing on modern-day heroines within parapsychological scenarios that explored the period's interest in the occult and the paranormal while simultaneously addressing the contradictory female condition in contemporary society.

Other filmmakers came up with idiosyncratic takes on the Gothic canon. Argento developed the irrational elements of his *gialli* into a pair of ambitious efforts, *Suspiria* (1977) and *Inferno* (1980), which revised old-style Gothic elements (the damsel in distress, the menacing castle, the 'return of the past') alongside psychoanalytic ones and nods to current cultural trends (such as the rediscovery of Thomas De Quincey's work on the part of the Italian intellectuals) through the director's unique visual flair and taste for over-the-top violence.

Finally, with *La casa dalle finestre che ridono* (1976), Pupi Avati developed a self-styled 'gotico padano' [Po Valley Gothic] (Adamovit and Bartolini 138), removed from the typical Northern and Eastern European settings as well as from the urban dimension of 1970s Italian *gialli*. Deeply rooted in Italian folklore and closely linked to a geographically localised rural environment, the Po delta, Avati's film offered an original approach to Gothic tropes (the lone traveller, the perturbing painting, the return of the past) which the director would develop over the next decades, in his sporadic returns to the genre.

Bibliography

Adamovit, Ruggero, and Claudio Bartolini, *Il gotico padano. Dialogo con Pupi Avati* (Recco, Genova: Le Mani, 2010).
Carpi, Pier, 'Editoriale', *Horror*, 1, 1969, p. 2.
De Feo, Sandro, 'I vampiri tema di moda nelle conversazioni di via Veneto', *Corriere della Sera*, 28 July 1959, p. 3.
De' Rossignoli, Emilio, *Io credo nei vampiri* [1961] (La Mesa, CA: Gargoyle Books, 2009).
Faldini, Franca, and Goffredo Fofi (eds), *L'avventurosa storia del cinema italiano raccontata dai suoi protagonisti 1960–1969* (Milan: Feltrinelli, 1981).
Fofi, Goffredo, 'Terreur in Italie', *Midi-Minuit Fantastique*, 7, 1963, pp. 80–4.
Freda, Riccardo, *Divoratori di celluloide* (Milan: Edizioni del Mystfest – Emme Edizioni, 1981).
Kavka, Misha, 'The Gothic on Screen', in Jerrold E. Hogle (ed.), *The Cambridge Companion to Gothic Fiction* (Cambridge: Cambridge University Press, 2002), pp. 209–28.
Lucas, Tim, *Mario Bava: All the Colors of the Dark*, (Cincinnati, OH: Video Watchdog, 2007).
Mora, Teo, 'Elegia per una donna vampiro. Il cinema fantastico in Italia 1957–1966', in Teo Mora (ed.), *Storia del cinema dell'orrore, vol. II.*, 2 vols (Rome: Fanucci, 2001–2, II, 2002), pp. 159–96.
Morandini, Morando, 'I vampiri', *La Notte*, 16–17 April 1957.
Pezzotta, Alberto, 'Il boom? È gotico (e anche un po' sadico)', *Bianco e nero*, 579, 2014, pp. 34–48.
Pezzotta, Alberto, 'Doppi di noi stessi', *Segnocinema*, 85, 1997, pp. 25–31.
Todorov, Tzvetan, *The Fantastic: A Structural Approach to a Literary Genre* [1970], trans. Richard Howard (Ithaca, NY: Cornell University Press, 1975).
Venturini, Simone, *Galatea Spa (1952–1965): storia di una casa di produzione cinematografica* (Rome: Associazione italiana per le ricerche di storia del cinema, 2001).
Venturini, Simone, *Horror italiano* (Rome: Donzelli, 2014).

Chapter 6

The Decline of the Gothic: 1980–2020
Marco Malvestio

The last four decades have been an ambivalent period for the Gothic in Italian culture. The 1980s and the 1990s saw the transformation of Gothic cinema into more markedly horror cinema, with an emphasis on splatter and gore, while the quantity of horror films produced in Italy thereafter significantly decreased. As far as fiction is concerned, the 1980s opened with the debate on the fantastic, which (together with the diffusion of postmodernism and its characteristic merging of different cultural codes) in many ways helped cast a new light on overlooked areas of Italian literature, including the Gothic. While this debate caused an expansion of the Italian literary canon, its critical premises were extremely narrow and prevented an open discussion of genre fiction and popular texts – despite the growing and persistent success of Gothic mass products such as the comic-book series *Dylan Dog* (1986–present).[1] Contemporary Italian Gothic fiction is polarised into, on the one hand, highbrow works reappropriating Gothic imagery without regard for popular products and, on the other, genre fiction that has no space in the mainstream literary debate. Gothic tropes can be found also in the most recent forms of Italian supernatural fiction, as evidenced by the debate on the so-called 'New Weird'. Nevertheless, the presence of Gothic elements within mainstream fiction is filtered through prejudices against popular forms that prevent this mode from being fully embraced.

Italia magica or *Italia gotica*? Gothic Fiction in Italy between 1980 and 2020

The 1980s in Italy were characterised by the debate on the fantastic. Starting with the translation of Tzvetan Todorov's *Introduction à la littérature fantastique* (1970) in 1977, Italian critics began to examine the fantastic in Italian literature and produced a series of anthologies of texts belonging to this tradition. In 1984, Enrico Ghidetti edited two volumes on the 'racconto nero' [dark tale] of the nineteenth and twentieth centuries respectively (the latter with Leonardo Lattarulo). Italo Calvino published the anthology *Racconti fantastici dell'Ottocento* in 1983 (though this did not include any Italian author) and later reprised the debate in a series of articles and conferences. Finally, in 1988, Einaudi published a new edition of Gianfranco Contini's *Italia magica*, which had originally appeared in France in 1946 and had remained almost unknown in Italy.[2] Although its theoretical taxonomy deliberately omitted the concept of the Gothic, as we have seen in the introduction, this debate contributed to the re-emergence of several texts and authors that can be considered Gothic and indeed to the rediscovery of a Gothic vein in Italian culture, even if this was mislabelled. While the fantastic and the Gothic are two different forms, and while critics generally chose more established and canonical authors over popular texts, the anthologies collecting fantastic stories or *racconti neri* by Italian authors contributed to shedding new light on a previously underdeveloped area of Italian studies, as well as starting a debate that expanded to involve the general public.

However, the editors of these anthologies tended to exclude Gothic texts and popular authors. By omitting Italian authors from his anthology of fantastic tales of the nineteenth century, Calvino implicitly endorses what Contini argued in the preface to *Italia magica*: that it is the twentieth century (a century of magical realism, surrealism and avant-gardes) that produced the most interesting examples of this genre. According to Calvino, the philosophical and speculative apologues of Giacomo Leopardi's *Operette morali* are the only nineteenth-century Italian example of the fantastic worth studying. Ghidetti maintains that Italian literature in the nineteenth century only accepted the more rational manifestations of Romanticism, centred on national history and patriotic claims, and not its horrific effects. Thus, in Ghidetti's anthology dedicated to the nineteenth century (the earliest text included here was published in 1868), we find only the works of the *Scapigliati* and the minor works of authors renowned for other, more 'serious' and 'respectable' efforts, like Giovanni Verga or Antonio Fogazzaro.

While the very spirit of this companion contradicts the ideas outlined by these critics, it is undeniable that the debate on the fantastic that started in those years facilitated the re-evaluation of the Italian literary canon and the creation of an alternative genealogy of Italian literature. For instance, Ghidetti's anthology was used as a polemical starting point in *Il cuore oscuro dell'Ottocento* (2008), edited by Riccardo Reim, and *Ottocento nero italiano. Narrativa fantastica e crudele* (2009), edited by Claudio Gallo and Fabrizio Foni, which are definitely more inclusive and more oriented towards popular fiction.

Importantly, the debate on the fantastic was not confined to academia, but was, rather, widespread among the general public. In fact, it contributed to creating favourable conditions for the publication of novels dealing with the fantastic, including several contemporary Gothic texts. This was also encouraged by the cultural attitude of postmodernism and its double-coding poetics, which advocated the merging of different cultural codes and the reuse of the narrative and thematic structures of popular fiction (as is the case of Umberto Eco's *Il nome della rosa*, itself a Gothic text, which inaugurated the decade in 1980). The poetics of postmodernism focused on the merging of highbrow and lowbrow models, intertextuality, metafictional devices and a new critical consideration of popular art forms. This last point, in particular, was the reason for the renewed attention paid by critics to comics as an art form (especially in the context of the DAMS faculty at the University of Bologna, founded in 1971) and the development of comics as a serious means of artistic expression. Postmodernist authors often employed popular literature such as Gothic narratives, science fiction and detective novels as models for more theoretically layered works; the utilisation of generic trappings was typically carried out in an ironic fashion, with the lowbrow sources constituting the material for a pastiche.

Paola Capriolo and Michele Mari were among the Italian Gothic authors influenced by postmodern poetics.[3] Capriolo's first novels (*La grande Eulalia*, 1988, *Il nocchiero*, 1989, and *Il doppio regno*, 1991) deal with Gothic atmospheres, settings and themes such as the double and the ambiguous relationship between art and life in a way that is coherent with postmodernism's contestation of grand narratives.[4] A significant amount of Mari's work can be labelled as Gothic, especially novels such as *Di bestia in bestia* (1989), *Io venìa pien d'angoscia a rimirarti* (1990), *La stiva e l'abisso* (1992) and the stories collected in *Fantasmagoriana* (2012). Mari's work is often pervaded by monstrous doubles and intergenerational hauntings, but, most importantly, it presents a strong metatextual component, evidencing the postmodern influence on the Italian Gothic at the time. In particular, *Io venìa pien d'angoscia a rimirarti*, a retelling of the life of Italian poet Giacomo Leopardi as if he were a werewolf, is a great example of the author's postmodern imagination, as well as his plastic and metatextual understanding of the Italian literary canon and icons.

As previously stated, the debate on the fantastic had an ambivalent effect on the reception of the Gothic in Italy. On the one hand, it contributed to the rediscovery of authors and texts that had not previously been considered Gothic or fantastic, thereby *de facto* opening up new provinces of the literary world to critics. On the other hand, however, the debate focused mostly on highbrow texts and authors and, most significantly, it did so in a way that not only did not recognise the Gothic, but even deliberately omitted it: while the debate on the fantastic often encompassed Gothic texts, the critical concept of the Gothic was never employed. Therefore, while the 1980s and 1990s constitute a period of great interest in terms of fantastic fiction at large, they were also decades of critical misunderstandings and partisan appropriations. Finally, it is worth noting again that the omission of the Gothic from the debate on the fantastic occurred immediately after the decades of greatest success for Italian Gothic cinema and at a time when Italian Gothic comic series such as *Dylan Dog* were selling up to half a million copies a month.

One of the ways in which the new interest in different forms of literature manifested itself was the wave of splatter texts published in the 1990s (a consequence of Italian cinema's predilection for splatter and gore in the previous decade). Between 1989 and 1991, the magazine *Splatter* was a great success, while the collection of short stories *Primi delitti* by Paolo Di Orazio (1989), himself on the editorial board of the magazine, caused a huge scandal in Italy and was the object of a parliamentary inquiry. Following the success of these publications, in 1996, mainstream publisher Einaudi, aiming to give a new direction to its authoritative catalogue, published *Gioventù cannibale*, an anthology edited by Daniele Brolli containing the work of young authors. Although it was a marketing operation more than a serious critical attempt to define a genre, *Gioventù cannibale* represents an important moment in the assimilation of genre fiction (and in particular of horror) into mainstream discourse.

Similarly, mainstream publishers occasionally attempted to capitalise on the widespread interest in horror and the Gothic. So it was with Feltrinelli and Pietro Grossi's *Orrore* (2018) and Bompiani and Loredana Lipperini's *Magia nera* (2019), neither of which were particularly original or successful. Adelphi published the work of Edgardo Franzosini, whose literary biography *Bela Lugosi* (1998) questions the boundaries between artistic invention, cultural mythologies and private life, making it an example of Gothic non-fiction. Similarly, Francesco Permunian's *Cronaca di un servo felice* (1999) and *Camminando nell'aria della sera* (2001, both re-issued in 2017 by il Saggiatore as a single volume entitled *Costellazioni del crepuscolo*) consistently deal with Gothic themes and settings (palaces, small towns hiding secrets) and the grotesque. Furthermore, Nicola Lagioia's Strega prize-winning *La ferocia* (2014) is interesting from a Gothic perspective, as it merges (not always successfully) elements of the *impegno* [social engagement] typical of Italian literature (social critique, ecologism) with topoi associated with the international Gothic novel (a mansion, intergenerational hauntings, ghosts, the queering of heteronormative sexuality). Such an interest in the most refined expressions of the genre can also be found in the vogue of translations of horror classics for otherwise mainstream publishers, as in the case of Shirley Jackson for Adelphi, Thomas Ligotti for il Saggiatore, and, for non-fiction, of Mark Fisher for minimum fax. Horror and the Gothic appear to have become fashionable and appealing for mainstream publishers, as long as this does not imply having to deal with its popular and occasionally chaotic manifestations.

As far as specialised, genre-oriented authors are concerned, there are a number of interesting contemporary Italian Gothic and horror novelists, with a prevalence of folk horror and small-town horror texts evidently derived from Anglo-American fiction.[5] Danilo Arona is the author of several Gothic novels, most notably *Melissa Parker e l'incendio perfetto* (2006), which is based on the urban legend of a ghost hitchhiker that Arona himself contributed to creating and circulating online, and *L'estate di Montebuio* (2009), a small-town horror set in the Ligurian Alps. Nicola Lombardi is the author of several novels of psychological horror set in small provincial towns, such as *I ragni zingari* (2014) and *Il letto rosso* (2018). Sergio Bissoli, who is also the author of pioneering research on *I racconti di Dracula* and other Gothic series of popular fiction (Bissoli and Cozzi), published *Il paese stregato* (2012), which collects writings from the 1970s to the present on the Veneto countryside and its legends. Other authors explore the Gothic tones of dark fantasy, as in the case of Barbara Baraldi (also a writer for *Dylan Dog*), who has written several novels that merge thriller and horror, such as her dark fantasy *Scarlett* trilogy (2010–15) and the *Striges* trilogy (2013–14), centred on witchcraft. Similarly, Gianfranco Nerozzi places Gothic tropes within the structure of a detective novel, most significantly in *Genia* (2004) and *Resurrectum* (2006). Horror and the Gothic are also employed to investigate urban spaces and the evolutions of modern metropolises. The musician and comics writer Gianfranco Manfredi wrote some of the most fascinating Gothic novels of recent decades, which appeared for important publishers such as Feltrinelli and Mondadori. *Magia rossa* (1983) and *Cromantica* (1985) are two urban wyrd novels set in contemporary Milan, while *Ultimi vampiri* (1987) and *Ho freddo* (2008) explore vampirism in a chronological time frame ranging from the eighteenth century to the present. The most compelling stories by Samuel Marolla, including 'Tenebra al neon', 'Una notte al Ghibli' and 'Ultima sambuca al bar dell'ortica', collected in *La mezzanotte del secolo* (2012), are a convincing mixture of Gothic and weird elements in the unlikely setting of old-fashioned Milan and the peripheries of Lombardy. Similarly to Marolla's work, Luigi Musolino's *Uironda* (2013) and *Pupille* (2021) bring weird elements into Italian provincial life, while Lucio Besana's notable *Storie della serie cremisi* (2021) are more explicitly linked to the imagery of weird author Thomas Ligotti, but develop it in a personal and original way (Besana also contributed to the screenplays of Roberto De Feo's *The Nest*, 2019, and *A Classic Horror Story*, 2021, the latter a Netflix production). Finally, it is also worth mentioning Valerio Evangelisti: arguably the most successful and accomplished science-fiction writer in Italy, Evangelisti's *Inquisitor Eymerich* saga is deeply rooted in Gothic imagery. With few exceptions (Manfredi, Evangelisti, Palazzolo), these authors are published by small, independent publishers, often specialising in genre fiction.[6]

Among genre practitioners, two exceptionally relevant and original authors stand out. Tiziano Sclavi is not only the creator of *Dylan Dog*, possibly the most important Gothic production in contemporary Italy, but also a writer. Sclavi's novels have never been as successful as his comics, but they are particularly noteworthy. *Film* (1974) and *Tre* (1977) are interesting works of fiction in which Sclavi adopts a cinematic and fragmentary narrative to represent provincial habits and discuss the absurdity of life, while *Dellamorte Dellamore* (1991) is an exemplary mix of folk horror fiction and black humour. In the collection of short stories *Sogni di sangue* (1992), Sclavi employs horror fiction to depict the persistent and oppressive atmosphere of the 'years of lead'. Finally, *Mostri* (1994) and *La circolazione del sangue* (1995) reprise a recurring theme in Sclavi's work: monstrosity. Here, the diversity of the 'freaks' (to quote one of his masterpieces, *Dylan Dog* 81, 'Johnny Freak') is used as a polemical alternative to normality and everyday life.

Chiara Palazzolo is the author of the trilogy *Non mi uccidere* (2005), *Strappami il cuore* (2006) and *Ti porterò nel sangue* (2007), which relate the adventures of the young vampire Mirta Luna and her fight against the witches (who, in a reprise of Carlo Ginzburg's folkloric research, are called *benandanti*) hunting her kind. Palazzolo's work has been marketed as an Italian version of the *Twilight* saga, but her books are more thematically nuanced and stylistically refined than Stephanie Meyer's. *La casa della festa* (2000), *I bambini sono tornati* (2003) and *Nel bosco di Aus* (2011) are profoundly Gothic stories concerned with intergenerational hauntings, guilt and social criticism. These are not only extremely well-written but also unapologetically reprise Gothic imagery (in *Nel bosco di Aus*, the plot of which centres on a coven of witches), leaving behind the intellectualism and metatextuality of the postmodern Gothic. Palazzolo's work, therefore, is a significant example of stylistically refined Italian contemporary Gothic fiction that has been stripped of postmodern irony.

Finally, the last few years have been characterised by the production and circulation of works labelled as weird or New Weird, which spawned a debate that has taken place in newspapers and literary magazines. In Anglo-American fiction, 'weird' describes a relatively precise genre that evolved from the Gothic and is concerned with cosmic horror,[7] while 'New Weird' refers to a wave of contemporary writers merging horror, fantasy and science fiction (Ann and Jeff VanderMeer). In Italy, instead, the concept of weird has been generally adopted to describe texts that exhibit non-realistic tendencies. Like the debate on the fantastic, that on the weird is relevant to our examination of the Gothic for two reasons. The first is that it contradicts the long-standing prejudice against non-realistic fiction in Italy (especially in the 2000s, which were characterised by a return to the concept of *impegno*).[8] Secondly, while this label is, again, partial and misleading, several of the works that it is used to describe are markedly Gothic.[9]

The idea of weird was first evoked in 2016 when writer and journalist Alcide Pierantozzi used the term 'weirdness' in a review of Gabriele Di Fronzo's *Il grande animale* and Luciano Funetta's *Dalle rovine* (both published in 2016).[10] Pierantozzi considers Di Fronzo's and Funetta's novels to be similar in scope and intentions to a series of texts published in the previous ten years – *Sirene* (2007) by Laura Pugno, *La casa madre* (2008) by Letizia Muratori, *Zoo col semaforo* (2010) by Paolo Piccirillo, *Settanta acrilico trenta lana* (2011) by Viola Di Grado, *Mio salmone domestico* (2013) by Emmanuela Carbé, *Questa vita tuttavia mi pesa molto* (2015) by Edgardo Franzosini, *Panorama* (2016) by Tommaso Pincio, *Il cinghiale che uccise Liberty Valance* (2016) by Giordano Meacci, *Io e Henry* (2016) by Giuliano Pesce – and, more generally, to the editorial policies of the publisher Tunué, then managed by writer Vanni Santoni. These texts are all characterised by an anti-realistic tendency and a choice of unlikely and odd narrative material that occasionally plays on the tropes of Gothic and fantastic literature, despite the fact that these forms are seldom fully embraced. Despite this, however, the label of 'weird' (or 'weirdness') masks a great categorical confusion, as none of these authors' texts are nods to cosmic horror or a mixture of fantasy, horror and science fiction. On the contrary, their work (which can be Gothic, as in the cases of Di Fronzo, Funetta and Muratori, openly science-fictional, as in the case of Pugno, or just fantastic, as in the case of Meacci) is assimilated into the 'weird' on the basis of a general refusal of realism and the reuse of an uncanny atmosphere and, occasionally, supernatural elements.

Although it provides an idea of the extent of the phenomenon that has been labelled New Weird in Italy and that covers similar grounds to the Gothic and the fantastic in general, this list also reveals the notable absence of genre fiction, several examples of which were cited above. Despite the persistent hybridisation of genres and highbrow and lowbrow forms of literature, Italian so-called New Weird fiction still seems to be modelled on the parameters of the Italian fantastic, even if these have been loosened somewhat. That is to say that these texts are characterised by an erudite, often ironic style, centred on cognitive estrangement. Again, we can note a strong ambiguity in the widespread diffusion of themes and forms related to the Gothic: on the one hand, their presence testifies to the attempt to subvert traditional views of literature as based on commitment and social critique; on the other hand, this subversion operates in a way that is very much in keeping with Italy's long-standing disregard toward popular culture and supernatural fiction.

Imitations, Remakes and Mockbusters in Late Italian Horror Cinema

As with fiction, the decades between the 1980s and the 2010s can be considered a period of general decline for Italian Gothic cinema. This is even more significant considering both the high quality and the great success of Gothic films in the 1960s and 1970s. Specifically, after the 1980s and the early 1990s, Italian horror and Gothic productions lost much of their cultural and commercial significance.[11] As Roberto Curti argues, this was at least partly due to the growing importance of private productions (most notably by Silvio Berlusconi's Reteitalia) in the Italian film market, to which the national television company reacted by increasing its production of genre movies. However, as Curti writes, 'the massive presence on the market of Reteitalia and RAI meant the Italian movie industry would gradually set out to make films aimed more and more at a television audience, with easily understandable consequences: tamer products, devoid of the sexual and violent excesses of the past' (Curti). The taming of the contents was also a result of the growing importance of 'committees, associations and other guardians of the public moral', which led to the soft censorship introduced by the 1990 Mammì law,

> which severely limited the TV airing of films, by forbidding to broadcast films with a V.M.18 rating and relegating those with a V.M.14 rating after 10:30 p.m. A movie had to be certified for all audiences to be aired on prime

time, which led to a massive resubmitting of old films that had been rated V.M.14 and V.M.18 to the rating boards, in order to obtain a new screening certificate after several cuts. In fact, it was a powerful weapon of barely disguised censorship, and a much more effective one than there had ever been. (Curti 17)

During the 1980s, however, Italian horror cinema was still a strong industry, consistently relying on the international market, as 'can be seen in the transnational dimension of the production based on co-production agreements, employment of international cast, use of English pen-names, foreign settings and locations, and the involvement of American distributors for the financing of the films' (Baschiera 46). The invention of VHS technology also gave an initial boost to the circulation of Italian horror films on foreign markets (competition with American movies, however, later became unbearable in this sector; Baschiera 54–6).

In the case of private productions in particular, Italian films of this period had to maximise profits, resulting in a number of mediocre and formulaic TV and direct-to-video movies. One way in which this was done was by producing 'mockbusters', that is, movies exploiting ideas and images from more successful foreign films. This was not new in Italian cinema: for example, after William Friedkin's *The Exorcist* came out in 1973, scenes were added to Mario Bava's 1972 *Lisa e il diavolo* to insert a demonic possession subplot, so that the movie could be marketed in the United States as *La casa dell'esorcismo*. Producers, however, started commissioning fake sequels to American movies, in order to profit from the audience's mistaken conflation of the two. This was the case with Lucio Fulci's masterpiece *Zombi 2* (1979), which is presented as a sequel to George Romero's *Dawn of the Dead* (1978), translated into Italian as *Zombi*. It was also true of the fake sequels to Sam Raimi's *Evil Dead* trilogy (in Italian, *La casa*), produced by Joe D'Amato's Filmirage. The three movies produced, entitled *La casa 3, 4* and *5* (directed by Umberto Lenzi, Fabrizio Laurenti and Claudio Fragasso respectively), bear no resemblance whatsoever to their alleged model.

Furthermore, the Gothic was no longer the prevalent mode in Italian horror cinema. Although the golden age of Italian Gothic, the 1960s, was over, key elements of the genre persisted in the *giallo filone* of the 1970s. However, horror productions in the 1980s attempted to attract new audiences by heavily investing in gory effects and shocking images, as in the zombie sub-genre (consisting of movies such as Lucio Fulci's *Zombi 2*, Marino Girolami's *Zombi Holocaust*, 1980, Bruno Mattei and Claudio Fragasso's *Virus*, 1980, Andrea Bianchi's *Le notti del terrore*, 1981) and cannibal movies (Ruggero Deodato's *Cannibal Holocaust*,

1980, Umberto Lenzi's *Mangiati vivi!*, 1980, and *Cannibal Ferox*, 1982, Aristide Massaccesi's *Antropophagus*, 1980, and *Rosso sangue*, 1982). These *filoni* marked a decisive turning point in Italian horror cinema, as they inaugurated a gorier and more shocking approach to filmmaking, as well as a form of storytelling that was based more on adventure than mystery.

As Curti notes, 1980 marks a symbolic moment for Italian Gothic and horror cinema: Mario Bava died and both his son Lamberto's debut *Macabro* and Dario Argento's ambitious and expensive *Inferno* were released (Curti 17). Generally speaking, it was in the 1980s that the great directors of Italian horror, such as Mario Bava, Argento and Lucio Fulci, gained critical recognition (at least abroad). In the cases of Argento and Fulci, they were so highly esteemed by the public that their names became a guarantee of quality, with Argento producing several young directors and appearing on national television to introduce the segment 'Gli incubi di Dario Argento' on the TV show *Giallo* (1987–8) and Fulci supervising a series of movies marketed as 'Lucio Fulci presenta' for Alpha Cinematografica.

However, the 1980s was also a decade of both maturity and decline for celebrated horror directors. Dario Argento's supernatural thrillers *Inferno* (1980, the second instalment of the *Three Mothers* trilogy, after *Suspiria*) and *Phenomena* (1985) and the giallo *Tenebre* (1982) are accomplished movies that contain some of the best moments of Argento's work (as the underwater sequence in *Inferno* or the flies sequence in *Phenomena*). *Inferno* and *Tenebre* were also 'among the few titles not belonging to the comedy genre that managed to enter the top ten of the national box office' (Baschiera 46). After these films, however, Argento's work became increasingly confused and convoluted, although he remained resourceful in his use of special effects. All of the flaws of Argento's early work (sketchy characters, senseless plots, random plot twists) are exaggerated in his later movies, without being counterbalanced by the poetic inspiration of the mise en scène of *Profondo rosso* (1975) or *Suspiria* (1977). Despite being motivated by 'his desire to achieve auteur status by choosing respectable and literary sources' (Aldana Reyes 229), Argento's approach to Gothic classics such as *Il fantasma dell'opera* (1998) and *Dracula 3D* (2012) results in a gratuitous and superficial exploitation of the original texts without any significant auteurial contribution.

Lucio Fulci was a prolific filmmaker with experience in virtually all of the genres of Italian cinema, from sword-and-sandal and western to *giallo* and horror, though the quality of his work has always been extremely varied. Along with a series of unremarkable direct-to-video works (*Quando Alice ruppe lo specchio* and *Il fantasma di Sodoma*, both 1988) and uninspired horror movies (*Aenigma*, 1987, and *Demonia*, 1989), Fulci directed some of his masterpieces in the 1980s. Besides the supernatural *giallo Gatto nero* (1981), loosely based on Edgar Allan Poe's story 'The Black Cat' (1843), at the beginning of the decade Fulci directed the visionary trilogy *Paura nella città dei morti viventi* (1980), *. . . E tu vivrai nel terrore! L'aldilà* (1981) and *Quella villa accanto al cimitero* (1981), merging Gothic atmospheres with Lovecraftian cosmic horror and sensationally gory special effects. While occasionally weak in terms of their plot and script, these movies were acclaimed for their macabre atmosphere and their pervasive sense of dread. In particular, *L'aldilà*, with its insistence on the blindness of the female protagonist and the mysterious, evocative ending scene, can be considered a connection between splatter aesthetics, aiming to shock the viewers, and metaphysical horror. Fulci's last film, *Le porte del silenzio* (1991), is a lowkey psychological horror and a poetic reflection on death (already unwell, Fulci died a few years later, in 1996).

In the 1980s, Lamberto Bava, son of the pioneer of Italian Gothic cinema Mario Bava, directed several horror movies: the aforementioned *Macabro*, *La casa con le scale nel buio* (1983), and the successful *Dèmoni* (1985) and *Dèmoni 2 . . . L'incubo ritorna* (1986). However, due to the poor conditions of the film industry at the time, Bava moved to TV productions (most notably, all five seasons of the fantasy *Fantaghirò*, 1991–5). Michele Soavi's career followed a similar trajectory: having directed several horror movies between the 1980s and the 1990s, he has mostly worked on TV series since then. After the *giallo*/slasher *Deliria* (1987), Soavi directed the *Dèmoni*-inspired *La chiesa* (1989) and *La setta* (1991), the latter a nod to Roman Polanski's *Rosemary's Baby*. In 1994, Soavi directed *Dellamorte Dellamorte*, based on Tiziano Sclavi's novel of the same name and bearing striking similarities to the comic-book series *Dylan Dog* (whose title character's physical appearance was modelled on the actor playing the protagonist of this movie, Rupert Everett).

As we have seen, the 1980s saw the diffusion of postmodern poetics in Italy and a certain postmodern influence can be noted in Italian cinema as well. Bava's *Dèmoni*, one of the most representative films of the decade, can be analysed as a postmodern work. Like other important horror works of those years, such as Clive Barker's short story 'Son of Celluloid' (in the third volume of *Books of Blood*, 1984–5) and Joe R. Landsdale's *The Drive-In: A 'B' Movie with Blood and Popcorn, Made in Texas* (1988), the set of Bava's horror is a movie theatre (extensively decorated with memorabilia and posters of other horror films).

By setting his film in a theatre and presenting a movie-within-the-movie as the source of a demonic curse, Bava conducts a complex metatextual operation aimed at reflecting on the boundaries between art and life, an inherently Gothic topos characteristic of postmodern Gothic works.[12] A similar attitude is evident in Lucio Fulci's *Un gatto nel cervello* (1990). The protagonist of the movie is Fulci himself, a horror movie director who is tormented by a series of nightmares depicting horrible and gory homicides. Interestingly, the homicide scenes are taken from the movies of the 'Lucio Fulci presenta' series, which the director was able to reuse after a legal dispute regarding copyright issues. While the reasons behind this choice are purely commercial (that is, to use pre-existing films to create a new motion picture with a theatrical release), the result is both humorous and disturbing. By representing the character Fulci as tormented by the movies that the director Fulci produced in real life, Fulci plays on an image of himself as an author tarnished by his reputation for making cheap B-movies.

It would not be correct to state that horror disappeared from Italy in the 2000s. Several horror movies have been produced, some of them of good quality. However, the genre is not even remotely as commercially significant as it was from the 1960s to the 1990s and these movies are not widely distributed in Italy or abroad. Pupi Avati has continued to direct horror movies, such as the acclaimed *L'arcano incantatore* (1996) and the less impressive *Il nascondiglio* (2007) and *Il signor diavolo* (2019). The Roman brothers Marco and Antonio Manetti directed the horror comedy *Zora la vampira* (2000), imbued with references to classic Italian horror films and comics. Ivan Zuccon has adapted several of H. P. Lovecraft's stories to cinema, such as *La casa sfuggita* (2003), *Colour from the Dark* (2008) and *Herbert West: Reanimator* (2017). Jonathan Zarantonello's *La stanza delle farfalle* (2012), starring the iconic Italian Gothic cinema star Barbara Steele, pays homage to the genre with a story of monstrous motherhood, while Roberto De Feo's *Il nido* (2019) is an elegant example of psychological and atmospheric horror. The output of female directors should also be noted, such as Rossella De Venuto's *Controra – House of Shadows* (2013) and Laura Girolami's *Surrounded* (2014, with Federico Patrizi).[13]

Luca Guadagnino's *Suspiria* (2018), an international remake of Dario Argento's movie of the same name (1977), could be considered the most significant event in contemporary Italian horror: despite (or because of) the international production and cast of his movies, Guadagnino is one of the most internationally popular Italian directors. *Suspiria* is imbued with all of the Gothic elements present in the original motion picture, from deviant femininity to monstrous motherhood, from the unmappable architecture of the school to the atmospheric use of the weather. However, by setting it in Berlin in 1970, Guadagnino adapts Argento's movie from a fairy tale-like coming-of-age story into a reflection on political power, with references to the Holocaust. The reception of Guadagnino's work has been extremely polarised between those who praise its style and technical features and those who find its intellectualism questionable. Nevertheless, it is noteworthy that the most-discussed horror movie by an Italian director of the twenty-first century is not an exclusively Italian production and, most significantly, that it is a remake. Guadagnino's decision to remake one of the most celebrated horror movies in the history of Italian cinema was certainly ambitious. At the same time, we can note in this choice the haunting presence of old-fashioned Italian horror and the inability of the genre to look forward and develop a new autonomous language.

Bibliography

Aldana Reyes, Xavier, 'The Cultural Capital of the Gothic Horror Adaptation: The Case of Dario Argento's *The Phantom of the Opera* and *Dracula 3D*', *Journal of Italian Cinema and Media Studies*, 5.2, 2017, pp. 229–44.
Ania, Gillian, 'Inside the Labyrinth: The Thematics of Space in the Fiction of Paola Capriolo', *Romance Studies*, 18.2, 2000, pp. 157–71.
Baschiera, Stefano, 'The 1980s Italian Horror Cinema of Imitation: The Good, the Ugly and the Sequel', in Stefano Baschiera and Russ Hunter (eds), *Italian Horror Cinema* (Edinburgh: Edinburgh University Press, 2016), pp. 45–61.
Beville, Maria, *Gothic-postmodernism: Voicing the Terrors of Postmodernity* (New York: Rodopi, 2009).
Bissoli, Sergio, and Luigi Cozzi (eds), *La storia dei Racconti di Dracula* (Rome: Profondo Rosso, 2013).
Botting, Fred, *Gothic* (London and New York: Routledge, 1996).
Calvino, Italo, 'Definizioni di territori: il fantastico', in Mario Barenghi (ed.), *Saggi 1945–1985*, 2 vols (Milan: Mondadori, 2001, I), pp. 266–8.
Calvino, Italo, 'Il fantastico nella letteratura italiana', in Mario Barenghi (ed.), *Saggi 1945–1985*, 2 vols (Milan: Mondadori, 2001, II), pp. 1672–82.
Calvino, Italo, 'Un'antologia di racconti "neri"', in Mario Barenghi (ed.), *Saggi 1945–1985*, 2 vols (Milan: Mondadori, 2001, II), pp. 1689–95.
Calvino, Italo (ed.), *Racconti fantastici dell'Ottocento* (Milan: Mondadori, 1983).
Catalano, Walter, Gian Filippo Pizzo and Andrea Vaccaro (eds), *Guida ai narratori italiani del fantastico* (Bologna: Odoya, 2018).
Contini, Gianfranco (ed.), *Italia magica* (Turin: Einaudi, 1988).
Cooper, Andrew, 'Demon Media: Horrific Representations of the Transformative Global Image', *Horror Studies*, 4.2, 2013, pp. 241–58.
Curti, Roberto, *Italian Gothic Horror Films, 1980–1989* (Jefferson, NC: McFarland and Company, 2017). Kindle edn.

De Camilla, Lauren, 'Contemporary Italian Horror Cinema: Female Directors and Framing the Maternal', *L'avventura*, 1, 2019, pp. 79–91.

Donnarumma, Raffaele, and Gilda Policastro, 'Ritorno alla realtà? Otto interviste a narratori italiani', *Allegoria*, 57, 2008, pp. 9–25.

Ghidetti, Enrico (ed.), *Notturno italiano: Racconti fantastici dell'Ottocento* (Rome: Editori Riuniti, 1984).

Ghidetti, Enrico, and Leonardo Lattarulo (eds), *Notturno italiano. Racconti fantastici del Novecento* (Rome: Editori Riuniti, 1984).

Joshi, S. T., *The Weird Tale* (Holicong, PA: University of Texas Press, 1990).

Lovecraft, Howard Phillips, *Supernatural Horror in Literature* (New York: Ben Abramson, 1945).

Luckhurst, Roger, 'The Weird: A Dis/Orientation', *Textual Practice*, 31.6, 2017, pp. 1041–61.

Luperini, Romano, *La fine del postmoderno* (Naples: Alfredo Guida Editore, 2005).

Machin, James, *Weird Fiction in Britain 1880–1939* (London: Palgrave Macmillan, 2018).

Malvestio, Marco, 'New Italian Weird? Definizioni della letteratura italiana del soprannaturale nel nuovo millennio', *The Italianist*, 41.1, 2021, pp. 1–16.

Palumbo Mosca, Raffaello, *L'invenzione del vero* (Rome: Gaffi, 2014).

Palumbo Mosca, Raffaello, 'Notes on Hybrid Novel and Ethical Discourse', *MLN*, 128.1, 2013, pp. 185–205.

Pierantozzi, Alcide, 'New Italian Weirdness', *Rivista Studio*, 26 June 2016, <https://www.rivistastudio.com/tunue-funetta-di-fronzo/> (last accessed 29 July 2022).

Sica, Beatrice, *L'Italia magica di Gianfranco Contini: storia e interpretazione* (Rome: Bulzoni, 2013).

Simonetti, Gianluigi, 'I nuovi assetti della narrativa italiana (1996–2006)', *Allegoria*, 57, 2008, pp. 95–136.

Smith, Andrew, *Gothic Literature* (Edinburgh: Edinburgh University Press, 2013).

Vandermeer, Ann and Jeff (eds), *The New Weird* (San Francisco: Tachyron Publications, 2008).

Wilson, Rita, 'Paola Capriolo's Mythic Fantasies', in Francesca Billiani and Gigliola Sulis (eds), *The Italian Gothic and Fantastic. Encounters and Re-writings of Narrative Traditions* (Madison, NJ: Fairleigh Dickinson, 2007), pp. 210–26.

Notes

1. In this chapter, I have omitted an extensive discussion of comics, which are an essential part of Gothic production in Italy from the 1980s onwards, as they are discussed in greater detail by Fabio Camilletti in Chapter 11.
2. On the composition and publication of the volume, see Sica.
3. On the postmodern Gothic, see Smith 141, Botting 170–1, and Beville.
4. On the use of Gothic spaces and postmodern tendencies in Capriolo's work, see Ania; and Wilson.

5. On genre authors in Italian fiction, see Catalano, Pizzo and Vaccaro.
6. In recent years, several new publishers have been created that deal exclusively with horror and Gothic texts, such as Hypnos Edizioni, Acheron Press, Kipple Officina Libraria and Independent Legions (founded by horror veteran Alessandro Manzetti, also known as Caleb Battiago, the only Italian ever to win a Bram Stoker Award).
7. In regard to 'weird', besides Howard Phillips Lovecraft's genre-defining *Supernatural Horror in Literature*, see Joshi; Luckhurst; and Machin.
8. See Luperini; Donnarumma and Policastro; Simonetti; and Palumbo Mosca 'Notes' and *L'invenzione*.
9. As for *Gioventù cannibale*, the self-promoting nature of the New Weird 'brand' has to be underlined, since this label is mostly used to refer to the work of certain publishers (e.g. Tunué, il Saggiatore, Chiarelettere) and many individuals involved in this debate work or worked for these very publishers (e.g. Vanni Santoni and Michele Vaccari).
10. For details on the debate on the New Weird and the several novels and authors that exhibit New Weird tendencies, see Malvestio.
11. In the 1980s, the folk horror wave that characterised the 1970s continued with less intensity, but with some remarkable works, such as Pupi Avati's *Zeder* (1983). See Chapter 16 for further details.
12. On Lamberto Bava's *Dèmoni* as a postmodern film, see also Cooper.
13. On female directors in Italian horror cinema, see De Camilla.

Part II

Media

Chapter 7

Gothic Poetry
Simona Di Martino

The thorny task of composing a 'prehistory' of the Italian Gothic drives us back to the late eighteenth century and to a cluster of authors who, although extremely popular during their time, have been generally classified as minor by contemporary compendia of Italian literature. Their poems are characterised by constellations of words semantically related to death, which many Gothic scholars seem to identify as one of the foremost terrors at the heart of their cultural field of enquiry (Davison 2). Deathly motifs emerge from words describing the imagery of the night, with its darkness and melancholic states; the imagery of tombs and graves, strictly linked to macabre portrayals of corpses in decay; and finally, all images related to incorporeal bodies, such as *fantasmi* [ghosts], *larve* and *ombre* [shadows], and pertaining to the realm of visions and dreamlike experiences.

However, all the representations of death exposed here are not to be considered 'Gothic' just because they pivot around the horrific image of death. Rather, they are all characterised by specific traits that make them 'Gothic', namely widespread exaggeration and abjection. As far as exaggeration is concerned, Gothic writings rely on an over-abundance of imaginative frenzy, against conventional eighteenth-century needs of simplicity, which results in a trespass of reason into visionary outcomes (Botting 2). In this respect, sepulchral poems embody a trend towards a new aesthetics, which is no longer based on reality and exemplarity, as classicism would prescribe, but rather on the spontaneity of feelings and emotions. In this way, sepulchral poems exemplify propensity for magnificence and grandeur, tending to the idea of the sublime (Botting 2). The concept of abjection is applied to poetical representations of death and the new aesthetics is the means through which such abjection is exemplified. Indeed, sepulchral texts abound in depictions of corpses where the decay of the human body is strongly represented as something to be parted from, a waste to be rejected, yet carrying a certain degree of fascination (Kristeva 3). Therefore, in order to shed light on the Gothic filigree that crosses Italian late eighteenth-century poems, one needs to key on all those representations of death where exaggeration and abjection play a role.

Due to the brief nature of this chapter, only a selection of authors and texts from a vast array is tackled.[1] An exhaustive repertoire of such sources is currently missing from scholarship, although dated anthologies and collections of eighteenth-century works can offer a partial picture. Particularly, this chapter selects its texts from three sources: *Poesia del Settecento* edited by Carlo Muscetta and Maria Rosa Massei, where section IX is devoted to lugubrious matters; *Poeti minori del Settecento*, edited by Alessandro Donati; and *Lirici del Settecento* edited by Bruno Maier. Although the authors included in these anthologies are quite heterogeneous, what can be noticed is that most of them share their geographical provenience and a Jesuitical education, a fact that can help understand the formation of a sepulchral stream, or, at least, spark some curiosity for further examination. Indeed, the vast majority of such authors came from Emilia Romagna, Marche and Veneto regions. Considering that both Emilia Romagna and Marche were part of the Papal State during the eighteenth century, one can hypothesise that religious influences played an important role in shaping a deathly imagery with excessive and horrific depictions in both sermons and visual representations in churches. These aspects also seem in line with the rigidity of the Counter Reformation spirit and the severity of the punishments for sinners, aspects that are fully part of the authors' background. Furthermore, it has to be noted that a large part of these poetical works had a huge number of reprints in a variety of volumes and formats (van Vliet 423). The popularity of this stream of literature cannot be stressed enough in this essay, but it actually demonstrates how texts that are now considered low-brow and marginal in the whole picture of Italian literature were very well received by readers of their time and had an important part in directing the taste of the epoch.[2] Given that popularity among a vast audience has always been a central element in defining Gothic novels, it is worth underlining that the success of sepulchral poetry and its deathly motifs constitute the first step towards a 'pre-history' of a later Italian Gothic development.

A Brief Theoretical Background

Is it possible to talk about an Italian 'graveyard poetry' stream? As explained by Eric Parisot, the term 'graveyard poetry' originally emerged in the late nineteenth century to indicate epitaphic verse, and was not applied to a specific brand of eighteenth-century poetics until the 1890s (1). Its critical application has been inconsistent, even though it has generally been used when referring to a loose conglomeration of British poetry meditating upon the transience of life, the imminence of death and the consolation accorded by a Christian afterlife.[3] Whereas the issue of taxonomy and influence was finally tackled by John W. Draper's *The Funereal Elegy and the Rise of English Romanticism* (1929), and the term 'graveyard poetry' achieved a critical consensus, the Italian context still suffers from a lack of investigation into its autochthonous origins: late eighteenth-century poems have generally been regarded as derivative from foreign models and not better named and characterised.

Indeed, criticism of the Italian sepulchral literature has been largely included within the context of pre-Romanticism and it begins as such in the late nineteenth century.[4] No substantial contributions on the subject appeared until the end of the Second World War, when Walter Binni published *Preromanticismo italiano* in 1947. In this book, Binni attempted, for the first time, to define Italian pre-Romanticism, clearly detaching it from both the previous bombast of Arcadia and the rationality of the Enlightenment. Consequently, he concentrated on the important role of Italian translations and translators of the 1770s, as several other critics had also done, particularly focusing on Melchiorre Cesarotti, who helped to define the figure and the role of the modern translator (Broggi). Two years later, Ettore Bonora contributed to the study of the subject with his *Il preromanticismo in Italia*, in which he focused on translations from foreign sources, seeking to delineate the impact of single European nations on the development of pre-Romanticism.

However, such a nationalistic approach does not help to understand a trans-national phenomenon such as the interest in sepulchral themes. It is evident that sepulchral literature flourished in the same time span in all Europe, fostered by intercultural exchanges of the cosmopolitan late eighteenth century, as well as the impact of translations and adaptations of foreign models. Even though poetry provided a common ground, prose worked differently, as exemplified by the fact that the Italian Gothic novel did not appear in concomitance with the circulation of the early British Gothic stories. It can be hypothesised that the fragmented Italian political situation and the control exerted by the Church fostered a kind of literature which was rooted in classical models, differently to what happened in the British context, where the Gothic pervaded literary prose. Where literary works were free to move away from neo-classical aesthetic rules, the Gothic bloomed, with novels set in gloomy castles haunted by ghosts and monsters. Conversely, Italy had to focus its energy on the building of its national identity, where the cruelty of death was considered an abjection to be avoided unless represented with the composure of a Canova's statue. Classical models were a more suitable foundation stone than scary ghosts, even though a golden past is always made of spectres.

Death is certainly the starting point when analysing eighteenth-century lyrics and their pre-Gothic traces. Over the century, a distinct taste for death-related matters and the macabre flourished and became extraordinarily popular, even though such a taste never really experienced a crisis in history, as will be highlighted. Notably, such matters have been already abundantly faced by Dante and Petrarch, who were used to sharing their lives with death and centred their poetics on the action of death. Whereas Petrarch's poetry does not allow macabre descriptions, sepulchral poets show that they master both the delicacy of Petrarch and the crudeness of Dante's lexicon. In this way, their poetry gives a nod to both sensitive and macabre depictions of death.

However, the Bible was unquestionably the original source which modelled a deathly imagery and had a dramatic impact on human ideas on life and death, globally (Davies 85). As Douglas J. Davies posits, 'the history of the death of Jesus contributed more to the history of the world than the death of any other figure' (92–3). Religion influenced earthly everyday life with the promise of a correspondent otherworldly one. Renderings of spiritual possibilities are evident since the Middle Ages in Dante's *Divine Comedy*, where Dante offers images of the three realms of hell, purgatory and paradise, and describes their occupants. Promises of eternal damnation for sinners, since medieval times, persisted in the seventeenth century with the impact of the Jesuits, who made an expert use of innovations of their time. For instance, they employed the recently invented magic lantern to project examples of the pains of hell in the aisles of churches to make their admonitions more tangible for adepts (Pesenti Campagnoni 30–2). At the same time, the teaching of Saint Ignatius from Loyola, whose texts contained encouragements of repentance, sacramental confession and contrition, had been the basis for the plethora of sacred and moral texts[5] in the eighteenth century (Endean 52–67). Concurrently, the ubiquity of skeletons and mementos across the entire seventeenth century left its legacy in churches, for instance in their floors where the graves were decorated with ephemeral symbols – death's-heads, skeletons, hourglasses and the like (Ariès, *The Hour of Our Death* 167). The importance of the caducity of life and its symbolism remain central to eighteenth-century authors. In their poems, indeed, there is the interplay and the incomprehensible contrast between divine goodness and creaturely sinfulness. This approach allows the authors to depict either pilgrims or their poetic-selves, in the wake of Dante's revival, in a state of quasi-death in which they experience all sort of visions: the souls of the dead showing pains for sinners, the beatitude of souls ascending to God, or even visions of their dead beloved ones.

Excess and Abjection: Nocturnal, Funereal and Macabre Repertoire

The presence of death in sepulchral poems produces narrations of mournful experiences. Their Gothic potential is disclosed when they manifest their exaggerations, create disturbing phenomena and foster gloomy settings. Gothic taste, indeed, seems to be fuelled by 'objects and practices that are constructed as negative, irrational, immoral and fantastic' (Botting 1). Specific constellations of words characterise such mournful experiences and outline a repertoire of images where excess and abjection shape nocturnal, funereal and macabre atmospheres. Excess and abjection are the two forces that forge the Gothic filigree overarching sepulchral texts. In so doing, both help maintain the intention to arouse some sort of fear-related emotional response constant in all the poems – and such is, after all, the same mechanism one can find in horror films (Soltysik Monnet 143–56). Such an emotional response manifests itself in nocturnal settings, funereal moments and macabre scenes, as will be shown.

In our corpus of sepulchral texts, the night appears under different shapes, and it is variously accompanied by nymphs, terror and fascination. Terms referring to it are countless – to name a few adjectives the night can be 'tenebrosa', 'ombrosa' and 'maestosa' [gloomy, shaded, grandiose] – and it is often associated with the ability of the poetic subject to recollect memories. At the same time, the night is inevitably coupled with death, because its dark horror prepares and inspires a quiet end. Antonio Capra, the author of *Sei notti poetiche sopra argomenti diversi* (1777), plunges his reader into the darkness from the very beginning of his work, when 'lugubri e torbidi pensieri' [lugubrious and murky thoughts] are sparked by the night 'fra i notturni, e tenebrosi orrori' [among nocturnal and dark horrors].[6] Funereal thoughts are evoked by the adjective 'lugubre' [lugubrious] as revealed by its etymology, which originates in the Latin form *lugŭbris* from the verb *lugēre*, meaning 'crying and mourning'.[7] Even though this adjective was primarily used to qualify clothes worn while mourning the dead, in the late eighteenth century the term is generally and largely applied to mournful environments, contrasting the contemporary denotation for a sense of oppression, angst, or sadness (Devoto and Oli 1179). The term is also effectively employed by Ambrogio Viale in his *Rime del solitario delle alpi* (1792). In the seventh of his lyrics, the initial powerful scene illustrates a night walk among the tombs. Viale invokes the 'ombre cave dei morti' [hollow shadows of the dead] asking for their re-emergence from their darkness, 'sepolcrale orrore taciturno' [sepulchral silent horror], while his poetic-self is walking 'pe' claustri miei fra il tenebror notturno' [through my cloisters in the night dark] (Muscetta and Massei 2130). As the invocation of the dead continues, one can see how the 'concavi occhi' [hollowed eyes] are characterised by 'cerchio di color di piombo' [lead-coloured circle], which resembles those of modern zombies. However, the adjective *lugubre* is the element that attracts the reader's attention. Indeed, it is iterated numerous times in different contexts: sometimes it concerns the allegory of Time described as 'lugubramente muto' [lugubriously silent], and sometimes it involved the dead's lament and their 'lugubre rimbombo' [lugubrious rumble]. Such insistence on adjectives underpins the sense of exaggeration and excess, thus conveying images rich in Gothic potential.

At night-time, though, other elements emerge, such as the invocation to death. Capra's poetic-self wishes to die and refers to death as 'sonno' [sleep] and 'bel ristoro' [good rest], for it would lead him to peace. The same concept is evoked in the works of Aurelio de' Giorgi Bertola and Ippolito Pindemonte. In Pindemonte's *Le quattro parti del giorno* (1817), and specifically in *La notte*, the poetic-self finds himself on a cliff, alone, and dives into the silence.[8] His thoughts are described as pleasant because he is possessed by a 'forza di malinconico diletto' [force of melancholic delight] and he is contemplating 'quell'orror bello, che attristando piace' [that beautiful horror that pleases, while saddening]. The eighteenth century is an epoque characterised by a 'fashionable melancholy', as Clark Lawlor calls it, a time in which the condition of being melancholic was very common and considered as a double-edged sword (Lawlor 25). Indeed, whereas melancholic subjects usually suffered for their murderous condition, melancholy often appeared less of an illness and more of a blessing for poets (Lawlor 26). Notably, poets felt a sort of inspiration that allowed them to produce great poetry, resulting in lyrics rich in causeless sadness, fear and desire for death, all features which characterise an actual disease.[9] The same sense of mental alienation suspended between actual disease and divine possession is effectively shown in Bertola's *La malinconia*, where the melancholic subject is characterised by an overabundant imagination and propensity to daydream, as suggested in the following lines: 'Tu [the melancholic nymph] i fantastici oggetti / moltiplichi, e colori / di quel dolce patetico,

/ per cui piaccion gli affetti / del cor laceratori' [You multiply objects of fantasy / and you colour them / of that sweet pathos, / whereby the tearing affections of the heart / are appreciated]. Here, the adjective *fantastico* defines a purely mental image, suggesting the natural inclination of the melancholic subject to being creative. Such alienation of the subject can be partially reconducted to what Kristeva identifies as the abjection of the self, because 'there is nothing like the abjection of self to show that all abjection is in fact recognition of the *want* on which any being, meaning, language, or desire is founded' (Kristeva 5).

Whereas melancholy represents an important element in the sepulchral repertoire, mourning, from which it is differentiated, gains a greater deal of attention (Freud).[10] Concrete references to graves and burials quilt the texts, and often the image is reinforced and exaggerated by rhymes, as is the case for the words *fossa* [dig] and *ossa* [bones], or by synonymies, such as *sepolcro* [sepulchre], *urna* [urn], *tomba* [tomb] and *chiostra* [cloister]. There exists a wealth of authors who resort to these literary devices, spanning from the brief, light and melodious poems by Jacopo Vittorelli *Anacreontiche a Irene* (1784), to the popular and more complex composition *Dei sepolcri* (1807) by Ugo Foscolo. A detailed portrayal of a burial site is the one provided by Salomone Fiorentino, whose *Elegie in morte di Laura sua moglie* (1790) received public acclaim and enjoyed vast popularity. The second elegy of his collection, *La morte*, describes a simple architecture where the corpse of his bride Laura rests: 'Opaca chiostra, e nel silenzio mesta, / quella è che or serba dell'estinta sposa / sul terreno inegual l'orma funesta' [It is an opaque cloister, and mournfully silent, / the one that now keeps the dead bride's / footprints on the uneven ground] (Fiorentino 6). Architectural features are also portrayed in Alfonso Varano's *Poesie sacre e morali* (1789), and especially in *Visione XI*, which is dedicated to the death of Amennira, the woman loved by the poet. Surrounded by high columns, the author describes a 'monumento di funebre lutto' [a mourning funeral monument] as if it was a work of art: 'Nella volta di cui con varie gonne, / e d'elette virtù coi segni vari / sculte in pietra sedean piangenti Donne' [in the vault of which with various skirts, / and outstanding virtues represented by various signs / weeping women were sitting sculpted in the stone] (Varano 269). Varano indulges in artistic descriptions, illustrating both structures, 'archi reggenti' [supporting arches] and decorations, 'marmi peregrini e rari' [rare marbles], outlining in so doing the originality of Italian sepulchral monuments in his lyric.[11] As for the urn itself, Varano transmits to the reader that particular sense of marvel and terror typical of the Gothic taste – for instance, when he says that 'ma ribrezzo in toccar l'urna mi assalse' [but I felt revulsion in touching the urn] – which ventures into the ground of necromancy and arcane ritual (Botting 4). Such terrors prove themselves to be the source of pleasure for human beings, and result in a blend of medieval fears, macabre details of the Baroque and the eighteenth-century scientific interest for material decay. Indeed, *Visione XI* is entitled to the caducity of earthly life and stresses how beauty is vain and perishable, in line with the religious *memento mori*. Therefore, macabre details are those employed to describe the corpse of Ammenira, where the semantic field stressed is that of the remains, such as 'spoglia' [remains] and 'cenere' [ashes], with emphasis on the excessive characterisation of such remains, as one can see in the word 'putredine' [rottenness]:

> Su letto di putredine schifosa
> giacea dal tempo nel suo morder forte
> l'estinta spoglia avidamente rosa:
> fitti i rai spenti entro l'occhiaie smorte
> guaste le labbra, aperto il petto, e l'anche
> gonfiate, e tinte di livida morte:
> rigide e impallidite le man bianche,
> dilacerato il grembo, e combattuto
> dalle serpi non mai nell'ira stanche:
> lezzo, noia, ed orror quel, che rifiuto
> fu degli ingordi vermi, ed era in lei
> la più vezzosa parte il cener muto. (Varano 270)

[Over a bed of disgusting rottenness / the extinct relic was lying avidly consumed: / extinguished rays in her lifeless eyes / ruined her lips, open the chest, and her hips / swollen, and stained with livid death: / rigid and faded the white hand, torn the womb apart, offended / by the snakes never tired in their rage: / stench, discomfort, and horror were the remains of that silent dust, / which refused by greedy worms, used to be / the most charming part of her.]

The photographic description of single parts of the body consumed by worms or snakes is another recurring feature in sepulchral literature, a legacy of the exaggeration' of the Baroque fashion. Worms are usually paired with bones and flesh and are depicted in a very expressionistic style in order to convey the idea of the corruption of the body in a very tragic way.

Sepulchral authors are also certainly indebted to the classical elegy and do not spare accurate descriptions of sickness – mainly women's – before death, matters that perfectly meet the concepts of excess and abjection. Models for the genre are both Ovid (*Heroides*) and Boethius (*Consolationes*), while Horace, in his *Ars poetica*, clarifies that elegy is the perfect genre to express 'miseria amoris' [misery of love] and 'dolores amantium' [pains of the lovers] (Carrai, 'Appunti' 1–15). Among those who composed elegiac poems and who could have served as an illustrious model is Petrarch. His earliest work known to us, *Elegia ritmica in morte di Laura* or *funereum carmen*, is an affectionate Latin elegy on the death of his mother, Eletta Canigiani, composed between 1318 and 1319, followed by another, *Laurus amena*, dedicated to his beloved Laura after her death. Both poems deal with premature death and the poet's desire to join the departed, each one concluding with the morbid image of the protagonist woman and her tomb (Grimes and Marsilio 161–75). The deathly reverie and the theme of the ill woman became popular features in the eighteenth and nineteenth centuries, as testified by the best-selling *Elegie* by Salomone Fiorentino, Ugo Foscolo's *All'amica risanata* and Giacomo Leopardi's *A Silvia*, to name a few. Based on the cutting-edge elegiac reading of Dante's *Vita Nuova* (1294) and Petrarch's *Rerum vulgarium fragmenta* (1336–74), the surge of new elegiac works in eighteenth-century poetry needs to be interpreted as a new interest in funereal and mourning matters.[12] In fact, sepulchral poems are not only indebted to the aforementioned *lirica dell'assenza*, but they also allow authors to portray death and the decay of the human body in a pathetic and plaintive way, while depicting the loss of a beautiful woman, which years later Edgar Allan Poe would describe as 'the most poetical topic in the world' (114–30).

The elegiac genre has been successfully employed by the already mentioned Fiorentino, who divided his work in four parts, each dedicated to a single step of his wife's departure from life: malady, death, vision and remembrance. The section dealing with Laura's death unveils an evident taste for the morbid and bodily decay. Fiorentino's first elegy is entirely dedicated to the malady of his wife Laura. The woman's face is described with just a few details: 'Come avvivar quelle tue labbra smorte / quella porpora estinta, e dalle gote / la squallida fugar ombra di morte?' [How to revive those dull lips of yours / that extinct purple, and from the cheeks / cancel the bleak shadow of death?] (Fiorentino 3). Fiorentino insists on her pain: 'Egro è il tuo corpo, e di vigor già scemo, / e il morbo che infierisce dispiegato, / e il flutto che ti tragge al giorno estremo' [Sick is thy body, and of vigor already devoid, / and the disease that rages unfolded, / and the flood that draws thee to the extreme day] (Fiorentino 3). However, the corpse gives way to the ecstatic vision of Laura's soul, who appears to the poetic-self, sometimes with the appearance and the modes of a ghost. Laura's vision is somehow uncanny, and the event of her manifestation is expressed by Fiorentino as an inexplicable supernatural force, something defined as 'sacro orror' [sacred horror]. Such an expression manifests the excess and the extraordinariness of the visionary repertoire, thus its Gothic potential. Indeed, Laura floats ('librata ambe le piante' [both her feet hovering in the air]) and is described as an angelic presence, in a Petrarchan way: 'Candide avea le vesti, e all'aura sparte, / e tutta l'avvolgea cilestre un velo, /che trasparir lasciava ogni sua parte' [Her garments were white, and scattered in the breeze, / and a veil enveloped her all, / which let every part of her shine through]. The astonishment of the poetic-self is caused by the contrast between the rotting corpse and the vision: 'Tal la vid'io oltre ogni creder bella, / che l'aspetto divin mi tenne in forse, / e un sacro orror mi chiuse la favella' [I saw her beyond all belief so beautiful, / that I wondered whether she was a goddess, / and a sacred horror impeded my speech] (Fiorentino 14). Yet, the ghost of Laura, although promoting a feeling of astonishment, soon turns into a haunting presence: 'Io so quanto l'immagin mi tormenta/ della perduta mia dolce consorte/ ovunque io sia, come ch'io guati, o senta' [I know how much torments me the image/ of my lost sweet wife/ wherever I may be, whatever I may see or hear] (Fiorentino 18) and Fiorentino calls it 'fantasia molesta' [disturbing fantasy] (Fiorentino 20).

It has to be noted that, even though the Italian literary tradition differs from the English one in the fact that the former does not involve ghosts and spirits as the latter does, such an obsessive presence of something hidden from the past, either a loss or an intimate matter, haunts the characters, psychologically, physically, or otherwise.[13] Even though these hauntings assume many forms, particularly in novels, they mainly embody the shapes of ghosts and spectres (Hogle 2). The prehistory of a Gothic thematic line is evident here, for the haunting presence is one of the parameters by which fictions can be identified as primarily or substantially Gothic (Hogle 2). The oneiric atmosphere typical of many eighteenth-century lyrics is an element which discloses a Gothic potential too, being a feature often related to the premonitions of the author/ poetic-self's death.

Sepulchral poets also portray death itself, foretelling its own arrival in dreams. In his poem *Alla lucerna* (1802), Francesco Cassoli depicts his poetic-self brightened by a close candlelight in the 'solingo orrore' [lonely darkness] of his room during his 'estrema sera' [last evening]. The Jesuit Clemente Bondi, instead, writes *La morte in sogno* (1804) (Donati 240–1). The main character does not realise whether what he sees is 'sogno' [dream] or 'vision dell'alma' [vision of the soul] but surely describes his 'corporea salma' [earthly body] following the canon already employed by other authors – white cheeks, pale lips, feverish state. In the background one can hear 'il cantico funebre' [funereal song] and the author seizes the moment in which the soul comes out of the body 'l'anima spaventata uscir io miro' [I see the frightened soul come out]. The floating ghost is horrified by the sight of its rotten body, a disgust expressed with a language of excess: 'ribrezzo nauseoso spettacolo' [disgust nauseous spectacle]. Moreover, the mortal body is described as 'già guasto / e ormai vicino a imputridir, distrutto / a ingordi vermi preparato pasto' [already dead / and now close to rotting, destroyed / a meal for greedy worms], consolidating the macabre repertoire of sepulchral poetry. The religious aim of the poem allows Bondi to illustrate the vision of God, 'ombra smarrita [...] trovossi in faccia a Dio nuda e romita' [lost shadow [...] found itself naked and lonely in the face of God], as well as to impart the lesson of asking for forgiveness and repenting, and pursues, in so doing, that sacred and moral goal so popular in eighteenth-century poetry. The awakening of the poetic-self concludes the poem with an abrupt vanishing of both the 'gelo mortale' [deathly frost] and 'ogni fantasma' [every ghost] leaving the poetic-self with the scaring premonition of his 'sognata morte' [dreamed death].

A similar subject, the vision of a supernatural force coming to predict the poet's death, endures in the work of the young Leopardi, whose inspiration could have arrived from the pantheon of acclaimed eighteenth-century authors selected by himself in his *Crestomazia poetica* (1828). In his *Appressamento della morte*, written in 1816, Leopardi narrates the coming of an angel sent from the Virgin Mary with the mission of guiding Leopardi himself through an 'ammiranda visione' [admiring vision] to prepare him for the upcoming death: 'Poco t'è lunge 'l dì che tu morrai' [the day you will die is not far away] (40–1). As Varano did in his *Visioni sacre e morali*, Leopardi employs the Dantean scheme of *terza rima* to describe his supernatural vision where the soul of the poetic-self embarks on a journey to be enlightened on human turmoil and vanity. Deathly feelings and cruel scenes pervade the poem, as suggested by lines such as 'orrendo un gel mi sdrucciolò per l'ossa' [horridly a chill crept through my bones] and 'la punta a mia gola e' ficcò dentro, / e caddi con la bocca in su rivolta' [he thrust the point of the sword into my throat, / and I fell with my mouth upturned], as well as episodes of transmigration of the soul from the corpse, such as 'l'ultimo ghiaccio là mi corse, / e svolazzò lo spirto sospirando' [the last frost went through me, / and the sighing spirit fluttered away] (Leopardi 47, 48). The poem is quilted with expressions indicating the end of life and the extreme hour (see 's'appressa il punto estremo' [the end point is approaching]; 'quando dell'ore udrà l'ultimo suono' [when he will hear the sound of his last hour]) (Leopardi 70) recalling Daniello Bartoli's terminology 'l'uomo al punto' [the dying man], and the devotional meaning is always stressed.[14]

As illustrated, sepulchral poetry oscillates between 'the earthly laws of conventional reality and the possibilities of the supernatural', exactly like Gothic texts (Hogle 3). The aforementioned works well combine the terror and the horror of the Gothic, taking the readers in suspense and presenting physical dissolution and the revolting and ineluctable consequence of death. The emphasis on exaggerated and excessive images is constantly maintained in the whole sepulchral production, as well as the sense of repulsion and disgust which characterises the overarching abjection for death and the dead. Obscurity, mourning, and the macabre synthetise the essence of an Italian Gothic repertoire which silently bloomed in eighteenth-century poetry and laid the foundation for a later prosaic development.

Bibliography

Antonelli, Roberto, 'Introduzione a Francesco Petrarca', in Francesco Petrarca, *Canzoniere*, ed. by Gianfranco Contini and Daniele Ponchiroli (Turin: Einaudi, 1992), pp. v–xxv.

Ariès, Philippe, *The Hour of Our Death: The Classic History of Western Attitudes Toward Death over the Last One Thousand Years* [1975] (New York: Vintage Books, 2008).

Ariès, Philippe, *Storia della morte in Occidente dal Medioevo ai giorni nostri* [1975] (Milan: Biblioteca Universale Rizzoli), 1994.

Bartoli, Daniello, *L'huomo al punto, Cioè l'huomo in punto di morte* (Rome: E. Ghezzi, 1667).

Bertana, Emilio, *Arcadia lugubre e preromantica* (Spezia: Edizioni dell'Iride, 1899).

Boito, Camillo, 'Un Corpo', in Gilberto Finzi (ed.), *Racconti neri della Scapigliatura* (Milan: Mondadori, 1980), pp. 36–69.

Botting, Fred, *Gothic* (London and New York: Routledge, 1996).

Broggi, Francesca, *The Rise of the Italian Canto: Macpherson, Cesarotti and Leopardi: From the Ossianic Poems to the Canti* (Ravenna: Longo Editore, 2006).

Camilletti, Fabio, 'Guerre, sequestri e tavolette ouija. Contributo a una storia parapsicologica del Novecento italiano', *The Italianist*, 39.1, 2019, pp. 82–95.

Camilletti, Fabio, *Leopardi's Nymphs: Grace, Melancholy and the Uncanny* (Oxford: Legenda, 2013).

Carrai, Stefano, 'Appunti sulla preistoria dell'elegia volgare', in Andrea Combini and Alessandra Di Ricco (eds), *L'elegia nella tradizione poetica italiana* (Trento: Editrice Università degli Studi di Trento, 2003), pp. 1–15.

Carrai, Stefano, *Dante elegiaco. Una chiave di lettura per la 'Vita Nova'* (Florence: Olschki, 2006).

Cian, Vittorio, 'Per la storia del sentimento sepolcrale in Italia e in Francia prima dei Sepolcri del Foscolo', *Giornale storico della letteratura italiana*, XX, 1892, pp. 205–35.

Cometa, Michele, *Il Trionfo della morte di Palermo. Un'allegoria della modernità* (Rome: Quodlibet, 2017).

Corradi, Morena, *Spettri d'Italia: scenari del fantastico nella pubblicistica postunitaria milanese* (Ravenna: Longo Editore, 2016).

Davies, Douglas J., *A Brief History of Death* (Malden, MA: Blackwell, 2005).
Davison, Carol Margaret, 'Introduction. The Corpse in the Closet: The Gothic, Death, and Modernity', in Carol Margaret Davison (ed.) *The Gothic and Death* (Manchester: Manchester University Press, 2017), pp. 2–17.
Devoto, Giacomo, and Gian Carlo Oli, *Il dizionario della lingua italiana* (Florence: Le Monnier, 1995.)
Donati, Alessandro (ed.), *Poeti minori del Settecento* (Bari: Laterza, 1912).
Duranti, Francesca, *La casa sul lago della luna*, (Market Harborough: Troubador, 2001).
Endean, Philip, 'The Spiritual Exercises', in Thomas Worcester (ed.), *The Cambridge Companion to the Jesuits* (Cambridge: Cambridge University Press, 2008), pp. 52–67.
Fiorentino, Salomone, *Elegie di Salomone Fiorentino in morte di Laura sua moglie* (Parma: co' i tipi Bodoniani, 1801).
Freud, Sigmund, 'Mourning and Melancholia', in James Strachey (ed.), *The Standard Edition to the Complete Psychological Works of Sigmund Freud*, 24 vols (London: Hogarth Press, 1953–74, 1964, xiv), pp. 243–58.
Frugoni, Chiara, and Simone Facchinetti, *Senza misericordia, Il Trionfo della Morte e la Danza Macabra a Clusone* (Turin: Einaudi, 2016).
Grimes, Kristen, and Maria Marsilio, 'Petrarch's Elegies for Mother and Beloved: Eletta, Laura, and the Humanist's Pursuit of Poetic Glory', *Latomus*, 71.1, 2012, pp. 161–75.
Hogle, Jerrold E., 'Introduction: The Gothic in Western Culture', in Jerrold E. Hogle (ed.), *The Cambridge Companion to Gothic Fiction* (Cambridge: Cambridge University Press, 2002), pp. 1–20.
Knöll, Stefanie, and Sophie Oosterwijk, *Mixed Metaphors: The Danse Macabre in Medieval and Early Modern Europe* (Newcastle-Upon-Tyne: Cambridge Scholars, 2011).
Kristeva, Julia, *Powers of Horror: An Essay on Abjection* [1980] (New York: Columbia University Press, 1982).
Landi, Ubertino, 'Il museo della morte', in *Poemetti italiani* (Rome: Società letteraria di Torino presso Michelangelo Morano), 1797.
Lawlor, Clark, 'Fashionable Melancholy', in Allan Ingram et al. (eds), *Melancholy Experience in Literature of the Long Eighteenth Century: Before Depression, 1660–1800* (Basingstoke and New York: Palgrave, 2011), pp. 25–53.
Leone, Giuseppe, *Le chiome di Thanatos* (Naples: Liguori Editore), 2011.
Leopardi, Giacomo, *Appressamento della morte*, ed. by Lorenza Posfortunato (Turin: Edizioni della Crusca, 1983).
Malone, Hannah, *Architecture, Death and Nationhood: Monumental Cemeteries of Nineteenth-Century Italy* (London: Routledge, 2017).
Muoni, Guido, *Poesia notturna preromantica* (Milan: Società Editrice Libreria, 1908).
Napoleone, Caterina, *Il Trionfo della morte a Palermo* (Fontanellato: Franco Maria Ricci Editore), 1998.
Neppi, Enzo, 'Ontologia dei Sepolcri', in Gennaro Barbarisi and William Spaggiari (eds), *'Dei sepolcri' di Ugo Foscolo* (Milan: Cisalpino, 2006), pp. 165–226.
Parisot, Eric, *Graveyard Poetry: Religion, Aesthetics and the Mid-Eighteenth-Century Poetic Condition* (Farnham and Burlington, VT: Ashgate, 2013).

Pesenti Campagnoni, Donata, *Verso il cinema. Macchine spettacolari e mirabili visioni* (Turin: UTET, 1995).
Poe, Edgar Allan, 'The Philosophy of Composition', in Rollo Walter Brown (ed.), *The Writer's Art: By Those Who Have Practiced It* (Cambridge: Harvard University Press, 1924), pp. 114–30.
Soltysik Monnet, Agnieszka, 'Body Genres, Night Vision and the Female Monster: *REC* and the Contemporary Horror Film', in Fred Botting and Catherine Spooner (eds), *Monstrous Media/Spectral Subjects: Imaging Gothic from the Nineteenth Century to the Present* (Manchester: Manchester University Press, 2015), pp. 143–56.
Tenenti, Alberto, *Il senso della morte e l'amore della vita nel Rinascimento* (Turin: Einaudi, 1989).
Tomasi, Grazia, *Per salvare i viventi. Le origini settecentesche del cimitero extraurbano* (Bologna: Il Mulino, 2001).
Tonelli, Natascia, 'I Rerum Vulgarium Fragmenta e il codice elegiaco', in Andrea Combini and Alessandra Di Ricco (eds), *L'elegia nella tradizione poetica italiana* (Trento: Editrice Università degli Studi di Trento, 2003), pp. 17–35.
van Vliet, Rietje, 'Print and Public in Europe 1600–1800', in Simon Eliot and Jonathan Rose (eds), *A Companion to the History of the Book* (Oxford and Malden, MA: John Wiley & Sons Ltd, 2020), pp. 423–36.
Varano, Alfonso, *Visioni sacre e morali*, ed. by Riccardo Verzini (Alessandria: Edizioni dell'Orso, 2003).
Viale, Ambrogio, 'Rime del solitario delle alpi', in Carlo Muscetta and Maria Rosa Massei (eds), *Poesie del Settecento. Volume II*, 2 vols (Turin: Einaudi, 1967).
Vigo, Pietro, *Le danze macabre in Italia* (Palermo: Il Vespro, 1980).
Zacchiroli, Francesco, *Il sepolcro. Ottave di Euripilo Naricio in morte di Lorenzo Ricci, ultimo generale della Compagnia di Gesù* (Lausanne: presso Francesco Martin, 1776).
Zumbini, Bonaventura, 'La poesia sepolcrale italiana e straniera e il carme di Foscolo' in *Studi di letteratura italiana* (Florence: Le Monnier 1894), pp. 79–172.

Notes

1. Apart from those discussed in this chapter, other relevant authors are Giuseppe Bottoni, Luigi Cerretti, Melchiorre Cesarotti, Giovanni Fantoni, Bernardo Laviosa, Angelo Mazza, Onofrio Minzoni, Agostino Paradisi, Carlo Rezzonico della Torre, Andrea Rubbi and Francesco Soave.
2. In the eighteenth century, books were chiefly octavos or small, handy-sized duodecimos. In the case of Italian sepulchral poetry, however, books were printed even in sextodecimo, and occasionally in octodecimo. This is the case for the best-selling *Elegie in morte di Laura sua moglie* by Salomone Fiorentino, which attained extraordinary success, as well as Aurelio de' Giorgi Bertola's *Le notti clementine*, which made it all the way to its tenth edition. This reveals important information about the works' circulation.

Smaller formats were indeed the easiest to carry and their popularity is evidence of the success that sepulchral works achieved.
3. As Parisot claims, at its narrowest, the term refers to four poems: Thomas Parnell's *Night-Piece on Death* (1721); Robert Blair's *The Grave* (1743); Edward Young's *Night Thoughts* (1742–5); and Thomas Gray's *Elegy Written in a Country Churchyard* (1751).
4. See Neppi; Cian; Zumbini; Bertana; and Muoni.
5. Poems dealing with sacred and moral matters were already popular in the seventeenth century. Evidence of this can be found in Monsignor Petrucci's *Poesie sacre morali, e spirituali* published in 1686, and in Giacomo Lubrano's *Scintille poetiche* published in 1690, whose subtitle states *Poesie sacre e morali*. More than a century later, in 1824, there appeared *Poesie sacre e morali* by the priest Luigi Fajeti, whose heading 'ad uso della studiosa gioventù' [for the scholarly youth] reveals a didactic aim. A few years later, the publisher Nicolò Bettoni issued a collection of works dealing with sacred and moral matters under the title *Scelta di poesie sacre e morali di vari autori* published in Milan in 1830, whose aim reminds the reader of Leopardi's *Crestomazia*, a collection of excellent poetical examples to be taken as models from young poets.
6. The *Sei notti poetiche* was written by Capra specifically in reply to Edward Young's *Night Thoughts on Life, Death and Immortality* (published between 1742 and 1745). The *Sei notti* have a similar structure, for they are divided into different parts called 'nights', but Capra detaches himself from Young's work due to Young's several flaws to be amended, as declared in Capra's note *A chi legge*.
7. According to the *Tesoro della Lingua Italiana delle Origini* (TLIO) the term *lugubre* in its first meaning is described as 'suitable to honour a deceased', first attested in Boccaccio's *Filostrato* (1336–8), and in its second meaning as 'funereal, apt to evoke deathly scenes'.
8. The poem is part of *Le prose e poesie campestri d'Ippolito Pindemonte con l'aggiunta d'una Dissertazione su i giardini inglesi e il merito in ciò dell'Italia*, Tipografia Mainardi, 1817.
9. Nympholepsy and melancholy were already feared in Ancient Greek culture and by medieval monks. A sort of possession from an external agent, for example, a nymph or a demon, which influences the human mind can be found in Italian literature already in Torquato Tasso and later on in Giacomo Leopardi, as described in Camilletti.
10. The melancholic subject is obsessed with the idea of possessing an object of desire situated outside the domain of actuality, and sometimes an object which is not even defined. Contrastingly, mourners are affected by actual losses and suffer for the lack of a dear person.
11. This is a feature that constitutes a certain degree of originality and independence from foreign sources, for Italian funereal architecture contrasts the essentiality of foreign cemeteries and enter sepulchral poems (Ariès, *Storia della morte* 64). In Italy, instead, cemeteries and tombs became monumental and such a development implied political consequences (Malone).
12. Stefano Carrai has recently attempted an elegiac reading of Dante's *Vita nuova* and Natascia Tonelli has posited that Petrarch's *Rerum vulgarium*

fragmenta marks a semantic and narrative continuity with the traditional elegy of Propertius. See Bibliography.
13. Spirits and presences of the dead became incredibly popular in the eighteenth century through the narration of séances, see Corradi; Camilletti. See also Foscolo; Boito; Duranti.
14. See Daniello Bartoli, *L'huomo al punto, cioè l'huomo in punto di morte*.

Chapter 8

The Gothic in Periodicals and Magazines
Fabrizio Foni

Towards a National Readership

In the years immediately following the unification of Italy, *Scapigliatura*'s fascination with Gothic themes and the occult in general – and that of authors who were influenced by the movement – found ample space in the pages of magazines (some more successful than others), which, however, could not rely on national, or at times even regional, distribution.[1] As noted by the historian Donald Sassoon, 'in 1872, the highest-circulation daily was the Milanese *Il Secolo* (1866), which sold only 30,000 copies' and 'Italian dailies [...] depended more on ministerial favour, government handouts and banking and business interests than on market demand' (323). The sociologist Fausto Colombo identifies 1881 as the actual beginning of an Italian cultural industry, although he notes that the process had already started in the first decade of unification (39).

Interestingly, despite the prolonged absence of an efficient national distribution system, numerous authors regularly contributed to newspapers and magazines whose offices and readerships were located in distant cities or regions. The Neapolitan Salvatore Di Giacomo – a versatile exponent of *Verismo*, who initially took inspiration from German fantastic literature, as well as Edgar Allan Poe and the Erckmann-Chatrian duo – readily springs to mind. 'La veglia al morto, ossia l'orologio dello zio Van Becke', one of the author's most distinctively Gothic stories, first appeared in the *Gazzetta Letteraria* of Turin, from 31 January to 7 February 1880, and, just a few days later, it appeared in the Naples-based *Corriere del Mattino* (9–12 February).[2] The *Gazzetta Letteraria* began as a weekly supplement of the *Gazzetta Piemontese* (which, in 1894, became the still-active newspaper *La Stampa*), having been founded in 1876 by Vittorio Bersezio, another author with a propensity for the Gothic.[3] Until it was discontinued in 1902, the *Gazzetta*

Letteraria distinguished itself by publishing writers from all parts of Italy and for acquainting its public with foreign artists and authors.

However, the periodical that ushered in an epochal change – being the first to assume a truly national character – was the *Fanfulla della Domenica*, launched in 1879 by Ferdinando Martini as a Sunday supplement of the daily *Fanfulla* (originally inaugurated in Florence nine years earlier, but which, after less than a year, relocated to the Kingdom of Italy's new capital, Rome). Alongside narratives of a more veristic or decadent tone, the *Fanfulla della Domenica* also featured stories about the eerie and the supernatural up until it stopped being printed in 1919.

Moreover, it is noted that *Verismo* had a far-from-superficial interest in psychical research and the more 'uncanny' states of alienation (an interest inherited from the *Scapigliati*, whose spasmodic search for 'truth' involved explorations of the darker aspects of reality).[4] 'A veglia (Bozzetto villereccio)' by Giuseppe Bargilli, published on 25 July 1880 in the *Fanfulla della Domenica*, is a narrative – which today might be defined as 'folk horror' – set against the backdrop of the Tuscan countryside. It takes place on a cold evening, during one of those habitual fireside gatherings at which country people exchange stories and anecdotes that often spill over into the miraculous and the frightening, and that are steeped in superstition. One of those present, Gaetano, contests the statement that the dead cannot return from beyond the grave. In this vivid and many-voiced context, he speaks of a time when he saw one of the dead walking and even heard the corpse speaking.

Other stories published in the *Fanfulla della Domenica* deserve to be rediscovered. These include 'Vampiro innocente' (16 August 1885) by Francesco Ernesto Morando and 'Fantasmi' (23 August 1885) by Gaetano Carlo Chelli.[5] In the former, an enigmatic patient in a lunatic asylum claims to have been compelled to kill his own little son because he had been absorbing his sister's life energies (in a sense, foreshadowing the psychic vampirism of Algernon Blackwood's famous 1911 short story, 'The Transfer'). In the second story, the narrator-protagonist accepts a bet to spend a night in a reputedly haunted country house, over which hangs the shadow of a suicide.

A Factory of Gothic Storytelling: *La Domenica del Corriere*, *L'Illustrazione Italiana* and *La Tribuna Illustrata*

A truly game-changing magazine was *La Domenica del Corriere*, which, whilst also emerging as the most popular and diffused periodical in Italy, was, for some decades, a receptacle of fantastic and horror narratives in the suspense tradition.⁶ Luigi Albertini, who was appointed editorial secretary in 1896 by Eugenio Torelli-Violler, the *Corriere della Sera* founder and editor, had personally examined, during a series of visits, the printing methods and editorial organisation of the most widely circulated German, French and British publications. In less than a year (8 January 1899), his own illustrated periodical made its first appearance: *La Domenica del Corriere*, which had front and back covers in full colour, depicting the most sensational events covered by news reportage at the time. Editorship of this Sunday supplement was entrusted to Attilio Centelli, who would remain at the helm until his death in 1915. The publication itself enjoyed unprecedented success in Italy: in the space of a year, its initial print run of 50,000 copies grew to 70,000, only to progressively increase thereafter (in 1900, its circulation reached 140,000 copies and, by the early 1960s, it surpassed one million).

In addition to regular columns and features, *La Domenica del Corriere* hosted tales (both stand-alone and in episodes), as well as serialised novels of various genres, opening its doors even to unknown or emerging authors, including its own readers who were metamorphosing into writers. It would be a mistake, however, to assume that its contributors were limited only to minor or amateur talents. The supplement also published contributions by famous and prestigious authors, both Italian and foreign, most notably Arthur Conan Doyle, whose Sherlock Holmes stories came to be popular throughout Italy after appearing in the supplement's pages. Although it underwent various transformations (which had a significant impact on the narrative content), *La Domenica del Corriere* remained largely identical in format until 1945 and continued being printed up until 12 October 1989.

A full list of the supernatural or macabre stories published in this periodical, from its very first year of circulation, would be surprisingly long. Giuseppe Tonsi's 'Il vampiro' (2 November 1902) may well have been inspired by the aforementioned Morando story, as it also involves a case of psychic vampirism narrated by the inmate of a facility for the criminally insane. Its villain – an occultist of sorts – absorbs the souls of highly intelligent people, which results in their deaths. In 1904, Tonsi – who had by then added the name 'Lucifero' [Lucifer] to his own – collected some of his short stories in the anthology *Il vampiro: Racconti incredibili*, which was published by Giannotta of Catania. In the version of 'Il vampiro'⁷ in this anthology, Tonsi inserts an epigraph from Poe's 'The Imp of the Perverse' (1845), as well as a dedication to Luigi Capuana. Capuana was a pioneer of Italian *Verismo* but also the author of the essay *Spiritismo?* (1884),⁸ which substantially supported the mediumistic phenomena, and the short story 'Un vampiro' (1904), arguably the most famous Italian vampire story ever written (it will be discussed later in this chapter).

Another writer who deserves to be mentioned is the Neapolitan author Daniele Oberto Marrama, whose Gothic and sensational stories mostly appeared in *La Domenica del Corriere*. Of the eight tales anthologised in his volume *Il ritratto del morto: Racconti bizzarri*, published by Perrella in Naples in 1907, seven had previously featured in the weekly supplement. The most notable of these include 'Il ritratto del morto' (published on 17 May 1903), which calls to mind 'The Signal-Man' (1866) by Charles Dickens; 'Il medaglione' (16 August 1903), which explores the topoi of reincarnation, the asylum and a homicidal severed hand – this latter detail probably inspired by 'La main d'écorché' (1875) and 'La main' (1883), both by Guy de Maupassant, but possibly also by Arthur Conan Doyle's 'The Brown Hand' (1899); 'Il Dottor Nero' (14 August 1904), one of the most convincing examples of Italian vampire literature, which is set in an ancient castle in Ireland and makes effective use of some of the most recognisable tropes of the genre, with an exotic touch in the form of superstitions from Tierra del Fuego. Also worthy of mention are another two short stories by the same author, both absent from the abovementioned anthology, but published in *La Domenica del Corriere*: 'Il ciclope' (6 January 1907) seems like a personal rewrite of Prosper Mérimée's 'La Vénus d'Ille' (1837), while 'Pulcinella' (13 September 1908) focuses on the transmigration of souls – evidently a topic that was dear to the author's heart – in relation to vivisection conducted on animals.

The subject of reincarnation, though addressed in positivist terms (that is, in light of the Darwinian concept of heredity), is at the core of one of the most eloquently Gothic stories published in *La Domenica del Corriere*, 'La mano di sangue' (24 June–1 July 1906) by Italo Toscani.[9] Toscani produced a large number of short stories combining the macabre, weird science and horror that were published in this and other widely read magazines up until the 1940s. His 'La mano di sangue' might also have inspired a televised miniseries on the Italian main RAI station, *L'amaro caso della Baronessa di Carini*, aired for the first time in 1975, in which the theme of metempsychosis is taken up again.[10]

Equally Gothic, in the most traditional sense of the word, is 'L'Antenato' by Alfonso di Palma (another of *La Domenica del Corriere*'s recurring bylines), published on 23 April 1911. Although it takes place in a castle, the story is broadly set in the contemporary period, as evidenced by an explicit reference to the use of telegraphy. However, in the castle in which the protagonist lives with his daughter, an ancient painting holds court, like a permanent omen from the past, and the canvas comes alive:

the portrayed titular ancestor emerges from the frame (thus recalling, among others, Horace Walpole's seminal *The Castle of Otranto* from 1764), pronouncing terrible threats of retribution to his fearful and craven descendant.

Even before *La Domenica del Corriere*, other weekly periodicals destined for a large audience had been fairly successfully launched: as well as the *Fanfulla della Domenica*, one could mention the Sunday magazine *L'Illustrazione Italiana*, by the Milanese publishing house Treves, or *La Tribuna Illustrata*, another Sunday supplement, issued with the Roman daily newspaper *La Tribuna*. *L'Illustrazione Italiana* was founded and edited by Emilio Treves towards the end of 1873, under the title *Nuova Illustrazione Universale*, which, after one year, absorbed the Roman weekly *L'Illustrazione*, only to acquire its final name in 1875. *La Tribuna Illustrata* first came out in January 1890, under the editorship of Vincenzo Morello. From 1893 onwards, the periodical opted for a monthly schedule but added a *Supplemento Illustrato della Domenica* [Sunday Illustrated Supplement], which – between 1897 and 1901 – was replaced by *La Tribuna Illustrata della Domenica*, a weekly supplement that also absorbed the monthly periodical. In 1902, it resumed the name *La Tribuna Illustrata*, with Luigi Dobrilla at its helm.

L'Illustrazione Italiana would shut down permanently in 1962, seven years before *La Tribuna Illustrata*. Together with *La Domenica del Corriere*, they constituted the most successful Italian periodicals, although, over the years, it was the *Corriere della Sera*'s Sunday supplement that functioned as a primary catalyst for the collective imagination and whose choices influenced the other two previously launched publications (as well as the magazine landscape as a whole). The fact that, for instance, more space was given to narratives with a Gothic atmosphere – even though such narratives had already occasionally been present – was clearly an effect of *La Domenica del Corriere*'s editorial policy. This is illustrated by stories such as 'Il braccio nudo' by Alfonso B. Mongiardini, published in *La Tribuna Illustrata* on 9 May 1915, which may have been inspired, again, by Conan Doyle's 'The Brown Hand'. The story's narrator-protagonist finds himself the guest of an unspecified English lord, lodged in an immense castle consisting of seven buildings from different eras, where he discovers an old manuscript attesting to a centuries-old gruesome legend.

Between Popular Fiction and Avant-Garde

Torelli-Violler died in 1900 and, within a few months, Albertini became both administrative and managing director, and eventually editor in chief, of the *Corriere della Sera*. Albertini favoured the creation of new periodicals to attach to the daily newspaper, such as the monthlies *La Lettura* (1901–46) and *Il Romanzo Mensile* (1903–45). Modelled on foreign publications (including Britain's *The Strand Magazine*), *La Lettura* attempted to be popular and informative, but also to attract a more selective audience. Its direction was entrusted to Giuseppe Giacosa and, upon his death in 1906, transferred to Renato Simoni.

The periodical proved receptive to the fantastic and horror, publishing, for instance, Capuana's 'Un vampiro' (July 1904), which merges traditional folklore and positivist science. The vampire of the story takes the form of a largely invisible physical force, emanating from the corpse of a woman's spouse and tormenting the widow and her new husband. The malevolent entity sucks the vital essence out of the couple's infant child and even talks through the entranced woman's mouth. The semi-visible manifestation of part of the dead body calls to mind Guy de Maupassant's 'Le Horla' (1886 and 1887). For Capuana – who was, among other things, one of the *Fanfulla della Domenica*'s editors in chief – writing short stories was almost a lifelong obsession and he often entrusted the publication of these stories to magazines, showing no disdain whatsoever for the more popular periodicals.[11] Many of his stories are sensational, lugubrious and proto-science fictional, often marrying the Gothic to theories that would, today, be ascribed to the realm of 'pseudoscience'.[12]

It is mostly due to Capuana that Luigi Pirandello developed his familiarity and ambiguous rapport with spiritualism, theosophy and the paranormal, as reflected in quite a number of his works.[13] Among Pirandello's many short stories, initially published in periodicals, mention must at least be made of 'La casa del Granella', which first appeared in the Florentine weekly *Il Marzocco* (27 August 1905). The plot focuses on a court case involving a house that is believed to be haunted. The former tenants reported having witnessed phenomena akin to the manifestations of a poltergeist.

During the first decades of the twentieth century, Gothic narratives in Italian magazines were inevitably influenced by positivism (still far from extinct in the collective imagination), though they emphasised the uncanniest sides of science. To this can be added the more (stereo)typical situations of the Grand Guignol theatre, brought to Italy in 1908 by the

Alfredo Sainati and Bella Starace company (though it was already well known for its excesses prior to this).[14] Under the influence of colonialism, this fiction did not hesitate to exploit the 'otherness' of exotic backdrops, predominantly presented in conventional form.

Such hybridisation is appositely exhibited by a competition, launched by *La Lettura* in April 1904, for a short story that, based on scientific premises, needed to arrive at surprising conclusions, preferably relying on the mysterious, the adventurous or the horrific ('Tre concorsi' 289). Just over a year later, both Gothic and science-fiction elements would merge in Onorato Fava's 'La casa bianca' (October–November 1905),[15] published in *Il Secolo XX*, a Treves magazine that had been created in 1902, presumably using *La Lettura* as a blueprint.

Within the ambit of the (pre-)avant-garde, the combative Florentine magazine *Leonardo* (1903–7), under the stewardship of Giovanni Papini and Giuseppe Prezzolini, gathered together the voices of various intellectuals who shared a common distrust of positivist rationalism. It was on the pages of the *Leonardo* that a debate on religion and mysticism was spawned; not without some reservations, the doors were flung open to occultism.[16] Both Futurism – to which Papini himself adhered, albeit problematically – and subsequent avant-garde movements would foster an existing interest in spiritualism, psychical research, magic and theosophy.[17]

L'Italia Futurista (1916–18), another Florentine periodical founded and edited by Emilio Settimelli and Bruno Corra, served as a magnet for those of such unorthodox inclinations.[18] One significant short story that featured in the latter is 'Romanticismo sonnambulo' (10 June 1917) by Rosa Rosà, which, two years later, would be anthologised in *'Non c'è che te!'* with the new title 'L'acquario'. The anonymous female narrator-protagonist, like a medium, one night finds herself compelled to write in a stranger's handwriting what appear to be the hallucinatory memories of a man. After a storm, he found part of his house swallowed up by the sea and – through a glass – witnessed the submerged corpses of his wife and all the guests who were with her engaged in a macabre spectacle.

Starting with its title, an equally hallucinatory atmosphere pervades the short novel *La casa allucinata* by Corra, serialised in the *Corriere della Sera* (from 1 to 20 June 1942) and, in December of that year, in an issue of the aforementioned *Il Romanzo Mensile*. By then, the author had detached himself from Futurism, focusing on the writing of comedies and popular novels. In *La casa allucinata*, set in Egypt, he amalgamates mystery, adventure, the Gothic, psychical research and science fiction, with a debt to H. G. Wells's *The Island of Doctor Moreau* (1896).

Travel and Adventure Magazines: The Italian Pulps

Magazines dedicated to travel and adventure remained in fashion until the 1940s. On 5 September 1878, the Milanese publisher Sonzogno inaugurated the weekly *Giornale Illustrato dei Viaggi e delle Avventure di Terra e di Mare*, after acquiring the rights to the French *Journal des Voyages et des Aventures de Terre et de Mer*, launched the preceding year. In addition to the title, the Italian magazine borrowed from the foreign model a template consisting of travel narratives and accounts, as well as geographical news, on which it based more or less all its first series, which came to an end in 1891. The success of this initiative rapidly gave rise to a proliferation of analogous periodicals.

It was in one of these – *La Valigia*, published by Ferdinando Garbini in Milan – that Emilio Salgari, destined to become the true progenitor of the Italian adventure novel, debuted in 1883, with a gory, cannibalistic tale. In 1904, Salgari founded and managed the weekly *Per Terra e per Mare* on behalf of the Genoese publisher Donath, to whom he was contractually bound. Already famous by then, the author – who had earlier shown a certain propensity towards the Gothic[19] – renewed the format of the travel/adventure magazine to open the door to proto-science-fiction, as well as macabre and supernatural stories, accepting as contributors even very young or emerging authors, some of whom would go on to develop professional writing careers of their own. Salgari published some novels and a number of short stories in *Per Terra e per Mare*, including three tales characterised by an eerie and mysterious tone: 'Lo scheletro della foresta' (vol. 1, nos 41–2, 1904), 'Il brik [sic] del diavolo' (vol. 2, no. 19, 1905) and – under the pseudonym 'Bertolini E.' – 'Il castello degli spiriti' (vol. 2, no. 25, 1905).[20]

Per Terra e per Mare stopped being published in 1906, but this was certainly not due to the lack of a readership: Salgari, much to Donath's disappointment, had breached his contract and was now bound to Bemporad of Florence. This popular firm promoted its new author by, among other things, publishing four of his short stories and serialising three of his novels in an innovative weekly magazine for children and teenagers: *Il Giornalino della Domenica*, which ran from 1906 until 1911 (only to be revived at the end of the war, from 1918 to 1927, by different publishers).[21] Though pitched at a younger audience, the periodical reserved space even for grim, lugubrious and supernatural tales, sometimes republishing stories originally written for adults (one example is the aforementioned tale by Di Giacomo, reprinted on 4 September 1910 with the title 'L'orologio dello zio Sigismondo') and sometimes hosting previously unpublished material such as 'I morticini' (30 October 1910) by Emma R. Corcos,[22] in which three prematurely deceased children decide to emerge from their graves, on the days traditionally consecrated to the dead, to visit the homes of their respective families.

On 28 December 1913, the third series of Sonzogno's *Giornale Illustrato dei Viaggi* debuted with Guglielmo Stocco at the helm. Stocco was an experienced storyteller who had already exhibited an attraction to horror. The second series, inaugurated in 1897, had come to an end in 1910, probably due to intense competition from magazines modelled on *Per Terra e per Mare*, which had, in its turn, been inspired by none other than the *Giornale Illustrato dei Viaggi*, of which Salgari was an avid reader.

Without changing too much of the magazine's format or visual appearance, Stocco progressively altered the editorial direction to ensure that the publication would have a long new life (in 1931, the periodical would be absorbed by its sister weekly *Il Mondo*, which would retain the subtitle 'Giornale Illustrato dei Viaggi' until 1937). The 'voyage' theme would become increasingly nominal, to the extent that it was altogether absent from various published stories. The magazine would also publish authors such as Poe, Dickens, Ambrose Bierce, W. W. Jacobs, Wells, Blackwood and André de Lorde, chief dramaturgist of the Grand Guignol. Moreover, it did not hesitate to republish stories that had already appeared in *La Domenica del Corriere* and other magazines or to rediscover a *Scapigliato* such as Igino Ugo Tarchetti. Nonetheless, the sheer quantity of new supernatural or proto-science-fiction narratives featured in the third series of the *Giornale Illustrato dei Viaggi* is truly impressive.

From the mid-1930s onwards, these popular travel and adventure magazines would struggle to keep up with comics,[23] which were gaining ever more ground. For instance, according to different sources, *L'Avventuroso* (1934–43) – an Italian weekly issued by Florence's Nerbini, dedicated to adventure-style comics – reached a circulation of 500,000 copies.[24]

However, as a result of the proliferation of popular periodicals, a veritable school of Italian genre-literature authors was born: although inspired by the nineteenth-century fantastic and Gothic, these writers more or less consciously aligned themselves with those new trends and tendencies that, in the United States, would come to fruition in seminal pulp magazines such as *Weird Tales* and *Amazing Stories*. For example, 'La vendetta del morto' by Alberto Enrico Puccio – published on 1 July 1906 in *L'Oceano*, edited by Luigi Motta and issued by the Società

Editoriale Milanese of Milan – demonstrates the author's familiarity with 'optogram fiction': that is, stories underpinned by the idea that the retina can preserve the last images it captures before the moment of death.[25]

At the crossroads of horror, detective fiction and science fiction, this hypothesis had already been imprinted onto the collective imagination by the novels *L'accusateur* (1897) by Jules Claretie and *Les Frères Kip* (1902) by Jules Verne. Even earlier, it had been explored in a novella by Villiers de L'Isle-Adam, *Claire Lenoir* (1867), and in a Rudyard Kipling short story called 'At the End of the Passage' (1890). In the Italian cinematic landscape, the same motif was exploited by a silent movie produced by Cines of Rome, *Dovere professionale* (1911) – both the director and actors of which are unknown[26] – and would be reprised by Dario Argento's *Quattro mosche di velluto grigio* (1971), as well as Stefano Bessoni's *Imago Mortis* (2009).

Moreover, in the pages of popular Italian publications, there was no lack of stories that could be unapologetically defined as *ante litteram* 'Lovecraftian' or otherwise in sync with the 'weird' fiction of American pulp magazines. One need only read Giuseppe Zucca's 'A Khorsabad', in *La Domenica del Corriere* (3 January 1904) and later republished as 'Prigioniero nel museo egiziano' in the *Giornale Illustrato dei Viaggi* (2 March 1924; a few months before *Weird Tales* published 'Imprisoned with the Pharaohs', a novelette ghost-written by H. P. Lovecraft for Harry Houdini).[27] Other stories include 'L'Incantata' by Gaetano Giacomantonio, which also appeared in *La Domenica del Corriere* (9 August 1908), and 'L'uomo vegetale' by Luigi Ugolini, published in the *Giornale Illustrato dei Viaggi* (1 July 1917), a story that Ann and Jeff VanderMeer included in their successful and much-debated anthology *The Weird* (2011).[28]

Gozzano, Landolfi and Vigolo

But, as had happened in the nineteenth century, even authors who were considered refined, and firmly established within the twentieth-century Italian literary canon, contributed to periodicals that were at the time regarded as popular or otherwise ephemeral. For example, Guido Gozzano – a major exponent of the so-called literary current *Crepuscolarismo* – published his 'Dopo il voto tragico' in the *Giornale Illustrato dei Viaggi* (30 August 1914), which had already appeared under the title 'Un voto alla Dea Tharata-Ku-Wha' in the daily newspaper *La Stampa* (30 January 1914)[29] and would, four years later, be included in the posthumous anthology *L'altare del passato*, published by Treves. This narrative, the first part of which is typical of the author's disenchanted tone, builds up to a genuinely uncanny finale. Gozzano's short stories, destined for the wide readership of periodicals, were collected for republication only after the author's death and were for a long time ignored by the critical establishment, which saw less merit in such 'minor' works than it did in Gozzano's poetic works. Yet many of these stories deserve to be read from a Gothic perspective, with attention being paid to their authentically mysterious and macabre aspects and, above all, to their consonance with the concurrent theosophical and spiritualistic context.

Even the elusive Tommaso Landolfi – one of the undisputed maestros of the Italian fantastic, whose works are often infused with self-reflexivity and the grotesque – published several of his stories in periodicals before they were collected in volumes. It was, after all, a widespread practice that some critics and scholars still unjustly tend to ignore to this day. Landolfi's works are frequently attuned to the Gothic, even though they showcase its internal mechanisms and its Romantic shortcomings, while at the same time making full use of its symbolic charge. Here, it suffices to mention 'Settimana di sole', originally published in *Letteratura* (January 1937, under the erroneous title 'Una settimana di sole'); 'Il racconto del lupo mannaro', in *Campo di Marte* (1–15 May 1939) and later in *Ansedonia* (October–November 1940); 'Il babbo di Kafka' in *Corrente di Vita Giovanile* (15 January 1940); 'La spada', in *Prospettive* (15 March 1940); as well as 'Il fuoco' and 'La paura', both published in the daily *Il Messaggero* (23 March and 16 May 1940, respectively).

Despite lacking any overtly supernatural elements, a transgressively Gothic atmosphere pervades Landolfi's *Le due zittelle*, published in its entirety in 1946 by Bompiani of Milan, after appearing in six episodes in the Florentine periodical *Il Mondo* (not to be confused with the weekly Sonzogno magazine of the same name), from 1 September to 17 November 1945. This short novel recounts the disarray, of theological nature even, provoked by a male – although castrated – pet monkey named Tombo, who belongs to the two devout titular spinsters. Having found his way into an adjacent nuns' convent, Tombo performs, in his own manner, a blasphemous 'mass', by both imitating and reinventing the ceremony, in a paradoxical event that subtly pays tribute to Poe's 'The Murders in the Rue Morgue' (1841).

The author who was perhaps most capable of breathing life into an intrinsically Italian Gothic was Giorgio Vigolo. Through his eyes (or, to be more precise, through the eyes of a narrator who is often ambiguously autobiographical), the so-called Eternal City becomes a nocturnal, mysterious and menacing city, in frightening contrast to the conventional image of Italy's capital. In the labyrinthine, stormy, secretive and magical Rome envisaged by Vigolo, pagan cults coexist alongside the most gloomy and enigmatic of Church rituals. Most of the Vigolo stories collected in the 1960 book issued by Bompiani *Le notti romane* – whose very title is reminiscent of the ancient spirits emerging from their sepulchres in Alessandro Verri's work of the same name (1792 and 1804)[30] – were originally published in periodicals. For instance, 'Il guardacaccia' (14 July 1939) appeared in the daily *Il Giornale d'Italia* and was later published in another newspaper, *Risorgimento Liberale*, under the title 'Il Signore delle tenebre' (25 July 1948); but also 'Racconto d'inverno' (27 December 1940), which is called 'La cena degli spiriti' in *Le notti romane*; and 'La mano tagliata' (27 April 1941), renamed 'La bella mano' in the later volume.

However, it is with 'Avventura a Campo di Fiori', which first appeared in *Risorgimento Liberale* (31 December 1947), that Vigolo seems to have influentially contributed to the portrayal of Rome in RAI's *Il segno del comando*, the miniseries that, in 1971, flung open the doors of Italian television to occultism and the Gothic.[31] This genealogy signals the lasting influence of newspapers and magazines on the Italian Gothic, an influence that is often overlooked by critics but that is by no means secondary.

Bibliography

Anonymous, 'Tre concorsi', *La Lettura*, 4.4, 1904, pp. 289–90.
Arduini, Carla, *Teatro sinistro: Storia del Grand Guignol in Italia* (Rome: Bulzoni, 2011).
Bernardini, Aldo, and Vittorio Martinelli, *Il cinema muto italiano: I film degli anni d'oro. 1911, prima parte* (Turin: Nuova ERI Edizioni RAI-Centro Sperimentale di Cinematografia, 1995).
Capuana, Luigi, *Mondo occulto* [1884 and 1896], edited by Simona Cigliana (Catania: Edizioni del Prisma, 1995).
Capuana, Luigi, *Spiritismo?* [1884], edited by Mario Tropea (Caltanissetta: Lussografica, 1994).
Casini, Paolo, *Alle origini del Novecento: Leonardo, 1903–1907* (Bologna: Il Mulino, 2002).
Cigliana, Simona, *Futurismo esoterico: Contributi per una storia dell'irrazionalismo italiano tra Otto e Novecento* (Naples: Liguori, 2002).
Colombo, Fausto, *La cultura sottile: Media e industria culturale in Italia dall'Ottocento agli anni novanta* (Milan: Bompiani, 2009).
Corradi, Morena, *Spettri d'Italia: Scenari del fantastico nella pubblicistica postunitaria milanese* (Ravenna: Longo, 2016).

Curti, Roberto, *Fantasmi d'amore: Il gotico italiano tra cinema, letteratura e tv* (Turin: Lindau, 2011).
Curti, Roberto, *Italian Gothic Horror Films, 1970–1979* (Jefferson, NC: McFarland, 2017).
Daniele, Antonio (ed.), *Vampiriana: Novelle italiane di vampiri* (Mercogliano: Keres, 2011).
de Turris, Gianfranco (ed.), *Le aeronavi dei Savoia: Protofantascienza italiana 1891–1952* (Milan: Editrice Nord, 2001).
Farnetti, Monica (ed.), *Racconti fantastici di scrittori veristi* (Milan: Mursia, 1990).
Foni, Fabrizio, *Alla fiera dei mostri: Racconti pulp, orrori e arcane fantasticherie nelle riviste italiane 1899–1932* (Latina: Tunué, 2007).
Foni, Fabrizio, *Fantastico Salgari: Dal 'vampiro' Sandokan al 'Giornale Illustrato dei Viaggi'* (Cuneo: Nerosubianco, 2011).
Foni, Fabrizio, *Piccoli mostri crescono: Nero, fantastico e bizzarrie varie nella prima annata de «La Domenica del Corriere» (1899)* (Ozzano dell'Emilia: Perdisa Pop, 2010).
Foni, Fabrizio, 'Romanzo febbrile, anzi un po' "frenetico": *Il bramino dell'Assam* (1911) tra ipnosi, sotterranei e misteri', in Luciano Curreri and Fabrizio Foni (eds), *Un po' prima della fine?: Ultimi romanzi di Salgari tra novità e ripetizione (1908–1915)* (Rome: Luca Sossella, 2009, pp. 124–36).
Foni, Fabrizio, and Irene Incarico, 'Drawing-Room Shivers: Spiritualism and Uneasy Presences on the Pages of *La Domenica del Corriere*', in Alessandra Aloisi and Fabio Camilletti (eds), *Archaeology of the Unconscious: Italian Perspectives* (Abingdon: Routledge, 2019), pp. 164–84.
Foni, Fabrizio (ed.), *Il gran ballo dei tavolini: Sette racconti fantastici da «La Domenica del Corriere»* (Cuneo: Nerosubianco, 2008).
Gallo, Claudio, and Giuseppe Bonomi, *Tutto cominciò con Bilbolbul . . .: Per una storia del fumetto italiano* (Zevio: Perosini, 2006).
Gallo, Claudio, and Giuseppe Bonomi (eds), *Il giornalino della Domenica: Antologia di fiabe, novelle, poesie, racconti e storie disegnate* (Milan: Edizioni BD, 2008).
Gallo, Claudio, and Fabrizio Foni (eds), *Ottocento nero italiano: Narrativa fantastica e crudele* (Milan: Aragno, 2009).
Gaspa, Pier Luigi, *Dal signor Bonaventura a Saturno contro la Terra: Agli albori del fumetto in Italia (1908–1945)* (Rome: Carocci, 2020).
Ghidetti, Enrico, *L'ipotesi del realismo: Storia e geografia del naturalismo italiano* (Milan: Sansoni, 2000).
Goulet, Andrea, *Optiques: The Science of the Eye and the Birth of Modern French Fiction* (Philadelphia, PA: University of Pennsylvania Press, 2006).
Gozzano, Guido, *Nell'Oriente favoloso: Lettere dall'India*, edited by Epifanio Ajello (Naples: Liguori, 2004).
Illiano, Antonio, *Metapsichica e letteratura in Pirandello* (Florence: Vallecchi, 1982).
Lattarulo, Leonardo (ed.), *Il vero e la sua ombra: Racconti fantastici dal Romanticismo al Primo Novecento* (Rome: Quiritta, 2000).
Melani, Costanza (ed.), *Fantastico italiano: Racconti fantastici dell'Ottocento e del primo Novecento italiano* (Milan: BUR-Rizzoli, 2009).

Milner, Max, *La fantasmagorie: Essai sur l'optique fantastique* (Paris: PUF, 1982).
Pagliaro, Annamaria, and Brian Zuccala (eds), *Luigi Capuana: Experimental Fiction and Cultural Mediation in Post-Risorgimento Italy* (Florence: Firenze University Press, 2019).
Pallottino, Paola (ed.), *L'irripetibile stagione de* Il giornalino della Domenica (Bologna: Bononia University Press, 2008).
Papini, Giovanni, 'Franche spiegazioni (A proposito di Rinascenza Spirituale e di Occultismo)', *Leonardo*, 5.2, 1907, pp. 129–43.
Papini, Giovanni, 'I sette peccati degli occultisti', *Leonardo*, 3, October–December 1905, pp. 184–7.
Pautasso, Guido Andrea, *Vampiro futurista: I futuristi e l'esoterismo* (Albissola Marina: Vanillaedizioni, 2018).
Porto, Silvia, 'L'Italia Futurista', in Ezio Godoli (ed.), *Il dizionario del futurismo* (Florence: Vallecchi-Mart, 2001), pp. 597–9.
Pozzo, Felice (ed.), *Il laboratorio magico di Emilio Salgari: Avventure, fantasmi, magie* (Cuneo: Nerosubianco, 2012).
Proietti, Biagio, and Mario Gerosa, *Daniele D'Anza: Un rivoluzionario della TV* (Piombino: Il Foglio, 2017).
Reghini, Arturo, 'Il punto di vista dell'occultismo', *Leonardo*, 5.2, 1907, pp. 144–56.
Reghini, Arturo, 'La Massoneria come fattore intellettuale', *Leonardo*, 4, October–December 1906, pp. 297–310.
Ruchin, Francesco, *Il paese delle oche: Il teatro del Grand Guignol in Italia* (Prato: Pentalinea, 2013).
Salgari, Emilio, *Per terra e per mare: Avventure immaginarie*, edited by Claudio Gallo (Turin: Aragno, 2004).
Santovincenzo, Leopoldo, and Carlo Modesti Pauer, *Fantasceneggiati: Sci-fi e giallo magico nelle produzioni Rai (1954–1987)* (Bologna: Elara, 2016).
Sassoon, Donald, *The Culture of the Europeans: From 1800 to the Present* (London: HarperPress, 2006).
Tenerelli, Domenico, *'Ai limiti della vita': Storia e letteratura nella Roma occulta di Luigi Pirandello (1891–1907)* (Bari: Giuseppe Laterza, 2020).
Tropea, Mario, *Nomi, ethos, follia, 'discordanze' negli scrittori siciliani tra Ottocento e Novecento, con uno scritto su Giuseppe Sciuti pittore* (Caltanissetta: Lussografica, 2014).
VanderMeer, Ann and Jeff Vandermeer (eds), *The Weird: A Compendium of Strange and Dark Stories* (New York: Tor, 2012).
Verri, Alessandro, *Le notti romane*, edited by Renzo Negri (Bari: Laterza, 1967).

Notes

1. See, for instance, Corradi.
2. Republished in Gallo and Foni 483–96.
3. See, by the author, the novella *La parola della morta* (1897), republished in Gallo and Foni 305–33.

4. See, for instance, Farnetti.
5. Both republished in Gallo and Foni 197–207 and 211–20.
6. See Foni, *Alla fiera* (especially 29–82); Foni, *Gran ballo*; Foni, *Piccoli mostri*, as well as Foni and Incarico.
7. Republished in Lattarulo (227–38), Melani (545–56) and Daniele (55–68).
8. See Capuana, *Spiritismo?*, but also Capuana, *Mondo occulto*.
9. Republished in Gallo and Foni 449–63.
10. See Curti, *Fantasmi* 378–81; Santovincenzo and Modesti Pauer 105–10; as well as Proietti and Gerosa 141–3.
11. See 'Il demonio della novella: storia di Capuana novelliere' in Ghidetti 197–248.
12. See, for instance, Pagliaro and Zuccala 145–256.
13. From the vast Pirandellian bibliography, it is worth mentioning Illiano and Tenerelli. On Capuana's relationship with the supernatural, see Tropea 117–214.
14. On the Grand Guignol in Italy, see both Arduini and Ruchin.
15. Republished in Gallo and Foni 379–98.
16. See Casini (164–73 in particular). See also, by Papini, 'Sette peccati' and 'Franche spiegazioni' and, by Reghini, 'La Massoneria' (published under the pseudonym 'Il Fratello Terribile' [The Terrible Brother]), as well as 'Punto di vista'.
17. See, for instance, Cigliana and Pautasso.
18. See Porto.
19. See Foni, 'Romanzo'; Foni, *Fantastico Salgari*; Pozzo.
20. The three short stories were republished in Salgari, *Per terra*, respectively 91–112, 113–26 and 140–54.
21. See Pallottino, but also Gallo and Bonomi, *Giornalino*.
22. Republished in Gallo and Bonomi, *Giornalino* 89–91.
23. On the dawning and first decades of the comic industry in Italy, see Gaspa.
24. See Gallo and Bonomi, *Tutto cominciò* 62.
25. See both Goulet 155–221 and Milner 191–201.
26. See Bernardini and Martinelli 158.
27. Zucca's short story was republished in Gallo and Foni 369–75.
28. First republished in de Turris (244–9), then in Ann and Jeff VanderMeer (97–100, translated into English by Brendan and Anna Connell).
29. Republished in de Turris (397–403) and Gozzano (15–24).
30. See the critical edition of 1967, edited by Renzo Negri.
31. See Curti, *Fantasmi* 374–8 and Curti, *Italian Gothic* 219–22; Santovincenzo and Modesti Pauer 81–91, 103 and 137–8; Proietti and Gerosa 106–12 and 225–36.

Chapter 9

Gothic Cinema
Giulio Giusti

The most prolific period in Italian horror filmmaking is commonly classified into two main cycles or *filoni*: the Gothic of the 1960s and the *giallo* of the 1970s. While the former describes a key trend in domestic horror that is marked by a distinctive approach to the stereotypical Gothic themes and motifs, the latter refers to a nationally specific hybrid form that is defined by a strict coexistence of crime fiction and graphic gore. That said, this chapter seeks to add nuance to this acknowledged distinction by further exploring the Gothic influence on the *giallo* as well as the close intertwining of the two cycles in relation to their narratives and style.[1] Internationally, this strict interrelationship has also served to differentiate the Gothic and *giallo* film production from its Anglo-American models and make it one of global popular culture's most iconic trademarks.

The purpose of this investigation is twofold. On the one hand, this chapter provides a critical understanding of both the Gothic and the *giallo* in a domestic context by outlining their historical phases, the dynamics of their production system as well as their major thematic affinities and shared practices. On the other hand, this chapter focuses on the narrative tropes and stylistic practices that distinguish three of its most representative figures, namely Riccardo Freda, Mario Bava and Dario Argento, from their foreign inspirations. It explores how and to what extent these directors have served to shape the two cycles and earn them cult status.

The Dawn of the Italian Gothic Horror

> To me, there is something strangely offensive about the idea of screen violence 'justified by the plot'.
> — Stephen Thrower, *Beyond Terror: The Films of Lucio Fulci*

The traditionally popular genre of horror 'was as much a foreign narrative form in the history of Italian cinema as was the western' (Bondanella 306). Unlike other Italian popular genres of the 1960s, such as the *commedia all'italiana* and the *peplum*, Italian horror film did not develop from an earlier cycle during the era of Italian silent cinema (1905–30). Throughout this period the domestic production companies were uninterested in the genre, the costume drama and the historical epic being the industry's most popular and profitable investment (Bondanella 5). During the silent era, in fact, the only recorded attempt at embracing the horrific and the macabre in Italy was Eugenio Testa's *Il mostro di Frankenstein* (1920), which is now lost (Günsberg 136; Paul 11–12; Bondanella 306; Hunter 19). Two previous examples dealing with the fantastic and the supernatural were Luigi Maggi's *Satana* (1912), a three-episode film about the devil, and Raimondo Scotti's *L'atleta fantasma* (1919), the story of a masked fighter of evil. Because of their farcical and operatic nature, however, these two examples showed no systematic approach to the genre and were never marketed as such (Hunt 329).[2]

This lack of interest continued during the Fascist Era (1922–45), in which the strictest regulation of censorship by the regime's *Direzione Generale per la Cinematografia* (DGC) tended to control the depiction of horrific themes and visually shocking images (McCallum 2; Günsberg 136; Bondanella 306; Gundle 32). Nor was there a consolidated and extended tradition of Italian Gothic literature and theatre equivalent to that of Anglo-American cultures (Günsberg 136; Venturini 5–9). As Louis Paul has pointed out, the only domestic attempt to use horrific images and themes in theatre is perceivable in the Italian branch of the French Grand-Guignol, which was based in Rome from 1908 to 1928 (8–9).

The narrative that lies behind the official birth of a Gothic tradition in Italian horror filmmaking with Riccardo Freda's *I vampiri* (1957) was thus imported from a variety of foreign sources.[3] Freda's film primarily consisted of a low-budget experiment aimed at domestic profit and in the wake of the previously commercially successful expressionist cinema – this includes Stellan Rye's *Der Student von Prag* (1913), Robert Wiene's *Das Kabinett Des Dr. Caligari* (1920) and Friedrich Wilhelm Murnau's *Nosferatu* (1922) – and the Gothic horror films produced in Hollywood by Universal Studios during the 1930s under expressionist influence, such as Tod Browning's *Dracula* (1931), Rouben Mamoulian's *Dr. Jekyll and Mr. Hyde* (1931) and James Whale's *Frankenstein* (1931) (Jancovich 53–4; Berenstein 14; Günsberg 137; Bondanella 306). It is not surprising, therefore, that *I vampiri* provided the paradigm for an aesthetic appreciation of the Gothic in Italy, as this film emerged on the eve of a second Anglo-American Gothic horror renaissance, which was marked by Terence Fisher's *The Curse of Frankenstein* (1957) for the low-budget British Hammer Film Productions, Alfred Hitchcock's *Psycho* (1960) and Roger Corman's *The House of Usher* (1960) (Bertellini 213–14).

In this regard, the birth of a domestic Gothic horror film production is due to the fact that post-Second World War Italian popular cinema had a history of making low-budget carbon copies of previous commercial successes in America and Britain (Newman, *Nightmare Movies* 187). As Mary Wood has discussed, in this period box-office popularity was central to the development and identification of Italian popular genres. As the production system in Italy in the period post-Second World War was not based on the large-scale studio filmmaking of the Hollywood companies, any single producer or distributor had the power to decide whether a film could be made or not, without concerted legislation and policies. Italian producers and distributors tended to present annually an output composed of different genres of film to minimise commercial risk and tried to respond creatively to changes in public taste and the dynamic development of domestic society (35). In the case of Freda's *I vampiri*, although the film grossed a very small amount of money at the box-office, the success of Terence Fisher's *Dracula* (1958) in Italy convinced the domestic production companies to pursue the genre mode with five films in 1960, paving the way for the so-called Italian Gothic cycle (Günsberg 138).[4] As these films also produced only modest successes at the box-office, Italian Gothic horror continued sporadically until 1966, the year arguably seen as marking its close with Mario Bava's *Operazione paura* and Camillo Mastrocinque's *Un angelo per Satana*. From 1957 to 1966, in fact, the Italian Gothic cycle never exceeded annual production of five or six films, totalling only around thirty films, like the Hammer output in the same period. In comparison with the numerous and commercially successful *pepla* (or 'sword and sandal') – around 300 from 1957 to 1967 – Italian Gothic horror still represented both quantitatively and financially a relatively minor domestic popular film production (Günsberg 138; Di Chiara 35).

The Gothic Cycle

Ignored by domestic critics and scholars until the mid-1970s, the Italian Gothic horror film production of the 1960s has constantly been accused of amounting merely to an imitation of its Anglo-American counterpart (Brunetta, *Storia del cinema italiano* 585–6). Together with the British Hammer Film Productions and Roger Corman's Poe stories, the Italian Gothic cycle has also come under attack for never transcending the B-movie level and for predominantly focusing on controversial and shocking themes, including bodily corruption and disfigurement, incest, gynophobia, necrophilia and torture at the expense of a coherent plot and complex character development (Hunt 326–7; Günsberg 139). Nevertheless, as Kim Newman has stated:

> While it is undoubtedly true that many Italian genre movies are simply worthless carbon copies with a few baroque trimmings, the best examples of most cycles are surprisingly sophisticated mixes of imitation, pastiche, parody, deconstruction, reinterpretation, and operatic inflation. ('Thirty Years in Another Town' 20)

Freda's *I vampiri* and Bava's *La maschera del demonio*, for example, have eventually gained cult status both domestically and internationally and have been recognised as offering a valid alternative to the Hollywood and British Hammer Film Productions in developing a certain degree of aesthetic and narrative autonomy (Brunetta, *Storia del cinema italiano* 409). *I vampiri* is not a film about vampires in the Anglo-American Gothic cinematic and literary tradition (Paul 84; Bondanella 308). The story of a demented scientist draining the blood of young women to rejuvenate his evil lover moves away from the classic depiction of the vampire as shown in Tod Browning's and Terence Fisher's loosely based adaptations of Bram Stoker's *Dracula* (1897). Rather, Freda's film anticipates some of the key narrative tropes and stylistic practices that would become embedded in the Italian *giallo* (plural *gialli*), a closely interrelated horror sub-genre inaugurated by Bava's *La ragazza che sapeva troppo* (1962) and *Sei donne per l'assassino* (1964) and further re-elaborated into a more sophisticated formula by iconic horror-master Dario Argento in his directorial debut *L'uccello dalle piume di cristallo* (1970).

Firstly, *I vampiri*'s sub-plot explores the fictional element of the civilian amateur detective that became a typical narrative device of the Italian *gialli* of the 1970s. Freda's film, in fact, also centres on the figure of a journalist investigating the scientist's crimes and eventually discovering the reason behind the disappearance of young women in contemporary Paris. Secondly, Freda's graphic depiction of murders, committed by the scientist while disguised with black gloves and black raincoat, paves the way for one of the major visual tropes of the *giallo* tradition, namely the aestheticisation of the act of murder by an elaborate use of camerawork, editing and soundtrack. The violence in *I vampiri* is presented with near-medical attention by the medium of the fast zoom in and out, the persistent close-ups on female bodies, and a powerful interplay of expressionistic backlighting and a disquieting soundtrack. Such a depiction of the act of murder is radically different from the relatively realist and restrained Anglo-American style. Finally, the scientist's psychological subjugation to his female lover to the extent of becoming her accomplice in the various crimes introduces another fundamental topic that will be further explored in Argento's *L'uccello dalle piume di cristallo*, namely the castrating and mentally deranged female 'monster' and the feminisation of the serial-killer.

As Maggie Günsberg has remarked, the Italian Gothic horror film production of the 1960s 'centres on the female body and the threat femininity poses to masculinity' (133). It is to the central figure of women as *femme fatale*, vampire, victim and witch that Teo Mora attributes the expressive autonomy and narrative unity of the whole Italian Gothic cycle, rather than to the stereotypical male 'monster' of the Anglo-American tradition (292).[5] American and British counterparts were strongly focused on male stardom, with iconic figures such as Boris Karloff in *Frankenstein* (1931) and Christopher Lee in *Dracula* (1958), and their misogynist aspects were exclusively related to both a masochistic female victim-identification and a sadistic behaviour by men toward them. Italian Gothic horror's most enduring cult figure throughout the 1960s, instead, was British actress Barbara Steele, an icon 'who seemed to exist simply to torture and be tortured, to terrify and be terrified' (Hunt 325). In Bava's *La maschera del demonio*, for example, Steele assumes the double role of a seductive vampire-witch and a virginal beauty who are identical in appearance. As far as Bava's style is concerned, it is especially in his persistent and prolonged use of the extreme close-ups combined with elaborate editing and different points of view (POVs), all in one single sequence, that the 1970s generation of domestic *gialli* also found inspiration in representing the effect of terror. According to William K. Everson, in *La maschera del demonio* Bava developed a rather unhealthy tendency to dwell on the detailed unpleasantness of death and torture (207–8). In a key sequence, Steele dies by having a spiky metal mask hammered onto her face before she is executed and buried. Throughout the sequence, Bava shoots the spiky mask from the executioner's POV then suddenly reverses the perspective by moving the camera through the mask's apertures and transferring the POV from that of the executioner to that of the victim. As soon as the mask is nailed to the victim's face by the executioner's hammer, blood explodes from the mask's apertures for eyes, mouth and nose. Indeed, this elaborate camerawork contributes to exalting the graphic scenes of violence with an almost clinical attention to the method by which they were achieved. In this regard, Bava's technical expertise in the film may have originated from the director's previous career as a cinematographer (Colombo and Tentori 25). Because of his talent in photography and self-confidence with the camera, Bava had been frequently asked by production teams to re-shoot technically complex scenes or to finish a film due to the absence of the original director, as was the case with Freda's *I vampiri* and *Caltiki: il mostro immortale* (1959). During this period, Bava gained considerable technical experience in working with extremely low budgets and fast production schedules and developed a sophisticated high contrast photographic style (Bondanella 311).[6] This photographic style, together with the director's tendency to deploy a plethora of technical devices in his documentary exploration of the body's responses to death and torture, served to shape and differentiate the Italian Gothic cycle from its Anglo-American counterparts and indicated the direction a whole generation of domestic horror directors would take from the 1970s onwards.

The *Giallo* Cycle

Bava's *Operazione paura* and Mastrocinque's *Un angelo per Satana* virtually signalled the end of the domestic Gothic cycle and the 1970s welcomed a strictly intertwined horror sub-genre known as *giallo*.[7] As James Gracey has remarked:

> *Giallo* films notoriously combine sex and violence, hyper-stylised and elaborate murders, lavish camerawork and set design, displaced protagonists who unwittingly stumble into the ensuing mayhem, ineffectual or non-existent police and copious gore. [...] Everything weaves together in a weak and often convoluted narrative, frequently interrupted by scenes of startling violence and bloodshed. More abstract modes of detection are utilised rather than the usual logical deduction of 'whodunnit'-style movies. (14)

Gracey's assertion demonstrates how Italian Gothic cinema and the *gialli* are not necessarily separate in narrative and style despite the *gialli*'s tendency to set their stories in the present and to privilege a more rational-scientific explanation over any supernatural involvement.[8] Indeed, because of their adoption of macabre atmospheres and transgressive themes and focus on the more exploitative aspect of crime fiction, namely the graphic depiction of murder and violence, the Italian *gialli* offer a clear continuity with the Gothic film productions of the 1960s. The main reason for their division into two different sub-genres may come from the production company's need to label or list these films for commercial purposes (Koven 9).[9] The cross-pollination of the Gothic with the *giallo* is also confirmed by the fact that some of the most representative figures of the Gothic, including Freda and Bava, also worked on the *giallo* with the result of transferring part of their narrative tropes and stylistic practices from one sub-genre to the other.[10] Although the sub-genre was first pioneered by Bava's *La ragazza che sapeva troppo* and *Sei donne per l'assassino* during the first half of the 1960s, the period of the Italian *gialli* officially started in 1970 with Argento's box-office hit *L'uccello dalle piume di cristallo* and ended in 1982 with Lucio Fulci's *Lo squartatore di New York*, with a peak in the period 1970–5 (Hardy 294; Koven 8).[11] Specifically, Argento's extraordinary commercial success convinced the Italian production companies to invest in this cinematic trend (Gervasini 175). As a result, between January 1971 and December 1972 more than seventy films that strongly rely on Bava-Argento's narrative and visual formulae were produced, many of them lacking the thematic and stylistic qualities of their precursors (Gervasini 179; Koven 6; De Sanctis 147).

As far as the literary background is concerned, several film scholars[12] agree in tracing the etymology of the name *giallo* to the American and British mystery and detective novels published in Italy by Mondadori from the late 1920s. The name *giallo* alludes to the yellow colour of the covers of these volumes. As Ken Hanke (111) and Mikel J. Koven (6–8) have pointed out, a similar source of inspiration is traceable in the *Krimi*, a parallel movement in German crime cinema based on Edgar Wallace and his son Bryan Edgar Wallace's detective stories and produced by the German company Rialto Film between 1959 and 1972. However, while in the traditional detective story, or whodunnit, the reader is provided with objective clues from which the identity of the murderer may be deduced before the solution is eventually revealed by a professional detective, the stereotypical *giallo*, as established by the Bava-Argento formula, is built on partial, ambiguous and often deceptive narrative information. As Gary Needham has discussed:

> The typical Argento protagonist is the victim/witness of trauma who must keep returning to the scene of the crime (the Freudian '*nachtragluichkeit*' or retranscription of memory; popularly represented via flashback sequences), often committed by a killer who just can't resist serial murder (the psychoanalytic 'compulsion to repeat').

Thus, the stereotypical *gialli* share an underlying Gothic component in their structure as their narratives are often based on the fragmented memory of the protagonist relative to what really happened and the whole plot is sometimes impressively convoluted until the revelation of the killer's identity. As David Punter and Glennis Byron have remarked:

> From its beginnings, the literary Gothic has been concerned with uncertainties of character positioning and instabilities of knowledge. Far from knowing everything, like an omniscient narrator, characters – and even narrators – frequently know little or nothing about the world through which they move or about the structures of power which envelop them. (273)

Bava's *La ragazza che sapeva troppo*, for example, focuses on a young displaced American tourist who witnesses a mysterious murder in the city of Rome. Not certain she can recall a specific detail of the crime she witnessed or recognise the killer, the woman is haunted by the feeling of something amiss and decides to investigate on her own. In 1964, the director returned to the sub-genre with *Sei donne per l'assassino* and introduced some of the visual tropes that had been pioneered in Freda's Italian Gothic forerunner *I vampiri*, such as the graphic violence of the murder act and the introduction of what was to become the archetypal *giallo* killer's disguise: black leather gloves and raincoat (Met 202). Argento kept the basic story idea from *La ragazza che sapeva troppo* in his *L'uccello dalle piume di cristallo* and imbued the film with the graphic violence and the distinctive killer's disguise from *Sei donne per l'assassino* (Gervasini 176–7; Menarini 30; Koven 4; Pezzotta 85). It is this combination of narrative and visual tropes that defines the typical *giallo* format of the 1970s and the early 1980s (Koven 4).

In addition to this, what closely relates Bava's *La ragazza che sapeva troppo* and Argento's *L'uccello dalle piume di cristallo* to the domestic Gothic cycle of the 1960s is their focus on threatening femininity and the feminisation of the serial-killer. However, while in Bava's film the final denouement that implies the feminisation of the serial-killer still relies on the narrative conventions of the classic detective fiction, as it involves financial greed as the reason for the murders, Argento is the first *giallo* director to explore a series of psychosexual issues behind the killer's motives in the wake of the American film noir's depiction of excessively dysfunctional family behaviour and sexual motivations behind crimes (Wood 57).[13] In *L'uccello dalle piume di cristallo*, the figure of the accomplice is identified with a husband who tries to cover up the murders of his wife, who had been sexually abused in the past and now derives her pleasure in killing from identifying with her male rapist. Similarly, in a very consistent number of *gialli* after *L'uccello dalle piume di cristallo* the killer's motives, whether they are male or female, are often of a psychosexual nature or directly linked to the murderer's experience of some event or trauma which occurred either in childhood or in a relatively recent past (Koven 104). This implies that the generation of domestic filmmakers of the 1970s and 1980s tended to passively accept Argento's introduction of psychological insights into the *giallo* and that these final denouements were metabolised to such an extent as to become potentially identifiable with the sub-genre itself (Koven 109).

As far as the graphic depiction of violence is concerned, another significant feature indicating the strict interrelationship between the domestic Gothic cinema of the 1960s and the *giallo* is reflected in the persistent focus on elaborate set-pieces during the murder sequences. As Donato Totaro has remarked:

> A set-piece is a choreographed scene that usually, though not exclusively, takes place in one location. By an 'elaborate' set-piece, I mean a situation or set of actions where narrative function [. . .] gives way to 'spectacle'. In other words, the scene plays on far longer than is strictly necessary for the narrative purposes. (162)

The typical Bava-Argento *giallo*, in fact, 'places equal (if not more) importance on the actual method of killing as well as solving the crime' (Guins 141). Grabbing the audience's attention through a combination of aural and visual signs, both filmmakers created in the murder set-piece a kind of film within the film around which the whole plot is constructed.

According to Bengt Wallman, an additional explanation for the introduction of murder set-pieces into the *gialli* may be found in the influence of the *fumetto nero* of the 1960s, an adult Italian comic-strip series featuring sadism, graphic sex and protracted violence (11–13). Interestingly, the publication of the first Italian *fumetto nero* in 1962, Angela and Luciana Giussani's *Diabolik*, coincides with both the golden age of the Gothic cycle and the release of Bava's seminal *giallo La ragazza che sapeva troppo*. Thus, all three modes can be placed within the same cultural and thematic framework at a time of 'hedonistic excess when Italian popular culture ventured to explore every dimly lit corner of the underworld and erotic, generously dwelling upon crime, violence, sadomasochism and fetishism' (Guidotti 13). Moreover, some of these *fumetti neri* were also made into films, such as in the cases of Umberto Lenzi's *Kriminal* (1966), Piero Vivarelli's *Satanik* (1967) and Bava's *Diabolik* (1968), thus testifying to the mutual influences shared between both industries. The *fumetto nero* described the horror of modern cities and daily life in a very brutal and violent way. *Satanik* also proposed a wide range of Gothic horror themes, including a potion with an unexpected side effect, evil creatures and vampires. Similarly, this blend of eroticism and horror are common ground in any given *giallo*, where violence is often sexualised and the set-pieces are designed to be appreciated within a larger filmic context and are included to make the audiences of graphic horror aware of the beauty the sub-genre can impart, both aesthetically and emotionally, by an effective use of camerawork, editing and soundtrack (Freeland 256–7; Hunt 257; Koven 127). In this regard, Bava's *Sei donne per l'assassino* is the seminal *giallo* to introduce a radical split between a narrative progression that is typical of the traditional detective fiction and a series of highly choreographed murder sequences. Specifically, this is the first film within the sub-genre to mix a traditional blackmailing plot behind the killer's motives and a series of murders during which the sheer variety of tools and weapons, such as medieval spiked armoured gloves, knives and razor blades, imparts a spectacle in itself and increases the levels of excessive Gothic gore and graphic violence. Like in his previous Gothic classic *La maschera del demonio*, in this *giallo* Bava makes use of repeated extreme close-ups, fast zooms, both in and out, and POV shots to increase the suspense both emotionally and visually. Particularly, the shift to a handheld killer-cam perspective is the most common device in Bava's *Sei donne per l'assassino* which creates a temporary subjective position within the psychotic mind of the serial-killer stalking the victim. The film avails itself of different kinds of subjective camera devices to reflect the emotional and psychological states of both the killer and the victim. Thus, the series of POVs, whether killer-cam or any of the other subjective camera devices, provide moments of cinematic virtuosity within the film by effectively fusing together the character's subjective mental states and the camera itself.

Bava's experimentation with style within the murder set-pieces was eventually perfected and re-invented by Argento throughout the 1970s and 1980s. Belonging to a domestic popular tradition that places more emphasis on spectacular rather than narrative pleasures, Argento has eventually been able to carve out an authorial niche for himself by creating the perfect format within which the visual tropes typical of both the Italian Gothic cycle and the *gialli*, such as an avant-garde soundtrack, prohibited camerawork and sophisticated technologies, could be put on display. Such sophistication was only possible with the higher budget he could command. By doing this, Argento not only worked together with Bava to create the *giallo* sub-genre, but also provided some of the most audio-visually sophisticated and technically accomplished murder set-pieces in the history of the Italian horror cinema, leading to international acclaim and recognition for himself that remains to this day (Bertellini 6).

Conclusion

In the Italian context, the Gothic cycle and the *gialli* are more closely interrelated than has been generally accredited. During the 1960s and 1970s, in fact, there was an inextricable overlap between these two cycles in terms of narrative and style. Domestic films constantly shifted from supernatural themes to a gruesome depiction of contemporary society whilst maintaining an underlying point of aesthetic affinities and shared production system dynamics.

At an international level, Italian Gothic horror and the *gialli* have been able to guarantee a certain artistic distance from the consolidated Anglo-American tradition and to offer a 'more assaultive, explicit, disturbing and potentially transgressive' cinematic experience (Hutchings 82). As Francesco Di Chiara has discussed, 'because of their graphic violence, eroticism and visual flair' both sub-genres 'soon gained a cult following outside of Italy, and especially throughout the 1970s with the increasing international success of Italian *giallo* and with the emergence of horror cult directors like Dario Argento' (30). Despite producing modest successes at the domestic box-office, during the 1960s both Freda and Bava had served to pioneer a distinctively Italian narrative and stylistic repertoire that Argento reworked in his 1970s and early 1980s *gialli* through a range of sophisticated visual tropes, such as complex camerawork, flamboyant *mise-en-scène* and unsettling soundtrack, all made possible by the higher budgets his films have commanded (Hunt 328). What distinguishes the work of Freda, Bava and more predominantly Argento from their foreign inspirations is thus not to be found in the brutal murder set-pieces and the unhealthy atmosphere charged with sexual symbolism, but rather in the directors' technical concern and visual sensibility.

From the first half of the 1980s onwards, however, Italian horror as a whole faced a significant moment of generational crisis and structural changes in the film production system. On the one hand, the decades ahead did not 'offer sufficient originality, either in terms of style or industrial approach to be considered as an "age" on its own' (Baschiera 47). On the other, by the end of the 1980s and the beginning of the 1990s, domestic producers had lost their ability to attract foreign investments and suffered from a sheer competition in the home video market with low-budget American films, thus leaving Argento as the only author to stand out from the crowd in a very fragmented cinematic landscape.

Bibliography

Aldana Reyes, Xavier, *Gothic Cinema* (London: Routledge, 2020).
Baschiera, Stefano, 'The 1980s Italian Horror Cinema of Imitation: The Good, the Ugly and the Sequel', in Stefano Baschiera and Russ Hunter (eds), *Italian Horror Cinema* (Edinburgh: Edinburgh University Press, 2016), pp. 45–61.
Berenstein, Rhona, *Attack of the Leading Ladies: Gender, Sexuality and Spectatorship in Classic Horror Cinema* (New York: Columbia University Press, 1996).
Bertellini, Giorgio, '*Profondo rosso/Deep Red*. Dario Argento, Italy 1975', in Giorgio Bertellini (ed.), *The Cinema of Italy* (London: Wallflower Press, 2004), pp. 213–22.
Bondanella, Peter, *A History of Italian Cinema* (New York: Continuum, 2009).
Brunetta, Gian Piero, *Cent'anni di cinema italiano* (Bari: Laterza, 1991).
Brunetta, Gian Piero, *Storia del cinema italiano: dal miracolo economico agli anni novanta 1960–1993*, 4 vols (Rome: Editori Riuniti, IV, 1993).
Colombo, Maurizio, and Antonio Tentori, *Lo schermo insanguinato: il cinema italiano del terrore 1957–1989* (Chieti: Solfanelli Editore, 1990).
Curti, Roberto, *Italian Gothic Horror Films, 1957–1969* (Jefferson, NC: McFarland, 2015).
De Sanctis, Pierpaolo, 'Il rosso e l'argento: uccelli, gatti, mosche e altre specie nel thrilling Italiano', in Vito Zagarrio (ed.), *Argento vivo: il cinema di Dario Argento tra genere e autorialità* (Venice: Marsilio Editori, 2008), pp. 147–54.
Di Chiara, Francesco, 'Domestic Films Made for Export: Modes of Production of the 1960s Italian Horror Film', in Stefano Baschiera and Russ Hunter (eds), *Italian Horror Cinema* (Edinburgh: Edinburgh University Press, 2016), pp. 30–44.
Everson, William K., *Classics of the Horror Film* (Secaucus, NJ: Citadel Press, 1974).
Freeland, Cynthia A., *The Naked and the Undead: Evil and the Appeal of Horror* (Boulder, CO: Westview Press, 2000).
Gervasini, Mauro, 'Il rosso segno del delitto. Ispirazione e novità del giallo argentiano', in Giulia Carluccio, Giacomo Manzoli, and Roya Menarini (eds), *L'eccesso della visione: il cinema di Dario Argento* (Turin: Lindau, 2003), pp. 175–80.
Gracey, James, *Dario Argento* (Hampenden: Kamera Books, 2010).
Guidotti, Roberto, 'Nude, Transgressive, Pop', in Stefano Piselli and Riccardo Morrocchi (eds), *Esotika, Erotika, Psichotika: Kaleidoscopic Sexy Italia 1964–1973* (Florence: Glittering Images Edizioni D'essai, 2000), pp. 1–15.
Guins, Ray, 'Tortured Looks: Dario Argento and Visual Displeasure', in Andy Black (ed.), *Necronomicon: The Journal of Horror and Erotic Cinema: Volume One* (London: Creation Books, 1996, pp. 141–53.
Gundle, Stephen, *Mussolini's Dream Factory: Film Stardom in Fascist Italy* (New York and Oxford: Berghahn, 2013).
Günsberg, Maggie, *Italian Cinema: Gender and Genre* (Basingstoke and New York: Palgrave, 2005).
Hanke, Ken, 'The "Lost" Horror Film Series: The Edgar Wallace Krimis', in

Steven Schneider (ed.), *Fear without Frontiers: Horror Cinema Across the Globe* (Godalming: FAB Press, 2003), pp. 111–23.

Hardy, Phil, *The Aurum Film Encyclopedia 3* (London: Aurum Press, 1985).

Hunt, Leon, 'A Sadistic Night at the Opera: Notes on the Italian Horror Film', *The Horror Reader* (London and New York: Routledge, 2000), pp. 324–35.

Hunter, Russ, '*Preferisco l'inferno*: Early Italian Horror Cinema', in Stefano Baschiera and Russ Hunter (eds), *Italian Horror Cinema* (Edinburgh: Edinburgh University Press, 2016), pp. 15–29.

Hutchings, Peter, 'Bavaesque: the Making of Mario Bava as Italian Horror Auteur', in Stefano Baschiera and Russ Hunter, *Italian Horror Cinema* (Edinburgh: Edinburgh University Press, 2016), pp. 79–92.

Jancovich, Mark, *Horror* (London: B. T. Batsford, 1992).

Kavka, Misha, 'The Gothic on Screen', in Jerrold E. Hogle (ed.), *The Cambridge Companion to Gothic Fiction* (Cambridge: Cambridge University Press), pp. 209–28.

Koven, Mikel J., *La Dolce Morte: Vernacular Cinema and the Italian Giallo Film* (Lanham, MD: Scarecrow Press, 2006).

Lowenstein, Adam, 'The *Giallo*/Slasher Landscape: Ecologia del delitto, *Friday the 13th* and Subtractive Spectatorship' in Stefano Baschiera and Russ Hunter (eds), *Italian Horror Cinema* (Edinburgh: Edinburgh University Press, 2016), pp. 127–44.

Lucas, Tim, *Mario Bava: All the Colours of the Dark* (Cincinnati, OH: Video Watchdog, 2007).

McCallum, Lawrence, *Italian Horror Films of the 1960s: A Critical Catalog of 62 Chillers* (Jefferson, NC: McFarland, 1998).

McDonagh, Maitland, *Broken Mirrors/Broken Minds: The Dark Dreams of Dario Argento* (New York: A Citadel Press Book-Carol Publishing Group, 1994).

Menarini, Roy, 'Dal thriller all'horror. Tra modernità, postmodernità e manierismo', in Giulia Carluccio, Giacomo Manzoli, and Roya Menarini (eds), *L'eccesso della visione: il cinema di Dario Argento* (Turin: Lindau, 2003), pp. 29–38.

Met, Philippe, '"Knowing Too Much" About Hitchcock: The Genesis of the Italian *Giallo*', in David Boyd and R. Barton Palmer (eds), *After Hitchcock: Influence, Imitation, and Intertextuality* (Austin, TX: University of Texas Press, 2006), pp. 195–215.

Mora, Teo, *Storia del cinema dell'orrore 1957–1977*, 2 vols (Rome: Fanucci, 1977–8, II, 1978).

Needham, Gary, 'Playing with Genre: An Introduction to the Italian *giallo*', *Kinoeye*, 2.11, 2002, <www.kinoeye.org/02/11/needham11.php> (last accessed 1 August 2022)

Newman, Kim, 'Thirty Years in Another Town: The History of Italian Exploitation', *Monthly Film Bulletin*, 53.626/1, 1986, pp. 20–4.

Newman, Kim, *Nightmare Movies: A Critical History of the Horror Movies from 1968* (London: Bloomsbury, 1988).

Palmerini, Luca, and Gaetano Mistretta, *Spaghetti Nightmares: Italian Fantasy-Horrors as Seen through the Eyes of Their Protagonists* (Key West, FL: Fantasma Books, 1996).

Paul, Louis, *Italian Horror Film Directors* (Jefferson, NC: McFarland, 2005).

Pezzotta, Alberto, 'La modernità imperfetta', in Vito Zagarrio (ed.), *Argento vivo: il cinema di Dario Argento tra genere e autorialità* (Venice: Marsilio, 2008), pp. 83–9.
Punter, David, and Glennis Byron, *The Gothic* (Oxford: Blackwell, 2004).
Slater, Jay, *Eaten Alive: Italian Cannibal and Zombie Movies* (London: Plexus Publishing Limited, 2002).
Thrower, Stephen, *Beyond Terror: The Films of Lucio Fulci* (Godalming: FAB Press, 1999).
Totaro, Donato, 'The Italian Zombie Film: From Derivation to Reinvention', in Steven Schneider (ed.), *Fear Without Frontiers: Horror Cinema Across the Globe* (Godalming: FAB Press, 2003), pp. 161–73.
Venturini, Simone, *Horror Italiano* (Rome: Donzelli, 2014).
Wallman, Bengt, *Il Thrilling Italiano: Opening up the Giallo*, Stockholm University, MA Thesis, 2007.
Wood, Mary P., *Italian Cinema* (Oxford: Berg, 2005).

Notes

1. This chapter, therefore, will focus solely on the coalescence of the Gothic and the classic *giallo* format of the 1970s in terms of narratives and aesthetics. The other sub-genres and *filoni* that form the domestic horror of the 1970s and 1980s, such as the cannibal, the possession, and the zombie films, will not be discussed as they do not fit the purpose of this investigation.
2. For a comprehensive list of horror-related films during the Italian silent period, see Palmerini and Mistretta (8).
3. As Misha Kavka has pointed out, Gothic film is not an established genre. Rather, the term 'Gothic' should be considered as an aesthetic marker involving characters, images, plots and styles and that is often found in the broader category of horror cinema (209). For a clear definition as well as engaged analysis and understanding of Gothic cinema as an aesthetic mode within the horror genre, also see Aldana Reyes.
4. The five films include Mario Bava's *La maschera del demonio*, Giorgio Ferroni's *Il mulino delle donne di pietra*, Anton Giulio Majano's *Seddok, l'erede di Satana*, Renato Polselli's *L'amante del vampiro* and Pietro Regnoli's *L'ultima preda del vampiro* (Brunetta, *Cent'anni di cinema italiano* 616–17 and *Storia del cinema italiano* 408–11).
5. On threatening femininity in the domestic Gothic cycle, see Curti.
6. For a highly detailed and engaged analysis of Bava's cinematic career, see Lucas.
7. Throughout the 1970s and 1980s, supernatural horror continued to be present in Italy. Since the films of the Gothic cycle produced only modest successes at the domestic box-office, Italian producers and distributors decided to invest in two new supernatural horror sub-genres in the wake of two successful American films. While William Friedkin's *The Exorcist* (1973) launched a new craze for possession films – these include Ovidio Assonitis's *Chi sei?* (1974), Alberto De Martino's *L'Anticristo* (1974) and

Holocaust 2000 (1977), the box-office success in Italy of *Dawn of the Dead* (1978) by American director George A. Romero generated a series of zombie films, such as Lucio Fulci's *Zombi 2* (1979), *Paura nella città dei morti viventi* (1980) and *Zombi 3* (1988). For a historical contextualisation and critical analysis of these two sub-genres, see Colombo and Tentori (139–47; 149–54), Slater and Bondanella (326–34).
8. A few *gialli* of the 1970s, including Francesco Barilli's *Il profumo della signora in nero* (1974), Dario Argento's *Profondo rosso* (1975) and Lucio Fulci's *Sette note in nero* (1977), however, still rely on some sort of supernatural agency in their plots as they also focus on a series of mental abilities and practices, ranging from clairvoyance to spiritualism, that constantly invade the legitimate investigative sphere and challenge the adequacy of rational-scientific discourses.
9. In a selected corpus of *gialli*, including Emilio P. Miraglia's *La notte che Evelyn uscì dalla tomba* (1971), *La dama rossa uccide sette volte* (1972) and Sergio Martino's *Tutti i colori del buio* (1972), the continuity with the domestic Gothic cycle is made more explicit. These films, in fact, perfectly combine the detective element typical of the *giallo* sub-genre with a series of stereotypical Gothic themes and motifs, including spooky castles, the supernatural, and Satanism.
10. Throughout the 1970s Bava returned to the Gothic with *Gli orrori del castello di Norimberga* (1972), *Lisa e il diavolo* (1972), *Shock* (1977) in collaboration with his son Lamberto, and *La Venere d'Ille* (1978). In addition to this, apart from the already mentioned *La ragazza che sapeva troppo* and *Sei donne per l'assassino*, Bava's long and wide-ranging career includes three other *gialli*. These are *Il rosso segno della follia* (1969), *Cinque bambole per la luna di agosto* (1970) and *Reazione a catena* (1971). *Reazione a catena* has frequently been invoked as anticipating the American *slasher* trend of the 1980s inaugurated by John Carpenter's *Halloween* (1978) and Sean S. Cunningham's *Friday the 13th* (1980) (see McDonagh 25 and 49–51; Bondanella 380; Hutchings 86; Lowenstein 137).
11. As Bengt Wallman has discussed, any Italian film prior or post the period 1970–82 with similar narrative and stylistic traits to the *giallo* immediately encourages one to consider whether it is a *giallo*. While films such as Mario Mattoli's *Labbra serrate* (1942), Luchino Visconti's *Ossessione* (1942), Pietro Germi's *Un maledetto imbroglio* (1959) and Giacomo Gentilomo's *Atto d'accusa* (1960) tend to privilege a more realist and restrained style rather than focusing on the often convoluted and hyper-stylised visual tropes typical of the sub-genre, an argument could be advanced that any *giallo* post-1982 is either 'revival *giallo*' like Argento's *Non ho sonno* (2001), widely acknowledged as a return to the director's cinematic origins, or 'neo-*giallo*' like Michele Soavi's *Deliria* (1987), which was closely inspired by American *slasher*-movies in the wake of John Carpenter's *Halloween* (1978) and Sean S. Cunningham's *Friday the 13th* (1980) (4).
12. These include, among others, Wood (53), Koven (2; 17), Bondanella (372) and Lowenstein (127–8).
13. In Argento's *Suspiria* (1977) and *Inferno* (1980), female figures continue to represent a transmutation of the deranged women of both his *gialli* of the early 1970s and the narrative framework established by the domes-

tic Gothic cycle of the 1960s. As Leon Hunt has pointed out, Argento's *Suspiria* and *Inferno* show a combination of foregrounding Gothic themes, including the depiction of alchemy, the supernatural and witchcraft, and the visual tropes that are typical of the *gialli*, such as black-gloved and black raincoated killers (332).

Chapter 10

Comics and the Gothic
Fabio Camilletti

You know you're successful when you've pissed off your parents.
— David J. Schow

Those who wish to know, have whole libraries at their disposal. That spirit, however, is no longer available.
— Giorgio Pressburger

Introduction

Late twentieth-century Italian Gothic could only proliferate thanks to cinema and, most of all, comic books. The economic boom of the 1960s gave comics a broader audience than that of schoolchildren; and, consequently, new purposes, other than being 'funny' and 'instructive', as earlier strips were required to do. Mass alphabetisation, raising of the school age, and improvement of living standards shaped teenagers as a new category of customers, while new practices and rituals (commuting, use of public transport, mass holidays) required non-demanding readings for adults, aimed at generating immediate enjoyment. In the 1960s, producing comics seemed an easy way of making a profit, which resulted in a veritable proliferation of makeshift publishers (Preianò 274): the majority of them were based in Milan, the capital city of Italy's publishing industry since the nineteenth century. This vast, semi-piratical market would become a fertile ground for the development of Gothic-oriented comic books, also thanks to the popularity of Gothic horror films and the dissemination of 'occulture' throughout the decade and beyond (Camilletti). In the 1970s, Italy's comic-book industry was, by sales, the second biggest worldwide after the Japanese, then the vast crisis undergone by the market between the late 1970s and early 1980s decimated Italian publishers, and by the mid-1990s only a few had survived. Tellingly, the last Italian comic to become a mass phenomenon was a horror book, *Dylan Dog* – still one of the best-selling, most representative Italian products.

The birth of a distinctly Italian industry of Gothic horror comics, ranging from classic horror (Sansoni's *Horror*) to postmodernist experiments (*Dylan Dog*), exploitation (the sexy-horror pocket-books of the 1970s and 1980s), splatter and gore (ACME's *Splatter*), was primarily due to the extreme freedom in which the Italian comic-book market was accidentally allowed to develop. Certainly, like everywhere in the industrial world, Italian comics were subject to recurrent, moralising attacks on the part of media and institutions. However, unlike in the United States, such campaigns never took the shape of systematic lobbying, and were rather the initiatives of single magistrate's courts than symptoms of a wider 'scare' (Hajdu). As a consequence, in the absence of an actual censorial authority, Italian comics were often at the forefront in terms of explicitness, mirroring – and often heralding – the evolutions of popular cinema from the 1960s through to the 1980s (classic Gothic, Italian *giallo*, softcore erotica, exploitation films).

Even more importantly, Italian comic books benefited from being considered a niche product in the broader entertainment industry. Intellectuals generally ignored comics, viewing them at best as an irrelevant phenomenon and at worst as symptoms of moral and aesthetic degeneration, and therefore unworthy of any serious consideration; even the very few exceptions, such as Umberto Eco and Vittorio Spinazzola, focused on auteurs such as Schulz, Eisner or Crepax, without considering the wider, 'down and dirty' market in which *Satanik*, *Jacula* or *Splatter* lived and proliferated. From the 1960s through to the early 1990s, therefore, Italian Gothic horror comics remained relatively untouched by intellectualism and engagement – which does not mean, of course, that they were stupid or escapist, but that they could develop their discourses outside the pre-made frameworks of ideologies, and therefore intercept *abject* tensions and desires lying off the radars of 'highbrow' culture. Not incidentally, once they stopped being a mass phenomenon, rather addressing themselves to an increasingly self-referential fandom, Italian comics seemed to lose their cultural potential. The contemporary comics scene seems to be dominated by a 'retromaniac' attitude (Reynolds), constantly repeating and celebrating its own past.

As a consequence, the history of Italian Gothic horror comics is largely a thirty-year affair, spanning from 1962 (the appearance of *Diabolik* as a watershed moment, at the peak of the economic boom) to 1992 (Tiziano Sclavi's *Caccia alle streghe,* a homage paid to the short-lived season of

Splatterpunk comics, as well as a meta-reflection on the destabilising power of popular horror, at the collapse of the 'Second Republic'). This chapter will, therefore, primarily focus on this time span, analysing in order: the *fumetti neri* of the 1960s; the auteur experiments around 1968; the sexy-horror pocket-books of the 1970s and 1980s; the boom of *Dylan Dog* in the late 1980s; and, finally, the Splatterpunk vogue of 1989–92. In the conclusion, I will succinctly describe the post-1992 scene, particularly in its 'retromaniac' aspects.

Into the Black

Since the 1930s, nearly all Italian comic books had been incorporating Gothic-related themes (Castelli, *Horror* 8). Magazines such as *L'Avventuroso* and *L'Audace* had made their debut by publishing British and American comics featuring detectives or explorers, but soon began to create their own serials, often foraying into the 'dark' repertoire borrowed from popular literature and serial novels. All-Italian productions became a necessity after the mid-1930s and the increasing frictions between Fascist Italy and the international community, leading the regime to promote 'autarchy' in all fields, including the publishing industry. In 1938, Mussolini banned all translations from foreign comic books, with the exception of Walt Disney's productions: the great popularity of Disney characters, however, led Italian publishers to turn to local authors for new material, some of which possessed distinctly Gothic features. Federico Pedrocchi's and Nino Pagot's *Biancaneve e il Mago Basilisco* (1939) is a perfect example of a distinctly Italian tendency to exacerbate the grotesque, disturbing and uncanny elements of Disney imaginary, which would come to full maturity in the post-war years (Boschi, Gori and Sani 31). In 1949, Guido Martina and Angelo Bioletto published a quite explicit story (for Disney standards) entitled *L'Inferno di Topolino*, inspired by Dante's *Inferno* and graphically indebted to Gustave Doré's nineteenth-century illustrations (41–4). Later in the 1950s, Martina would impart new life to a minor villain of US comic strips, Macchia Nera, transforming him into an anti-hero of a sort that would be unthinkable in the United States, where the Comics Code Authority had just been introduced, following a most violent mass campaign against comics (57–8). The first story featuring Macchia Nera – Guido Martina's and Romano Scarpa's *Topolino e il doppio segreto di Macchia Nera* (1955) – is particularly disturbing, in that it involves hypnosis, mind control and attempted murder. The plot, indebted to the Alfred Hitchcock-like atmosphere that was popular at the time, even invites readers to suspect Mickey Mouse himself, thereby deteriorating the ideal of the hero being situated beyond all possible suspicion (57).

Chronologically, Macchia Nera anticipates the many anti-heroes dominating the Italian comic-book industry in the 1960s, through the so-called vogue of *fumetti neri*. The first and most famous of the *fumetti neri* is *Diabolik*, published by Astorina, which was created in 1962 by Angela Giussani and is still one of the best-selling Italian comic books. According to Giussani, the inspiration for *Diabolik* came from Marcel Allain's and Pierre Souvestre's Fantômas novels, and certainly, from a thematic viewpoint, Diabolik is a direct heir of the romanticised criminals/avengers of French popular literature, including Ponson du Terrail's Rocambole, Arthur Bernède's Judex and, precisely, Fantômas (Castelli *Fantômas*). The innovativeness of Giussani's operation, however, lies in the adoption of the comic-book format. With the help of her sister Luciana, Giussani wrote each issue of *Diabolik* as a self-contained episode, normally centred on one of Diabolik's criminal deeds, so that they could be enjoyed independently, even by the casual reader. The Giussani sisters and their cartoonists perfectly captured the aesthetics and mood of the economic boom, setting *Diabolik* in the Monte Carlo-like, imaginary state of Clerville, and modelling characters' features on those of popular film stars (for example, Grace Kelly provided the inspiration for Diabolik's partner, Eva Kant). First and foremost, *Diabolik* was the first Italian comic book explicitly labelled for 'adults only': the promise of explicit content cornered a large, heavily ignored chunk of the market, while the pocket-book format, expressly conceived for commuters and holiday readers, had the advantage of being both portable and easy to hide. This last element was particularly important given the severe condemnation, both moral and aesthetic, that *Diabolik* and its imitators met since their appearance. While the comic-book quickly became a bestseller, also thanks to its cheap price and to the Giussanis' hand-made yet effective marketing strategies, the *fumetti neri* became the object of judiciary sequestrations, attempts at censorship and disparaging press campaigns (Tesauro). As often happens in Italy, censure was not uniquely a prerogative of the conservative flank, and Communist intellectuals were particularly active in blaming *fumetti neri* for their disengagement, lack of morals and supposed escapism (see for example Quintavalle).

Diabolik was not strictly 'Gothic', but the Giussani sisters often adopted Gothicising strategies in order to emphasise the 'forbidden' flavour of their creation: labelled 'il fumetto del brivido' [the thrilling comic book], *Diabolik* featured episodes with titles such as 'Il re del terrore' [The King of Terror] or 'Sepolto vivo!' [Buried Alive!]; moreover, its first two issues featured illustrators possessing a remarkably Gothicising style, such as the so-far unidentified 'Zarcone' (nicknamed 'Il tedesco' [The German]) and Kalissa, the former's work being replaced by more traditional graphics in later reprintings. Epigones would make these Gothic connections more explicit: the protagonist of Max Bunker's and Magnus's *Kriminal* (Editoriale Corno, 1964–74) wears a skeleton costume; *Satanik*, also created by Bunker and Magnus (Editoriale Corno, 1964–74), centres on a scientist transformed into a killing witch thanks to a potion. Most of all, the connection of these comic books with the Gothic mode lies in the challenge they pose to public morals: by romanticising criminals, heroifying homicide, and portraying sexual unruliness, they deal with the same *abject* concurrently explored by Gothic cinema and popular literature.

Tales from the Crypt

With the exception of single horror-oriented stories in non-horror comic books, such as Bonelli's western series *Tex*, horror comics published in Italy in the 1960s were almost exclusively translations from American magazines such as *Creepy* and *Eerie*. Before the end of the decade, a selection from the former appeared as a pocket-book for Mondadori, testifying to an increasing interest in horror fiction on the part of mainstream publishers (Bianchi).

The watershed year is 1969 – perhaps not incidentally, quite a crucial year in Italy's contemporary history, characterised by protests, political turmoil and terrorist attacks, culminating in the bomb placed by a neofascist group, on 12 December, in central Milan. When the bomb exploded in the National Bank of Agriculture, killing seventeen people and harming eighty-eight, news stands displayed the freshly published first issue of *Horror*, one of the first horror magazines entirely made of Italian material. On the same day, the Cortina art gallery in central Milan was expected to host the launch of Dino Buzzati's *Poema a fumetti*, the first Italian graphic novel (and one of the first worldwide), revisiting the myth of Orpheus and Eurydice in a contemporary urban-Gothic setting: when the bomb exploded, all events across the city were cancelled, and the launch never took place.

Published in Milan by Gino Sansoni, *Horror* had been ideated by Pier Carpi, a specialist in esotericism and the managing editor of Sansoni's magazines, and by Alfredo Castelli, a versatile comic-book author with multiple interests in all aspects of pop culture. Although Castelli's immediate reference was the American EC Comics of the 1950s, *Horror* was by no means a pulp magazine: instead of the pocket-book format, it presented itself as an all-round journal, breaking up comics with articles, reportages and contributions from writers such as Giovanni Arpino and Guido Piovene. Stories were generally of excellent quality: Sansoni had a generous policy about royalties, and in its short life (only twenty-two issues) *Horror* managed to gather the élite of Italian illustrators (Castelli, *Horror* 12). Experimentalism was at the core of Carpi and Castelli's project. Although most stories followed the surprise-ending model of the EC Comics or *Creepy*, *Horror* hosted underground authors such as Max Capa and Maurizio Turchet, as well as experiments of various kinds: a comic strip coupled with a music stave (Carpi and Carlo Peroni's *Clown*, featuring the compositions of Alceo Guatelli) or a short story written by Castelli and entirely illustrated through the enlarged details of a banknote. The magazine's high production costs, however, caused its decline: the publisher was forced to keep a quite expensive cover price, and *Horror* closed in November 1972, although single stories were continuously reprinted in a series of pocket-books throughout the 1970s and beyond. The magazine left an indelible legacy in the history of Italian comics: the Splatterpunk vogue of the 1990s would pay homage to *Horror* by re-editing *Il nostro delitto quotidiano*, a selection of Castelli's stories which originally appeared in the magazine and were collected as a single volume in 1970.

Poema a fumetti is only apparently unrelated to publications such as *Horror*, and not exclusively for reasons of chronological proximity. Buzzati had been one of the very few Italian writers to speak of *fumetti neri* in non-derogatory terms; he knew Sansoni, and an interview with him appeared in *Horror*. The experimentalism bringing him to the graphic novel, in an age when the notion itself of 'graphic novel' was yet to come, is close, in terms of background and attitude, to the deliberate deconstruction of visual codes undertaken by Carpi and Castelli. The embarrassment and disdain displayed by critics, when *Poema* appeared, shows well how their misunderstanding of Buzzati's work was rooted in their lack of knowledge about comics and their potential as a medium (Buzzati 235–8). *Poema* should, instead, be read within the same cultural background from whence the experimentalist and auteurist side of *Horror* had emerged, influenced by the inputs and stimuli of pop art and counterculture. Whereas Castelli explored the narrative potential of comics, and Pier Carpi mixed esotericism and politics in a series of grotesque, surreal stories illustrated by Marco Rostagno, Buzzati employed the medium as a way of developing an elegant reflection on death and eternity, tended between Urban Wyrd (a small street in central

Milan as the anteroom of the otherworld) and folk horror (the pictures illustrating Orfi/Orpheus's song).

Dance of the Sexy-Vampires

The 1970s saw the firm presence of horror and Gothic themes in all areas of the comic-book industry. American comics, especially those published by Warren (*Creepy*, *Eerie*, *Vampirella*) were regularly translated, and, from 1974 to 1976, the Editoriale Corno published *Il Corriere della Paura*, an anthological magazine collecting the horror stories published by Marvel Comics in periodicals such as *Vampire Tales*, *Tales of the Zombie*, and *Haunt of Horror*. Non-horror series published by Daim Press (later Sergio Bonelli Editore) such as *Tex*, *Zagor*, or *Mister No* frequently hosted mad scientists, monsters and black magic, inspired by the 'Universal Classic Monsters' of the 1930s and 1940s; in 1974, in the magazine *Corriere dei Ragazzi*, Mino Milani and Aldo Di Gennaro created *Il Maestro*, an occult detective series heralding 1980s heroes such as Martin Mystère and Dylan Dog.

The most prominent phenomenon of this decade, however, was the proliferation of erotic-horror pocket-books, whose origins date to the late 1960s. Renzo Barbieri and Giorgio Cavedon's publishing house ErreGi had tried to enter the market of *fumetti neri* in their early days, but Barbieri had later discovered that erotica could be more rewarding in terms of sales: inspired by Angélique, the uninhibited adventuress portrayed by Michèle Mercier in a series of films, his comic book *Isabella* (published from 1967) quickly reached sales of over 100,000 copies. In 1969, while in the US Warren Publishing was launching *Vampirella*, Barbieri and Cavedon gave birth to *Jacula*, a series combining erotica and horror that would revolutionise the Italian comic-book market. The increasingly explicit adventures of the eponymous lady vampire remained in print until 1982, inspiring a series of imitators, as had happened with *Diabolik* a few years before. Generally entitled to a female heroine with supernatural powers and a 'diabolical' name (Jacula, Lucifera, Maghella, Belzeba, Zora, Sukia, Ulula, Cimiteria), these periodicals freely recombined plots and situations of Gothic-horror literature and cinema, with a peculiarly grotesque and humorous taste. Eroticism, more and more explicit throughout the years, was a constant element; erotic scenes and situations involved a broad set of sexual practices and paraphilias, usually treated without any sense of political correctness and with a distinctly libertarian approach (*Jacula*, quite unusually for the time, had a discreet number of female readers). Most of these comics were published by the two houses born out of the break-up between the two founders of ErreGi: while Cavedon renamed his publishing house as Ediperiodici, carrying on the publication of *Jacula* and launching new series such as *Oltretomba*, *Lucifera* and *Maghella*, Barbieri founded Edifumetto, whose most prominent periodicals were *Zora*, *Sukia* and *Belzeba*. All these periodicals disappeared in the 1980s, unable to face the competition of home video erotica, and have since then acquired a cult status.

Horror Fest

From the late 1970s and throughout the 1980s, the arrival of anime from Japan and the liberalisation of the TV market decimated the Italian comic-book industry. By the end of the 1990s (and nowadays), of the many publishing houses based in Milan, only Astorina and Daim Press/ Sergio Bonelli Editore survived. In both cases, evergreen series such as *Diabolik* and *Tex* doubtlessly made the difference. Bonelli, however, would not only endure the crisis, but would give birth to the last (for now) mass phenomenon of Italian comics: a horror comic book named *Dylan Dog*.

Dylan Dog was entirely the creation of Tiziano Sclavi, who had joined Bonelli – together with Alfredo Castelli – after the editorial team of *Corriere dei Ragazzi* disbanded in the late 1970s. In 1982, Castelli had created *Martin Mystère*, a comic book inspired by Pseudoarchaeology that significantly distanced itself from the traditionally exotic settings of the Bonelli series, mostly taking place in the Old West and/or in exotic countries: by proposing a sort of contemporary, New York-based Indiana Jones, *Martin Mystère* inaugurated a new wave of Bonelli comics, exploring the new trends of popular culture. *Dylan Dog* was conceived with the same attitude: a contemporary horror comic, mindful of the innovations which had been occurring in horror cinema (George Romero, Tobe Hooper, Wes Craven) and literature (Thomas Tryon, Stephen King) in the most recent decades. Although Bonelli himself did not particularly believe in it, the series was launched in September 1986, without fanfare. Four years later, it had become a veritable mass phenomenon: the issue of April 1990 had a run of 185,000, which increased to 200,000 in June, even surpassing the sales of *Tex* in the following months. Nowadays, Sclavi's *Dylan Dog* stories of 1986–92 may be regarded as one of the milestones of comic-book history worldwide, together with coeval works such as Frank Miller's *The Dark Knight Returns* (1986), Alan Moore and Dave Gibbons's *Watchmen* (1986–7), and Neil Gaiman's *Sandman* (1989).

It is difficult to account, even briefly, for the reasons behind this success. Certainly, *Dylan Dog* managed to attract a varied audience, including girls – a target that was traditionally excluded by Bonelli products, and which instead formed an important part of *Dylan Dog*'s fanbase. Sclavi's writing, saturated with citations from 'highbrow' literature, pop and heavy metal music, and the visual arts, could give the impression that *Dylan Dog* was somewhat 'more than a comic-book', justifying the interest of those readers who regarded comics as a childish pastime – an impression corroborated by illustrious endorsements, including that of Umberto Eco. *Dylan Dog*, after all, was a perfect example of the postmodernist attitude as defined by Eco in 1983, 'Irony, metalinguistic play, enunciation squared'. The very title of the first issue, *L'alba dei morti viventi*, was a citation from Romero (*Dawn of the Dead*, 1978); entire sequences were directly taken from Romero's earlier *Night of the Living Dead* (1968); Dylan Dog had the features of Rupert Everett, and Groucho, his assistant, was a Groucho Marx look-alike, as if nothing in the *Dylan Dog* universe could be but the citation of some already-existing figment of pop culture. And yet, first and foremost, *Dylan Dog* managed to capture a *Zeitgeist* that was beyond postmodernism, and had more to do with the mixture of uneasiness and disengagement, estrangement and lack of reference points that characterised the so-called Generation X, and which was voiced, in the same years, by grunge music or by novelists such as Bret Easton Ellis. From this viewpoint, writer Paolo Di Orazio perfectly pinpoints the question, when he writes that *Dylan Dog* was a 'fumetto *sull'*orrore, più che *del*' [more a comic book about horror than a horror comic book] (18): an aspect that was not caught by the many imitators that followed, merely reiterating the occult-detective formula without grasping the mixture of Romantic anarchism, ennui, and surrealism that characterised Sclavi's creature (e.g. *Elton Cop*, Edizioni Center TV, 1991–2; *Gordon Link*, Editoriale Dardo, 1991–3; *Demon Hunter*, Xenia Edizioni, 1993–6; *Dick Drago*, Fenix, 1994). The same misunderstanding would unfortunately characterise the work of several of Sclavi's successors, as well as other Bonelli experiments in the horror genre, including successful series such as *Magico Vento* (1997–2010) or *Dampyr* (2000, in press). One of the few exceptions is the work of Alessandro Bilotta, perhaps not incidentally a Generation X writer (b. 1977), who seemed to capture the essence of Sclavi's legacy in the short-lived comic-book series *Valter Buio* (Star Comics, 2010–11), and later in his own stories for *Dylan Dog*.

Witch-Hunt

In October 1986, distributors informed Sergio Bonelli that the first issue of *Dylan Dog* seemed to have sold well below the average: in slang, it was *morto in edicola* [a news stand stillborn]. One month later, official data confirmed that sales had slightly passed the threshold of 50,000 copies – which was, at that time, the minimum allowed for a publication to survive. Quite tellingly, on Halloween 1986 – between those two months in which the fate of *Dylan Dog* (and, indirectly, of Italian horror comic books) was decided – writer David J. Schow spoke at the World Fantasy Convention in Providence, coining an expression that perfectly captured the atmosphere of those years, the same influencing Sclavi's creature. The term was 'Splatterpunk': Paul Sammon's anthology *Splatterpunks*, which popularised the term by collecting tales by Joe Lansdale, Clive Barker and George R. R. Martin, would appear in 1990, when *Dylan Dog* was already a cult phenomenon.

The popularity of *Dylan Dog* showed that the ironic explicitness of contemporary horror could be appealing to Italian audiences. As early as June 1989, publisher ACME (founded by editor Francesco Coniglio and cartoonist Silver) launched the periodical *Splatter*: the idea was not so much to imitate *Dylan Dog*, but rather to combine the formula of Sansoni's *Horror* – short, direct and self-contained narratives; top-quality comics – with the absolute freedom and explicitness of the exploitation comics of the 1970s and 1980s. Experienced authors such as Attilio Micheluzzi and Roberto dal Prà were sided by newcomers, some of whom would later become famous in mainstream comics (e.g. Nicola Mari and Bruno Brindisi). *Splatter* jumped to selling around 30,000 copies per month while, at the same time, creating a vast and loyal fanbase, thanks to Paolo Di Orazio's editorship and his constant correspondence with readers (Rosati 12). In 1990, *Splatter* was followed by two more magazines: *Mostri*, managed by the same team and devoted to horror in the broadest possible sense, and *Nosferatu*, more focused on classic horror. The success of *Splatter* also invited minor publishers to align themselves with the new trend, giving birth to a cluster of anthological magazines inspired by the same formula – short narratives, gory taste, and normalisation of violence. The vast majority of these imitations were published by Ediperiodici, the forefront house of the horror-porn boom of the previous decades, bearing titles such as *Gore Scanners*, *Bloob* and *Follia sanguinaria* (1990–1), *Atroci delitti* (1990), and *Cervelli marci* (1991). Max Bunker Press launched *Angel Dark* (1990–1) – not an anthology magazine, but an exploitation series with distinctly gory aesthetics; Edizioni Scorpio and, later, Edizioni Eden published *Profondo Rosso* (1990–1), endorsed by Dario Argento.

All these publications entered the eye of the storm once the weekly magazine *L'Espresso* published a dossier on horror comics, including the sectarian, uninformed opinion of a psychoanalyst deliberately suggesting a connection between the popularity of *Splatter* and *Dylan Dog* and juvenile delinquency (Roberto Cotroneo 'Che horror!' [1990], now in Rosati 318–25). Soon after, Silver and Ferruccio Giromini (the director of *Splatter*) were reported and tried after a parent found his son reading *Primi delitti* [Early Crimes], Di Orazio's earliest book, published in December 1989 as a supplement to *Splatter*. The protagonists of Di Orazio's tales were children: the book was accused of 'pornography' (*L'Avvenire*, 18 October 1990, now in Rosati 314) or of being a 'guide', teaching children how to murder their parents (*L'Unità*, 18 October 1990, now in Rosati 317). Even a parliamentary inquiry was begun, asking for horror comics to be banned and meeting a high consensus from the whole parliamentary spectrum, including the left. The fear of new trials and the pervasiveness of the moralising campaign by the press was fatal to weak publishers such as ACME: after bargaining their plea, Silver and Giromini were forced to close *Splatter*. The last issue appeared in May 1991, and so happened to *Mostri* and *Nosferatu*; by the end of the same year, almost all of their imitators had disappeared. *Dylan Dog* could survive only because it was supported by the whole Bonelli house. Although Sclavi was slowly abandoning the series, in June 1992 he and Pietro Dall'Agnol published a story explicitly referring to the censure against horror comics and tellingly entitled *Caccia alle streghe*: the story's underlying message was that 'gli inquisitori sono ancora tra noi. [. . .] hanno tolto il saio e indossano un più rassicurante completo borghese' [inquisitors are still among us. They have removed their frocks and wear a more reassuring, middle-class business suit] (Sclavi and Dall'Agnol 103–4). Quite ironically, *Caccia alle streghe* would prove itself to be *Dylan Dog*'s all-time bestseller: since then, the publisher imposed that the series should abandon all splatter aesthetics and became a more conventional occult-detective comic. The 'New Wave of Italian Splatterpunk' (Di Orazio 34) was over, at least as far as comic books were concerned. It had been a short-seasoned yet prophetic phenomenon, not only in that it heralded the literary movement of *cannibali* of the late 1990s (Brolli), but primarily because it anticipated the upsurge of heinous crimes plaguing Italy in the following decades, triggering the morbid (and, often, truly pornographic) attention of the same general press that had so hastily condemned the portrayal of violence in works of fiction.

Conclusion

Normalisation killed the Italian Gothic-horror comic-book industry. In the 1990s, as we have seen, all the Milan publishers of the economic boom closed one after the other, incapable of adapting themselves to the new market and thereby depriving the scene of their often homemade yet vital editorial care. Japanese *manga* and American superhero comics started to massively invade news stands, while former readers grew up, and for the younger ones, cinema, videogames and literature could vastly supply all the extreme horror, violence, and gore they would have requested from comic-books in the past (attempts at resuscitating *Horror* and *Splatter*, in 2003 and 2013 respectively, were significantly unsuccessful). At the same time, the entire Gothic-horror segment of the market was about to be dominated by Retromania, as was already happening with pop culture broadly intended. In cinema, the 2000s would be characterised by endless remakes, reboots and adaptations of horror classics: the same happened with the inglorious yet most lively past of Italian Gothic-horror comics of the *trente glorieuses* 1962–92.

In recent years, *Diabolik* was celebrated by an exhibition at the Milano Urban Center, and *Satanik* was re-edited as a supplement to a football newspaper. We possess valuable, careful new editions of *Jacula* and *Zora*, and a whole series of new, glossy comic books in which contemporary artists pay homage to the sexy-vampires of Edifumetto and Ediperiodici. Complete collections of *Horror* are increasingly overpriced on Ebay, and Castelli has edited a selection of his own stories in a glazed volume, filled with apparatuses. Anthologies from *Splatter* are repeatedly re-assembled and re-sold with no clamour, and *Primi delitti* is widely recognised as a landmark of 1990s independent literature. Even *Dylan Dog* has undergone a reboot, through a six-issues miniseries (January–June 2020) that changed everything not to change anything; and although new comics still appear (the most striking example being 'Samuel Stern', published by Bugs Comics since 2019), they are mostly directed at a defined fanbase, without any possibility of becoming mass phenomena. As stated above, Gothic-horror comics are now a part of the country's memory landscape, but have lost all capacity for generating scandal. One may consider this a minor problem.

Bibliography

Bianchi, Pietro (ed.), *Le spiacevoli notti di Zio Tibia* (Milan: Mondadori, 1969).
Boschi, Luca, Leonardo Gori and Andrea Sani (eds), *I Disney italiani. Dal 1930 al 1990, la storia dei fumetti di Topolino e Paperino realizzati in Italia* (Bologna: Granata Press, 1990).
Brolli, Daniele (ed.), *Gioventù cannibale. La prima antologia italiana dell'orrore estremo* (Turin: Einaudi, 1996).
Buzzati, Dino, *Poema a fumetti* [1969], edited by Lorenzo Viganò (Milan: Mondadori, 2017).
Camilletti, Fabio, *Italia Lunare. Gli anni Sessanta e l'occulto* (Oxford: Peter Lang, 2018).
Castelli, Alfredo, *Fantômas. Un secolo di terrore* (Rome: Coniglio Editore, 2011).
Castelli, Alfredo (ed.), *Horror. La rivista italiana dell'insolito a fumetti. I racconti scritti da Alfredo Castelli* (Reggio Emilia: Editoriale Cosmo, 2019).
Di Orazio, Paolo, 'Primi relitti', in *Primi delitti 30 Years* (Trieste: Independent Legions Publishing, 2019), pp. 9–36.
Eco, Umberto, 'Postscript to *The Name of the Rose*', in *The Name of the Rose* [1983], trans. William Weaver and Richard Dixon (New York: Harcourt, 2014). Kindle edn.
Hajdu, David, *The Ten-Cent Plague: The Great Comic-Book Scare and How It Changed America* (New York: Farrar, Straus and Giroux, 2008).
Milani, Mino, and Aldo Di Gennaro, *Il Maestro* (Bologna: Nona Arte, 2017).
Preianò, Anna, 'Personaggi Horror. Intervista ad Alfredo Castelli', in Massimiliano Boschini, Fabio Camilletti and Anna Preianò (eds), *L'uomo che credeva nei Vampiri* (Rome: Profondo Rosso, 2018), pp. 273–6.
Quintavalle, Arturo Carlo (ed.), *Nero a strisce. La reazione a fumetti* (Parma: Istituto di Storia dell'Arte, 1971).
Reynolds, Simon, *Retromania: Pop Culture's Addiction to Its Own Past* (London: Faber and Faber, 2011).
Rosati, Edoardo (ed.), *Splatter* (Milan: Rizzoli, 2013).
Sclavi, Tiziano, and Pietro Dall'Agnol, *Caccia alle streghe* [1992] (Milan: Bao Publishing, 2015).
Tesauro, Alessandro, *Neri come il carbone. I fumetti neri degli anni Sessanta* (Giffoni Valle Piana: Alessandro Tesauro Editore, 2014).

Chapter 11

Gothic Music
Eduardo Vitolo

In Italian music, the Gothic (meaning a musical style as well as an aesthetic category, variously dealing with the macabre, the lugubrious, the excessive and the occult) has assumed several different forms over the decades, from progressive rock to the recent wave of Italian Occult Psychedelia and different styles of Metal – Heavy, Doom, Black. These underground manifestations were seldom visible in Italian mainstream culture (in which, however, references to Gothic themes, albeit ironic, are not uncommon; Camilletti 41) and often had English lyrics in order to reach an international audience. Many of the bands in question, as we will see, come from provincial parts of Italy, rather than metropolitan centres, which illustrates the marginality and underground status of this current in Italian music. At the same time, by continuously presenting intermedial references, the different manifestations of the Gothic in Italian culture represent a long-standing element of disturbance and testify to the wide and persistent interest in these themes and styles.

Defining the Gothic in music is not a simple task. While there is a specific 'goth' current in contemporary alternative music, the influence of the Gothic cannot be limited to that particular form; rather, it needs to be investigated in a variety of genres and subcultures. Most importantly, the Gothic in music is not limited to lyrics and sound; it also manifests itself in several acts of self-fashioning that range from stage costumes to the use of make-up, from album covers to the interior design of clubs and venues. Before the explosion of the Gothic subculture in the 1980s, several bands were labelled as Gothic, from The Doors (in 1967, music critic John Stickney called their style 'Gothic rock') to The Velvet Underground and Nico, the latter's solo work and the Shock-rock of Alice Cooper. Nevertheless, these bands do not belong to the Gothic subculture in the strictest sense.

Gothic influences in contemporary alternative music manifest themselves in two main ways. Firstly, the term 'Gothic' (or 'goth') is used to describe Post-Punk bands such as The Cure, Siouxsie and the Banshees, Bauhaus, The Sisters of Mercy and Joy Division. The last of these was labelled as 'Gothic' in comparison with contemporary mainstream pop music by their manager Tony Wilson on the BBC TV show *Something Else* in 1978 (Bibby 239). Characterised by a minimal sound, a pulsating bass, the use of keyboards, insistent drums and lyrics focused mostly on love, loneliness and death, goth music rapidly became popular in the United Kingdom and abroad, inspiring countless bands and giving rise to a variety of ever-changing styles.

The second form the Gothic assumes in contemporary music goes beyond the Goth genre. It can be found in Progressive and Hard Rock and later in Heavy Metal, starting with the British band Black Sabbath. The album *Black Sabbath* (1970) established an aesthetic and musical imagery based on the excessive, the macabre and the occult, and on a dark and heavy sound that has influenced nearly all Heavy Metal bands since. As Bryan Bardine argues, in the 1970–83 period, 'bands including Black Sabbath, Iron Maiden, Judas Priest, Saxon and Motorhead, to name a few, incorporated various aspects of the Gothic into their lyrics, stage clothes, shows and album covers, and in doing so helped to give heavy metal a stronger, more powerful image with fans and media alike' (125).[1] As we will see, both tendencies proved to be hugely influential in Italian underground music scenes.

The Origins: The 1960s and 1970s

If the United Kingdom can be considered the homeland of both the literary Gothic and its musical descendants, in Italy, from the late 1960s, several bands contributed to creating a dark soundscape that, to quote Canadian music critic Martin Popoff, 'creeped people out a lot' in the following years (interviewed in Vitolo, *Children of Doom* 266). Defined either as a typically Italian 'Dark Sound' (a label recently used in specialised magazines)[2] or simply as a form of progressive rock with occult influences that was contemporary with Black Sabbath,[3] the origins of Gothic influences in Italian music can be traced back to the 1960s and the work of Antonio Bartoccetti. Through two parallel projects – Jacula (like the contemporary *fumetto nero* of the same name; see Chapter 11 of this companion) and Antonius Rex – Bartoccetti established a 'Mediterranean' approach to Gothic music. Besides the name of the former of these projects, the connection with vampire-themed erotic-horror comic books is strengthened by the logo of Jacula and, in the case of Antonius Rex, by the title and cover of the album *Zora* (Tickel,

1977; *Zora la vampira* was another important comic-book series at the time).

Since his early work, Bartoccetti distinguished himself not only through his music, but also through his relationship, deemed scandalous by many, with mediums and esoteric groups, which play an important role in his albums. According to Bartoccetti, the melodies on which his music is based were revealed to him by a spirit evoked by the medium Franz Parthenzy and later played on guitar and recorded. Only 300 copies were made of Bartoccetti's first album, *In Cauda Semper Stat Venenum* (1969) and, according to the author (Vitolo, *Magister Dixit* 43), many of these ended up in the hands of the members of several occult sects across Europe. Like Black Sabbath, whose debut album had yet to be released, Bartoccetti's music merges the ritual sound of a pipe organ with powerful guitar riffs, while he sings lyrics inspired by esotericism and European romantic and Gothic masterpieces, including James Macpherson's Ossian cycle (Vitolo, *Magister dixit* 45). Nevertheless, both critics and fans cast doubts on the alleged 300-copy release of this album, which was reissued (or released for the first time?) by Black Widow Records in 2001 (Vitolo, *Magister dixit* 209–10).

Bartoccetti's long career, which continues to this day, is rich in excursions into the occult. *Neque Semper Arcum Tendit Rex*, produced as part of the Antonius Rex project, was released in 1974 in 400 privately distributed copies and reissued in 2002 by Black Widow Records. It is characterised by obscure pipe organ insertions, lyrics condemning modern society, and the complete absence of percussion. In the song *Aquila non capit muscas*, for instance, Bartoccetti plays with a medieval imagery made of witches and tortures:

> Affidiamo questo compito
> alla più giovane delle nostre streghe,
> mentre il fabbro del castello
> ha già preparato la maschera di ferro
> con griglie sottili ed una porta.
> Ecco: questo è il momento,
> le mani di Wandessa
> stringono il topo più affamato.
> Apri la porta della maschera
> e libera la bestia
> che deturperà il tuo viso,
> che si nutrirà del tuo sangue,
> dei tuoi denti,
> dei tuoi occhi,
> nei secoli dei secoli.

[We assign this task / to the youngest of our witches / while the castle's blacksmith / has already prepared the iron mask / with a thin grill and a gap. / Here: now it is the moment, / Wandessa's hands / hold the hungriest rat. / Open the mask's split / and release the beast / that will ruin your face, / that will feed on your blood, / on your teeth, / on your eyes, / forever and ever.]

The image of the iron mask being used as a torture tool is reminiscent of the opening scene of Mario Bava's *La maschera del demonio* (1960), in which a similar device is used to kill the witch portrayed by Barbara Steele. Bartoccetti's other albums from the 1970s are connected to the deaths of some former collaborators, a circumstance that contributed to the sinister fame of the musician who, however, was rehabilitated by critics as an under-recognised precursor of Gothic manifestations in Italian music.

This hybridisation of Progressive Rock and Gothic themes can be found in some other bands from the period that failed to gain a considerable following – interestingly, in the 1970s, the genre was still called 'new pop'; in 1973, on the occasion of Black Sabbath's first Italian tour, the posters promoted them as 'il più rivoluzionario gruppo pop' [the most revolutionary pop band ever]. One such band is Spettri, established in Florence in 1964, whose album of the same name (1972) merges horror-inspired atmospheres and guitar tuning like that of Deep Purple and Black Sabbath. In their lyrics, however, the supernatural is employed only as a metaphor to comment on socio-political issues. Metamorfosi, a band formed in Rome at the end of the 1960s, does something similar on their album *Inferno*, which uses the model of Dante's *Divina Commedia* to discuss crime and politics in contemporary Italy. A different kind of literary inspiration, more markedly Gothic, predominates in the music of Tuscany's Goad, founded in the 1970s and still active to this day. Their lyrics continuously make references to the work of Howard Phillips Lovecraft and Edgar Allan Poe, and their album *The Wood* (2006) was recorded in a purportedly haunted mansion (Vitolo, *Sub terra* 277).

Inextricably connected to the international success of Italian horror and *giallo* cinema, Claudio Simonetti and Massimo Morante's Goblin is probably the band that achieved the greatest popular and critical success. Their suspenseful soundtracks for movies such as Dario Argento's *Profondo rosso* (1975), *Tenebre* (1982) and *Phenomena* (1985), Joe D'Amato's *Buio omega* (1978), George Romero's *Dawn of the Dead* (1978) and Michele Soavi's *La chiesa* (1989) represent a blend of Gothic atmospheres and Progressive Rock, which characterises Italian approaches to the genre and has influenced several other bands. Furthermore, Goblin's success is the result of their soundtracks, which reinforces the connection between Gothic music and genre cinema in Italy, a connection that has been reprised in recent years by Italian Occult Psychedelia. Given its purely instrumental dimension, Goblin's music cannot be considered strictly Gothic, but it has become the quintessential music *of* the Gothic and as such has been reinterpreted by other bands.

The end of the 1970s also saw the debut of Steve Sylvester (Stefano Silvestri) and Paul Chain (Paolo Catena)'s Death SS, from the Marche region, one of Italy's first Heavy Metal bands. Like Bartoccetti, Death SS, especially in the beginning, showed great interest in the occult and a strong taste for the macabre and provocation, as evidenced by the band's name, a shortening of 'The Death of Steve Sylvester', alluding (even in the artwork) to Nazi Germany's military corps. As Sylvester states in his autobiography (*Il negromante* 78), the members of the band have a taste for scenographic settings, such as cemeteries, abandoned houses and deconsecrated churches. Furthermore, the band's musicians are recruited not only on the basis of their technical ability, but also for their interest in the occult. The search for tombstones and decadent settings for the band's photo sessions, the rituals allegedly celebrated in the hills near Pesaro and the frequent visits to deconsecrated churches in search of stage material are all key elements in the creation of the musical and, most importantly, aesthetic style of Death SS.

The originality of the extreme imagery of Death SS is evident in their first EP, *Evil Metal* (1983), and even more so in the later compilation of their early works *The Story of Death SS 1977–1984* (1987), which collects all the material composed with guitarist Paul Chain from 1977 onwards. The self-definition 'Evil Metal' is a good starting point for understanding Death SS's sound, which merges a lugubrious theatricality (reprised from Shock-rock bands such as Alice Cooper) and simple and straightforward songs, inspired by Punk and NWOBHM (the acronym for New Wave of British Heavy Metal, the predominant style of Heavy Metal music in Britain between the late 1970s and the 1980s, characterised by fast and aggressive songs). The tracks of their first full studio album, *. . . In Death of Steve Sylvester* (1988), exploit a whole variety of classic Gothic monsters, from *Vampire* to *Black Mummy*, from *Zombie* to *Werewolf*, and include a cover of Alice Cooper's ballad *I Love the Dead*.

Steve Sylvester has never hidden the importance not only of horror and supernatural fiction and cinema, but also of erotic-horror Italian comic books to his imagery. Published since the 1960s and already having influenced Bartoccetti, the *fumetti neri* played an important role in shaping Death SS's aesthetic. On several occasions ('Il fumetto erotico'), Steve Sylvester discussed how, as a child, he was fascinated by the excessive, bizarre, and colourful covers of such publications, which he came across at an uncle's house. Not only did Sylvester become an avid collector; he later commissioned the artists of the *fumetto nero*, in particular Emanuele Taglietti and Alex Horley (Alessandro Orlandelli), to design the covers of his albums. Consequently, Death SS's albums catalyse and celebrate a period in Italian comics that anticipated the plots and atmospheres of American and European horror and Gothic cinema.

The artistic journey of Death SS was tormented by polemics, (false) accusations of Satanism, break-ups and sudden deaths. Singer Steve Sylvester and guitarist Paul Chain finally parted ways in 1984. Sylvester, after a short hiatus, continued his work with Death SS (while simultaneously revealing his affiliation to Aleister Crowley's Ordo Templi Orientiis). Paul Chain, on the contrary, began a successful solo career, abandoning provocation and references to Satanism in favour of a personal spiritual path, as stated on the retro cover of the album programmatically titled *Detaching from Satan* (1984).

Goth or Metal? The 1980s

In Italy as well as abroad, the 1980s were characterised by the diffusion of Goth Rock (which, in Italy, is known by the more generic label 'Dark Rock'), predominantly in the form of New Wave, a genre that reprises and discontinues some of the stylistic traits of the previous decade.[4] New Wave is not inherently Gothic, but it influenced the development of Dark Wave, characterised by slow tempos, low pitches and minor keys, which in turn reprises the innovations of Post-Punk Goth Rock (although the two genres often overlap). One of the first and most important New Wave works in Italy is Diaframma's debut album *Siberia* (1984); significantly, the band started as a Joy Division covers band. Diaframma's lyrics depict a depressive, hopeless world, illuminated by a dim and oblique sunlight (the song that gives the name to the album opens with the line 'Il ghiaccio si confonde con il cielo' [The ice merges with the sky]), and where sentimental relationships are confined to the past ('Scordati di me al più presto' [Forget me as fast as you can], Miro Sassolini sings in *Desiderio del nulla*). Other bands made similar debuts but later moved to a more mainstream sound, as in the case, for instance, of Litfiba, whose *Trilogia del Potere* (*Desaparecido*, 1985, *17 re*, 1986, and *Litfiba 3*, 1988) merges Dark Wave and Punk with politically-committed lyrics, which gained them a significant following.

The three albums by Modà, founded by Andrea Chimenti, tend toward the New Romantic side of New Wave and certain aspects of David Bowie's work, especially from his Berlin period. Neon, after a successful debut album (*Rituals*, 1985) and a twenty-five-date tour around Europe, broke up in 1990 only to reunite at the end of the decade.

While the bands mentioned all come from the Florence area, other parts of Italy also contributed to the diffusion of New Wave's aesthetics and musical style. Giancarlo Onorato's Underground Life, formed in Monza in the late 1970s, produced an English-language debut album titled *The Fox* in 1983 and, in 1984, signed a record deal with Alberto Pirelli's I.R.A. Records. Together with Diaframma, Modà and Liftiba, Underground Life ended up on the compilation *Catalogue Issue*, which is greatly representative of the New Wave scene of the time. Far from being relegated to the underground scene, however, New Wave sounds can be found in mainstream music of the time, in the work of artists such as Franco Battiato and Giuni Russo. Other bands were characterised by a darker sound and greater use of electronic instruments, such as Kirlian Camera (whose name comes from a machine purported to be able to photograph the aura of the human body). The band became famous both in Italy and internationally thanks to a collaboration with Vangelis for their single *Pulsar* and was the first Italian band to sign a contract with Virgin Records.

Gothic elements in Italian music from the 1980s are not limited to the Dark/New Wave, but can also be identified in Heavy Metal, especially Doom Metal, a genre typified by slow tempos, low-tuned guitars and funereal and melancholic imagery, heavily influenced by Black Sabbath. Robert Measles (Roberto Morbioli) formed the band Black Hole in Verona in 1981. The band's first album, *Land of Mystery* (1985), is marked by deliberately rough production and a spectral sound, with lugubrious keyboards, and the album cover depicts a stylised cemetery surmounted by a skull. The lyrics underline and enhance this lugubrious atmosphere. *Bells of Death* open with the image of a funeral ('There's silence for a moment of remembrance. / With a slow motion a coffin enters in a great church. / All the presents kneeled pray for the dead'), while *Spectral World* recounts an out-of-body experience ('My body is divided in two parts. / I'm suspended in the air, I haven't a weight / Strange imagines and magic visions around me. / I'm a spirit. I haven't a body and shape. Now I'm inside the darkness / Under control of the evil's eyes'). As is often the case with Italian Metal bands, the lyrics are not always written in stylistically and grammatically correct English. This is, however, the international language of Heavy Metal, and Italian bands singing in Italian are extremely rare.

Abruzzo-based Requiem, led by Mario Di Donato, employed sacred vestments (all authentic, not replicas) and attempted to create a ritual atmosphere on stage, 'per fuggire dalle fasi ossessive della vita moderna dove tutto è permesso e concesso, senza paura di sconfinare in campi pericolosi per se stessi e per gli altri come l'esoterismo' [to escape the obsessive rhythms of modern life in which everything is allowed and granted, without the fear of trespassing on fields that might be dangerous for one's self and for others, such as esotericism] (Di Donato in Vitolo, *Sub terra* 271). Upon Requiem's premature break-up, Di Donato insisted on an aesthetic merging of the sacred and the blasphemous with the band The Black, which is still active to this day. In particular, in the album *Infernus Paradisus Et Purgatorius* (1990), Di Donato and The Black made reference to an ancestral, pre-modern religiosity, which, in later works, is inspired by elements of Abruzzo's landscape and folklore, such as St Clemens Abbey at Casaunia in *Abbatia Scl Clementis* (1993) and the Capestrana warrior in *Capistrani Pugnator* (2004).

The 1990s and the Italian Black Metal Scene

The Black is one of several bands that combines Goth/Dark, Progressive Heavy Metal and Black Sabbath-inspired Doom, and explores macabre and occult themes. Many of these bands, moreover, are produced by Black Widow Records, a record company founded in Genova in 1990 that played a major role in the history of the genre. Along with Jacula, Antonius Rex, Requiem, Goad, The Black and some international bands (e.g. High Tide, Black Widow, Bram Stoker, Pentagram), Black Widow Records releases several Italian bands that make direct reference to the Gothic tradition: Malombra (from the title of Antonio Fogazzaro's 1881 novel), Abiogenesi (which has produced vampire-themed albums like *Io sono il vampiro* and *Le notti di Salem*), L'impero delle ombre, and Il segno del commando (a name that pays homage to Daniele D'Anzia's Gothic TV series from 1971). Also thanks to the efforts of Black Widow Records, the 1990s was a decade of success for Italian Heavy Metal in all its forms: a great many professional magazines were sold monthly in kiosks (*Metal Shock*, *HM*, *Flash*, *Psycho* and *Metal Hammer*),[5] taking the place of the numerous fanzines of the previous decade.[6]

The aforementioned bands convincingly continued the stylistic discourse of their predecessors, merging a fascination with the occult with a sound influenced by contemporary grunge music. The aesthetic of these bands, moreover, plays with Italian Gothic products that had already gained a cult status, such as *Il segno del comando* or Lucio Fulci's movies. Fulci himself is referenced in Black Widow Records' 2000 compilation ... *e tu vivrai nel terrore! – L'aldilà* (named after Fulci's 1981 movie), whose cover was designed by the Swiss artist H. R. Giger. In the compilation, many of the bands re-elaborated the soundtracks of classic Italian horror films, from Fulci to Argento, Mario Bava and Pupi Avati, strengthening the close relationship between Gothic Italian music and genre cinema and inaugurating a hauntological retromania that persists in the twenty-first century.

In 1987, the partly Italian and partly Slovenian Devil Doll, one of the most peculiar bands in the field, began its activity. Founded in Venice by Mr Doctor (Mario Panciera), Devil Doll recorded its debut album *The Mark of the Beast* in Ljubljana with Jurij Toni, the sound technician of legendary Industrial Rock band Laibach. The band, however, decided not to proceed with the publication. It was only in 1989 that the band debuted with *The Girl Who Was ... Death*, a concept album inspired by an episode of Patrick McGoohan's TV series *The Prisoner* that bears the same title. The album fuses Goth Rock with more pronounced Classical music influences. Devil Doll's career has been marked by a certain snobbishness towards traditional promotional channels and the band has released only limited-edition albums at their concerts. After their debut, Devil Doll released four other albums characterised by long symphonic and experimental compositions, a sinister sound and a theatrical use of recitative. Their imagery makes ample use of literary and cinematic Gothic references: *Dies Irae* (1996), their last album, derives from Edgar Allan Poe's poem 'The Conqueror Worm' (1843).

Most importantly, the 1990s was the decade of the diffusion of Black Metal in Italy (a genre that originated in the late 1980s). Black Metal is an extreme and low-fi evolution of the early style of Venom merged with the theatricality of King Diamond's Mercyful Fate. It reached its peak of quality and popularity in the Scandinavian scene, especially in Norway. Stylistically, Black Metal is characterised by deliberately poor and rough productions, simply structured songs, and a tendency towards ambient music (sometimes with the addition of synthesisers); aesthetically, it brings the medieval look of NWOBHM to the extreme, with an abundance of studded leather, and makes extensive use of corpse paint, a black-and-white make-up applied to the face in order to make the wearer resemble a corpse.[7]

The first band to adopt the genre in Italy was Mortuary Drape, a band formed in 1986 in Alessandria that is still active today. In 1987, the band released its first demo tape, which centred on necromancy and death and was dedicated to the victims of witch-hunts. Mortuary Drape's debut album, released in 1994, is titled *All the Witches Dance* and has an extremely disturbing cover: shot by the band members, the photographic image depicts the exhumed corpse of an old woman. Songs like *Tregenda (Dance in Shroud)*, *Occult Abyss* and *Astral Bewitchment* celebrate the powers of witchcraft, the latter showing the world taken over by supernatural, presumably Satanic, forces:

> We'll take your soul, we'll take your mind,
> We'll take your fate under the ground.
> He has begun, unleashed his wrath.
>
> [...]
>
> All presents conjured, explosive force and lethal current.
> Soon you will be fallen into the hand of a sinister doom.

Necromass, based in Florence, is another important band of that early period. Its debut, *Mysteria Mystica Zothyriana* (1994), traces another connection between esotericism and Italian music, with lyrics explicitly referring to occult rites.

The importance that Black Metal accorded to the Middle Ages, a real or imaginary past, and local traditions (exemplified by the use of their native Norwegian by bands such as Ulver and Darkthrone, in contrast to the traditional use of English in Heavy Metal) makes it possible for Black Metal to be fruitfully appropriated and re-shaped by different cultures. This was what happened in the case of Sicilian Black Metal, which mingles Black Metal, Folk Metal and Dark Ambient with Mediterranean sounds and the use of dialect. As Kristopher F. B. Fletcher noted, 'Mediterranean metal is the logical outcome of another key development within the history of metal, the birth of Viking metal' (10), which is a sub-genre of Black Metal with lyrics that centre on Scandinavian history. Agghiastru (Michele Venezia), head of the band Inchiuvatu, is the main exponent of Sicilian Black Metal (which includes a wide range of bands, including Astimi, Lamentu, Tenebra, La Caruta di Li Dei, Ultima Missa and Malefici Sanctificatu). *Addisìu* (1997), Inchiuvatu's debut album, can be considered a manifesto for the local scene and summarises the features mentioned above. Their lyrics deal heavily with Satanism, from *Inchiuvatu*, which opens with an invocation to 'santu patri de lu 'nferno' [holy father in hell], to *Cristu crasto* (a title which translates into Italian as 'Cristo caprone' [goat-Jesus]), to *Luciferu Re*. Other songs tend to portray the world of the spirits with references to a more local imagery, as happens in *Lu jocu di li spiddi*:

> Si japi na' lu cielu 'na potta 'nmaliritta,
> si japi na' la terra la fossa di li motti.
> Luna è no' cielu,

sangu e focu sunnu pronti già.
Agghiastru conza alivi 'nmaliritti.
Agneddi spaccati hannu lu cori na' li petti.
Luna è no' cielu,
tuttu è prontu pi' lu jocu di li spiddi.

[A cursed door opens in the sky, / the dead's grave opens in the earth. / The moon is in the sky, / blood and fire are ready. / The oleaster prepares cursed olives. / Opened-up lambs show their hearts. / The moon is in the sky, / everything is ready for the spirits' play.]

In the 1990s, Black Metal spread to other parts of Italy as well. In Padua, the band Evol took inspiration from the genre's use of medieval aesthetics to create a sound that combined Dark Ambient, litanies and obscure guitar riffs. The band developed imagery connected to the Middle Ages, influenced both by fantasy fiction and the local folklore of Northern Italy, particularly legends about the devil and witchcraft. The devil (or the horned god of the witches?) also appears on the cover of the debut album by Opera IX (founded by guitarist Ossian), titled *The Call of the Wood* (1994). Formed in Biella, the band featured one of the first female lead singers in Italian Metal, Cadaveria (Raffaella Rivarolo, who started a solo career in 2001), and its work touches on themes such as nihilism, horror fiction and paganism. Equally from Piedmont, Maldoror released a Black Metal album with the title *Ars Magika* in 1998, but became more influenced by Dark Wave and Industrial in the years that followed.

Macabre imagery also typifies the work of the doom band Cultus Sanguine, from Milan. The cover of the band's debut album *Shadow's Blood* (Candlelight Records, 1997) portrays a dead baby in a coffin and the lyrics of the songs are imbued with decadent imagery. The band's guitarist, Aqua Regis (Roberto Mammarella), is one of the most influential figures of the European underground in the 1990s. Not only is Mammarella the founder and lead member of Monumentum, a Gothic/Dark Wave band that is quite famous internationally and remains active to this day; he is also the manager of the record company Avantgarde Music, which has been promoting Funeral Doom and Black Metal both in Italy and abroad since the 1990s.

More recent explorations of Black Metal have been carried out by two bands from Parma: Forgotten Tomb (which merges doom and black metal) and Caronte (influenced by Black Sabbath). In Genoa, Abysmal Grief formed in 1996, but did not release their debut album until a decade later, with Black Widow Records (*Abysmal Grief*, 2007). *Abysmal Grief* is a concept album that attempts to create a musical narration of the spiritistic process, presenting the main conceptual and practical points of this discipline. Finally, the internationally famous

Theatres Des Vampires, from Rome, created a unique blend of Black Metal, Gothic Metal and Symphonic Metal, which they combine with an insistence on vampirism in their lyrics and elaborate, decadent stage sets and costumes. The name of the band is taken from the Paris-based group of vampires in Anne Rice's classic 1979 novel *Interview with the Vampire*. Their first demo, which came out at a time when the band still had only two members (Lord Vampyr, guitar and voice, and Agaharet, drums), is titled *Nosferatu, Eine Simphonie Des Grauens* (1995), which is a direct reference to Friedrich Wilhelm Murnau's 1922 movie. The following year, they released their debut album, *Vampyrìsme, Nècrophilie, Nècrosadisme, Nècrophagie*, which makes great use of the macabre imagery typical of the genre, but is poorly produced, for which reason it was re-recorded in 2003. The lyrics contain direct references to *Dracula* ('I was born in this ancient land, in Transylvania', in *Intro/Twilight Kingdom*, or 'Blood will be life', in *Wood of Walacchia*) as well as depictions of vampirism as it has been codified in countless movies and books, but with attention to gory and unsettling details: 'Cold wind in the castle. / In the unholy walls / nocturnal sacrifices of virgins / raped from the lord of darkness' (*Ancient Vampires*). After another album centred on literary vampirism, *The Vampire Chronicles* (1998; a further reference to Rice), the band moved towards Death Rock, thanks to the influence of vocalist Sonya Scarlet, who took the leading role in the band after Lord Vampyr's departure.

The Future and the Past: Italian Occult Psychedelia

The diffusion of the internet at the end of the twentieth century did not diminish the interest in underground genres and subcultures, but rather facilitated their circulation and consumption. At the same time, the cataloguing function of the web has led to a hauntological reprise of occult and Gothic aspects of Italian music (a phenomenon that, as we saw, began as early as the 1990s). This is what Italian musical journalist Antonio Ciarletta, in the January 2012 issue of *Blow Up*, labelled Italian Occult Psychedelia.

Italian Occult Psychedelia should not be confused with Psychedelia, a music genre from the 1960s. Rather, it is a hybrid of various musical influences (from Pink Floyd's early work to New Wave and Krautrock) and soundtracks of Italian B-movies (most notably Riz Ortolani's *Cannibal Holocaust*, 1980), as well as vintage documentaries, news bulletins, radio dramas and TV series. The variety of inspirations spans from Goblin and Antonius Rex to Morricone and the soundtracks of

Mario Bava's movies. 'Addicted to its own past', to quote the title of Simon Reynolds's influential essay on pop culture's retromania, Italian Occult Psychedelia is a genre that perfectly summarises the processes of remediation typical of trans-medial Gothic.[8]

The most representative projects of this new expression of Italian Gothic music include La piramide di sangue, with its hypnotic and ritualistic sound, Cannibal Movie, whose name refers to the sub-genre of Italian horror cinema, the hallucinatory atmospheres of Squadra Omega, the progressive sound of Hermetic Brotherhood of Lux-or and the one-man band Spettro Family. Since 2012, Fabio Frizzi, the Italian composer and long-term collaborator of horror director Lucio Fulci, has presented, in Italy and abroad, live performances of his soundtracks for Fulci's movies, as part of a project titled *Frizzi to Fulci*.

After having started out as a series of isolated experimentations by a few musicians with eccentric interests, the Gothic vein in Italian music is still alive after sixty years and its precursors have attained cult status. Even though it has yet to achieve definitive popular success (and most of the bands discussed often had more success abroad), there are several bands that reprise and innovate the sound of the pioneers of the genre, building a thematic and stylistic bridge between past and future. Just as the first British Gothic novel, Horace Walpole's *The Castle of Otranto*, is set in southern Italy, two centuries later the *Belpaese* produced a rich Gothic musical scene that, compared with the indifference of mainstream music, developed a strong individual identity. It is not by chance, after all, that Black Sabbath, which contributed so much to defining the genre, got its name from the American version of one of the greatest Italian Gothic films, Mario Bava's *La maschera del demonio* (1960).

Bibliography

Bardine, Bryan, 'Elements of the Gothic in Heavy Metal: A Match Made in Hell', in Gerd Bayer (ed.), *Heavy Metal Music in Britain* (Farnham: Ashgate, 2009), pp. 125–39.

Bibby, Michael, 'Atrocity Exhibitions: Joy Division, Factory Records, and Goth', in Lauren M. E. Goodlad and Michael Bibby (eds), *Goth: Undead Subculture* (Durham, NC: Duke University Press, 2007), pp. 233–56.

Caccamea, Francesco, *Shocking metal. La storia del giornalismo metallaro in Italia* (Falconara Marittima: Crac Edizioni, 2016).

Camilletti, Fabio, *Italia lunare* (Oxford: Peter Lang, 2018).

Farabegoli, Francesco, 'Ascesa e declino delle riviste metal', *Prismo*, 20 January 2016, http://www.prismomag.com/stampa-metal/ (last accessed 1 August 2022)

Fletcher, Kristopher F. B., and Osman Umurhan, 'Introduction. Where Metal and Classics Meet', in Kristopher F. B. Fletcher and Osman Umurhan (eds), *Classical Antiquity in Heavy Metal Music* (London and New York: Bloomsbury, 2019), pp. 1–22.

Mattioli, Valerio, *Remoria. La città invertita* (Rome: Minimum fax, 2019).

Patterson, Dayal, *Black Metal: Evolution of the Cult* (Minneapolis, MN: Feral House, 2013).

Perasso, Massimo, 'Doom Made in Italy: Il Dark Sound Italiano degli Anni 80', *Tomorrow Hit Today*, 26 May 2019, <https://www.tomorrowhittoday.it/2019/05/26/doom-made-in-italy-il-dark-sound-italiano-degli-anni-80/> (last accessed 1 August 2022).

Reynolds, Simon, *Retromania: Pop Culture's Addiction to Its Own Past* (New York: Faber and Faber, 2011).

Stickney, John, 'Four Doors to the Future: Gothic Rock is Their Thing', *The Williams Record*, 24 October 1967.

Sylvester, Steve, *Il negromante del rock* (Falconara Marittima: Crac Edizioni, 2011).

Sylvester, Steve, 'Il fumetto erotico tra amore e morte', *Loud and Proud*, 28 October 2019 <https://loudandproud.it/steve-sylvester-intervista-fumetto-erotico/> (last accessed 1 August 2022).

Tosoni, Simone, and Emanuela Zuccalà, *Italian Goth Subculture: Kindred Creatures and Other Dark Enactments in Milan, 1982–1991* (Cham: Palgrave, 2020).

Van Elferen, Isabella, *Gothic Music: The Sounds of the Uncanny* (Cardiff: University of Wales Press, 2012).

Van Elferen, Isabella, and Jeffrey Weinstock, *Goth Music: From Sound to Subculture* (Abingdon: Routledge, 2015).

Vitolo, Eduardo, *Children of Doom* (Milan: Tsunami Edizioni, 2018).

Vitolo, Eduardo, *Magister dixit. La leggenda esoterica di Jacula e Antonius Rex* (Milan: Tsunami Edizioni, 2015).

Vitolo, Eduardo, *Sub terra. Rock estremo e cultura underground in Italia, 1977–1998* (Milan: Tsunami Edizioni, 2012).

Walser, Robert, *Running with the Devil: Power, Gender, and Madness in Heavy Metal Music* (Hanover, IN and London: Wesleyan University Press, 2013).

Notes

1. See also Walser.
2. See Perasso.
3. Progressive rock is a music genre that developed in the United States and United Kingdom in the late 1960s. Influenced by jazz, folk, and classical music, progressive rock is characterised by electronic instrumentation, eclectic compositions, and long phrasing.
4. On the goth, see Van Elferen (2012, 2015); for the goth on the Italian scene, see Tosoni and Zuccalà.
5. See Farabegoli.
6. On the fanzines, see also Vitolo (*Sub terra* 18–24) and Caccamea.
7. See Fletcher and Umurhan (9). For a history of black metal, see Patterson.

8. At Mattioli's request, Reynolds devoted a blogpost to Italian Occult Psychedelia on 30 January 2012; it is available at: http://blissout.blogspot.com/2012/01/why-so-glum-chums-interesting-piece-by.html. Mattioli's essay *Remoria. La città invertita* (2019) touches upon similar themes, albeit transferred to the Italian scene.

Part III
Themes

Chapter 12

The Gothic Body
Catherine Ramsey-Portolano

The resonance of the Gothic genre in Italy can be noted most strongly within the literary production of certain *fin-de-siècle* writers, particularly those active within the *Scapigliatura* and naturalist movements, who were especially receptive to literary influences from beyond national borders. The adoption of Gothic elements such as the supernatural, mystery, decay, madness and death went hand-in-hand with the exploration of female malady and deformities in the works of writers such as Igino Ugo Tarchetti, Luigi Capuana, Antonio Fogazzaro and Matilde Serao. These authors' portrayal of femininity, in a period characterised by derogatory and paradoxical theories about women's nature, interweaves themes of contaminated beauty, illness and madness with plot structures that combine romance, mystery, suffering, alienation and sometimes death. A focus on the female condition within the Gothic tradition features early in the genre's origins, as Ellen Moers notes in the chapter 'Female Gothic' of *Literary Women: The Great Writers*: 'as early as the 1790s, Ann Radcliffe firmly set the Gothic in one of the ways it would go ever after: a novel in which the central figure is a young woman who is simultaneously persecuted victim and courageous heroine' (91). In this essay I examine those novels in the *fin-de-siècle* Italian context, specifically Tarchetti's *Fosca* (1869), Fogazzaro's *Malombra* (1881), Capuana's *Profumo* (1892) and Serao's *La mano tagliata* (1912), which utilise the suffering female body as a means of exploring female oppression within society. The heroines of these novels demonstrate characteristics of vulnerability, expressed through illness and madness, but also strength of character in their attempts to control their fates and escape their oppressive surroundings. The focus on the female body and its physical and mental deformities, central to these authors' portrayal, points to the female characters' struggle to overcome situations which posit them as victims of suffering, persecution and oppression. In their rebellion against society's restrictions, often embodied by a male aggressor, the female protagonists transgress traditional norms for female passivity and their mental and physical illness represents the manifestation of their deviance.

It is important to note that few Italian *fin-de-siècle* women writers adopt the Gothic tradition in their portrayal of female realities, privileging instead domestic realism as a means of portraying and denouncing women's limited options outside the domestic realm (Mitchell). Although Moers's 1976 seminal text identifies the Female Gothic according to authorial gender, that is novels in the Gothic mode by women writers, more recently literary critics have argued against such a strict categorisation. Anna Shajirat suggests a rethinking of the Female Gothic tradition to recognise works not 'because they were written by women, or even because they tell stories about women, but because they highlight the gendered horrors that structure their heroines' maturation to expose the trauma of the ordinary for women' (384–5). It is possible to observe within the Italian context that the Male Gothic represents as much as the Female Gothic the vehicle of expression for 'anxieties over domestic entrapment and female sexuality' (Ledoux 2) recognised by second-wave feminists as central to the concept of Female Gothic.

Female degeneracy featured prominently within late nineteenth-century European scientific and intellectual circles, in the works, for example, of sociologists such as Auguste Comte, evolutionary theorists such as Charles Darwin and Herbert Spencer, criminologists such as Cesare Lombroso, neurologists such as Paul Julius Moebius and philosophers such as Otto Weininger. Most based notions of female mental inferiority on physiological deficiency, often comparing women to children, deformed men or lower forms on the evolutionary scale. The alignment of women with irrationality and emotion, in contrast to men's command of reason and logical analysis, harkens back to Aristotelian theory and assertions of female inferiority have circulated for at least as long. However, in the second half of the nineteenth century the apparently undeniable truth of evolutionary biology lent authority to theories concerning the underdeveloped and inferior female brain. Female physical and intellectual inferiority were posited as logical conclusions of the natural selection worldview, which posited the male species as exposed to far greater selective pressures and therefore more evolved physically and intellectually than the female species. The justification for female inferiority presented in the works of Darwinist and positivist thinkers often derived from the physical evidence offered by the female body. Darwin and others posited women's inferiority and subordination within society as deriving from biology, overlooking cultural factors, such as familial environment, constraining social roles and the fact that relatively few occupational and intellectual opportunities existed for women.

Italian criminologist Cesare Lombroso, strongly influenced by positivism and social Darwinism, published his studies on physiognomy, criminality and social deviance in works such as *Genio e follia* (1864), *L'uomo delinquente* (1876) and *La donna delinquente, la prostituta e la donna normale* (1893), in which he proposed statistics from his study of the differences between male and female exemplars in the animal world to support the theory that women were physically as well as morally and mentally inferior to men. Lombroso presented theories of women's deficiency as fact, based on concrete evidence provided by the female body. Janet Oppenheim notes in *Shattered Nerves* that for 'several decades beginning in the late 1860s, nothing was believed to underscore the biological basis of female mental inadequacy more resoundingly than craniology' (185). Lombroso's theories legitimised the identification of those considered 'different' by bourgeois standards: the prostitute, the criminal and the mentally ill fulfilled such roles within society, Lombroso's theories suggest, because their physiological and biological constitution, which determined their capacity for moral and intelligent behaviour, rendered them incapable of executing other roles. In *The Gothic Body: Sexuality, Materialism, and Degeneration at the Fin de Siècle*, Kelly Hurley notes the mutual 'threat' to society represented by female degeneracy: 'in a vicious circle of causes and effects, a poisonous society (locus of both environmental and moral contaminants) infected the individual, the individual passed the infection to its offspring, and the degenerate offspring reinfected society' (69).

The portrayal of female degeneracy, tied to the 'estetica dell'orrido e del terribile' [aesthetic of the horrid and the terrible] (Praz 33), was a trope in European *fin-de-siècle* literature, as Mario Praz notes in *La carne, la morte e il diavolo nella letteratura romantica*:

> [l]a scoperta dell'orrore come fonte di diletto e di bellezza finì per reagire sul concetto stesso della bellezza: l'orrido, da categoria del bello, più per diventare uno degli elementi propri del bello: dal bellamente orrido si passò per gradi insensibili all'orribilmente bello. (33)

> [The discovery of horror as a source of pleasure and beauty ended up affecting the very concept of beauty: causing the horrid, from the category of beauty, to become one of the actual elements of beauty: one passed by imperceptible degrees from beautifully horrid to horribly beautiful.]

Stories of malady, madness and death in the works of writers such as Ernst Theodor Amadeus Hoffman, Charles Baudelaire, Johann Wolfgang von Goethe, John Keats, Percy Bysshe Shelley and Edgar Allan

Poe, testify to a common literary interest in the *fin de siècle* in exploring Gothic tendencies that combined elements of romance, horror and suffering. In *The Italian Gothic and Fantastic: Encounters and Rewritings of Narrative Traditions* Francesca Billiani notes the influence of such tendencies within the Italian literary context: 'Italian writers adopted the fictional modes provided by foreign gothic and fantastic narrative traditions with the intent of subverting current literary paradigms, especially those proposed by realist narration' (15). I will examine the contribution by Tarchetti, Capuana, Fogazzaro and Serao to creating a Gothic tradition in the Italian context, at the centre of which the portrayal of female malady features as a vehicle for exploring supernatural and mysterious contexts that exist outside of the objective reality proposed by positivist culture. Furthermore, I will discuss how instances of female mental and physical malady serve in the works of these authors to mark the female character's difference and bring attention to her situation of oppression, reflecting, as Shajirat observes, 'the physical and mental decay the Gothic heroine undergoes on the path from childhood innocence to adult experience' (383).

In Igino Ugo Tarchetti's *Fosca* the female character's illness is central to the novel's plot and defines her identity before she is even presented. Fosca does not appear initially in person but rather through the sound of her bone-chilling screams and the descriptions provided by other characters, including her doctor's analysis of her condition as a kind of phenomenon which science has failed to understand and for which there is no cure. When Fosca finally appears in person, her body is presented as ravaged by illness, disproportionate in its features and demonstrating an extreme, almost skeletal thinness. Her identity is intertwined with the notion of infirmity; although her doctor refers to her as a walking collection of all possible maladies, the source of her ailments is identified as hysteria. Tarchetti, however, presents Fosca's malady as deriving principally from her inability to satisfy societal standards for female beauty and behaviour. In fact, she recounts to her love interest Giorgio that she has always been considered ugly and narrates her failed experiences as wife and mother. Tarchetti problematises Fosca's illness by portraying her as a conscious victim who subverts the established order through her condition. Her ugliness, illness and ultimately her condition of being different allow her to evade society's conventions and expectations. Fosca utilises her status to achieve what she wants and what would otherwise be considered inappropriate and unacceptable behaviour for women, such as her ravenous appetite for reading and her aggressive actions to obtain Giorgio's love and spend time alone with him. Giorgio eventually comes to love and even desire Fosca, and the novel's conclusion describes their night of passion together. This encounter, however, is marked by an uncontrollable sense of fear and horror on Giorgio's part, recalling Praz's affirmation noted previously regarding 'un'attrattiva proprio in quel senso d'orrore' [an attraction exactly toward that sense of horror] (244). Adding to the theme of decay and illness associated with their union is the transference of qualities from one character to another when Giorgio, afterward, takes on characteristics that had been associated previously only with Fosca. Tarchetti's portrayal of Fosca's condition reflects techniques and objectives typical to the Female Gothic, as Shajirat notes:

> Through these constructions of female subjectivity as simultaneously regressive and progressive, as unstable as any decaying castle or monument, the Female Gothic locates horror not in supernatural monsters and spectacularized violence as in other Gothic works of the period, but in the mundane realities that women must learn about their subjugation in worlds dominated by men. (383)

As noted earlier, Tarchetti's *Fosca* is an example of how within the Italian Male Gothic, female malady serves as the vehicle of expression for 'anxieties over domestic entrapment and female sexuality' (Ledoux 2) typically associated only with the Female Gothic.

Contemporary to *Fosca* is Tarchetti's short story 'Lorenzo Alviati' (1869), which also features the portrayal of a diseased female body and the attraction of illness and death. The story's protagonist Lorenzo finds true love, which he describes as 'una malattia della mia anima' [a disease of my soul] (Tarchetti, *L'amore nell'arte* 28), in Adalgisa, who is dying of tuberculosis, but her illness only increases his attraction for her:

> Essa era anzi più bella. Che ti dirò delle contraddizioni inesplicabili della mia natura? ... Io me ne innamorai in quei giorni; e quanto più ella si andava approssimando al suo fine, quanto più io acquistava la certezza del suo abbandono, tanto più si rafforzava in me questo affetto. [...] In poco tempo il mio amore raggiunse tutta la sua pienezza, assunse tutta la forza d'una passione indomabile. Sola, mia, sofferente, purificata dalla morte – così e non altrimenti io poteva amare una donna! (Tarchetti, *L'amore nell'arte* 32)

> [She was instead more beautiful. What can I tell you about the inexplicable contradictions of my nature? ... I fell in love during those days; and the closer she got to her end, the more I obtained the certainty of losing her, only served to increase my affection. [...] In a short amount of time my love reached its fullness, took on all the force of an uncontrollable passion. Alone, mine, suffering, purified by death – only this way could I love a woman!]

In this short story the female body seduces not because of its sensuality but rather because of its resemblance to death: the beloved's body is referred to as a 'cadaver' [corpse] and there are references to the paleness of her face, the emptiness of her eyes and the whiteness of her hands (Tarchetti, *L'amore nell'arte* 35). After Adalgisa's death, Lorenzo's love grows even stronger, becoming what he describes as 'una passione che mi divorava la vita, senza che potessi spegnerla, che mi dominava senza che potessi combatterla' [a passion that devoured my life, without my being able to extinguish it, that dominated me without my being able to fight it] (Tarchetti, *L'amore nell'arte* 33). Lorenzo describes the development of his feelings for her in one line: 'L'aveva dimenticata viva, l'aveva amata morente, l'adorava già morta' [I had forgotten her alive, I had loved her dying, I loved her once dead] (Tarchetti, *L'amore nell'arte* 33). Adalgisa prefigures Fosca, whose illness and skeletal appearance both repulse and fascinate Giorgio. Tarchetti's portrayal of female illness and death in *Fosca* and 'Lorenzo Alviati' reveals a clear and distinctive fascination with the macabre and the influence of Gothic literary models on this Italian *scapigliato* writer, as David Del Principe notes:

> The complex spate of foreign influences to which Tarchetti was receptive and which posited the representation of Reality in the dichotomy between the natural and preternatural [...] do seem to indicate that his narrative sits more comfortably among the Gothic novelists, such as Walter Scott and Edgar Allan Poe than among his late Romantic contemporaries in Italy. (33)

Tarchetti's contribution to the Gothic tradition in Italy is undeniable and relies principally on his portrayal of female malady and contaminated beauty.

In Luigi Capuana's *Profumo* the novel's protagonist Eugenia suffers from a strange and mysterious condition that manifests itself in the emission of the smell of orange blossoms from her fingertips. The portrayal of Eugenia's condition, beyond any scientific explanation and of almost supernatural origin, reveals how Capuana, largely recognised as one of the leading figures within Italian *verismo*, distanced himself from the goals of literary objectivity of that movement to explore other literary genres, as Del Principe affirms: 'Capuana explored, in the tradition of Tarchetti, spiritualism, ghosts, mesmerism, hypnotism, the occult, vampires, and monstrosity' (97). Eugenia's condition is first revealed after an argument with her husband Patrizio regarding the interfering presence in their lives of his mother Geltrude. The fight for possession of Patrizio by both mother and wife reaches macabre tones when Geltrude accuses Eugenia of usurping Patrizio's health in vampire-like fashion: 'Lei se lo beve il tuo sangue! Lei se l'assorbisce la tua carne, il midollo delle tue ossa, la tua vita! ... Io sono impotente a lottare con lei. È giovane, è bella, è amata. Ti ha stregato!' [She drinks your blood! She absorbs your flesh, the marrow of your bones, your life! . . . I am powerless to fight against her. She is young, beautiful, loved. She has enchanted you!] (Capuana 43). Paola Azzolini notes the symbolic juxtaposition between the two female characters in *Profumo*: 'è evidente il gioco oppositivo: la madre ha dato il latte e la vita; "colei" si beve il sangue, come una *belle dame sans merci*' [The game of opposites is evident: the mother gave him milk and life; 'the other' drinks his blood, like a *belle dame sans merci*] (viii). The hovering presence of the mother-in-law, both in life and after her death, prevents Patrizio from expressing intimacy with his wife; his feelings of guilt for opposing his mother lead him to avoid Eugenia and her claims for attention, choosing even after the mother's death to spend his time visiting her tomb rather than seeing Eugenia. The couple's marital difficulties play out in a typical Gothic setting, that of the ex-convent that has been designated as Patrizio's office and residence in his new position in the *Agenzia delle Tasse* in the town of Marzallo. Eugenia leaves behind family and friends to find herself alone with Patrizio and his mother in a large, empty and isolated building set atop a rock precipice, reminiscent of a medieval castle, with its vast and echoing corridors. The novel's Dr Mola, a small-town physician unfamiliar with cases such as Eugenia's, studies her condition as a rare phenomenon, describing it as an indication of the great delicacy of the female nervous system (Capuana 59). The doctor is hesitant to cast a verdict on Eugenia's condition, confirming stereotypical notions regarding the mystery of femininity: 'Con le malattie nervose, non si sa mai. [. . .] Noi mediconzoli, imbattendoci in un caso che c'imbarazza, specialmente se si tratta di donne, sogliamo uscirne pel rotto della cuffia, dicendo: "Nervi! Nervi!"' [With nervous diseases, you never know. [. . .] We small-time doctors, when we encounter a case that embarrasses us, especially if it regards women, we usually muddle through, saying: 'Nerves! Nerves!'] (Capuana 59). As in *Fosca*, however, the real cause of Eugenia's condition can be found in her dissatisfaction with suppressing her desire for physical love. She reveals a transgressive sexuality for women of the time by attempting to emancipate herself from traditional restrictions regarding the expression of sexual desire, demanding attention and physical love from her husband. In *Profumo* Capuana adopts a typically Gothic theme and setting in his portrayal of female illness as metaphor for analysing a situation of female oppression.

In Antonio Fogazzaro's *Malombra* the themes of female entrapment and illness are explored literally and metaphorically through the experiences of two female characters: Marina di Malombra, the young, beautiful and rebellious protagonist who represents the epitome of the Gothic heroine with her pale complexion, 'fiumi di capelli' [long, flowing hair] and 'grandi occhi penetranti fatti per l'impero e per la voluttà' [big penetrating eyes made to command and for voluptuousness] (Fogazzaro 47), and Cecilia, Marina's ancestor accused by her husband of infidelity and subsequently enclosed within her room until she succumbs to madness and death. Marina lives with her elderly uncle, Cesare d'Ormengo, in his dark and gloomy castle on the shores of a lake in Lombardy, inhabiting the room which years before had belonged to Cecilia. Set within the walls of a castle haunted by what are described as strange legends, the novel presents a typically Gothic setting and plot, perfect for the exploration of the themes of reincarnation, the occult and supernatural forces. Reflecting Fogazzaro's interest in spiritualism and personality disorders, a pathology which was believed at that time to be common to cases of female hysteria, the novel presents Marina's obsession with being the reincarnation of Cecilia and the ruinous actions that follow.

Through the careful construction of Marina's character as hysterical, Fogazzaro explores not only how character predisposition gives way to psychic illness but also how mental instability acts as a sort of medium between reality and the supernatural. The cause for Marina's illness is linked to her discovery of a letter left by Cecilia in a secret compartment of the desk in her room. Cecilia's literal entrapment becomes Marina's metaphoric binding due to the act of reincarnation, as the words from Cecilia's letter predict: 'ebbene, qualunque sia il tuo nome, tu che hai ritrovato e leggi queste parole, conosci in te l'anima mia infelice. Avanti di nascere hai sofferto TANTO, TANTO' [So, whatever your name is, you who have found and read these words, bring my unhappiness into your soul. Before being born you suffered SO, SO MUCH] (Fogazzaro 62). Cecilia explains the reasons for her madness in the letter: 'Il conte Emanuele e sua madre mi assassinano lentamente – sono condannata! Ogni pietra di questa casa mi odia. Nessuno ha pietà di me' [Count Emanuele and his mother are slowly killing me – I am condemned! Every stone in this house hates me. No one pities me] (Fogazzaro 63). Cecilia, the Gothic heroine 'whose anxieties and desires are projected onto her environment' (Showalter 92), transfers her anxiety onto the objects that surround her so that they become portals of persecution. Marina is also a prisoner, bound by her uncle's expectations for her future and his attempts to arrange her marriage to a relative. Shajirat notes as characteristic of Gothic novels the tendency to 'stage their heroines' development in terms of irrevocable disruption in the dangers they experience from the world of reality, from men in positions of power who perpetually threaten their autonomy and integrity with sexual violence' (383). Marina, like Cecilia before her, is a victim of men seeking to control their options for fulfilment. Unlike Cecilia, however, Marina manages to escape a destiny of confinement and death, carrying out her revenge against the male descendant of Cecilia's husband before she flees the castle never to return, indicating *Malombra* as another example of the Italian Male Gothic for its attention to exploring the issues of female malady, suffering and persecution.

In Matilde Serao's *La mano tagliata* the traditional Gothic elements of suspense, the supernatural and female captivity abound in the bizarre account of aristocratic Roberto Alimena's discovery, under mysterious circumstances, of a box containing a female hand. Serao provides a lengthy description of the hand, presented as lying delicately positioned within a velvet-lined box, 'ingemmata' [bejewelled] and 'bellissima' [beautiful] with 'unghie, rosee, lucide, [. . .] lunate e tagliate a mandorla' [pink, shiny fingernails, [. . .] curved and cut in an almond-shape] (18). The hand seems healthy, as if it were still attached to its owner:

> era color carne, color naturale, del bianco avorio con una velatura di sangue dietro la pelle liscia, senza una ruga. Mano di tinta viva, di persona che era giovane, bella e sana: nulla di esangue, di cereo, di oscuro, in quella mano. Le vene si scorgevano appena; ma guardando bene, dall'indice e dall'anulare, si vedevano partire, in una tinta azzurro-violetta, le due vene più importanti della mano: e parevano quasi gonfie di vita. (18)

> [It was flesh-colored, a natural color, ivory white with a veil of blood behind the smooth skin, without a wrinkle. It was the hand of a living person, of a person who was young, beautiful, and healthy: nothing was bloodless, waxy, or dark in that hand. The veins were barely visible; but if you looked closely, starting from the index and ring fingers, you could see the two most important veins of the hand in a blue-violet hue: and they seemed almost swollen with life.]

Roberto becomes obsessed with the hand, even falling in love with it, and with finding its owner, whom he is convinced is still alive. He often dreams of the hand and its owner, who appears to him in his dreams as a

> bellissima giovane, pallida, dai capelli nerissimi, dalla bocca rossa e carnosa, dalla fronte breve di Dea, avvolta in un classico vestito bianco, a grandi pieghe, che nascondesse il braccio troncato, mentre l'altra mano, la compagna, la sorella, esciva da quel biancore, seducente e tenue come un petalo di fiore. (44)

> [beautiful young woman, pale, with very black hair, with a red and fleshy mouth, with the short forehead of a Goddess, wrapped in a classic white dress, with large pleats, that hid the truncated arm, while the other hand, the companion, the sister, came out of that whiteness, seductive and tenuous as a flower petal.]

Attempting to resolve the mystery of the hand, Roberto takes it for analysis to Professor Silvio Amati, 'uno scienziato di prim'ordine' [a first–

rate scientist] (44). After examining the hand and admitting that there are secrets that not even science can uncover, the doctor declares that it belongs to a young, healthy, beautiful woman, no more than twenty-five years of age, whose temperament and physical appearance he describes as follows: 'una donna di temperamento sanguigno, nervosa, di carnagione chiara e vivida, di capelli castagni che piegano al nero, di statura media, molto ben fatta' [a woman of sanguine temperament, nervous, with a clear and vivid complexion, chestnut hair that is almost black, of medium stature, very well-built] (49). The physical and personality characteristics identified by the doctor reflect those typically associated at the time with Gothic heroines as well as with women who suffered from nervous disorders such as hysteria and neurosis (see Esquirol; and Baker Brown 19–31). The doctor is also able to explain the mystery of the well-preserved condition of the hand: the amputation took place not only while its owner was alive but while she was 'immersa in un sonno, in un torpore, cloroformizzata o catalettica' [immersed in a sleep, in a torpor, chloroformed or cataleptic] (50). The doctor hypothesises however that the amputation resulted in the death of the woman, who was possibly even cut into pieces. Roberto refuses nonetheless to believe that the beloved owner of the hand is dead and undertakes as his mission to find her. After a rather intricate narration of encounters with mysterious, threatening and at times even ghost-like characters in cities such as Rome, Naples, Genoa and Ventimiglia, the novel's conclusion resolves the mystery of the hand and its owner: it belongs to Maria Cabib, who has been imprisoned for the past fifteen years by the novel's antagonist Marcus Henner. Serao's novel explores typical themes of the Gothic genre, such as the supernatural, mystery, romance and death, together with themes specific to the Female Gothic, such as female entrapment, alienation and suffering, which are portrayed through the experiences of mental and physical decay that accompany women in their development toward adulthood.

The portrayal of oppressive conditions experienced by the female characters in the novels examined above, often channelled through physical or mental malady and decay, reveals a commonality of objectives in the *fin-de-siècle* Italian Male and Female Gothic, one that has been associated exclusively only with the Female Gothic in other contexts, as Shajirat notes:

> The traumatic maturation process the heroine experiences in the pages of the Female Gothic novel, marked and marred by repeated threats of sexual assault, reflects the reality of maturity for eighteenth-century women who were subject to literal and figurative forms of violence from both private and public spheres, from intimate relationships and the law. (387)

Malady and degeneracy suggest a character's immorality and deviancy while at the same time serving to invoke a sense of horror and repulsion within the reader. Illness becomes a reflection of the character's inner self, serving to underline that these characters exist outside the realm of normalcy. In their struggle for independence and autonomy, characters such as Fosca, Marina, Eugenia and Maria attempt to break free from society's restrictive roles for women of the time. Through their deviancy, these characters are marked as different and as such achieve a privileged status within society, escaping its restrictive gender-based expectations and limitations.

Bibliography

Azzolini, Paola, 'Introduction', in Luigi Capuana, *Profumo* (Milan: Mondadori, 1996), pp. v–xxv.

Baker Brown, Isaac, *On the Curability of Certain Forms of Insanity, Epilepsy, Catalepsy, and Hysteria in Females* (London: Robert Hardwicke, 1866).

Billiani, Francesca, and Gigliola Sulis (eds), *The Italian Gothic and the Fantastic: Encounters and Rewritings of Narrative Traditions* (Madison, NJ: Fairleigh Dickinson University Press, 2007).

Breuer, Joseph, and Sigmund Freud, *Studies in Hysteria* [1895] (Boston, MA: Beacon Press, 1937).

Capuana, Luigi, *Profumo* [1900] (Milan: Mondadori, 1996).

Comte, Auguste, *Corso di filosofia positiva* [1830] (Turin: UTET, 1967).

Darwin, Charles, *The Descent of Man, and Selection in Relation to Sex* (London: John Murray, 1871).

Del Principe, Davide, *Rebellion, Death, and Aesthetics in Italy: The Demons of Scapigliatura* (Madison, WI: Fairleigh Dickinson University Press, 1996).

Esquirol, Etienne, *Mental Maladies: A Treatise on Insanity* [1845], trans. E. K. Hunt (New York: Hafner, 1965).

Fogazzaro, Antonio, *Malombra* [1881] (Rome: BEN, 1997).

Freud, Sigmund, 'Studies on Hysteria (1893–95)', in James Strachey (ed.), *The Standard Edition of the Complete Psychological Works of Sigmund Freud*, 24 vols (London: Hogarth Press, 1953–74, 1955, II).

Hurley, Kelly, *The Gothic Body: Sexuality, Materialism, and Degeneration at the Fin de Siècle* (Cambridge: Cambridge University Press, 1996).

Ledoux, Ellen, 'Was There Ever a "Female Gothic"?', *Palgrave Communications*, 3.1, 2017, https://doi.org/10.1057/palcomms.2017.42

Lombroso, Cesare, and Guglielmo Ferrero, *La Donna delinquente, la prostituta e la donna normale* [1893] (Turin: Bocca, 1915).

Mitchell, Katharine, *Italian Women Writers: Gender and Everyday Life in Fiction and Journalism, 1870–1910* (Toronto: University of Toronto Press, 2014).

Moebius, Paul Julius, *L'inferiorità mentale della donna* [1900] (Rome: Castelvecchi, 1998).

Moers, Ellen, *Literary Women: The Great Writers* (New York: Oxford University Press, 1985).
Oppenheim, Janet, *Shattered Nerves: Doctors, Patients, and Depression in Victorian England* (New York and Oxford: Oxford University Press, 1991).
Praz, Mario, *La carne, la morte e il diavolo nella letteratura romantica* [1930] (Milan: RCS Libri, 1999).
Serao, Matilde, *La mano tagliata* (Florence: Salani, 1912).
Shajirat, Anna, '"Bending her gentle head to swift decay": Horror, Loss, and Fantasy in the Female Gothic of Anna Radcliffe and Regina Maria Roche', *Studies in Romanticism*, 58, 2019, pp. 383–412.
Tarchetti, Igino Ugo, *Fosca* [1869] (Milan: Mondadori, 1981).
Tarchetti, Igino Ugo, *L'amore nell'arte* [1869] (Florence: Passigli, 1992).
Weininger, Otto, *Sesso e carattere* [1903] (Rome: Mediterranee, 1992).

Chapter 13

The Female Gothic
Francesca Billiani

The Public Voices of the Italian Female Gothic

The question about what constitutes the Italian Gothic – and implicitly the Female Gothic – remains an open one. If Italy has been defined as the country without the fantastic, could something similar be said about Gothic literature? Was Italy really the country where this Northern literary genre did not live an independent life?[1] The arrival of the Gothic in Italy followed a trajectory of interferences and intertextual moments that rejected the paradigm of mimesis which shaped the *vero* of the historical novel, as Guido Mazzoni wrote in his *Theory of the Novel*: 'The English gothic novel and the German Romanticism expanded the territory of mimesis to imaginary universes that lay very distant from common sense' (215), or, he explained further, quoting from Defoe's *Robison Crusoe*, it challenged the 'middle station of life' (218–22).[2] The adjective 'middle' in this instance is to be read as 'middle-class' as well as moderation and accomplishment, or else those social and personal attributes which were directly questioned by the British Female Gothic while only challenged obliquely, but comprehensively, by the Italian one.

In this chapter, we will discuss what might constitute the nineteenth-century Italian Female Gothic and how its female protagonists conveyed critical socio-political messages. By drawing on feminist theories, we argue for only a seemingly subaltern position occupied by the female protagonists of Italian Gothic novels, precisely because from such a stance they can nonetheless articulate forms of social critique, and thus make their voices heard publicly. Since the public realm was necessarily male dominated, and could not be emasculated, the private sphere was, and would continue to be, female. Furthermore, since the tension between these two domains had to remain veiled and unspoken, in order to sustain social order, an alternative means of conveying and sublimating the repressed had to be found. Accordingly, the Female Gothic permits a shift in perspective: the protagonists of these stories allow for a multiplicity of feminine models which did not present a unitary view, but rather a multifaceted understanding of the social fabric of the nation. Our case studies are taken from medusa-like female characters, blessed or cursed by such a beauty, portrayed in novellas and novels by Iginio Ugo Tarchetti (1869), Camillo Boito (1883) and later Luigi Capuana (1904), because they best exemplify the relationship between the Female Gothic and instances of social critique.[3]

Theorising a Female Gothic for the Italian Case

The relationship between the Gothic and the female body has been exhaustively discussed. We should like to mention, among other scholarly contributions, Elisabeth Bronfen's study *Over Her Dead Body* (1992) because of how she uses the discourse on the body as a psychoanalytical tool to read and bring together a wide-ranging set of disparate texts.[4] About the Gothic she wrote that the body itself is a liminal site where boundaries can be transgressed in such a way as to question the foundation of the reality we perceive:

> While Jean-Martin Charcot was experimenting with the use of hypnosis to treat patients for hysteria, spiritualists maintained that at the site of a figuratively deadened feminine body the immaterial realm of the beyond could become visible, a contact between the living and the dead be established or secured, and the boundary between the here and the beyond blurred. (Bronfen 4)

The female protagonists' bodies of the stories of Gothic fiction are liminal sites where conventions, norms and accepted wisdom can be challenged. An assumption we subscribe to in principle but we also alter in its focus. It is not the body the liminal site we are interested in, but the self as a site of social critique.

Feminist critics have also spoken about a distinction between Female/Male Gothic as well as about the relationship of the female characters with the villain-hero of the novel, at least as far as the British tradition was concerned.[5] If the Female Gothic challenged the secrets of family life, the Male Gothic explored those at the core of gender paradigms differences. For, Ferguson Ellis continues, in the 'feminine Gothic the heroine exposes the villain's usurpation and thus reclaims an enclosed space that should have been a refuge from evil but has become the very opposite, a prison. [. . .] It works to subvert the idealization of the home, and by implication the ideology of "separate spheres" on which that idealization depends' (xiii). Because of how it oversteps the boundaries of what a community recognises as familiar, the Gothic challenges the psychological and communal rules prescribed by the social contract. Specifically, according to Ferguson Ellis, the conventions of this thematic system preoccupied with the anthropological and political sphere of the foreign can problematise and speak 'to and of' what is forbidden by the rules and conventions established by the middle-classes. Yet, as Helene Mayers points out in her assessment of the Female Gothic from the origins to the present day, this binary approach to the Gothic has to make sure it avoids the pitfalls of victimisation of women as well as that of creating new essentialist views on the female sphere to encourage a more 'relational interpretation' of interpersonal relations (10–15).[6]

Such an analysis is certainly pertinent for the British case, but for the Italian one such a distinction is no longer valid because the female and male characters play interchangeable roles which are solidified in the notion of 'self' rather than that of gender affirmation. Therefore, the definition Ellen Moers gives of the Female Gothic, as 'the work that women writers have done in the literary mode that, since the eighteenth century, we have called the Gothic' (90), can hardly be applied to the Italian Female Gothic, which was written both by male and female authors and which did not respect traditional gender distinction. Rather, we uphold Mayers's argument that 'the Gothic [. . .] becomes a site to negotiate between the scripts of "male vice and female virtue" associated with cultural feminism and "gender scepticism"' (xii).

Therefore, to make sense of the working mechanism of an eccentric Gothic mode and of its eccentric heroines-heroes such as the Italian ones, in what will follow, we will take a more comprehensive look at the themes and areas the Female Gothic challenges. Namely, we will read some key texts populated by Gothic heroines to analyse how their subject-position is articulated within the public and personal sphere, and how their modes of self-affirmation are described often according to androgynous physical and behavioural patterns. The Gothic's encounter with the Other is not necessarily with an external other, but also with the inner contradictions of its self-functioning within the public sphere.

Fosca Can Speak, but How About the Others?

Before moving to the classic Gothic heroines of the Italian nineteenth century, it is worth considering a novella by Luigi Capuana titled 'Un vampiro' (1904) and dedicated to his friend Cesare Lombroso, the founder of the Italian school of positivist criminology and an extremely influential figure within the Italian scientific community of the time. In this early twentieth-century novella, the classic Gothic theme of the male vampire is intertwined with a realistic narrative mode – and it is used to challenge both the certainties of the positivist science and of medicine as well as the narrative paradigm of realism, rather than seeing the vampire as 'the embodiment of authorial neuroses and as the coded expression of more general cultural fears of which the author is, consciously or unconsciously, an observer' (Hughes 145; see also Della Coletta 192). Capuana's male vampire undermines and threatens the female protagonist, but such an interpersonal dynamic of victim and abuser had been already subverted in the works of bohemian *Scapigliati* artists, such as Igino Ugo Tarchetti, who famously portrayed female vampires in Gothic stories such as *Fosca* (1869), and in Antonio Fogazzaro's *Malombra* (1881).[7] Centred on the female protagonist Marina, *Malombra* in particular was a *romanzo nero* which was meant to address the social problems of contemporary society, as the author himself claimed, while simultaneously hiding social conflict by displacing it in the realm of the supernatural (Caesar, 'Sensation' 99–103). In other words, the world of the Female Gothic was a world of displaced dissent, as already made clear in the female characters populating the works by Tarchetti, Arrigo Boito, Giovanni Faldella, Carlo Dossi and Luigi Gualdo amongst others.

Tarchetti's short novel *Fosca* was published posthumously in 1869, after the author's death by typhus. The novel is divided into two main chronologically organised narrative blocks telling the story of Giorgio's liaison with a married woman, Clara, which takes place during a period of leave from his regiment due to illness in Milan, and subsequently of his dark affair with Fosca, a woman he meets once he returns to his regiment in the countryside: both loves are 'fatali e formindabili' [fatal and formidable] (Tarchetti 21).[8]

In the best tradition of the Gothic, the main first-person intradiegetic character and narrator Giorgio remembers those frightening, sublime events with a mixture of terror and attraction, and with some gratitude towards both the empirical sciences and his own luck, perhaps, for having survived such devastating passions, which he also describes as illnesses (Tarchetti 22), thereby placing himself in a subaltern position in comparison to those of the female protagonists of this story. Giorgio's seemingly linear narrative is a mixture of Gothic motifs: on the one hand, he describes a Burkean universe filled with sublime terror; and on the other, the past becomes obsessively present in his life so much that only the act of writing can help his healing.

Giorgio exists because Clara and Fosca enable him to do so, thereby deconstructing the binary distinction between victim and abuser, private and public sphere, male and female. Moreover, all these characters inhabit simultaneously diverse spaces (the home, the castle, the public sphere), whilst fulfilling different roles: that of the mother, the monster, the wife, the femme fatale. These two female protagonists in particular are interesting representations of the Female Gothic (especially if taken together with Giorgio, the male protagonist) since they both dismantle consolidated Western, nineteenth-century behavioural patterns, to which women were expected to adjust, and that can be classified according to an alternation of: activity and passivity, sun and moon, culture and nature, logos and pathos, rationality and emotions, day and night, authentic and inauthentic life.[9]

As their names suggest in a somewhat formulaic manner, Clara is the symbol of good health and light while Fosca is the symbol of darkness and illness, but within the context of the Gothic novel even Giorgio admits that such clear-cut categorisations did and do not work. Clara is a frustrated, married woman who has an affair with an army officer: for him and for her contemporary society she is a source of life, almost a nurturing figure, a 'patria perché è per amor tuo che adoro codesto angolo di terra' [homeland, for it is because of my love for you that I adore this corner of the earth] (Tarchetti 40). But she is also the embodiment of a seemingly ordinary but instead failed marriage: 'suo marito era giovine e avvenente, occupava una carica distinta in un'amministrazione governativa; non erano ricchi, ma parevano agiati e felici; avevano un figlio' [her husband was young and good-looking, he had a dignified position in the governmental administration; they were not rich, but they seemed comfortable and happy; they had a son] (Tarchetti 29). In the light of day, Clara occupies an ideal social position, and we could even say that, by embracing a medietas which is enviable by most peoples' standards, she appears to live an authentic life. She nonetheless subverts these very same standards by eluding them and risking her respectability to follow a passionate love affair with a bohemian officer who suffers from a heart complaint, thus inevitably breaking the association of propriety, nature and authenticity.

If Clara accepts a subversive social position, Fosca adds to the social problem that of her mental state: the physical disability of an era, hysteria. Fosca, the colonel's cousin, suffers from the most fashionable illness of the time, and one exclusively to be found in women because of their bodily anatomy and of the mysteries such anatomy still posed to the medical sciences. Fosca enters the narrative in absentia. At first we only hear her screaming from her bedroom, because of an attack of hysteria which signifies both a loss of self-control and a threat to the social order. Yet again, this attack represents a challenge to the reason-emotions divide. More suggestively however, Giorgio is attracted to Fosca's lack of self-control, her intelligence, her subversive sexuality and to how she exceeds social norms (see Tarchetti 64, 68, 81–2). Or else, because, in the words of Toril Moi, 'laying claim to all possible subject-positions, the speaking subject can indeed proudly proclaim herself as a "feminine plural"' (116).

Fosca does not conform to the canonically beautiful of her time: her bodily features do not fit with the stereotype of accepted female beauty which was based on an idea of harmony and symmetry. According to the first definition of the genre produced in the contest of architecture, the Gothic embodies anything which is not regular, which defies widely accepted mathematical rules about uniformity and proportion established by Vitruvius. Fosca functions on the premises of excess since she lacks centre and symmetry, both physically and emotionally. In this, she fits perfectly with the Female Gothic model, which is primarily *attractive and formidable at the same time* because of its illusion of classical composition, as in the case of Gothic architecture.

Fosca's past is filled with romances which do not fulfil the expectations of middle-class decorum; and she does make Giorgio aware of all this while seducing him. When at boarding school, Fosca had a lesbian affair with another student who, according to our protagonist, was far too puerile and superficial to understand the depth of their mutual feelings. This woman was then married and, unlike Fosca, had become socially acceptable, albeit unable to express herself as a plural self. Fosca defends her fluid sexual orientations because they enable her to express herself to her full potential without being subjected to castrating social norms. In a 1908 essay, Freud himself attributed to bisexuality a stabilising social role because as such it could normalise erotic desires which could not be channelled by binary oppositions (IX, 164–6).

Fosca's sexuality grants her a position of strength: Giorgio is afraid of this formidable, eccentric, androgynous and polymorphous woman and rejects her. In turn, she rejects and humiliates him. Giorgio's conclusions about the nature of his fatal passion for Fosca is that love is about the body, a Darwinian conglomeration of 'nervi, fluidi, di armonie animali: l'identità dei caratteri, la stima lo fortificano, non lo creano' [nerves, fluids, animal harmonies: the complementarity of personalities, the mutual respect do fortify it, do not create it] (Tarchetti 76). Giorgio's association of love with the body once more reveals how passive an actor he is in the story and how much he is forced to rely on social conventions to survive.[10] Fosca is not a subaltern subject because she is more intelligent, cultured and rational than Giorgio. Furthermore, Fosca's fluid sexual identity allows her to occupy a powerful subject-position which challenges the binary distinction between nature and culture that the social contract validates through marriage.

In this Gothic version of the story, Giorgio plays the part of the female heroine. During a walk in the garden of an abandoned castle, he describes himself as a decentred and isolated individual, just like the ruins of a Gothic castle, because he is unable to marry either Clara, already married, or Fosca, due to her psychological disposition and disregard for social conventions (Tarchetti 62).

Having said that, before meeting Giorgio, Fosca had been married to a proper Gothic villain, a certain Count Ludovico B. This man, claiming to have fled his country of origin, Dalmatia, for political reasons, was actually only a libertine in search of money and adventures, in not too dissimilar a way from that of the male protagonist of *Senso*. Ludovico was an attractive man who had used his physical beauty, coupled with some limited artistic talent and feminine mannerisms, to charm his way into the world (Tarchetti 106). Like Giorgio, Ludovico is an ambiguous, androgynous male figure who does not possess the strength and acumen with which Fosca is gifted. Moreover, Ludovico employs his physical qualities to survive by cheating on others. Not only does he dilapidate Fosca's family money but he also abandons her, leaving her to become socially disreputable and, after the loss of her child, sterile and only able to occupy liminal, nocturnal spaces in absentia.

In his work on the Italian Gothic, David Del Principe has argued that Fosca is a female vampire who vampirises Giorgio because she has already been the victim of another vampire, the self-proclaiming Count Ludovico (90–100). In this way, Tarchetti reverses the power structures and influences of Capuana's vampire by introducing a female character who can be at the same time subaltern and hegemonic.

Tarchetti's social vision comes to life by waving patterns of deconstruction of traditional social and gender paradigms and by fashioning a non-unitary selfhood, whether male or female. The novel ends with Fosca's demise in recognition of her excessive modernity. She can only acknowledge the conventional beauty of Giorgio (and his stereotypical opportunism) when, himself debilitated by an illness, he holds a mirror where both of them can be reflected. Such a symbolic exchange allows Giorgio to survive by running away in a somnambular state, shocked by Fosca's appearance (Tarchetti 136–7, 178). Fosca's cousin, the Colonel, must avenge her death by means of a manly and decorous duel at dawn in the garden of a Gothic castle in ruin. Giorgio survives this final duel not because of any virile act of courage on his part, of course, but because he falls 'victim' to a hysterical attack, once again reversing gender dynamics (Tarchetti 108).

The proper closure of this short novel comes in the guise of a letter from the doctor to reassure Giorgio about the transitory nature of his attacks of hysteria. The doctor, the scientific authority, just like in the case of Capuana's vampire, confirms with some degree of certainty that Giorgio is not responsible for what has happened to him because the agent who directed his actions, and his hand, was an extraordinary and mysterious being which could not be found in the realms of science, nor in those of history, but only in those of a Gothic tale (Tarchetti 171). This self-assuring end reverses the initial subject position occupied by its protagonists by attributing to Giorgio a clear male role, however artificial and precarious this might appear to be, and thus leaving this Gothic story suspended in ambiguity about the future and about its 'reality'.

The Countess in the Castle

The Milanese publisher Treves published *Senso* by Camillo Boito in 1883. This short novel narrates the adventures of Countess Livia, the heterodiegetic narrator, and specifically her affair with a young Austrian officer named Remigio Ruiz in Venice and Trento between 1865 (at the imminent start of the Third Italian War of Independence) and 1866. Therefore, *Senso* is a contemporary tale launching an explicit attack on the institution of marriage.

Married for interest to an older man, bored and frustrated, Livia falls in love with an enemy of the Italian nation who takes advantage of her emotionally and financially; once all his deceptions come to light, she hands him over to his superior with the charge of betrayal and facing the martial court. The story, stored in a draft manuscript Livia has penned in the heyday of her destructive torrid affair, is published several years after the events have occurred, following a standard Gothic narrative pattern. In a similar fashion to what we have seen in *Fosca* (and in the female protagonists of the trilogy *L'amore nell'arte*, 1869), Gothic narrative motifs and textual strategies appear within a largely realistic and historical novel which even starts with the typical Manzonian (and indeed Gothic) topos of the found manuscript.

Livia is the epitome of the decadent heroine described by Mario Praz: a victim as well as a perpetrator, trapped in an unhappy marriage of convenience, who struggles in finding an independent voice to assert herself through forms of creative and productive thinking (McNay 64). In an ideal continuation with the end of *Fosca*, but differently from Giorgio, this fresh incarnation of a medusean-mephisphelean female Gothic character starts her story by reflecting herself in a mirror to admire narcissistically the longevity of her beauty (Boito 21–2). Livia's power over men can be exercised only in the private sphere, because within the public sphere she is another disempowered subject, married to an older man she despises but who can give her a higher social status (Boito 23–4). Livia has signed a social contract to survive and, to meet the demands of the material conditions of existence, she has accepted a so-called inauthentic life.

However, it is the naked body which reigns over the personal sphere, and she exists because of her sexual desire towards Remigio, who combines, like Giorgio, feminine and masculine traits in a somewhat ambiguous manner. Remigio displays some statuesque attributes (see Tarchetti's collection entitled *L'amore nell'arte* and its three different portrayals of women annihilated and silenced by dominant masculine creative powers), leading to a physical attraction which is lethal (eventually for him and not for her) and not profitable socially. When Remigio is away, Livia's physical state deteriorates and she starts suffering from hysteria. In her case too, it has all to do with her nerves, and in order to recover she needs some fresh air: she needs to resolve the conflict between nature and her mind (Boito 37). With exactly the same formulation used for Fosca, since this was once more a matter concerning the nervous system, the doctor could not but recommend focusing exclusively on the recovery of the body.

Once her moment of madness and her revenge have been sealed and signed off, Livia is back in the comfort of the interior where the novel ends. In a perfect symmetry with the incipit, the explicit shows Livia in front of another narcissistic mirror ready to dismiss without any mercy her last, insignificant lover, a young lawyer named Gino, who had just left his fiancé for Livia. While dismissing Gino, Livia is almost compelled to remember the passion she once felt for Remigio with a sense of regret and nostalgia (Boito 61). Livia is a Gothic heroine who accepts her condition, her longing for the Gothic villain who lives outside her upper-class circles, as well as the inevitability of the social contract from which she cannot escape.[11]

This last scene brings us back to her home, where the same sense of fakeness and unhappiness is reinstated, thus challenging the idea that the home is a safe haven. On this occasion, the home represents the unity of matrimony and endurance of the social contract, and anything outside of these safe boundaries can only be classified as a fantasy, a malady, a melodrama, or even a Gothic tale. Or ultimately, any deviance is only a disease of the uterus, not of the mind, which does not call into question any form of affirmation of the self as an autonomous being or, even, as a citizen in their own right.

Livia, Clara, Fosca and all the Others who Entered the Public Sphere

Livia as a predatory self, Clara as an unfaithful wife and Fosca as a femme *castratrice* affirm to the point of self-annulation their feminine selves through their varied forms of rebellion against the rule of the monogamous bourgeoise marriage (McNay 4). Fosca will die as a result of her marriage, while Livia and Clara will survive physically by adjusting to the social rules of austerity and self-mastery, since only 'a political genealogy exposes the contingent and socially determined nature of sexuality', a genealogy which could only be established according to an organisation of the state and of the public sphere which lets women speak (McNay 30).

The idea of the family is profoundly tested to the point of disintegration. In these tales, the home is barren and cold and not the reassuring comfortable place it is meant to be. At the heart of the bourgeois family, the female Gothic heroine is a disempowered figure who cannot guarantee any form of unity because she is a fragmented self who defies unity (Ferguson Ellis 8; McNay 37). By not subjecting their sexuality or indeed their desires to the rules imposed by the common good, these Gothic heroines do not accept the separation between the personal and the private spheres which defined modern, bourgeois society. If the realist novel had the political and public obligation to try and speak of a unitary nation, albeit divided by cultures and languages, these Gothic heroines had freedom to speak of their private selves; and thus cast doubts on the shape of the new nation. And, crucially, the suspension of disbelief of the Gothic genre gave them a narrative configured for doing so without providing definite answers.

Their modern outlook consisted in their new understanding of their own selves, once they are placed outside binary distinctions between victim and perpetrator, night and day, authentic and inauthentic life, nature and culture. Their own conscious and unconscious desires speak and enable them to speak of what is not supposed to be spoken about. Not only a physical craving to possess their lovers but a desire to occupy an autonomous position within the public sphere allows these women to behave in ways that can contrast, if not subvert, those patriarchal models upon which the new Italian society was built. More interestingly perhaps, such a change had not to be realised once and for all, but rather to be deferred to the future, and to the imaginary utopias Gothic literature could build around alternative ways of configuring the self.

The twentieth-century Female Gothic capitalised on its nineteenth-century precursors' attempts at shaping spaces to accommodate alternative selves and indeed others, and created narrative scenarios in which the heroines can continue to speak of that which society marginalises due to perceiving it as either threatening, or disquieting, or both. For instance, such interpersonal utopianism can be found in the works of Annie Vivanti (*Sua altezza*, 1923), Paola Masino (*Ponte Ignoso*, 1931), Anna Maria Ortese (*L'iguana*, 1965) and Paola Capriolo (*Con i miei occhi*, 1997), in which the female characters establish an empathic relationship with an Other – often a monstrous creature, which lives outside social norms or has a closer relationship with the natural universe (most notably in the case of Ortese). These female writers adopted the Gothic mode in a spurious manner in order to reframe what disturbs the order of the polite middle-class world, by challenging once again the binary categories of activity and passivity, sun and moon, culture and nature, logos and pathos, rationality and emotions, day and night, authentic and inauthentic life that we have been discussing in this chapter. In this way these twentieth-century Gothic heroines problematise not simply the meaning of the 'real', but also what constitutes the 'female difference' in constructing a socially viable option for community life.

Bibliography

Billiani, Francesca, 'Eroi ed eroine nazionali manquée in *Fosca* di Igino Ugo Tarchetti e *Senso* di Camillo Boito', *Italica*, 88.2, 2011, pp. 78–96.

Billiani, Francesca, 'The Italian Gothic and Fantastic: An Inquiry into the Notions of Literary and Cultural Traditions (1869–1997)', in Francesca Billiani and Gigliola Sulis (eds), *The Italian Gothic and the Fantastic: Encounters and Rewritings of Narrative Traditions* (Madison, WI: Fairleigh Dickinson University Press, 2007), pp. 11–34.

Boito, Camillo, *Senso* [1883] (Milan: Bur, 1999).

Brabon, Benjamin, and Stépahnie Genz (eds), 'Postfeminist Gothic', *Gothic Studies*, 9.2, 2007 (monographic issue).

Bronfen, Elisabeth, *Over Her Dead Body: Death, Femininity and the Aesthetic* (Manchester: Manchester University Press, 1992).

Caesar, Ann H., 'Construction of Character in Tarchetti's *Fosca*', *The Modern Language Review*, 82.1, 1987, pp. 76–87.

Caesar, Ann H., 'Sensation, Seduction, and the Supernatural: Fogazzaro's *Malombra*', in Francesca Billiani and Gigliola Sulis (eds), *The Italian Gothic and the Fantastic: Encounters and Rewritings of Narrative Traditions* (Madison, WI: Fairleigh Dickinson University Press, 2007), pp. 98–118.

Camilletti, Fabio, 'Gertrude e il Nome del Padre', *Italian Studies*, 71.1, 2016, pp. 82–97.

Capuana, Luigi, *Un vampiro* [1907], <https://freeditorial.com/en/books/un-vampiro> (last accessed 2 August 2022).

Cesaretti, Enrico, *Castelli di carta. Retorica della dimora tra Scapigliatura e surrealismo* (Ravenna: Longo, 2001).

Del Principe, Davide, *Rebellion, Death, and Aesthetics in Italy: The Demons of Scapigliatura* (Madison, WI: Fairleigh Dickinson University Press, 1996).

Della Coletta, Cristina, 'Teoria realista e prassi fantastica: "Un Vampiro" di Luigi Capuana', *MLN*, 110.1, 1995, pp. 192–208.

Farnetti, Monica, 'Patologie del romanticismo. Il gotico e il fantastico fra l'Italia e l'Europa', in Gian Marco Anselmi (ed.), *Mappe della letteratura europea e mediterranea*, 4 vols (Milan: Bruno Mondadori Editore, 2000–1, II, 2000), pp. 340–66.

Ferguson Ellis, Kate, *The Contested Castle: Gothic Novels and The Subversion of Domestic Ideology* (Chicago: University of Illinois Press, 1989).

Freud, Sigmund, 'Hysterical Phantasies and their Relation to Bisexuality', in James Strachey (ed.), *The Standard Edition of the Complete Psychological Works of Sigmund Freud*, 24 vols (London: Hogarth Press, 1953–74, 1959, ix), pp. 159–66.

Hughes, William, 'Fictional Vampires in the Nineteenth and Twentieth Centuries', in David Punter (ed.), *A Companion to the Gothic* (Cambridge and New York: Cambridge University Press, 2000), pp. 143–54.

Mangini, Angelo M., *La voluttà crudele. Fantastico e malinconia nell'opera di Igino Ugo Tarchetti* (Rome: Carocci, 2000).

Mazzoni, Guido, *Theory of the Novel* (Cambridge, MA: Harvard University Press, 2017).

McNay, Lois, *Foucault and Feminism* (Cambridge: Polity Press, 1992).

Meyers, Helene, *Femicidal Fears: Narratives of the Female Gothic Experience* (Albany, NY: Suny Press, 2001).

Moers, Ellen, *Literary Women: The Great Writers* (New York: Oxford University Press, 1985).

Moi, Toril, *Sexual Textual Politics: Feminist Literary Theory* (London: Routledge, 1985).

Praz, Mario, *La morte, la carne, il diavolo* (Florence: Sansoni, 1988).

Smith, Andrew, and Diana Wallace (eds), 'Female Gothic', *Gothic Studies*, 6.1, 2004 (monographic issue).

Tarchetti, Igino Ugo, *Fosca* [1869] (Milan: Mondadori, 1981).

Tellini, Gino, *Il romanzo italiano dell'Ottocento e Novecento* (Milan: Bruno Mondadori, 2000).

Von Mücke, Dorothea, *The Seduction of the Occult and the Rise of the Fantastic Tale* (Stanford, CA: Stanford University Press, 2003).

Notes

1. For a further analysis on the need to consider these two genres as working together, and on the role of women in the Italian Gothic and fantastic literature, see Billiani 22–4.
2. See also Gino Tellini for a discussion of the place of the Gothic within the

national tradition (121–38). To note that in his history of Italian literature, Tellini dedicates very little space to the Gothic, and he rather treats it as a minor occurrence within the national paradigm. For a more detailed account of the reception of Gothic literature in Italy, see Del Principe and Farnetti.
3. Mario Praz's seminal *La carne, la morte e il diavolo* established an enduring paradigm for the definition of the fallen woman in terms of victim and abuser which has been consistently challenged by feminist scholarship (31–53).
4. For an overview of this problem in Italy, see Catherine Ramsey-Portolano's chapter in this volume.
5. Dorothea von Mücke observed that, since the beginning of the eighteenth century, writers resorted to anti-realist narrative models in order to portray forms of sexuality which exceeded current social norms (1–2).
6. The debate on the Female Gothic has been particularly lively, especially when, more recently, it has also set out to account for the transition from feminist to postfeminist readings of Gothic tales; for further insights see two special issues of *Gothic Studies* co-edited by Andrew Smith and Diana Wallace (Female Gothic, 2004) and by Benjamin Brabon and Stéphanie Genz (Postfeminist Gothic, 2007) respectively.
7. The same pattern can be found in other works by Tarchetti and more specifically in his trilogy *L'amore nell'arte* (1869).
8. *Fosca* has been read and analysed extensively; for further details see Billiani; Caesar 'Construction of Character'; and Mangini. All these contributions explore *Fosca* from different points of view: respectively the Gothic within the national discourse, Fosca as a character, and the novel as an example of fantastic fiction.
9. For a discussion of how such categories have been elaborated by feminist thinkers and by Cixous in particular, see Moi (103–4).
10. See Moi (110) for a discussion of masculine values and of propriety as a compass establishing what constitutes social acceptance.
11. On this point, see Cesaretti for the Italian case, Ferguson Ellis for the British, and Meyers for a response to Ferguson Ellis (19).

Chapter 14

Gothic Criminology
Stefano Serafini

Criminology, due to its inherent association with deviance and transgression, is particularly prone to Gothicisation.[1] It is not a coincidence that it originated in the second half of the nineteenth century, in conjunction with the resurgence of the Gothic novel, and that its founding father was the Italian physician Cesare Lombroso, who has been labelled by historians of crime Nicole Rafter and Per Ystehede as a truly 'Gothic scientist' (265). Lombroso's highly controversial theories of deviance as biologically determined and identifiable on the basis of physical traits – expanded and developed by his collaborators, who formed the famous Italian school of criminal anthropology – transcended national and disciplinary boundaries, reinforcing the symbiotic relationship between biology and transgression that continues to haunt contemporary Western cultures.

Lombroso's science aroused so much interest, attracting and repulsing at the same time, not only because it was built on common prejudices and widespread anxieties that were fuelled by literature and the press, but also because it was imbued with Gothicism. As Rafter maintains, Lombroso shifted criminology's focus 'away from the mind (a construct compatible with the idea of an immortal soul) to the brain (an organ whose physicality ruled out metaphysical speculation of any sort)' (87), thereby severing criminology's connection with morality and religion. His theories destabilised accepted boundaries and traditional assumptions about human identity and sexuality, converting 'Gothic anxieties', such as the spectre of degeneration, the bestiality within humans, and the divided nature of the self, into 'scientific concerns' (Rafter and Ystehede 276).

Starting from the premise that the *fin de siècle* was distinguished by the interplay of scientific and Gothic discourses, in this chapter I will explore precisely why and how Lombroso's criminology is deeply Gothic in its methods, applications and implications. Focusing on the literary, visual and occult components of Lombroso's multifarious and far-reaching work, I will seek to show how Gothic narratives on the construction of deviance influenced Lombroso's criminological thinking, ultimately transforming the transgressor from, in Karen Halttunen's perceptive words, a 'common sinner with whom the larger community of sinners were urged to identify in the service of their own salvation' into a moral monster 'from whom readers were instructed to shrink, with a sense of horror that confirmed their own "normalcy" in the face of the morally alien' (4–5).

Literary and Visual Monsters

Drawing on positivist approaches – positivism being a philosophical theory that, by the late 1860s, had become the official culture of the governing elite – Lombroso published, in 1876, the first version of his major work, *L'uomo delinquente*, with the aim of establishing the study of criminal behaviour on strictly scientific foundations through an analysis that prioritised biological causes. By means of this book, he popularised the category of the 'born criminal', whose supposed innate propensity for delinquency was explained by his reversion to a subhuman type of man, characterised by physical features reminiscent of savages and primitive peoples. The idea of the born criminal tapped into widespread fears of degeneration in the post-Darwinian Western world, both giving shape to and providing scientific validation for a purely Gothic figure, a throwback to an earlier evolutionary era that was both physically and mentally abnormal.

Lombroso's criminal bodies can be compared to what Kelly Hurley, in her landmark work on *fin-de-siècle* Gothic writing, identifies as the abhuman, that is, Gothic liminal bodies that occupy the ambiguous space between the human and the beast, the civilised and the primitive. These bodies, which threaten the integrity of human identity, are the product not of uncanny supernatural forces, but rather of scientifically explicable processes. It is thus the duty of criminologists and diagnosticians such as Lombroso to provide the necessary tools for identifying and categorising these elements of abnormality and dissolution. In doing so, as I argue, Lombroso dived into the literature of terror.

Cristopher Pittard has convincingly suggested that Lombroso's famous and widely cited description of the birth of criminal anthropology, that is, the medical analysis of the body of the brigand Giuseppe Vilella in 1871, is, in its very essence, a Gothic story. In *Criminal Man, According to the Classification of Cesare Lombroso*, mostly written by his daughter Gina and published in English in 1911, the Italian physician employs the motif of metaphoric enlightenment to convey the extraordinary importance of his discovery, namely the infamous median occipital fossa, an impression that he found both in criminals and inferior animals, especially rodents: 'this was [...] a revelation [...] at the sight of that skull, I seemed to see all of a sudden, lighted up as a vast plain under a flaming sky, the problem of the nature of the criminal' (*Criminal Man* xiv–xv). While this scene reminds Pittard of the 'flash of light' that illuminates Victor Frankenstein in Mary Shelley's Gothic novel *Frankenstein* (1818), the depiction of the born criminal and his abnormal tendencies closely resembles that of literary vampires, which widely populated nineteenth-century Gothic narratives (Pittard 107–8): the biologically predisposed delinquent, Lombroso contends, is 'an atavistic being who reproduces in his person the ferocious instincts of primitive humanity', which include 'the desire not only to extinguish life in the victim, but to mutilate the corpse, tear its flesh, drink its blood' (*Criminal Man* xv). Luigi Guarnieri significantly views Lombroso's most interesting and enduring feature as located in the scientist's narrative style: before Freud, 'Cesare Lombroso is the greatest narrator of the nightmare, the novelistic apex of horror, the encyclopedist of crime, insanity, and perversion [...] His style is approximate, confusing, anecdotal, colorful (in one word Italian)' (117–18).

As can be seen, Lombroso's research on crime as a pathological re-emergence of primitive, animalistic habits was shaped by Gothic narratives while simultaneously encouraging and legitimising the creation of literary figures of monstrosity – from Dracula to Mr Hyde – that leave the spatially and temporally remote locales of early Gothic fiction in order to threaten the realm of the contemporary reader, infiltrating the new urban landscape and penetrating the bourgeois domestic world. Such mutual interaction between Gothic and scientific narratives contributed to changing the location of the monstrous. As Fred Botting has explained, whereas in late eighteenth-century Gothic literature horrors tended to be external to the human form – ghosts and evil monks who threatened the protagonists from outside – in the nineteenth century the horrors became internal and the perversions that menaced Gothic figures came from inside their own degenerating brains (135–54).

The power of Lombroso's science derived from its combination of a literary component and a strong visual dimension. As Rafter has noted, 'no criminologist has ever drawn more heavily on the visual, or revelled more in the imagery of crime' (130). From a contemporary perspective, Lombroso's macabre collection of images and objects now held at the Museum of Criminal Anthropology in Turin – which includes skulls, skeletons, brains, tattoos, 'deviant' faces considered to be crucial data for criminal identification – is inevitably profoundly troubling. The visual, however, was the key to Lombroso's popular appeal. As Elena Past remarks, his dizzying rows of portrait photographs, which he shared with his American and European colleagues, remain one of the most reproduced aspects of his work nowadays (148). For Kate West, an undergraduate criminology lecture would seem odd 'without Lombroso's infamous portraits flickering past students' eyes' (273).

Indeed, it is well known that, in order to make the reader visualise his Gothic creations, Lombroso filled his books with horrific images and illustrations of delinquents. He gradually came to appreciate the importance of the visual. While the first edition of *L'uomo delinquente* (1876) was not particularly rich in images, the volume *La donna delinquente, la prostituta e la donna normale*, originally published in 1893, contained eight plates and eighteen figures. The fifth and last edition of *L'uomo delinquente*, which came out in 1897, had been enlarged so much by the inclusion of photos that Lombroso had to create a separate volume, the *Atlante*, to include all of them. What is remarkable is that he deliberately invites his readers to participate in the construction of the criminal man. By supplying various materials, including illustrations and verbal portraits, he builds a community of followers and interpreters. In the preface to the *Atlante*, Lombroso explains its importance for his work, actively interpolating the reader into the interpretive community. The main aim of the atlas, he claims, is to give readers the opportunity to understand and verify the real nature of criminality on their own:

> Il fine prefissomi nel pubblicare questo atlante è quello di offrire al lettore il mezzo di controllare da sé la verità delle mie asserzioni, senza d'altra parte danneggiare l'economia dello spazio che esige un libro. Quest'atlante è dunque non solo una parte integrante dell'opera, ma anzi la più importante. (Lombroso, *L'uomo delinquente* iii)

> [The main goal of this atlas is to offer readers the means to substantiate the truth of my affirmations, without compromising the economy of the space that a book necessitates. This atlas is thus not only part and parcel of this work but actually its most important section.]

It is therefore clear that Lombroso is perfectly aware of the way in which the visual can help disseminate, shape and reinforce knowledge on criminal behaviour.

Illustrations were a particularly powerful instrument in the hands of Lombroso. Although many other scientists working on heredity and criminality relied on images and photos to spread and legitimise their theories, Lombroso did so in a unique way. His rich and composite material did not serve to prove a specific and clearly defined hypothesis, but rather more generally conveyed an impression of scientific prowess. As most scholars have shown, Lombroso used photographs inconsistently, but this was precisely his intention. Apparently relying on the realism and accuracy of photography, he actually conventionalised the images to further his own ends. Rafter and Gibson have drawn attention to two different line-drawn portraits, one appearing in the first edition and one in the fourth edition of *L'uomo delinquente*, which was published in 1889. Although the criminal in each portrait looks different, it is actually the same man, who assumed a drastically different physiognomy between the publications. The portrait, as they point out, 'underwent considerable uglification' in order to make the image correspond to the archetype of the wicked man, who is naturally always ugly (Gibson and Rafter 23).

As David Horn claims, Lombroso had to 'negotiate between a popular folkloric recognition of the criminal, and a more distancing effort to establish a new discipline that was not based entirely on the "wisdom" seemingly available to all' (69). However, particularly when it comes to the visual data, Lombroso relied heavily on the idea that people could instinctively recognise the features of the delinquent due to their deformity and was confident that popular culture would cement such associations. As Giorgio Colombo originally noted in his old but insightful study, the passage from photo to drawing and from drawing to engraving is a gradual process of deformation, which transforms the criminal into a monster (116). Elements of physical monstrosity and moral inferiority served to consolidate a racialised scheme of the interpretation of differences, from class to gender, on which the new-born state was constructed. Thus, the Gothic dimension of Lombroso's science ultimately has the effect of demonising a vast and indiscriminate range of cultural others – not only criminals, but all 'deviant' figures at the margins of the social body, such as prostitutes and vagrants – onto whom Italians could project their fears and concerns about the state and the prospect of a deeply fragmented country.

Building on this, borrowing Glennis Byron and David Punter's words, we can also say that Lombroso's work is Gothic because it ultimately sheds light on the monster's artificial nature, drawing attention 'to the mechanisms of monster production' and revealing precisely 'how the other is constructed and positioned as both alien and inferior' (264). Lombroso's consistent obsession with the inherent constituents of crime both signals and conceals an insuppressible need to exorcise the possibility, raised by both his theories and Gothic narratives, that all of the abnormalities that we would divorce from ourselves, as Jerrold Hogle reminds us, 'are part of ourselves, deeply and pervasively' (12).

Crime and the Occult

Although Lombroso was not the first thinker to scientifically address the question of the supernatural, he was certainly the thinker who most persistently explored the nature of occult phenomena and their relation to crime, encouraging a large number of followers and collaborators to follow the same path. Lombroso's involvement with occult phenomena dated back to the mid-1850s, when he was a graduate student at the University of Pavia and developed a friendship with his teacher, Bartolomeo Panizza, a renowned physician who had experimentally studied thought transmission under hypnosis while he was a member of a medical commission in Milan in September 1850. However, Lombroso's dramatic turn to occultism occurred in the mid-1880s, when hypnotism began to assume a controversial yet prominent position in the discourse of crime across Europe.[2]

In that period, particularly in France, debates concerning the nature, inner workings and broad repercussions of hypnotism were extremely heated. While Jean-Martin Charcot and his disciples at the Paris school maintained that only the already hysterical (mainly female patients) were hypnotisable and that hypnosis was a manifestation of illness, the exponents of the Nancy school, including Ambroise-Auguste Liébault and Hippolyte Bernheim, challenged the notion that hypnosis was rare or pathological, claiming that everyone was hypnotisable under the right conditions and that suggestibility was a universal human condition. In Italy, where scientists generally followed the Nancy School,[3] scientific studies focusing on the relationship between the hypnotist and the hypnotised, and the consequences this had on autonomous agency, proliferated.[4] There were, however, several controversies over the origins and functioning of hypnotic phenomena that eventually destabilised the solidity of the entire scientific community. As Stewart-Steinberg remarks, this meant that 'the categorization of individuals according to visible or at least determinable criteria was potentially threatened' (69).

The conflict between Italian scientists revolved around the controversial figure of Donato, in particular. Donato was the pseudonym of the theatrical magnetiser of crowds Alfred D'Hont. He had apparently revolutionised hypnosis through the discovery of a phenomenon that he called 'fascination' and performed an astonishing and memorable event at the Teatro Scribe in Turin in 1886, hypnotising an exceptional number of young and healthy men, with the effect of shifting the more traditional sexual dynamic whereby the compelling magnetiser is male and his victim invariably female. The event, which called into question the deep-rooted idea that only fragile, female subjects could be hypnotised, had an enormous influence at the time. As Stewart-Steinberg observes, the theatre became the 'true home' of the hypnotic subject (70), a Gothic domain of magic and illusion, where the audience is forced to put aside rationality and instead embrace the irrational.

Donato's performances elicited different reactions. Most politicians and clergymen immediately perceived the danger that magnetisers might cause by directing people's will and reacted with horror and alarm. The Jesuit Giuseppe Giovanni Franco, for instance, published *L'ipnotismo tornato di moda* (1886) in order to denounce the diabolical element inherent in hypnotic phenomena. Enrico Morselli, professor of psychiatry at the University of Turin, who had witnessed and succumbed to the fascination of Donato, drew a generally favourable portrait of the hypnotiser in his *Il magnetismo animale: la fascinazione e gli stati ipnotici* (1886) and challenged the idea that animal magnetism was unquestionably evil. In contrast, influential figures such as Lombroso and Angelo Mosso found Donato's powers difficult to explain and hence highly disturbing, and agreed that a solution was urgently needed, which eventually resulted in the official prohibition of public performances of hypnotism by the Superior Council of Health.[5] In order to avoid misunderstandings, the Superior Council of Health decided from its first meeting that 'it was no longer necessary to discuss the scientific and technical aspects of induced somnambulism or hypnotic suggestion, since both were integral part of modern neurological doctrine' (Guarnieri, 'Theatre and Laboratory' 131). Although some kind of order had apparently been restored, in reality persistent doubts and uncertainties remained.

The possible use of hypnotism as a criminal tool, in particular, started generating intense discussions. Despite having divergent opinions, Italian scientists agreed that hypnosis involves the deactivation of the inhibitory function of the subject's brain and the consequent loss of autonomous agency. For Morselli, the hypnotised subject demonstrates two fundamentally interconnected psychological features, namely automatism, defined as a lack of spontaneity, and suggestion, or the capacity to receive an infinite number of external stimuli or feelings (92). Likewise, for Lombroso, during hypnotic suggestion the subject's free will is often erased and replaced with that of their hypnotiser (*Ricerche* 27).[6] This debate had a profound effect on the popular imaginary, raising the issue of whether and to what extent a person could be hypnotised and forced to commit criminal acts, which created further problems for the legal system. While Giulio Campili suggests that only the hypnotist should be held accountable and prosecuted (129), Salvatore Ottolenghi uses the general terminology 'crime of suggestion' to criminalise a diverse range of practices that, to a greater or lesser degree, involve the inexplicable forces of the mind (588, 599). According to Stewart-Steinberg, it was precisely 'the possibility of getting someone else to commit a crime that caused the whole system to unravel, for now the criminal was not only the bad leader but also the victim' (75). The disturbing possibility that '*any* crime could be committed by *any member* of the population on the basis of a perverse suggestive instigation' (Stewart-Steinberg 75) blurred the boundary between right and wrong, sanity and insanity, the normal and the pathological, and upset the already precarious certainties of the Italian criminological school.

The Donato affair thus eroded the confidence of scientists and created an atmosphere of uncertainty and doubt. Lombroso unhappily acknowledges that 'tutti o quasi i fenomeni offertimi dagli ipnotizzati mi parvero escire dalle norme della fisiologia e della patologia, per entrare in quelli dell'ignoto' [almost all the phenomena exhibited by hypnotised subjects seemed to defy the rules of physiology and pathology, veering towards the unknown] (*Ricerche* 27), and concludes rather sharply that 'la verità è che una spiegazione scientifica assolutamente non può darsi di questi fatti, i quali entrano nel vestibolo di quel mondo che deve giustamente chiamarsi ancora occulto, perché inesplicato' [the truth is that a scientific explanation for these events cannot be provided, as they enter the domain of that world which must still be called occult because it remains unexplained] (7). The long-term consequences of these debates have never really been addressed by scholars. In short, although there was no time for the 1889 criminal code to incorporate the ideas arising from discussions involving hypnotic powers, it is worth asking, as Clara Gallini aptly does, whether they contributed to re-forging cultural and legal understandings of external influence, coercion and subjugation.[7]

Nevertheless, this complex climate, as I show in my other essay in this volume, opened up liminal and uncharted spaces, offering fictional opportunities that Italian writers eagerly embraced. The debate on criminal hypnosis provided new, exciting models of self and intersubjectivity for the Gothic, new language and frameworks for producing spectral identities, and new possibilities for plot and narration. The figure of Donato revived a fascination with the eyes of the magnetiser that the rise of hypnotism as a scientific discipline in the second half of the nineteenth century had increasingly contributed to marginalising (Gallini 190). Morselli, for instance, draws attention to Donato's 'sguardo fulmineo ed insistente' [quick and insistent gaze] (*Il magnetismo* 295), while Franco defines it as 'selvaggio' [savage] (34), which is further identified as the trigger for hypnotic subjugation. Not surprisingly, the monstrosity of the criminal hypnotist in European literature is more and more denoted by the eyes, as testified by Herold Voltaire's 'terrible eye' (Kindle) in Joseph Hocking's *The Weapons of Mystery* (1890), Dracula's 'red, gleaming eyes' that shine in the moonlight (Stoker 88), or the gender-blending creature in Richard Marsh's *The Beetle* (1897), whose enormous eyes 'ran, literally, across the whole of the upper portion of his face' (Marsh 53). Criminals increasingly used the power of their eyes to induce their victims to commit acts against their will, thus probing the dangerous possibilities offered by the phenomenon of post-hypnotic suggestion. An excellent example is Luigi Capuana's 'Ofelia' (1893), in which a painter who has personally attended Donato's performances hypnotises his unfaithful wife and forces her to commit suicide.

In this period, criminological research delved into previously unexplored territories, investigating the controversial effects of the latest medical and technological discoveries. By the end of the century, for instance, thought transference had become a popular subject of debate in Europe, especially thanks to the influential work of the Society for Psychical Research, originally established in 1882.[8] Unsurprisingly, Lombroso found the topic extremely intriguing. In January 1890, he met Belgian professional magician and mind-reader Jean-Lambert Pickman, who was sojourning in Italy at the time, in order to study him and assess whether he was potentially prosecutable for fraud. Lombroso worked on Pickman's medical and psychological profile, performing thought transmission tests with him that were substantially inconclusive; he eventually affirmed that the individual was generally lucid, though he suffered from neuropathy with incipient ataxia.[9]

Lombroso also worked on a rich variety of unusual and seemingly supernatural phenomena, including cases of premonitions and haunted houses, subjects on which he published a significant amount of articles in criminological journals such as the *Archivio di Psichiatria, Scienze Penali ed Antropologia Criminale*.[10] Spiritualism was one of his principal interests towards the end of his life.[11] This should not come as a surprise, as the last decade of the nineteenth century, as Massimo Biondi has demonstrated, was truly the Golden Age of spiritualism in Italy.[12] Fascinated, in particular, by the elusive and ambiguous figure of Eusapia Palladino,[13] Lombroso was interested in the phenomenon of mediumship for the same reason he studied criminality: both mediums and delinquents are deviant subjects, the examination of which can bring to light the physical and mental abnormalities that set them apart from normal people.

The analysis that I have conducted in this chapter demonstrates why criminal anthropology, which directly participated in the construction and normalisation of the new body politic by re-conceptualising the idea of delinquency while also turning to the scientific study of occult practices, perfectly encapsulates the ambivalence of the period that spans at least from national unification to the rise of Fascism. My contention is that the work of criminal anthropologists constitutes an important field of research that can shed a unique light on Italy's crucial role as a laboratory for the understanding and containment of crime and transgression within a wider European context in the age of positivism and beyond.

Scholars have traditionally situated criminal anthropology exclusively within the context of post-unification Italy and explained it as a Gothic aberration. For Daniel Pick, for instance, Lombroso spoke powerfully to a particular crisis and provided a 'new language of social representation' (111) that related to post-unification politics and to socialism. This narrative has been reinforced by English-speaking critics, who have consistently downplayed the transnational circulation and cultural impact of Lombroso's theories.[14] I believe that this critical orthodoxy should be called into question; the lens of the Gothic, as I have sought to show in this chapter, might be the right tool for doing precisely that.

As well as the mutual influence exerted by Lombroso's theories and Gothic narratives of deviance on each other, the long-term implications of such intersections deserve closer attention. Scholars have perceptively noted that Lombroso's legacy, far from disappearing, survived into the twentieth century and influenced the Fascist regime's police and social policies.[15] Others have even suggested the existence of a direct link between Lombrosian theories and Fascist and Nazi politics. Henry Friedlander, for example, observes that 'the Nazi killers used the language of Lombroso to target the same victim groups' (3). Richard Weikart claims that positivist theories fed dictatorial regimes such as Nazism in Germany after the end of the First World War, which spread the idea that only through racial extermination could humanity improve biologically and advance to higher cultural levels, since the lower races were not mentally capable of producing culture (203). Likewise, Joseph Crawford argues that, within the Gothicised world that lies behind Lombroso's rhetoric, the otherness of marginalised groups appeared not as relative and situational 'but as innate and essential, the result of a basic, ineffable monstrousness that could be erased only by extermination' (160).

Ultimately, Lombroso's Gothic discourses involving innate evil, biological monsters and ghosts that team up with diabolical human beings found their way into the ideology of eugenics and scientific racism, which continue to resonate widely and disturbingly in our world. Since the early 1980s, indeed, there has been a significant growth in studies that again purport to trace the aetiology of crime to physical factors, without neglecting social components.[16] Although this trend has been facilitated by moral discourses concerning addiction, as well as techniques in the fields of genetic engineering, neuroanatomical imaging and virology, it is indisputable that this complicated and alarming resurgence of biological explanations for deviant behaviour has its deepest roots in the historical period I have analysed in this chapter. It does not come as a surprise, then, that historians of crime have increasingly turned their attention to the modalities through which Lombroso's work anticipated the current genetic and neurological theorisations of crime.[17] These new studies have affected legal proceedings and court decisions across Western societies, especially in Italy, and their growing popularisation by the media has somewhat re-framed the nature of the debate on the origin of evil.[18] Contemporary criminology is once again tinged with the Gothic and the examination of its broad cultural and socio-political repercussions seems to be more important than ever for the cultural historian.

Bibliography

Baudi di Vesme, Cesare, *Storia dello spiritismo*, 2 vols (Turin: Roux Frassati e co., 1896–7).
Belfiore, Giulio, *Magnetismo e ipnotismo* (Milan: Hoepli, 1898).
Biondi, Massimo, *Tavoli e medium: storia dello spiritismo in Italia* (Rome: Gremese, 1988).
Blair, James R., 'The Emergence of Psychopathy: Implications for the Neuropsychological Approach to Developmental Disorder', *Cognition*, 101.2, 2006, pp. 414–42.
Blair, James R., 'Psychopathy: Cognitive and Neural Dysfunction', *Dialogues in Clinical Neuroscience*, 15.2, 2013, pp. 181–90.
Botting, Fred, *Gothic* (London and New York: Routledge, 1996).
Brofferio, Angelo, *Per lo spiritismo* (Milan: Briola, 1892).
Byron, Glennis, and David Punter (eds), *The Gothic* (Oxford: Blackwell, 2004).
Cadoret, Remi J., et al., 'Evidence for Gene-Environment Interaction in the Development of Adolescent Antisocial Behavior', *Behavior Genetics*, 13, 1983, pp. 301–10.
Campili, Giulio, *Il grande ipnotismo e la suggestione ipnotica nei rapporti col diritto penale e civile* (Turin: Bocca, 1886).
Colombo, Giorgio, *La scienza infelice: il museo di antropologia criminale di Cesare Lombroso* (Turin: Paolo Boringhieri, 1975).
Crawford, Joseph, *Gothic Fiction and the Invention of Terrorism: The Politics and Aesthetics of Fear in the Age of the Reign of Terror* (London: Bloomsbury,

2013).

Davie, Neil, *Tracing the Criminal: The Rise of Scientific Criminology in Britain (1860–1918)* (Oxford: Bardwell Press, 2005).

Dunnage, Jonathan, 'The Legacy of Cesare Lombroso and Criminal Anthropology in the Post-War Italian Police: A Study of the Culture, Narrative and Memory of a Post-Fascist Institution', *Journal of Modern Italian Studies*, 22.3, 2017, pp. 365–84.

Franco, Giovanni Giuseppe, *L'ipnotismo tornato di moda* (Prato: Tipografia Giachetti, 1886).

Friedlander, Henry, *The Origins of Nazi Genocide: From Euthanasia to the Final Solution* (Chapel Hill, NC: University of North Carolina Press, 1995).

Gallini, Clara, *La sonnambula meravigliosa: ipnotismo e magnetismo nell'Ottocento italiano* (Milan: Feltrinelli, 1983).

Gibson, Mary, *Born to Crime: Cesare Lombroso and the Origins of Biological Criminology* (Westport, CT: Praeger, 2002).

Gibson, Mary, and Nicole Rafter, 'Editors' Introduction', in Cesare Lombroso, *Criminal Man* (Durham, NC: Duke University Press, 2006), pp. 1–38.

Guarnieri, Luigi, *L'atlante criminale: vita scriteriata di Cesare Lombroso* (Milan: Mondadori, 2000).

Guarnieri, Patrizia, 'Theatre and Laboratory: Medical Attitudes to Animal Magnetism in Late-Nineteenth-Century Italy', in Roger Cooter (ed.), *Studies in the History of Alternative Medicines* (Houndmills: Palgrave Macmillan, 1988), pp. 118–39.

Halttunen, Karen, *Murder Most Foul: The Killer and the American Gothic Imagination* (Cambridge: Harvard University Press, 1998).

Harris, Ruth, 'Murder Under Hypnosis', *Psychological Medicine*, 15, 1985, pp. 477–505.

Harris, Ruth, *Murders and Madness: Medicine, Law, and Society in the Fin-De-Siècle* (Oxford: Clarendon, 1989).

Hocking, Joseph, *The Weapons of Mystery* [1890], Kindle edn.

Hogle, Jerrold E., 'Introduction: The Gothic in Western Culture', in Jerrold E. Hogle (ed.), *The Cambridge Companion to Gothic Fiction* (Cambridge: Cambridge University Press, 2002), pp. 1–20.

Horn, David G., *The Criminal Body: Lombroso and the Anatomy of Deviance* (New York and London: Routledge, 2003).

Hurley, Kelly, *The Gothic Body: Sexuality, Materialism, and Degeneration at the Fin de Siècle* (Cambridge: Cambridge University Press, 1996).

Legrenzi, Paolo, and Carlo Umiltà, *Neuro-mania. Il cervello spiega chi siamo* (Bologna: Il Mulino, 2009).

'List of Members and Associates (December, 1890)', *Proceedings of the Society for Psychical Research*, 6, 1890, pp. 679–707.

Lombroso, Cesare, 'Caso singolare di premonizione', *Archivio di Psichiatria, Scienze Penali ed Antropologia Criminale*, 17, 1896, pp. 128–30.

Lombroso, Cesare, *Criminal Man, According to the Classification of Cesare Lombroso* (New York and London: G. P. Putnam's Sons, 1911).

Lombroso, Cesare, 'Eusapia Palladino: cenni biografici', *La Lettura*, 7, 1907, pp. 389–95.

Lombroso, Cesare, 'Fenomeni medianici in una casa di Torino', *Archivio di*

Psichiatria, Scienze Penali ed Antropologia Criminale, 22, 1901, pp. 101–6.

Lombroso, Cesare, 'The Haunted Houses which I Have Studied', *Annals of Psychical Science*, 3, 1906, pp. 361–72.

Lombroso, Cesare, 'Inchiesta sulla trasmissione del pensiero', *Archivio di Psichiatria, Scienze Penali, ed Antropologia Criminale*, 12, 1891, pp. 58–108.

Lombroso, Cesare, 'Le spiritisme et la psychiatrie: explication psychiatrique de certains faits spirites', *Annales des Sciences Psychiques*, 2, 1892, pp. 143–51.

Lombroso, Cesare, *L'uomo delinquente in rapporto all'antropologia, alla giurisprudenza ed alla psichiatria. Atlante* (Turin: Bocca, 1897).

Lombroso, Cesare, 'Mon enquête sur la transmission de la pensée', *Annales des Sciences Psychiques*, 14, 1904, pp. 257–75.

Lombroso, Cesare, 'Pickman e la trasmissione del pensiero', *Archivio di Psichiatria, Scienze Penali, ed Antropologia Criminale*, 11, 1890, pp. 207–18.

Lombroso, Cesare, 'Psychology and Spiritism', *Annals of Psychical Science*, 7, 1908, pp. 376–80.

Lombroso, Cesare, *Ricerche sui fenomeni ipnotici e spiritici* (Turin: Unione Tipografico-Editrice Torinese, 1909).

Lombroso, Cesare, *Studi sull'ipnotismo* (Turin: Bocca, 1886).

Lombroso, Cesare, 'Sui fenomeni spiritici e la loro interpretazione', *La Lettura*, 6, 1906, pp. 978–87.

Lombroso, Cesare, 'Sulle proibizioni degli spettacoli ipnotici', *Archivio di psichiatria*, 7, 1886, pp. 504–5.

Luckhurst, Roger, *The Invention of Telepathy 1870–1901* (Oxford and New York: Oxford University Press, 2002).

Marsh, Richard, *The Beetle* [1897] (Plymouth, Sydney, Ontario and Orchard Park, NY: Broadview Press, 2004).

Mighall, Robert, *A Geography of Victorian Gothic Fiction: Mapping History's Nightmares* (Oxford: Oxford University Press, 1999).

Morselli, Enrico, *Il magnetismo animale: la fascinazione e gli stati ipnotici* (Turin: Roux & Favale, 1886).

Morselli, Enrico, *Psicologia e spiritismo* (Turin: Bocca, 1908).

Mosso, Angelo, 'Fisiologia e patologia dell'ipnotismo', *Nuova antologia*, 21, 1886, pp. 56–74.

Musumeci, Emilia, 'New Natural Born Killers? The Legacy of Lombroso in Neuroscience and Law', in Paul Knepper and P. J. Ystehede (eds), *The Cesare Lombroso Handbook* (London and New York: Routledge, 2013), pp. 131–46.

Ottolenghi, Salvatore, *La suggestione e le facoltà psichiche occulte in rapporto alla pratica legale e medico-forense* (Turin: Bocca, 1900).

Pappalardo, Armando, *Spiritismo* (Milan: Hoepli, 1898).

Past, Elena, *Methods of Murder: Beccarian Introspection and Lombrosian Vivisection in Italian Crime Fiction* (London: University of Toronto Press, 2012).

Picart, Carolin Joan, and Cecil Greek (eds), *Monsters In and Among Us: Towards a Gothic Criminology* (Madison, WI and Teaneck, NJ: Fairleigh University Press, 2007).

Pick, Daniel, *Faces of Degeneration: A European Disorder c. 1848–1918* (Cambridge: Cambridge University Press, 1989).

Pittard, Cristopher, *Purity and Contamination in Late-Victorian Detective*

Fiction (Farnham and Burlington, VT: Ashgate, 2011).
Rafter, Nicole, *The Criminal Brain: Understanding Biological Theories of Crime* (New York: New York University Press, 2008).
Rafter, Nicole, 'Introduction', *Theoretical Criminology*, 18.2, 2014, pp. 128–33.
Rafter, Nicole, and Per Ystehede, 'Here Be Dragons: Lombroso, the Gothic, and Social Control', in Mathieu Deflem (ed.), *Popular Culture, Crime, and Social Control* (Bingley: Emerald, 2010), pp. 263–84.
Raine, Adrian, *The Anatomy of Violence: The Biological Roots of Crime* (London: Penguin, 2013).
Rowe, David, *Biology and Crime* (Los Angeles, CA: Roxbury Publishing Company, 2002).
Scipio, Sighele, *La coppia criminale: studio di psicologia morbosa* (Turin: Bocca, 1893).
Stewart-Steinberg, Suzanne, *The Pinocchio Effect: On Making Italians (1860–1920)* (Chicago, IL and London: University of Chicago Press, 2007).
Stoker, Bram, *Dracula* [1897] (New York: Norton and Company, 1997).
Thurschwell, Pamela, *Literature, Technology, and Magical Thinking, 1880–1920* (Cambridge: Cambridge University Press, 2001).
Turiello, Pasquale, *Dello spiritismo in Italia* (Naples: Golia, 1898).
Valier, Claire, 'Punishment, Border Crossings and the Powers of Horror', *Theoretical Criminology*, 6.3, 2002, pp. 319–37.
Weikart, Richard, *From Darwin to Hitler. Evolutionary Ethics, Eugenics, and Racism in Germany* (Basingstoke: Palgrave Macmillan, 2004).
West, Kate, 'Visual Criminology and Lombroso: In Memory of Nicole Rafter (1939–2016)', *Theoretical Criminology*, 21.3, 2017, pp. 271–87.

Notes

1. It is therefore surprising that, although much has been written about the Gothic in the fields of literature and the visual arts, very few studies have been devoted to the way in which Gothicism has historically affected the development of criminology. Exceptions include Mighall; Picart and Greek; and Valier.
2. See Harris 'Murder under Hypnosis' and *Murder and Madness*.
3. See Guarnieri.
4. See, among others, Campili; Lombroso *Studi*; Sighele; Belfiore; Ottolenghi.
5. See Lombroso 'Sulle proibizioni' and Mosso.
6. For a definition of automatism, which indicates the elimination of free will, see Morselli *Il magnetismo*, 92.
7. Clara Gallini cites article number 603 of the 1930 criminal code, which revolves around a vague 'delitto di plagio' [murder by coercion] that was used to legitimise forms of police repression during the Fascist regime. See Gallini 233.
8. See Thurschwell; Luckhurst.
9. See Lombroso 'Pickman', 'Inchiesta' and 'Fenomeni'. All of these works reveal the depth of Lombroso's knowledge of contemporary research

on telepathy, including that of Pierre Janet and the Society for Psychical Research. In fact, in 1890, Lombroso was listed as a corresponding member of the society. See 'List of Members and Associates' 680.
10. See Lombroso 'Inchiesta'; 'Caso'; 'Fenomeni'.
11. See, among others, Lombroso 'Le spiritisme'; 'The Haunted'; 'Psychology'.
12. See Biondi. Many Italian scientists turned their attention to spiritualist phenomena. See, among others, Brofferio; Baudi di Vesme; Turiello; Pappalardo; Morselli *Psicologia*.
13. She was undoubtedly the most famous Italian medium of the time. See Lombroso 'Eusapia'.
14. See Davie.
15. See Gibson; Dunnage.
16. Neuro-criminology, for instance, has provided increasing amount of evidence of how brain structures and functions are implicated in subjects with psychopathic traits, while molecular genetics has identified specific genes that increase the risk of criminal behaviour. See Cadoret et al.; Rowe; Blair; Raine.
17. See Musumeci.
18. See Legrenzi and Umiltà.

Chapter 15

Ecogothic and Folk Horror
Marco Malvestio

Given the importance of folklore in Italian nation-building processes, as well as the variety of regional cultures in Italy and the predominance of small towns and underdeveloped areas, it is no surprise that Italian Gothic is so often imbued with elements of folk horror. Folk horror pays attention to landscape and establishes a structural opposition between modernity and the past (which is an aspect of the inherently Gothic opposition between civilisation and barbarism), making it an important mode for reflecting on ecological issues that should be considered alongside the ecogothic. As the ecogothic and folk horror are modes rather than genres, discussing them in relation to certain texts or films does not necessarily imply that these products are Gothic, but rather that they contain Gothic elements (Hillard, 'Gothic Nature').

'Folk horror' is a recently coined label that was initially employed by British director Piers Haggard to describe a 'trilogy' of (unrelated) movies produced in Great Britain in the late 1960s and 1970s: Michael Reeves's *Witchfinder General* (1968), Haggard's *The Blood on Satan's Claw* (1971) and Robin Hardy's *The Wicker Man* (1973). The term was later popularised by Mark Gatiss's BBC series *A History of Horror* (2010) and has been used to describe a variety of cultural products, from video games to TV series to movies to literature, and extended both chronologically and spatially (Keetley and Heholt). Folk horror is usually defined as insisting on four key elements: landscape ('where elements within its topography have adverse effects on the social and moral identity of its inhabitants'), isolation ('the landscape must in some way isolate a key-body of characters, whether it be just a handful of individuals or a small-scale community'), skewed belief systems and morality (that is, folklore, superstition, twisted forms of religiosity) and a happening/summoning in which the plot culminates (Scovell 17–18).

Although it is just as recent as folk horror, the concept of the ecogothic has already been the subject of a vast series of academic publications

(Hillard, 'Deep Into That Darkness Peering'; Yi-Fu Tuan; Smith and Hughes; Keetley and Tenga; Keetley and Sivils; Parker; Heholt and Edmundson). As the term itself suggests, ecogothic relates to representations of nature, the environment and the landscape not only in Gothic texts, but also in a Gothic fashion. As Dawn Keetley and Matthew Wynn Sivils remark, while 'ecocriticism has devoted itself to studying the literary and cultural relationships of humans with the nonhuman world – to animals, plants, minerals, climate, and ecosystems [. . .], adopting a specifically *Gothic* ecocritical lens illuminates the fear, anxiety, and dread that often pervade those relationships' (Keetley and Sivils 1). In other words, ecogothic is a tool for investigating the ecophobic sentiment that is latent in many Gothic and non-Gothic textualities, by which I mean the fear of a lack of agency that is triggered by uncontrollable aspects of nature and the landscape that, in the case of the ecogothic, often take monstrous and hostile forms.[1]

Given the relative novelty of these two concepts, very little has been written on the ecogothic and folk horror in Italian artistic products. David Del Principe's monographic issue of *Gothic Studies* (16.1, 2014) contains two essays on Antonio Fogazzaro and Tommaso Landolfi that will be discussed later in this chapter. As for folk horror, Fabio Camilletti's *Italia lunare* (2018) deals with occultural beliefs in Italy from the late 1950s to the 1970s and provides a reading of Lucio Fulci's *Non si sevizia un paperino* (1972) as a folk horror film (Camilletti 135–6; see also DeGiglio-Bellemare), while I have discussed Pupi Avati's *La casa dalle finestre che ridono* (1976) in the same terms in Keetley and Heholt (2023). Camilletti and Fabrizio Foni also edited the volume *Orrore popolare* (2021), which focuses on the interaction between horror, popular/pop culture and Italian folklore. Since this chapter is an entry in a companion, I will attempt to offer as comprehensive an overview as possible on the subject; however, the reader should keep in mind that the authors and directors discussed represent but a few of a wide range of examples that could be cited. Moreover, I will refrain from discussing those authors (Fogazzaro, Landolfi, Fulci and Avati) who have already been discussed elsewhere in order to provide more textual space to previously unexamined authors.

It is worth reminding that the ecogothic and folk horror are two distinct aspects of Gothic Studies. The ecogothic is not necessarily concerned with popular belief systems, but rather it deals with the landscape, the environment and non-human agency. At the same time (and especially in the Italian case, as we will see), the ecogothic and folk horror are closely linked by the attention they pay to the relationship between the environment and human communities. In other words, although not all ecogothic textualities can be considered folk horror (as they could, for instance, discuss the boundaries between humans and animals or represent post-apocalyptic landscapes), folk horror always has ecogothic features. Furthermore, folk horror's insistence on ancestral traditions and beliefs in opposition to the cultural logic of the present challenges industrialised modernity and presents an alternative yet problematic genealogy of a society's relationship with the landscape. The attention folk horror pays to folklore and popular beliefs coincides with the attention paid to the (isolated, archaic, hostile) places where these beliefs have been generated.

The Gothic Ecology of Verismo

Tracing ecogothic and folk horror elements in the Italian literary canon is complex, as most authors and critics refused to use conceptual categories like the Gothic and to be associated with such literary forms. Italy's most notable nineteenth-century Gothic texts, such as the works of the *Scapigliatura*, contain few, if any, elements of these modes. This is not surprising as the *Scapigliati* came from the great industrialised towns of Northern Italy and so their work is more concerned with urban settings. Notably, in Igino Ugo Tarchetti's *Fosca* (1869), there are strong ecogothic elements in the representation of the desolate provincial landscape as a counterpart to the protagonist's anguish, while the short story 'Uno spirito in un lampone' (in *Racconti fantastici*, 1869) presents an interesting case of reincarnation as a vegetable, as well as the novelty of a Calabrian setting for a Gothic story. Nevertheless, Tarchetti's main focus is social issues (as in 'Uno spirito in un lampone' or in 'Un osso di morto'), as well as morbid sexuality and vampirism (as in *Fosca*).

Besides Fogazzaro and Landolfi, whose works have already been discussed in detail from an ecogothic perspective by Maria Parrino[2] and Keala Jewell[3] respectively, I argue that among the most interesting examples of the ecogothic in Italian fiction are those novels addressing the harshness of agricultural life and the difficult conditions experienced by farmers and shepherds in a significantly underdeveloped country. Specifically, the *Verismo* movement, which flourished in post-unification Italy, put great emphasis on the representation of social inequalities, most frequently between the North and the South, and underdevelopment in the country. Giovanni Verga's *Vita dei campi* (1880), *Novelle rusticane* (1883) and *Mastro-don Gesualdo* (1888) are the most notable examples of this style, and influenced the more markedly Decadent *Il trionfo della morte* (1894) and *Novelle della Pescara* (1902) by Gabriele D'Annunzio. While less imbued with ecogothic imaginary, the work of Luigi Capuana, one of the main authors of *Verismo* who also wrote Gothic tales and had a strong interest in spiritualism, can be read in this perspective.

The 'anti-pastoral' novel of *Verismo* realistically depicts the countryside and agricultural life, in contrast to the idealisation of Greek, Latin and Renaissance models, and aims to denounce the conditions of the poor. In these novels, nature has a pre-eminent role, as it plays a huge part in the life of the characters. However, it is often described as a cruel, supernatural power, which is coherent with the ecophobic sentiment at the core of the ecogothic. 'Anti-pastoral' novels focus on agricultural traditions, ancestral beliefs, superstitious Catholicism and the parallel between human interiority and the landscape, which often assumes anthropomorphic features. By focusing attention on the harsh conditions of peasants and their superstitions and rituals, these texts also investigate the peasants' relationship with the environment and its modernisation. In other words, the attention paid to 'barbaric' areas of Italy is intended to function as a kind of critical conscience of the newborn nation, as well as serving to gather information about, and represent, underdeveloped areas.

At the same time, the interest in these novels is not just social and ethnographic; there is also a strong symbolic undertone, with nature being represented as almost supernatural. D'Annunzio, for instance, idealises the lives of farmers and shepherds, however harsh, as such lives are more savage, free and nature-bound than the life of the intellectual (see Galbo). The most celebrated *Verismo* author, as well as an experienced writer of Gothic stories,[4] Verga always presents the landscape as hostile to human life; when his characters attempt to tame it, they are inevitably defeated. Verga's characters are bound to the environment in which they live: it determines their characteristics and behaviour and makes them almost indistinguishable from animals. In 'Rosso Malpelo', for instance, the cave is explicitly described as possessing a hostile agency ('La rena è traditora' [The cave is treacherous]; Verga 179) and the protagonists are always assimilated to animals (Misciu Bestia and Ranocchio, but also Malpelo himself, who is often described as ferine and wild). This is also evident in 'La lupa', a story in which female sexual agency is represented through the traditional affiliation with witchcraft and lycanthropy (see Klein). In 'Malaria', we find a portrayal of an eerie landscape, plagued by disease and death, where everything, from the houses to the animals, from the mist to the sun itself, appears as emaciated and sick as the humans that inhabit the area. In *Mastro-don Gesualdo*, the sunburnt

Sicilian landscape of the *controra* is described as a space where it would most certainly be possible to meet the devil – and not just figuratively (Mazzacurati 37–68; Luperini 209–32). While none of these stories and novels can be labelled as strictly Gothic, the presence of ecogothic elements, in the form of a malignancy of nature or the sense of a lack of agency, is undeniable. The lack of agency that typifies Verga's characters is enhanced by the consistent use of a homodiegetic omniscient narrator who presents the events described as inevitable. This choice also reinforces the omnipresent folkloric dimension of Verga's work, as the narrator evokes a world in which superstitions and legends are as true as (and possibly truer than) historical facts. The ecological dimension and the folkloric merge together perfectly in the final page of 'Rosso malpelo', when the protagonist, having disappeared into the cave, is said by the narrator to have turned into a ghost – to have turned, in other words, into a part of the cave itself.

Legendary, Mysterious, Unusual, Fantastic Italy: Folk Horror in Italian Non-Fiction

The mixture of ethnographic enquiry, interest in supernatural folklore and attention to the environment that characterise *Verismo* would cast a long shadow on Italian culture, and is also exhibited in the twentieth century by two academics whose work excited great popular interest and, most importantly, exerted a significant influence on later folk horror productions: Ernesto De Martino and Carlo Ginzburg. A pioneering anthropologist and ethnographer, De Martino extensively studied the survival of popular superstitions in Southern Italy in the 1950s and 1960s, especially in the underdeveloped region of Lucania (now Basilicata). He studied the diffusion of common magic in Italy at the time, as well as the singular blending of magical practices and the Catholic Church (De Martino 10–11). Interestingly, De Martino explicitly links the diffusion of magical beliefs to the underdevelopment of the region and thus to the prevalence of agriculture:

> Se ci chiediamo quali sono le ragioni che fanno ancora sopravvivere una ideologia così arcaica nella Lucania di oggi, la risposta più immediata è che tuttora in Lucania un regime arcaico di esistenza impegna ancora larghi strati sociali, malgrado la civiltà moderna. E certamente la precarietà dei beni elementari della vita, l'incertezza delle prospettive concernenti il futuro, la pressione esercitata sugli individui da parte delle forze naturali e sociali non controllabili, la carenza di forme di assistenza sociale, l'asprezza della fatica nel quadro di una economia agricola arretrata, l'angusta memoria

di comportamenti razionali efficaci con cui fronteggiare realisticamente i momenti critici dell'esistenza costituiscono altrettante condizioni che favoriscono il mantenersi delle pratiche magiche. (De Martino 89)

[If we ask ourselves why such an archaic ideology is still alive in present-day Lucania, the most immediate answer is that even today in Lucania, despite modern civilisation, large parts of society are still characterised by an archaic way of living. And certainly, the precariousness of elementary goods, the uncertainty of future prospects, the pressure of uncontrollable natural and social forces on individuals, the lack of welfare, the harshness of labour in an underdeveloped agricultural economy, and the short memory when it comes to rational ways of facing critical existential moments all constitute favourable conditions for the persistence of magical practices.]

In De Martino, the attention to the folkloric is connected to a commentary on socio-political and environmental issues, while pre-modern beliefs are inextricably linked to pre-modern ways of life. All these elements would prove extremely important to Italian folk horror, as testified by their inclusion in Brunello Rondi's *Il demonio* (1963), a story of witchcraft and exorcism set in Matera. While the movie is built around a rather melodramatic and conventional plot, it includes ethnographic curiosities that are a direct reference to De Martino's research. For instance, a scene in which farmers perform a magic rite to dissipate an approaching storm is taken almost word for word from an identical rite described by Ernesto De Martino in *Sud e magia* (64–7), and De Martino himself is mentioned in the opening credits as one of the consultants for the film.

An authoritative cultural historian and an academic who has worked both in Italy and in the United States, Carlo Ginzburg is the author of two important works on folklore and belief in the supernatural: *I benandanti* (1966) and *Storia notturna* (1989). In *I benandanti*, Ginzburg studies the inquisitorial trials of a group of people who, in sixteenth-century Friuli, claimed that they fought witches in their dreams in order to prevent them from spoiling the crops. This study is of great interest from an ecogothic and folk horror perspective, as it sheds light on a previously misrepresented part of Italian folklore concerned with both the supernatural and the environment, transfiguring known agricultural landscapes into an animated space filled with spirits and ghosts fighting against fertility. It is also worth noting that *Storia notturna*, which elaborates on the materials uncovered in *I benandanti* from a comparative perspective, partially reprises Margaret Murray's discredited theories about the survival of a pagan cult, disguised as witchcraft by its persecutors, into the modern age. Despite their disregard for the scientific method, Murray's theories were extremely influential in shaping the modern understanding of witchcraft and greatly contributed to the formation of contemporary neo-pagan movements (Hutton 194–201). Ginzburg's work has neither the superficiality nor the partiality of Murray's; however, this coincidence is significant in tracing a continuity between Italian culture at the time and the neo-pagan elements of British folk horror.

By investigating a previously forgotten folkloric belief, Ginzburg's *I benandanti* is timely with a series of publications dealing with the mysteries and the legends of Italy. Significantly, most Italian folk horror films were produced after two decades (the 1950s and 1960s) of unprecedented economic and technological development in Italy, which coincided with and contributed to increased connectedness of previously physically and culturally distant parts of the country. As a result of the economic boom, a network of motorways was developed and automobiles became widely available, which led to an increase in tourism and to new ways of experiencing the Italian landscape (Corona chapter IV; Hom 127–51). Furthermore, the development of national television enhanced the diffusion of both a standardised Italian language and a shared popular imagery (Marazzini 434–52). The new interest in forgotten corners of Italy is evidenced by the many tourist guides to the mysteries, legends and superstitions of Italy, such as Mario Spagnol and Giovenale Santi's *Guida all'Italia leggendaria misteriosa insolita fantastica* (1966–7), Dino Buzzati's *I misteri d'Italia* (1978, posthumously collecting articles that had been published in the newspaper *Corriere della sera* in 1965), or Peter Kolosimo's *Italia mistero cosmico* (1977). The 'Gothicisation' of Italy operated by De Martino and Ginzburg, as well as by these popular tourist guides, reveals a persistent interest in Italian culture for the uncanny parts of the country and of national heritage – an interest that was being explored, in the same years, by Italian cinema.

Ethnographies of Terror: Italian Folk Horror Cinema[5]

In keeping with the enduring notion that Italy is not an appropriate setting for Gothic fiction, when Gothic movies were first produced in Italy, they mostly had a foreign setting, as well as a foreign cast and occasionally English pseudonyms for the directors. Thus, it is difficult to cite examples of Italian folk horror from the 1950s and 1960s, but things changed in the following decades. In the 1970s and 1980s, many movies that could be labelled as folk horror were produced: Lucio Fulci's *Non si sevizia un paperino* (1972), Armando Crispino's *L'etrusco uccide ancora* (1972), Renato Polselli's *Riti, magie nere e segrete orge nel Trecento* (1973), Dario Argento's *Suspiria* (1977), Antonio Bido's *Il gatto dagli occhi di giada* (1977) and *Solamente nero* (1978), Ugo Liberatore's *Nero veneziano* (1978), Joe D'Amato's *Buio omega* (1979) and Sergio Martino's *Assassinio al cimitero etrusco* (1982), together with the more recent Michele Soavi's *Dellamorte Dellamore* (1994) and Federico Greco and Roberto Leggio's mockumentary *Road to L.* (2005). A large part of Pupi Avati's extensive filmography is also markedly dedicated to folk horror: *Balsamus, l'uomo di Satana* (1968), *Thomas (gli indemoniati)* (1970), *La mazurka del barone, della santa e del fico fiorone* (1975), *La casa dalle finestre che ridono* (1976), *Tutti defunti . . . tranne i morti* (1977), *Le strelle nel fosso* (1978), *Zeder* (1983), *L'arcano incantatore* (1996) and *Il signor diavolo* (2019). It is worth noting that, when we talk about Italian folk horror films, we are discussing a mode that is similar to its British counterpart, but largely independent. British folk horror developed from a series of movies and TV shows that had little or no distribution in Italy (significantly, Hardy's *The Wicker Man* has never been released in Italy).

What is remarkable is that all these films were set in Italy, especially in very specific parts of the country. Far from focusing only on Italy's major cities, horror films of the 1970s and 1980s privilege less well-known corners of the nation. The focal point is, in other words, 'volutamente nazionale [. . .] e deliberatamente provinciale' [intentionally national [. . .] and deliberately provincial] (Camilletti 131), as if to topographically and ethnographically enquire into national horrors (Venturini 87).[6] Like Rondi's *Il demonio*, *Non si sevizia un paperino* is set in the archaic and underdeveloped region of Lucania and the dialect spoken by the local people is contrasted by the variety of regional dialects spoken by the journalists and police officers who arrive in the town after the first homicide. The opening scene of Fulci's movie encapsulates the conflict between modern and rural Italy by showing the Lucania mountains crossed by a recently built highway, at the border of which the *maciara* is performing a magic rite. *L'etrusco uccide ancora* and *Assassinio al cimitero etrusco*, both centred on a series of homicides, are set in Tuscany, not among the monuments of the Renaissance, but rather amid the remnants of the Etruscan civilisation, which has become synonymous with death in Italian imagery due to the fact that most of what we know about it comes from necropolises and tombs.[7] Although there are no supernatural elements in these movies and none of the characters actually believe in a curse from the time of the Etruscans, the choice of Etruscan civilisation reveals an interest in a different and obscure part of Italian history, as opposed to the history of the Romans that has so often been evoked in nation-building processes. Other movies exploit the somnolent yet uncanny provincial corners of Italy: *Il gatto dagli occhi di giada* is set in Padua, *Buio Omega* in the mountains of Trentino, *Dellamorte Dellamore* and *Road to L.*, like Avati's works, in forgotten parts of the Po valley. *Solamente nero* and *Nero veneziano* are both set in Venice and make great use of the city's decadent atmosphere and putrescent colours. Venice is not represented as it once was, an important metropolitan area made rich by tourism and commerce, but rather as declining and demoted to the status of a provincial town.

Pupi Avati's movies also have eccentric, provincial locations, which gained for his style the label of *gotico padano* [Po Valley Gothic].[8] The Po Valley where his horror movies take place (with the exception of *L'arcano incantatore*, which is set in Umbria) is a mysterious province, where vast metropolitan areas and mass tourism can coexist with isolated communities and occult beliefs. As Roberto Curti argues about *La casa dalle finestre che ridono*, the traditional stereotypes of the Gothic genre are 'revisited not from an aristocratic perspective, but from a rural, peasant-like one' (*1970–1979*, 159): instead of the nineteenth century, the movie is set after the Second World War; the haunted manor is replaced by humble country houses lost in the mists of Polesine; and suspicious peasants and eccentric public officers have taken the place of the aristocracy that was protagonist of the Gothic *filone*. As a result of these choices, the very term 'Po Valley Gothic' sounds – and indeed sounded when it was coined – nonsensical, as it merges two completely separate realms: Italy (and specifically its countryside) and the Gothic. While the communities depicted by Avati do not necessarily share a common belief system, Avati's insistence on physical deformity and grotesqueness, as well as regional stereotypes and accents, contributes to portraying these communities as separate from contemporary and urban life.

Italian folk horror movies were produced after the economic boom of the 1950s and 1960s, which, as we have seen, was a time of great change and modernisation for the country. In this historical context, Italian folk horror movies portray a literal return of the repressed that embodies archaic folkloric traditions mixed with a twisted version of Catholicism and takes the form of geographical spaces usually not employed in the Italian Gothic. At the same time, as with 'anti-pastoral' novels, the attention to lesser-known and pre-modern parts of Italy facilitates reflections on the inequalities generated by the unification process that contributed to neglecting several parts of the country in favour of the industrial and cultural centres.

The insistence of many of these movies on Catholicism is a trait peculiar to Italian folk horror. While British folk horror deals with paganism (as in *Penda's Fen*, 1974), neo-pagan beliefs (as in *The Wicker Man*) or secret cults opposing the authority of the Church (as in *Blood on Satan's Claw*), and American folk horror and ecogothic are very much concerned with the wilderness and the myth of the frontier (Murphy; Keetley and Sivils 1–20), Catholicism is often the focus of Italian folk horror.⁹ Despite increasing secularisation, Italy was ruled by the Christian Democratic Party for most of the second half of the twentieth century (1946–92). Thus, when Catholicism is discussed, it does not represent just a spiritual institution, but rather a very secular one. It is notable that the Catholic Church fought (and lost) two important political battles in those crucial decades, lobbying against the two referendums on divorce and abortion (in 1974 and 1981 respectively).

Italian folk horror directors criticise the Church's role in the repression of sexuality: in *Non si sevizia un paperino*, the priest confesses to the homicides of young children, which he committed to prevent them from being corrupted; in *Solamente nero*, the killer is once again a local priest and one of his victims is a nurse who perform abortions illegally. The critique of Catholicism is also pivotal in the work of Pupi Avati. In particular, Avati satirises religious repression in his depiction of the female priest in *La casa dalle finestre che ridono*. In this movie, the symbolic and ideological violence of the Catholic Church is explicitly connected to a chain of homicides in that the religious painter Buono Legnani used to base the expressions of his martyrs on real-life victims.

Folk horror also reflects the diffidence toward traditional sources of power that was preponderant during the so-called *anni di piombo* [years of lead] (Venturini 88–9), two decades of profound socio-political turmoil during which thousands died at the hands of far-right and far-left terrorists – the secret service was also suspected of being involved. By representing sinister plots in isolated communities, these movies show how the ruling classes of the country can be beyond such plots. In a period plagued by terrorism and a profoundly suspicious attitude towards state institutions, Italian folk horror films insist either on the collective dimension of the plot against their protagonists (as in *La casa dalle finestre che ridono*) or on the responsibilities of traditional institutions (as in *Non si sevizia un paperino* and *Solamente nero*).

Pupi Avati's *Zeder* is an excellent example of the conflation of a critique of the Church, a reflection on the past, and attention being paid to previously underrepresented parts of the country. The movie pivots on a mysterious Vatican plot to cover up the existence of a certain piece of land where those who are buried come back to life and, like *La casa dalle finestre che ridono*, the end of the movie involves a monstrous priest. Again, the setting is Emilia Romagna; however, it is not the liminal Polesine area of *La casa dalle finestre che ridono*, but rather the sunny

Adriatic coast, one of Italy's most renowned sites of mass tourism. The second part of the film is set there, among the ruins of a touristic colony from the Fascist era (such colonies were the sites of state-sponsored holidays for children and thus an instrument of propaganda). As Curti argues, 'the huge, ghastly cement building in Zeder becomes a sort of relic, whose bare cement pylons stand out in the landscape like the carcass of a monstrous "white whale" stranded near the beach, a gigantic and looming memento of a wiped-out past' (and in fact, he adds, a *fascio littorio* can clearly be seen behind the protagonist's back during the film's climax) (*1980–1989* 303). In *Zeder*, Avati brings together an inquiry into the power of the Church in Italy, the remnants of Fascism and its transformation into mass consumerism, and the environmental impact of mass tourism.

As regards the relationship between Italian folk horror films and environmental history, most of the movies discussed above pay particular attention to landscapes that, for one reason or another, belong to the past and thus to a different synergy with the environment than that of the present. At the same time, the landscapes portrayed in these movies consistently play a role in creating a dreadful atmosphere, pivoting on ecophobic imagery. Both of these elements can be clearly observed in *La casa dalle finestre che ridono*, in which the eerie liminal space of the lagoon enhances the sense of imminent menace, but also (particularly in the opening scenes) signals an opposition between the complexity and fastness of modern metropolitan areas and the pre-modern rhythms of the local community. Again, these films present the return of a social and environmental repressed, as they focus on the rural countryside and agricultural life during a period when Italian agriculture was undergoing massive changes and the number of people working in the sector was drastically diminishing (from 8,261,000 in 1951 to 4,023,000 in 1969 to less than 3,000,000 in the early 1980s; Corona chapter II). At the same time, urban areas were growing fast, at the expense of rural areas and mountain communities (Corona chapter IV). In other words, folk horror became, in Italy, a means to reflect, without succumbing to idealisation, on the disappearance of past ways of life into the uniformity of modern times.

The Eternal Present of Folk Horror

As in the case of horror and Gothic cinema in general, the last few decades saw a drastic decrease in folk horror productions in Italian cinema (with the notable exception of the mockumentary *Road to L.*, whose non-fictional approach and low-budget production effectively merge Lovecraftian horror with Po Valley atmospheres). Attempts to revive the genre for an international audience, such as the Netflix-produced TV series *Curon* (2020) and *Luna nera* (2020) and the film *A Classic Horror Story* (2021), tend to offer a rather stereotypical portrayal of the Italian province and its folklore, failing to capture the significant environmental and social changes the country has undergone in recent years.

As far as fiction is concerned, however, folk horror has become much more widespread among Italian authors, especially due to the influence of the critical re-evaluation of the genre operated overseas. Nevertheless, while Italian folk horror films are, to a certain extent, distinct from their foreign counterparts, folk horror fiction tends to imitate foreign models and tropes, while simultaneously trying to recover Italian traditions and folklore (such an influence, however, does not seem to be confined to genre authors, but appears to have reached Italian mainstream fiction as well, as testified by Marco Peano's *Morsi* and Michele Orti Manara's *Consolazione*, both published in 2022).

Recent examples of Italian folk horror include works by Sergio Bissoli, Eraldo Baldini and Chiara Palazzolo. Bissoli is a somewhat extravagant and self-taught writer. His *Il paese stregato* (2012), published by Hypnos with a preface by Giuseppe Lippi, is made up of the short novel *La ragazza del paese stregato*, the collection *Racconti gotici* and the autobiographical *Vita di scrittore*. Bissoli's work is entirely devoted to the exploration of the provincial town of Cerea (Verona), where he spent his whole life. The town becomes the setting for magical and mysterious events involving both classic Gothic tropes and local folklore. At the same time, most of his stories are set in the crucial decades of the economic boom, and testify, through the lenses of Gothic imagery, the transformation of a predominantly rural region into a landscape of 'campagna industrializzata' [industrialised countryside] and 'industrializzazione diffusa' [spread industrialisation]. The haunted *ville* and *casali* of Bissoli's stories are already the remnants of a kind of life that has been surpassed by modernity.

Eraldo Baldini's horror fiction is almost invariably set in provincial small towns of the lower Po Valley, in the same areas featured in Pupi Avati's movies. Baldini, who also wrote several volumes on local folklore and legends, gave his collection of short stories the revealing title *Gotico rurale* (2013; lit. 'Rural Gothic', a term which, as is well-known, was a precursor of 'folk horror'). Baldini's stories attempt to adapt the most common topoi of Anglo-American horror cinema and fiction to the geographical frame of the Italian countryside, which is represented as a mysterious place full of dark secrets. He imports certain topoi of American cinema and television more or less unaltered: UFOs in 'Arrivano dal buio' and the ghost of a local serial killer in 'Foto ricordo', while 'Re di Carnevale' is an almost literal rendition of the topos of the stranger lured as a victim, as already seen in *Wicker Man*, Thomas Tryon's *Harvest Home* and Thomas Ligotti's 'The Last Feast of Harlequin'. However, he also tries to innovate by merging these traditional elements with indigenous beliefs and traditions, such as Saint John's Night ('Notte di San Giovanni') and the Befana ('La Befana vien di notte').

Finally, Chiara Palazzolo's work consistently deals with folkloric elements. Besides *Nel bosco di Aus* (2011), a story of witchcraft set in a small Sicilian town, her trilogy *Non mi uccidere* (2005), *Strappami il cuore* (2006) and *Ti porterò nel sangue* (2007) is particularly noteworthy. Intended for a young adult audience and marketed as the Italian version of *Twilight*, the trilogy is set in Umbria, another unlikely setting for a Gothic story, revealing the author's intention both of introducing novel elements into the usual patterns of Italian fiction and rediscovering unusual areas of the country. Interestingly, Palazzolo's imagery is based on a blend of romanticised vampirism and Carlo Ginzburg's *benandanti*, who are the antagonists of the novel – a reference that testifies to the widespread cultural impact of Ginzburg's research.

Complicated by the sometimes-overwhelming influence of Anglo-American models, contemporary Italian folk horror is perhaps less interested in cogent social and environmental matters than its nineteenth- and twentieth-century counterparts. However, the persisting interest in this mode from Italian authors is a sign of the deepness of its roots in Italian culture. From the Gothicised and malignant nature of *Verismo* to today's representations of the uncanniness of provincial life, from the desolate landscapes of Italian *giallo* and horror cinema to new approaches to dark tourism, Italian culture has shown a vast array of disturbing and disrupting ways to deal with its ethnographic and environmental heritage.

Bibliography

Adamovit, Ruggero, and Claudio Bartolini (eds), *Il gotico padano. Dialogo con Pupi Avati* (Recco: Le mani, 2010).
Barlozzetti, Guido, 'Il (poco) cinema dell'Etruscità', in Giuseppe Della Fina (ed.), *Gli Etruschi nella cultura e nell'immaginario del mondo moderno* (Rome: Quasar, 2017), pp. 255–69.
Buzzati, Dino, *I misteri d'Italia* (Milan: Mondadori, 1978).
Camilletti, Fabio, *Italia lunare. Gli anni Sessanta e l'occulto* (Oxford: Peter Lang, 2018).

Corona, Gabriella, *Breve storia dell'ambiente in Italia* (Bologna: il Mulino, 2015), Kindle edn.
Curti, Roberto, *Italian Gothic Horror Films, 1970–1979* (Jefferson, NC: McFarland, 2017).
Curti, Roberto, *Italian Gothic Horror Films, 1980–1989* (Jefferson, NC: McFarland, 2017).
De Berti, Raffaele, 'Fotogrammi etruschi', *L'uomo nero. Materiali per una storia delle arti della modernità*, 5.6, 2008, pp. 114–22.
De Martino, Ernesto, *Sud e magia* [1959] (Milan: Feltrinelli, 2019).
DeGiglio-Bellemare, Mario, 'Lucio Fulci's Poetics of Attractions: The Cinema of Poetry and the 'Southern Question' in *Don't Torture a Duckling*', *Monstrum*, 1.1, 2019, pp. 58–89.
Estok, Simon C., *The Ecophobia Hypothesis* (New York: Routledge, 2018).
Estok, Simon C., 'Painful Material Realities, Tragedy, Ecophobia', in Serenella Iovino and Serpil Opperman (eds), *Material Ecocriticism*, (Bloomington, IN: Indiana University Press, 2014), pp. 130–40.
Estok, Simon C., 'Theorising the EcoGothic', *Gothic Nature*, 1, 2019, pp. 34–53.
Estok, Simon C., 'Theorizing in a Space of Ambivalent Openness. Ecocriticism and Ecophobia', *Interdisciplinary Studies in Literature and Environment*, 16.2, 2009, pp. 203–25.
Fisher, Austin, 'Political Memory in the Italian Hinterland: Locating the Rural *Giallo*', in Stefano Baschiera and Russ Hunter (eds), *Italian Horror Cinema* (Edinburgh: Edinburgh University Press, 2016), pp. 160–74.
Galbo, Joseph, 'A Decadence Baedeker: D'Annunzio's *The Triumph of Death*', *The European Legacy*, 22.1, 2016, pp. 49–67.
Ginzburg, Carlo, *I benandanti. Ricerche sulla stregoneria e sui culti agrari tra Cinquecento e Seicento* (Turin: Einaudi, 1966).
Ginzburg, Carlo, *Storia Notturna. Una decifrazione del Sabba* (Turin: Einaudi, 1989).
Heholt, Ruth, and Melissa Edmundson (eds), *Gothic Animals: Uncanny Otherness and the Animal With-Out* (London: Palgrave, 2020).
Hillard, Tom J., '"Deep Into That Darkness Peering": An Essay on Gothic Nature', *Interdisciplinary Studies in Literature and Environment*, 16.4, 2009, pp. 687–95.
Hillard, Tom J., 'Gothic Nature Revisited: Reflections on the Gothic of Ecocriticism', *Gothic Nature*, 1, 2019, pp. 21–33.
Hom, Stephanie Malia, *The Beautiful Country: Tourism and the Impossible State of Destination Italy* (Toronto: University of Toronto Press, 2015).
Hutton, Ronald, *The Triumph of the Moon: A History of Modern Pagan Witchcraft* (Oxford: Oxford University Press, 1999).
Jewell, Keala, 'Italian Rural Gothic: The Powers of Were-Goats in Tommaso Landolfi's *La pietra lunare (The Moonstone)*', *Gothic Studies*, 16.1, 2014, pp. 55–69.
Keetley, Dawn, and Angela Tenga (eds), *Plant Horror: Approaches to the Monstrous in Fiction and Film* (New York: Palgrave, 2016).
Keetley, Dawn, and Matthew Wynn Sivils, 'Introduction. Approaches to the Ecogothic', in Dawn Keetley and Matthew Wynn Sivils (eds), *Ecogothic in Nineteenth-Century American Literature* (New York: Routledge, 2017), pp. 1–20.

Klein, Ilona, 'When Good Girls Go Bad (Or Do They?): Nymphomania and Lycanthropy in Verga's "La Lupa"', *MLN*, 134.6, 2019, pp. 272–85.

Luperini, Romano, *L'incontro e il caso. Narrazioni moderne e destino dell'uomo occidentale* (Rome: Laterza, 2007).

Malvestio, Marco, 'Catholicism, Unification, and Liminal Landscapes in Italian Folk Horror Cinema', in Dawn Keetley and Ruth Heholt (eds), *Folk Horror: New Global Pathways* (Cardiff: University of Wales Press, 2023). Forthcoming.

Marazzini, Claudio, *La lingua italiana. Profilo storico* (Bologna: il Mulino, 2002).

Mazzacurati, Giancarlo, *Stagioni dell'apocalisse. Verga, Pirandello, Svevo* (Turin: Einaudi, 1998).

Murphy, Bernice M., *The Rural Gothic in American Popular Culture: Backwoods Horror and Terror in the Wilderness* (Basingstoke: Palgrave, 2013).

Parker, Elizabeth, *The Forest and the EcoGothic: The Deep Dark Woods and Popular Imagination* (New York: Palgrave, 2020).

Parrino, Maria, '"L'orrida magnificenza del luogo". Gothic Aesthetics in Antonio Fogazzaro's *Malombra*', *Gothic Studies*, 16.1, 2014, pp. 85–97.

Pasolini, Pier Paolo, *Scritti corsari* (Milan: Garzanti, 1975).

Piperno, Martina, *L'antichità 'crudele'. Etruschi e italici nella letteratura italiana del Novecento* (Rome: Carocci, 2020).

Piperno, Martina, 'Mario Signorelli e la "nuova etruscologia" metapsichica', in Fabio Camilletti and Fabrizio Foni (eds), *Orrore popolare* (Bologna: Odoya, 2021), pp. 121–30.

Scovell, Adam, *Folk Horror: Hours Dreadful and Things Strange* (Leighton Buzzard: Auteur, 2017).

Smith, Andrew, and William Hughes (eds), *EcoGothic* (Manchester: Manchester University Press, 2013).

Spagnol, Mario, and Giovenale Santi (eds), *Guida all'Italia leggendaria misteriosa insolita fantastica*, 2 vols, Sugar, 1966–7.

Tuan, Yi-Fu, *Landscapes of Fear* (Minneapolis, MN: University of Minnesota Press, 2013).

Venturini, Simone, *Horror italiano* (Rome: Donzelli, 2014).

Verga, Giovanni, *Tutte le novelle* (Milan: Mondadori, 1979).

Xavier Mendik, 'The Return of the Rural Repressed. Italian Horror and the Mezzogiorno Giallo', in Harry M. Benshoff (ed.), *A Companion to the Horror Film* (Malden, MA: Wiley Blackwell, 2014), pp. 390–405.

Notes

1. On ecophobia, see Estok 'Theorizing in a Space of Ambivalent Openness'; 'Painful Material Realities'; *The Ecophobia Hypothesis*; 'Theorising the EcoGothic'.
2. According to Parrino's convincing argument, Fogazzaro creates a continuous parallel between the convoluted emotions of his protagonists and the obscurity and untamedness of the setting, from the villa on the lake to the nearby *orrido*, in a constant blending of the human and the non-human.

3. Jewell has argued that Landolfi's *La pietra lunare* (1939) represents a critique of the agricultural policies of the Fascist regime and a commentary on the social, cultural and environmental changes during the shift in the main source of income from pasturage to agriculture.
4. For example, 'Le storie del castello di Trezza', in *Primavera e altri racconti* (1876), or 'La festa dei morti', in *Vagabondaggio* (1887).
5. This section reprises and condenses the remarks on Italian folk horror made in Malvestio.
6. A similar attitude can be detected in what Xavier Mendik defines as 'mezzogiorno *giallo*', Italian *giallo* films set in Southern Italy and addressing the Southern Question and the economic and social gap between the North and the South of the country. Curiously enough, Mendik lists among the 'mezzogiorno giallo' movies Avati's *La casa dalle finestre che ridono*, which is set near Ferrara. On the rural element of *giallo* movies, see Fisher.
7. On the influence of Etruscan and ancient Italian peoples more generally on folk horror, see Piperno (2020; 2021). See also De Berti; and Barlozzetti.
8. The definition appears in many of Avati's interviews. See Adamovit and Bartolini.
9. It is worth noting, however, that Avati reprises the image of the 'female priest' from a folk tale heard as a child, thus linking his critique of the Catholic Church to a wider folkloric belief system (see Curti *1970–1979*).

Notes on Contributors

Francesca Billiani is Professor of Italian at the University of Manchester, where she teaches contemporary Italian literature and culture. Her research focuses on the Fascist period, censorship, literary journals, modernism, the history of publishing, and intellectual history. She is the author of a monograph on the politics of translation in Italy (*Culture nazionali e narrazioni straniere, Italia 1903–1943*), co-author of a monograph on architecture and the novel during the Fascist regime (*Architecture and the Novel under the Italian Fascist Regime*, 2019), editor of a collection of essays on translations and censorship, and co-editor of a volume on the Italian Gothic and Fantastic and of three special issues of scholarly journals. Her new monograph *Fascist Modernism in Italy: Arts and Regimes* is out with I. B. Tauris/Bloomsbury, 2021. She is currently working on a project about public art in Italy in the twentieth century.

Fabio Camilletti is Professor of Italian Literature at the University of Warwick. In 2018, he published a *Guida al gotico* (Odoya) and the monograph *Italia lunare. Gli anni Sessanta e l'occulto* (Peter Lang). He is also active as a translator: his editions and translations from the English and French include *Fantasmagoriana*, the writings of John Polidori, Ann Moberly's and Eleanor Jourdain's *An Adventure*, and a collection of ghost stories (*La casa infestata di Place du Lion d'Or*, ABEditore, 2020).

Morena Corradi is Associate Professor at Queens College and at the Graduate Center of CUNY (City University of New York). She holds a *Laurea in lingue e letterature straniere* (English) from the Università degli Studi of Bologna, and a PhD in Italian Studies from Brown University (Providence, RI). Her main teaching and research areas are nineteenth- and twentieth-century literature, the printing press, Gothic and fantastic literature, nation building and education in united Italy. She has published articles and essays on nineteenth-century Italian literature and culture (Tarchetti, Arrigo Boito, magnetism and spiritualism, journalism in post-unification Italy) as well as the monograph *Spettri d'Italia. Scenari del fantastico nella pubblicistica postunitaria milanese* (Longo, 2016). With Silvia Valisa (Florida State University), she co-edited the volume *La carta veloce. Figure, temi e politiche del giornalismo italiano dell'Ottocento* (FrancoAngeli, 2021).

Roberto Curti is an Italian film critic and film historian. He is a regular contributor to *Il Mereghetti – Dizionario dei Film* and to Italian magazines *Blow Up*, *Nocturno* and *Film TV*. He has published many volumes focusing on popular cinema, genres and film censorship, in various languages. Italian-language books include *Sex and Violence. Percorsi nel cinema estremo* (Lindau, 2003, with Tommaso La Selva), *Italia odia. Il cinema poliziesco italiano* (Lindau, 2006), *Demoni e dei. Dio, il diavolo, la religione nel cinema horror americano* (Lindau, 2009), *Fantasmi d'amore. Il gotico italiano tra cinema, letteratura e tv* (Lindau, 2011) and *Visioni proibite. I film vietati dalla censura italiana* (2014–15, with Alessio Di Rocco), a two-volume history of Italian film censorship. English-language books include *Italian Crime Filmography 1968–1980* (McFarland & Co., 2013); *Diabolika: Supercriminals, Superheroes and the Comic Book Universe in Italian Cinema* (Midnight Marquee Press, 2016), *Tonino Valerii: The Films* (McFarland & Co., 2016), *Riccardo Freda: The Life and Works of a Born Filmmaker* (McFarland & Co., 2017), *Mavericks of Italian Cinema: Eight Unorthodox Filmmakers, 1940s–2000s* (McFarland & Co., 2018); a trilogy of volumes on *Italian Gothic Horror Films (1957–1969; 1970–1979; 1980–1989)* (McFarland & Co., 2015, 2017, 2019 respectively); *Blood and Black Lace* (Auteur Publishing, 2019), *Elio Petri: Investigation of a Filmmaker* (McFarland & Co., 2021) and *Italian Giallo in Film and Television: A Critical History* (McFarland & Co., 2022).

Simona Di Martino is a final-year PhD student in Italian Studies at the University of Warwick (UK). Her research investigates the representations of death, human bodies and ghosts in late eighteenth- and early nineteenth-century Italian poems. Simona's interests span from the Gothic to folklore, and from children's literature and female roles to family novels. She participated in several international conferences, including the AAIS, CAIS, AIPI and ADI congresses, the Annual Society for Pirandello Studies Conference (September 2021), and finally the conference 'Women in Sardinia: Creativity and Self-Expression' at the

University of Cambridge (September 2021). Among her publications, a chapter on the Italian family novel '"Questo è il libro per cui sono venuto al mondo". L'epopea storico-familiare in Antonio Pennacchi's *Canale Mussolini*' (Pisa University Press, 2020); and two journal articles entitled 'The Figure of the Wet Nurse from Vittorelli to Pirandello' in *Notes in Italian Studies* (2021) and '"Orecchie rose e labbra mozze" and Other Bodily Suffering in Alfonso Varano. Dantean Reminiscences in Eighteenth-Century Sepulchral Poetry', in *Bibliotheca Dantesca* (2021). She is currently the editor of a special issue of *Quaderni d'Italianistica* on the theme of the night in Italian literature from the eighteenth century to the present day.

Fabrizio Foni is Senior Lecturer in the Department of Italian and member of the Institute of Anglo-Italian Studies at the University of Malta, with a specialisation in popular culture. His research interests and publications are in the areas of the Gothic, thriller and science fiction, the adventure novels of Emilio Salgari and his followers, comic-book series as well as the multifaceted fictional representations of sideshows and freaks. He co-authored, with Stefano Lazzarin, Felice Italo Beneduce and others, the most comprehensive annotated bibliography of criticism on the fantastic in Italian literature: *Il fantastico italiano: Bilancio critico e bibliografia commentata (dal 1980 a oggi)* (Le Monnier Università, 2016).

Giulio Giusti is Senior Lecturer in Italian Studies and European Cinema at Sheffield Hallam University (UK). His principal research interests are in the interrelationships between cinema and the other arts, inter-mediality and self-reflexivity in film and genre cinema, with particular focus on European Gothic fiction and Italian horror. He has also collaborated as a film critic and reviewer for a variety of journals and magazines, including *Cinergie*, *Filmcritica*, *Mediacritica*, *Segnocinema* and *Séquences*.

Marco Malvestio is EU Marie Skłodowska-Curie Postdoctoral Fellow at the University of Padua and at the University of North Carolina at Chapel Hill. His project, 'EcoSF', explores the presence of ecological issues in Italian science fiction. He holds a PhD in Comparative Literature from the University of Padua and was previously a Postdoctoral Fellow in the Department of Italian Studies at the University of Toronto. He has published *The Conflict Revisited: The Second World War in Post-Postmodern Fiction* (Peter Lang, 2021) and *Raccontare la fine del mondo. Fantascienza e Antropocene* (nottetempo, 2021). He co-edited with Valentina Sturli the volume on contemporary horror fiction and film *Vecchi maestri e nuovi mostri. Tendenze e prospettive della letteratura horror all'inizio del nuovo millennio* (Mimesis 2019).

Catherine Ramsey-Portolano (BA, The University of Tennessee-Knoxville, Laurea LUMSA, MA, The University of Wisconsin-Madison and PhD, The University of Chicago) is Associate Professor and Director of Italian Studies at The American University of Rome in Rome, Italy, where she teaches courses on Italian language, culture, literature and film. Her principal areas of research are Gender Studies, nineteenth- and twentieth-century Italian literature, with a focus on Italian women writers and the representation of femininity, and Italian film from the early and Fascist periods. She is author of numerous articles, book chapters and books on the above topics, including most recently the monographs *Nineteenth-Century Italian Women Writers and the Woman Question: The Case of Neera* (Routledge, 2020) and *Performing Bodies: Female Illness in Italian Literature and Cinema 1860–1920* (Fairleigh Dickinson University Press, 2018). She has edited *The Future of Italian Teaching: Media, New Technologies and Multi-Disciplinary Perspectives* (Cambridge Scholars Publishing, 2015) and, with Katharine Mitchell, a special issue of *The Italianist* titled *Rethinking Neera* (2010). Ramsey-Portolano has served as an invited peer reviewer for *ISSA* (Italian Studies in Southern Africa), *Italian Studies*, *Spunti e Ricerche*, *Modern Italy*, Edizioni Ca' Foscari and the Swiss National Science Foundation and she is a member of the *ISSA* editorial board.

Stefano Serafini holds a PhD in comparative literature and cultures from Royal Holloway, University of London. He was postdoctoral fellow in Italian Studies at the University of Toronto in 2020–1. His contributions have appeared in journals such as *Italian Studies*, *The Italianist*, *Quaderni del 900*, *Transalpina*, *Clues: A Journal of Detection* and the *Revue des littératures européennes*.

Eduardo Vitolo is a freelance journalist, underground music essayist, blogger, author and radio speaker. He is the author of *Horror Rock. La musica delle tenebre* (Arcana Publishings, 2010), *Sub Terra. Rock estremo e cultura underground in Italia, 1977–1998* (Tsunami Publishings, 2012), *Black Sabbath. Neon Knights: Testi commentati* (Arcana Publishings, 2012), *Magister Dixit. La leggenda di Jacula e Antonius Rex* (Tsunami Publishings, 2015) and *Children Of Doom* (Tsunami Publishings 2018).

Index

abjection, 107–8, 111, 113
Abysmal Grief, 177
Adelphi, 92
adventure literature, 64–5, 130–2
agency, 55, 215, 226, 228, 229
Albertazzi, Giorgio, 85
Albertini, Luigi, 125, 128
Alice Cooper, 167, 171
Aloisi, Alessandra, 2
animated pictures, 37–8
Antonelli, Giuseppe, 34
Argento, Dario, 10, 138, 145–6, 147, 148
   Dracula 3D, 98
   Il fantasma dell'opera, 98
   Inferno, 87, 98
   L'uccello dalle piume di cristallo, 141, 142, 144, 145
   Phenomena, 98
   Profondo rosso, 98, 170
   Quattro mosche di velluto grigio, 132
   Suspiria, 87, 98, 100–1, 232
   Tenebre, 98
Arona, Danilo, 93
Arpino, Giovanni, 159
avant-garde, 128–9
Avati, Pupi,
   Balsamus, l'uomo di Satana, 232
   Il signor diavolo, 100, 232
   L'arcano incantatore, 100
   La casa dalle finestre che ridono, 87–8, 226, 232, 233, 234
   La mazurka del barone, della santa e del fico fiorone, 232
   Thomas (gli indemoniati), 232
   Tutti defunti . . . tranne i morti, 232
   Zeder, 234–5
Azzolini, Paola, 191

Balbo, Cesare, 8, 30, 33, 38–40
Baldini, Eraldo, 236–7
Baraldi, Barbara, 93
Barbey d'Aurevilly, Jules, 64
Barbieri, Renzo, 160
Bardine, Bryan, 168
Bargilli, Giuseppe, 124
Barilli, Francesco, 87
Barker, Clive, 99
Barma, Claude, 85
Bartoccetti, Antonio, 168–70
Bartoli, Daniello, 117
Battiato, Franco, 173
Batzella, Luigi, 87
Bauhaus, 168
Bava, Lamberto, 98, 99–100
Bava, Mario, 10, 81, 82, 138, 148, 175, 178–9
   Diabolik, 146
   Ercole al centro della terra, 79
   Gli orrori del castello di Norimberga, 86
   I tre volti della paura, 80
   La casa dell'esorcismo, 80, 97
   La frusta e il corpo, 80

Bava, Mario (*cont.*)
  La maschera del demonio, 79, 80, 141, 142–3, 170, 179
  La ragazza che sapeva troppo, 141, 144, 145
  La venere d'Ille, 86
  Lisa e il diavolo, 86, 97
  Operazione paura, 80, 140, 143
  Sei donne per l'assassino, 141, 144, 145, 146, 147
  style, 142–3, 147
Bazzoni, Giambattista, 8, 30, 33, 38
  Il Castello di Trezzo, 36
  short stories, 37
Beckford, William, 84
Bemporad, 130
Bennati, Giuseppe, 85
Berlusconi, Silvio, 96
Bernardi, Gaetano, 67
Bersezio, Vittorio, 123
Bertolotti, Davide, 34
Besana, Lucio, 94
Bessoni, Stefano, 132
Bevilacqua, Giuseppe, 71
Bianchi, Andrea, 87, 97
Bible, 110
Biblioteca italiana, 24–5
Bido, Antonio, 232
Billiani, Francesca, 7, 11, 188, 197–209
Bilotta, Alessandro, 162
Binni, Walter, 109
Bioletto, Angelo, 156
Biondi, Massimo, 54
Bissoli, Sergio, 93, 236
The Black, 174
Black Hole, 173
Black Sabbath, 168, 169, 173, 179
Black Widow Records, 169, 174–5
Blasi, Silverio, 85
Blavatsky, Madame, 55
Boethius, 114
Boito, Arrigo, 200
Boito, Camillo, 198
  Senso, 204–5, 206
Bollini, Flaminio, 85

Bompiani, 84, 92
Bondi, Clemente, 116–17
Bonelli, Sergio, 160, 161, 163
Bonora, Ettore, 109
Bordoni, Carlo, 31–2
Botting, Fred, 212
Bowie, David, 173
Bracci, Tullio Alpinolo, 70
Bracco, Roberto, 72–3
Braid, James, 55
Brolli, Daniele, 92
Bronfen, Elisabeth, 198
Browning, Tod, 77, 139, 141
Bruno, Sergio, 65
Bunker, Max, 158
Bürger, Gottfried August, 33
Buzzati, Dino, 74, 86, 158, 159, 231
Buzzi, Paolo, 9, 70–1
Byron, Glennis, 145, 214
Byron, Lord, 22

Caiano, Mario, 82
Calvino, Italo, 6, 63, 90
Cameroni, Felice, 40
Camilletti, Fabio, 2, 5, 7, 10, 19–29, 154–66, 226
Campiglio, Giovanni, 34
Campili, Giulio, 217
Camporesi, Piero, 33
Capa, Max, 159
Capra, Antonio, 111–12
Capriolo, Paola, 91, 207
Capuana, Luigi, 11, 55, 56, 188, 198, 203, 204, 228
  'Ofelia', 56, 218
  Profumo, 185, 190–1
  'Un vampiro', 57, 125–6, 128, 199–200
Carbé, Emmanuela, 95
Carpi, Pier, 84, 158
Carr, John Dickson, 85
Cassoli, Francesco, 115
Cassone, Giuseppe, 66
Castelli, Alfredo, 84, 158–9, 161
Catholic Church, 54, 55, 108, 229, 233–5

Cavedon, Giorgio, 160–1
censorship, 67, 76, 86, 96–7, 139, 157
Centelli, Attilio, 125
Cervi, Tonino, 87
Cesaretti, Enrico, 74
Cesarotti, Melchiorre, 109
Ceserani, Remo, 7–8
Chain, Paolo (Paolo Catena), 171, 172
Charcot, Jean-Martin, 55, 215
Chelli, Gaetano Carlo, 124
city-mysteries, 50–1
Claretie, Jules, 132
Classicism, 5, 19
  Classicist-Romantic quarrel, 20–1, 24–5, 26
Collins, Wilkie, 85
Collodi, Carlo (Carlo Lorenzini), 8, 50
Colombi, Marchesa, 54
Colombo, Fausto, 123
Colombo, Giorgio, 214
comics, 10–11, 89, 91, 92, 131, 154–66
  adults-only comics, 86, 157
  censorship, 157
  decline of, 165
  development of, 154–6
  Disney themes, 156–7
  erotic-horror pocket-books, 160–1
  fumetto nero, 146–7, 157
  Gothic-related themes, 156–8
  horror comics, 161–4
  music connections, 168–9
Comte, Auguste, 186
Conan Doyle, Arthur, 65, 125
Contini, Gianfranco, 6, 90
Corcos, Emma R., 131
Corio, Lodovico, 51, 53
Corman, Roger, 65, 140
corpses, 71, 107–8, 114
Corra, Bruno, 129
Corradi, Morena, 8, 30–47
Corvetto, Giovanni, 64
Crawford, Joseph, 219

Crespi, Pietro, 55
crime and criminology, 11–12, 50, 51, 52, 55, 56, 210–24
  born criminal concept, 211, 212
  crime fiction, 67–70
  and hypnotism, 215–18
  imagery, 212–15
  literary and visual monsters, 211–15
  and the occult, 215–20
  resemblance between criminals and vampires, 212
  thought transference, 218
Cultus Sanguine, 177
The Cure, 168
Curti, Roberto, 9, 76–88, 96, 98, 233, 235
Curtiz, Michael, 77

Dadone, Carlo, 56
dal Prà, Roberto, 163
Dall'Agnol, Pietro, 164
Dalmazzo, Enrico, 54
D'Amato, Joe (Aristide Massaccesi), 86, 97, 98, 170, 232
dangerous classes concept, 50, 61n
D'Annunzio, Gabriele, 57, 227–8
Dante, 20, 110, 115, 170
D'Anza, Daniele, 85
Darwin, Charles, 126, 186–7, 202
Davies, Douglas J., 110
D'Azeglio, Massimo, 44
De Amicis, Ugo, 66
De Feo, Roberto, 100
de' Giorgi Bertola, Aurelio, 112–13
De Martino, Alberto, 82
De Martino, Ernesto, 229–30
De' Medici, Carlo H., 64
De' Rossignoli, Emilio, 78
De Sanctis, Francesco, 35, 44
de Staël, Madame, 24, 33
De Venuto, Rossella, 100
Death SS, 171–2
Deep Purple, 170
Del Principe, David, 190, 203, 226
Deodato, Ruggero, 97–8
Devil Doll, 175

di Breme, Ludovico, *Il Romitorio di Sant'Ilda*, 32–4
Di Chiara, Francesco, 148
Di Donato, Mario, 174
Di Fronzo, Gabriele, 95
Di Gennaro, Aldo, 160
Di Giacomo, Salvatore, 123, 130–1
Di Grado, Viola, 95
Di Martino, Simona, 10, 107–22
Di Orazio, Paolo, 92, 162, 163, 164
di Palma, Alfonso, 126–7
Diabolik, 10, 157–8, 161, 165
Diaframma, 172
Donati, Alessandro, 108
Donato (hypnotist), 215–16
The Doors, 167
Dossi, Carlo, 200
Draper, John W., 109
Dreyer, Carl Theodor, 77
du Maurier, George, 56, 66
Dylan Dog, 10, 89, 92, 94, 99, 155, 161–3, 164, 165

Eco, Umberto, 91, 155, 162
ecogothic *see* folk horror and ecogothic
Ediperiodici, 163
Einaudi, 90, 92
elegy, 114–15
Ellis, Ferguson, 198–9
Emmer, Luciano, 85
eroticism *see* sex themes
Evangelisti, Valerio, 94
Everson, William K., 142
Evol, 177

Falchi, Persio, 9, 71–2
Faldella, Giovanni, 200
Falletti, Ottavio, 34
Fanfulla della Domenica, 124
fantastic/*fantastico* concept, 6–7, 16n, 20, 63, 89–92, 113
films and cinema, 76–7
Farina, Corrado, 87
Farnetti, Monica, 6
Fascism, 67, 129, 156, 219, 235
Fava, Onorato, 129

Fellini, Federico, 8
Feltrinelli, 92, 93
female body/Gothic Body, 11, 185–96, 198, 202
Capuana's *Profumo*, 190–1
female degeneracy and inferiority, 186–7, 194–5
Female Gothic concept, 186
Fogazzaro's *Malombra*, 191–3
rebellion against society restrictions, 185–6
Serao's *La mano tagliata*, 193–4
Tarchetti's *Fosca*, 188–90
Female Gothic, 4, 87, 186, 197–209
Boito's *Senso*, 204–5, 206
public voices of, 197–8
Tarchetti's *Fosca*, 200–4, 206
theorising Female Gothic, 198–9
femininity, 11, 57, 145, 185
femme fatale, 68, 71–2, 77, 142
Ferrario, Vincenzo, 34
Ferroni, Giorgio, 68, 79, 86
films and cinema, 9, 10, 64, 76, 138–53, 225, 231
attitude to literary sources, 81–2
censorship, 96–7, 139
copying of plots, 82
early Gothic films, 79–81
fantastic cinema, 76–7
filming techniques, 142–3, 146, 147
folk horror cinema, 231–5
giallo cycle, 143–7
Gothic cycle, 140–3
Gothic horror, dawn of, 138–40
Gothic music, 170–1, 174–5
horror films, 89, 100–1
imitations, remakes and mockbusters in late horror cinema, 96–101
old-style Gothic, changing face of, 86–7
and popular fiction, 65, 68
private productions, 96, 97
psychosexual themes, 145–6
sex and violence, 83–4
vampire themes, 76–9, 80

Fiorentino, Salomone, 10, 113
  Laurus amena, 115–16
Fisher, Terence, 78, 140, 141
Fletcher, Kristopher F. B., 176
Florence, 48, 51, 52
Fogazzaro, Antonio, 11, 54, 90, 188, 226
  Malombra, 2, 49, 174, 185, 191–3, 200
folk horror and ecogothic, 225–40
  decline of, 235
  definitions, 225–6
  fiction, 236–7
  folk horror cinema, 231–5
  in Italian non-fiction, 229–31
  Verismo tradition, Gothic ecology of, 227–9
Foni, Fabrizio, 7–8, 9, 10, 63–75, 90–1, 123–37, 226
Foscolo, Ugo, 34, 113, 115
Foucault, Michel, 53
Fragasso, Claudio, 97
Franco, Giuseppe Giovanni, 216, 217–18
Franzosini, Edgardo, 92, 95
Freda, Riccardo, 10, 83, 86, 138, 144, 148
  I vampiri, 76–8, 81, 139–40, 141–2, 143, 145
Freud, Sigmund, 3
Friedkin, William, 86, 97
Friedlander, Henry, 219
Frizzi, Fabio, 179
Fulci, Lucio, 98–9, 174–5
  Dracula in Brianza, 87
  … E tu vivrai nel terrore! L'aldilà, 99, 175
  Gatto nero, 99
  Le porte del silenzio, 99
  Lo squartatore di New York, 144
  Non si sevizia un paperino, 226, 231, 232
  Paura nella città dei morti viventi, 99
  Quella villa accanto al cimitero, 99
  Un gatto nel cervello, 100
  Zombi 2, 97
fumetto nero, 146–7, 157, 159, 160, 171–2
Funetta, Luciano, 95
futurism, 70–2, 129

Galatea Film, 81
Gallini, Clara, 217
Gallo, Claudio, 90–1
Garfinkel, Paul, 50
Gatiss, Mark, 225
Gautier, Théophile, 8, 30, 66
Gazzetta Letteraria, 123–4
Gherardini, Giovanni, 25
Ghersi, Antonio, 64
Ghidetti, Enrico, 6, 90
Ghione, Riccardo, 87
Giacomantonio, Gaetano, 132
giallo, 10, 67–70, 76, 87–8
  and cinema, 138, 141, 143–8
  giallo filone, 97–8
Gibson, Mary, 214
Ginzburg, Carlo, 229, 230–1, 237
Giornale Illustrato dei Viaggi, 131, 132
Girolami, Laura, 100
Girolami, Marino, 97
Giromini, Ferruccio, 164
Giussani, Angela, 157–8
Giusti, Giulio, 138–53
Goblin, 170–1
Gogol, Nikolai, 80
Gothic Studies, 1
Gozzano, Guido, 132–3
Gracey, James, 143
graphic novels, 159
Gravina, Giovanni Vincenzo, 20
Greco, Federico, 232
Grossi, Pietro, 92
Guadagnino, Luca, *Suspiria*, 100–1
Gualdo, Luigi, 200
Guarnieri, Luigi, 212
Guerrazzi, Francesco Domenico, 8, 30, 33–4, 40–5
  Beatrice Cenci, 41, 42
  Indicatore Livornese, 44
  L'assedio di Firenze, 41, 42–3

Guerrazzi, Francesco Domenico (*cont.*)
  La battaglia di Benevento, 41–2, 43
Günsberg, Maggie, 142

Haggard, Piers, 225
Halttunen, Karen, 211
Hanke, Ken, 144
Hardy, Robert, 225, 232
Hawthorne, Nathaniel, 85
Heusch, Paolo, 80
Hillyer, Lambert, 77
historical novels and the Gothic, 30–47, 66–7
  early historical fiction, 34–40
  Risorgimento novel and Guerrazzi, 40–5
Hitchcock, Alfred, 140
Hocking, Joseph, 218
Hoffmann, E. T. A., 8, 19, 30, 31
Hogle, Jerrold E., 3, 4
  and the past, 4–5
Horace, 114
Horley, Alex, 172
Horn, David, 214
Horror, 84, 155, 158–9, 165
horror fiction, 93–4
Hurley, Kelly, 187, 211
Huysmans, Joris-Karl, 64, 69
hypnotism, 55–6, 215–18

I Gialli Moderni, 69
I Libri Gialli, 67
I Racconti dell'Occultismo, 68
I Romanzi del Disco Giallo, 68
Ignatius of Loyola, Saint, 110
Il Conciliatore, 26, 30, 32
Il Corriere della Sera, 56
Il Giornalino della Domenica, 130–1
Il Risorgimento, 38
Il Romanzo Mensile, 67
Il Romanzo Settimanale, 65
imagery, 48–9, 143, 212–15
impegno, 92–3
Inchiuvatu, 176–7
Invernizio, Carolina, 63

Iron Maiden, 168
Italian Gothic
  beginnings of, 19–29
  decline of, 1980–2020, 89–102
  definition, 1–16
  golden age of, 1957–1979, 76–88
  Gothic wave 1960–1966, 79–81
  lack of research on, 1
  permutations, age of 1915–1956, 63–75

Jacula, 160–1, 165
James, Montague R., 84
Jesuits, 110, 116–17, 216
Joy Division, 168
Judas Priest, 168

Kardec, Allan, 54
Keetley, Dawn, 226
King, Stephen, 49, 67
Kipling, Rudyard, 132
Kirlian Camera, 173
Kolosimo, Peter, 231
Koven, Mikel J., 144
Kristeva, Julia, 3, 113

La Domenica del Corriere, 56, 124–7
La Lettura, 128, 129
La Stampa, 66
La Tribuna Illustrata, 127
Lado, Aldo, 87
Lagioia, Nicola, 92–3
Landolfi, Tommaso, 74–5, 133, 226
landscapes, 12, 174, 225, 226–7, 228–9, 235
Landsdale, Joe R., 99
Lattarulo, Leonardo, 6
Lauria, Amilcare, 54–5
Lavezzolo, Andrea, 69
Lawlor, Clark, 112
Lazzarin, Stefano, 7
Le Grandi Films, 65
Leggio, Roberto, 232
Lenzi, Umberto, 98, 146
Leonardo, 129
Leopardi, Giacomo, 6, 24–5, 90, 91, 115, 117

Leroux, Gaston, 66
Lewis, Matthew, 30, 32, 33
Liberatore, Ugo, 232
Ligotti, Thomas, 94, 237
L'Illustrazione Italiana, 127
Lipperini, Loredana, 92
Lirici del Settecento, 108
L'Italia Futurista, 129
Litfiba, 172
Lo Castro, Giuseppe, 6–7
Lombardi, Nicola, 93
Lombroso, Cesare, 11–12, 54, 186, 199–200, 210–11, 219–20
   Atlante, 213
   Genio e follia, 187
   imagery, 212–15
   La donna delinquente, la prostituta e la donna normale, 187, 213
   L'uomo delinquente, 187, 211, 213
   and occultism, 215, 216, 217, 218
Londonio, Carlo Giuseppe, 25
Lorenzini, Carlo *see* Collodi, Carlo
Lorrain, Jean, 64
Lovato, Pietro, 21, 25–6
Lovecraft, Howard Phillips, 3, 100, 132, 170
lugubre, 111–12
Lukács, György, 32

Mabìl, Pier Luigi, 25
Macpherson, James, 169
magazines *see* periodicals and magazines
Maggi, Luigi, 139
Maier, Bruno, 108
Majano, Anton Giulio, 79, 85
Male Gothic, 186, 189, 198
Malvestio, Marco, 9, 12, 89–102, 225–40
Mammarella, Roberto, 177
Mamoulian, Rouben, 139
Manetti, Marco and Antonio, 100
Manfredi, Gianfranco, 93
Manini, Omobono, 37
Manzoni, Alessandro, 23, 30–1, 32, 33
   Fermo e Lucia, 20, 25, 26

I promessi sposi, 2, 5–6, 8, 25–6, 27
Marchesi, Marcello, 78
Margheriti, Antonio, 82, 86
Mari, Michele, 91
Mariotti, Vasco, 9, 67–8
Marolla, Samuel, 93–4
Marrama, Daniele Oberto, 57, 126
Marsh, Richard, 218
Martin Mystère, 161
Martina, Guido, 156
Martino, Sergio, 232
Marxism, 3–4, 77
Masino, Paola, 207
Massaccesi, Aristide *see* D'Amato, Joe
Massei, Maria Rosa, 108
Mastriani, Francesco, 51, 53, 143
Mastrocinque, Camillo, 81, 140
Mattei, Bruno, 97
Maturin, Charles, 30, 84
Mauri, Roberto, 80
Max Bunker Press, 163–4
Maxwell, Richard, 52
Mayers, Helene, 199
Mazzoni, Guido, 197
Meacci, Giordano, 95
Measles, Robert (Roberto Morbioli), 173
melancholy, 112–13
Méliès, Georges, 64
melodrama, 41
Merlini, Carlo, 55
Mesmer, Franz, 55
mesmerism, 55–6
Metamorfosi, 170
metempsychosis, 55
Meyrink, Gustav, 84
Micheluzzi, Attilio, 163
Middle Ages, 8–9, 34–7, 44, 176, 177
Milan, 21–2, 24, 25–7, 48, 51, 53
Milani, Mino, 160
mind-reading, 71
Miraglia, Emilio P., 85
Mistrali, Franco, 56
Modà, 173

modernity, 20, 21, 22, 23, 25, 49, 58, 203, 225, 227, 236
Moebius, Paul Julius, 186
Moers, Ellen, 185, 186, 199
Mondadori, 67, 144, 158
Mora, Teo, 142
moral influences, 41–2
Morando, Francesco, 57, 124
Morante, Massimo, 170
Morselli, Enrico, 54, 216, 217
Mortuary Drape, 175–6
Mosso, Angelo, 216
Motorhead, 168
mourning, 113
Muratori, Letizia, 95
Murnau, F. W., 65, 77, 139, 178
Murray, Margaret, 230–1
Muscetta, Carlo, 108
music, 11, 167–81
   and cinema, 170–1, 174–5
   Dark Wave, 172–3
   Goth rock and metal in the 1980s, 172–4
   Gothic in music, 167–8
   Hard Rock, 168
   Heavy Metal, 168, 171, 173, 174
   Italian Black Metal scene in the 1990s, 174–8
   Italian occult psychedelia, 178–9
   New Wave, 172–3
   origins of Gothic music: the 1960s and 1970s, 168–72
   Progressive Rock, 168, 170
   Sicilian Black Metal, 176–7
Musolino, Luigi, 94

Naples, 48, 51–2
Napoleon, 21–3, 25
Nazism, 219
Necromass, 176
Needham, Gary, 144
Neon, 173
Nerbini, 68
Nerozzi, Gianfranco, 93
New Weird, 89, 95, 96
Newman, Kim, 141
Nico, 167

night, 111–12
Noakes, Richard, 48
non-fiction, 229–31
Nordic influence, 5

occulture, 5, 8
   and religion, 54–5
Olcott, Henry Steel, 55
Onorato, Giancarlo, 173
Opera IX, 177
Oppenheim, Janet, 187
Orlando, Francesco, 6
Ortese, Anna Maria, 207
Orti Manara, Michele, 236
Ottolenghi, Salvatore, 217
Ovid, 114

Pabst, Georg Wilhelm, 77
Pagot, Nino, 156
Palladino, Eusapia, 218
Palazzolo, Chiara, 94–6, 236, 237
para-literature, 7–8, 12
Parisot, Eric, 108–9
Partridge, Christopher, 5
Past, Elena, 213
Paul, Louis, 139
Peano, Marco, 236
Pedrocchi, Federico, 156
Pellico, Silvio, 26
periodicals and magazines, 10, 123–37
   Gozzano, Landolfi and Vigolo, 132–4
   La Domenica del Corriere, *L'Illustrazione Italiana* and *La Tribuna Illustrata*, 124–7
   national readership, 123–7
   popular fiction and avant-garde, 128–9
   travel and adventure magazines, 130–2
Permunian, Francesco, 92
Pesce, Giuliano, 95
pessimism, 43–4
Petrarch, 110, 114–15
phenomena, 49
photo-novels, 79, 84

photography, 48–9, 143, 214
Piccini, Giulio, 51, 52–3
Piccirillo, Paolo, 95
Pick, Daniel, 219
Pickman, Jean-Lambert, 218
Pierantozzi, Alcide, 95
Pincio, Tommaso, 95
Pindemonte, Ippolito, 112
Piovene, Guido, 159
Pirandello, Luigi, 128
Pittard, Christopher, 211, 212
plague, 25–7
Poe, Edgar Allan, 8, 30, 64, 66, 72, 73, 77, 82, 115, 170, 175, 190
Poema a fumetti, 159
Poesia del Settecento, 108
Poeti minori del Settecento, 108
poetry, 10, 107–22
  excess and abjection: nocturnal, funereal and macabre repertoire, 111–18
  graveyard poetry, 108–9
  sepulchral poems, 107–8
  theoretical background, 108–11
Polidori, John, 22
Polselli, Renato, 79, 80, 86–7, 231–2
Pomba, Giuseppe, 38
Popoff, Martin, 168
positivism, 49, 54, 128, 129, 186–7, 188, 200, 211, 219
postmodernism, 91, 99–100, 162
Praz, Mario, 187
psychoanalysis, 3–4
Puccini, Mario, 73
Puccio, Alberto Enrico, 131–2
Pugno, Laura, 95
Punter, David, 1, 3–4, 145, 214
Puntoni, Renzo, 78
Pupillo, Massimo, 82, 84

Radcliffe, Ann, 19, 30, 32, 44, 185
radiesthesia, 69–70
Rafter, Nicole, 210, 212, 214
Raimi, Sam, 97
Ramsey-Portolano, Catherine, 11, 185–96

realism, 7, 51, 64, 79, 95–6, 186, 200
Reeves, Michael, 225
Regnoli, Piero, 79, 80
Reim, Riccardo, 90
reincarnation, 55, 69, 81, 85, 126, 192, 227
Requiem, 174
Retromania, 165
revenge themes, 42–3
Ridenhour, James, 51
Risorgimento novels, 40–5
Riva, Valerio, 78
Romagnoli, Sergio, 34
Romanticism, 5, 27, 33, 35, 70, 90
  Classicist-Romantic quarrel, 20–1, 24–5, 26
  as Gothic, 25
Romero, George, 97, 162, 170
Rondi, Brunello, 230, 232
Rosa, Giovanni, 41
Rosá, Rosa, 129
Rossi, Gastone, 56
Rostagno, Marco, 159
Russo, Giuni, 173
Rye, Stellan, 139

Saggini, Francesca, 8
Salgari, Emilio, 64, 130
Saluzzo di Roero, Diodata, 8, 30, 33, 34–5, 37–8
Sammon, Paul, 163
Santi, Giovenale, 231
Sassoon, David, 123
Sauli, Alessandro, 50
Savinio, Alberto, 73–4
Saxon, 168
Scapigliatura movement, 49, 61n, 70, 90, 123, 124, 200, 227
Schow, David J., 163
science, 48–9
Sclavi, Tiziano, 10, 71, 94, 161, 164
Scott, Walter, 31–2, 34, 36, 190
Scotti, Raimondo, 139
Semon, Larry, 64
Senizza, Giuseppe, 65–6
Serafini, Stefano, 9, 48–62, 210–24

Serao, Matilde, 11, 51, 52, 56, 185, 188
  La mano tagliata, 193–4
sex themes, 71, 83–4, 86–7, 202, 205
  eroticism, 76, 86–7, 160–1
Shajirat, Anna, 186, 188, 189, 194
Shelley, Mary, 19, 22, 67, 212
Shelley, Percy, 22
Sherman, Vincent, 77
Silver (Guido Silvestri), 163, 164
Simonelli, Giovanni, 86
Simonetti, Claudio, 170
Siodmak, Robert, 77
Siouxsie and the Banshees, 168
Sisters of Mercy, 168
Sivils, Matthew Wynn, 226
Soavi, Michele, 71, 99, 170, 232
Soldati, Mario, 8
Spagnol, Mario, 231
Spencer, Herbert, 186
Spettri, 170
Spinazzola, Vittorio, 155
spiritualism, 48–9, 54–5, 218
Splatter, 92, 155, 163, 164, 165
Steele, Barbara, 83, 142, 170
Stendhal, 21–2, 25
Stevenson, Robert Louis, 67, 79–80
Stewart-Steinberg, Suzanne, 215, 216, 217
Stickney, John, 167
Stilling, Heinrich, 23
Stocco, Guglielmo, 56, 131
Stoker, Bram, 56, 78
Sue, Eugène, 50, 52
Sulis, Gigliola, 7
Sylvester, Steve, 171–2

Taglietti, Emanuele, 172
Tarchetti, Igino Ugo, 11, 185, 198
  Fosca, 188–90, 200–4, 206, 227
  'Lorenzo Alviati', 189–90
Tardiola, Giuseppe, 57
telegraphy, 48
telepathy, 56
television, 10, 76, 85, 231
Terzoli, Italo, 78
Testa, Eugenio, 139

Tex, 158, 160, 161
Theatres Des Vampires, 177–8
thought transference, 218
Thrower, Stephen, 138
Todorov, Tzvetan, 6, 89
Tambora (volcano), 22–3
Tonsi, Giuseppe, 57, 125
Toscani, Italo, 9, 55, 64–5, 126
Totaro, Donato, 146
tourism, 231, 233, 235, 237
Tourneur, Jacques, 68
travel writing, 130–2
Tryon, Thomas, 237
Tunué, 95
Turchet, Maurizio, 159

Ugolini, Luigi, 132
Umbriano, Renato, 68–9
Underground Life, 173
urbanisation, 48
  urban Gothic, 50–3

Valera, Paolo, 51
vampire themes, 43, 56–7, 71–2, 76–9, 80, 125–6, 128, 139, 141–2, 177–8, 199–200, 212
Varano, Alfonso, 10
  Visione XI, 113–14
Vasari, Giorgio, 19
Velvet Underground, 167
Verga, Giovanni, 85, 90, 227–9
Verismo tradition, 12, 124
  Gothic ecology of, 227–9
Verne, Jules, 64, 70, 132
Viale, Ambrogio, 112
Vicario, Marco, 82
Vidler, Anthony, 52
Vigolo, Giorgio, 133–4
Villiers de L'Isle-Adam, Auguste de, 64, 132
violence, 83–4, 141–3, 145–7, 148, 163, 164, 192, 194
Vitolo, Eduardo, 11, 167–81
Vittorelli, Jacopo, 113
Vivanti, Annie, 207
Vivarelli, Piero, 146
Volta, Ornella, 78

Wallace, Bryan Edgar, 144
Wallace, Edgar, 144
Wallman, Bengt, 146
Walpole, Horace, 3, 8, 30
　The Castle of Otranto, 19, 32, 37, 127
war, 72–5
Waterloo, Battle of, 22–3
Weikart, Richard, 219
Weininger, Otto, 186
weirdness, 20, 69, 89, 94, 95, 132
Wells, H. G., 67
West, Kate, 213

Whale, James, 139
Wiene, Robert, 69, 139
Wier, Johannes, 64
Wilde, Oscar, 69
Willis, Martin, 48
Wood, Mary, 140
Woolrich, Cornell, 68

Ystehede, Peter, 210

Zampa, Pietro, 69–70
Zarantonello, Jonathan, 100
Zucca, Giuseppe, 132
Zuccon, Ivan, 100

EU representative:
Easy Access System Europe
Mustamäe tee 50, 10621 Tallinn, Estonia
Gpsr.requests@easproject.com

www.ingramcontent.com/pod-product-compliance
Lightning Source LLC
Chambersburg PA
CBHW051113230426
43667CB00014B/2568